GREGG SHORTHAND DICTIONARY

Diamond Jubilee Series

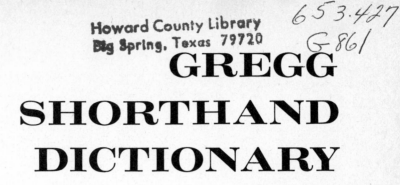

GREGG
SHORTHAND
DICTIONARY

A COMPILATION OF SHORTHAND OUT-LINES FOR 34,055 WORDS; 1,314 NAMES; AND 1,856 FREQUENTLY USED PHRASES

John Robert Gregg
Louis A. Leslie
Charles E. Zoubek

Shorthand written by Charles Rader

GREGG — **Diamond Jubilee Series**

McGraw-Hill Book Company

New York   St. Louis   San Francisco   Düsseldorf
London   Mexico   Sydney   Toronto

GREGG SHORTHAND DICTIONARY, DIAMOND JUBILEE SERIES

7 8 9 0 DODO 0 9 8 7 6

ISBN 07-024631-9

FOREWORD

Gregg Shorthand Dictionary, Diamond Jubilee Series, is divided into three parts:

Part One contains, in alphabetic order, the shorthand outlines for 34,055 words. These 34,055 words, however, represent a considerably larger vocabulary, as many simple derivatives of those words — those ending in *-ing* and *-s,* for example, which present no stenographic problem — have been omitted.

Part Two contains, in alphabetic order, the shorthand outlines for 1,314 entries for personal and geographical names.

Part Three contains, in alphabetic order, the shorthand outlines for 1,856 phrases frequently used in business dictation.

It is easily possible to construct briefer outlines for many of the scientific and literary words for which full outlines are given in this dictionary. It is not advisable to do so, however, unless the writer is certain that he will use those briefer outlines with sufficient frequency to justify the effort of learning them. Otherwise, the brief, but half-remembered, outlines will cause mental hesitation that will result in slower, rather than faster, writing.

Research techniques using high-speed motion pictures have proved that most shorthand writers actually write each outline at about the same speed, regardless of the speed of the dictation. That is why the writer who can take dictation at only 100 words a minute writes each outline as rapidly as it is written by another writer taking the same material at 200 words a minute. What, then, is the difference between the two writers?

The difference is that the writer who can write only 100 words a minute is wasting time thinking, pausing, hesitating. The writer who can write 200 words a minute does not need to stop to think. He writes the outlines little, if any, faster than the writer who can write only 100 words a minute, but the 200-word writer writes *continuously*.

The problem of increasing shorthand speed, therefore, is actually a problem of decreasing hesitations in writing. What causes hesitations in writing? They are caused by the struggle of the mind to remember and use the abbreviating material provided in the shorthand system.

The fewer shortcuts and exceptions the mind must remember and use, the easier it is for the writer to decrease or eliminate the hesitations that reduce speed. Therefore, any attempt by the writer to manufacture additional shortcuts is more likely to reduce his speed than to increase it, unless the new shortcuts are used in his daily work with such frequency that they readily become automatized.

The experience of expert shorthand writers of every system is conclusive in establishing the inadvisability of attempting to gain speed by devising and learning lists of brief outlines. Longer outlines that are quickly constructed by the mind under pressure of dictation give the writer more speed; the attempt to remember and use large numbers of abbreviated outlines tends to reduce the writer's speed.

There is often room for some difference of opinion as to the most appropriate outline for a word. This dictionary offers outlines that have been discussed and considered by experts. Sometimes an apparently obvious improvement in an outline will actually create the danger of a conflict in reading. More often an outline different from that provided in this dictionary would be individually satisfactory but would not be consistent with the outlines for other members of the same word family.

Of one thing the reader may be sure — every outline in this dictionary is the result of serious thought and consideration. Where possible alternate outlines exist, each alternate has been discussed and considered. This dictionary as a whole represents the accumulated experience of all those who have worked with Gregg Shorthand since its first publication in 1888.

It is hoped that this volume will render a useful service to the shorthand writer by placing at his disposal a facile and fluent outline for any word in which he may be interested.

The Publishers

PART ONE

Part One of *Gregg Shorthand Dictionary, Diamond Jubilee Series,* contains 34,055 word entries, alphabetically arranged. This is an increase of 7,957 words over the previous edition. Many of the new words were suggested by users of the previous edition or by the reading done by the authors.

Some words, like *sputnik, defector, plutonium, orbited, imperialistic, isotope,* and a number of others, were added because of their greatly expanded use in the field of "peaceful coexistence." Other words, like *stereophonic, transistor, tranquilizer, epoxy, fluoridate, video, togetherness, programed,* and *geriatrics,* were invented or came into general use in our speech in recent years. Some new words may be frowned upon, like *definitize, motivational, moonlighting,* but they have been included because the stenographer may have to write them from dictation.

Experience has proved that those using a shorthand dictionary often consult it for the simple words formerly omitted from shorthand dictionaries or for rare and unusual words likewise formerly omitted.

The present list, therefore, includes many of the apparently simple words formerly omitted. Most readily apparent will be the addition of the many rare and unusual words that experience has proved are wanted by users of a list such as this.

Many words are included because the shorthand learner, while still in school, has occasion to use them in his schoolwork. For this reason many mathematical, mineralogical, chemical, physical, botanical, and physiological terms are included. For the same reason many literary words are included, words that are usually of no business value but that the high school or college learner uses in his schoolwork. The bulk of the vocabulary, however, consists of words generally used in business-office dictation.

It must be remembered, too, that in many types of office work the stenographer may have occasion to use these scientific or literary words. The editor's stenographer will need the literary words. The professor's secretary will need many of the mathematical or chemical or physiological words—according to the professor's field of interest.

Consistency, rather than brevity of outline, has been the guiding principle in the construction of the shorthand outlines in this dictionary. The fastest shorthand outline (within reasonable limits) is the outline that requires the least mental effort, the outline that is written consistently and analogically.

The speed of a shorthand outline is not to be judged by its brevity to the eye, nor even by its facility for the hand; it is to be judged by the speed with which it may be constructed by the mind and supplied by the mind to the hand.

Many shorthand writers experience difficulty in understanding the principle that guides the shorthand author in devising shortcuts. If the preceding paragraph is true, why are there *any* shortcuts? Why not write out everything in full? The secret of the good shortcut is the frequency of use of the word or phrase. If a dictator says *as a matter of fact* day after day, the shorthand writer should, of course, use a very brief shortcut for that phrase. Because of this extreme frequency of use, the shortcut will come as quickly to the mind as though the phrase had been written in full.

There is no value, however, in having every shorthand writer learn a shortcut for the phrase *as a matter of fact,* for some dictators may never use the phrase, and if it should occur infrequently in the dictation, the mental effort needed to recall the phrase would require far more time than would have been necessary to write it in full.

It is strongly urged, therefore, that the outline in this dictionary be accepted as the normal outline for any expression unless that expression occurs so frequently in the writer's dictation that learning a shortcut for it is thoroughly justified. A long list of seldom-used shortcuts can be a very heavy burden on the mind and will almost invariably result in decreasing one's writing speed rather than increasing it. As a famous shorthand reporter of an earlier generation once said: "The longer I write shorthand, the *longer* I write shorthand."

aaaaaaaaaaaaaaaaaa
aaaaaaaaaaaaaaaaaa
aaaaaaaaaaaaaaaaaa
aaaaaaaaaaaaaaaaaa
aaaaaaaaaaaaaaaaaa
aaaaaaaaaaaaaaaaaa
aaaaaaaaaaaaaaaaaa

ab'a·cus

a·baft'

ab'a·lo'ne

a·ban'don

a·ban'doned

a·ban'don·ment

a·base'

a·based'

a·base'ment

a·bash'

a·bat'a·ble

a·bate'

a·bat'ed

a·bate'ment

ab'bess

ab'bey

ab'bot

ab·bre'vi·ate

ab·bre'vi·at'ed

ab·bre'vi·a'tion

ab'di·cate

ab'di·cat'ed

ab'di·ca'tion

ab·do'men

ab·dom'i·nal

ab·duct'

ab·duc'tion

a·bed'

ab'er·ra'tion

ab'er·ra'tion·al

a·bet'

a·bet'ted

a·bet'tor

a·bey'ance

ab·hor'

ab·horred'

ab·hor'rence

ab·hor'rent

a·bide'

a·bil'i·ty

ab'ject

ab'ju·ra'tion

ab·jure'

ab·jured'

ab·jure'ment

ab'la·tive

ab'laut

a·blaze'

a'ble

a'ble-bod'ied

ab·lu'tion

a'bly

ab'ne·ga'tion

ab·nor'mal

ab'nor·mal'i·ty

ab·nor'mi·ty

a·board'

a·bode'

a·bol'ish

a·bol'ished

ab'o·li'tion

ab'o·li'tion·ism

ab'o·li'tion·ist

a·bom'i·na·ble

a·bom'i·na·bly

a·bom'i·nate

a·bom′i·na′tion

ab′o·rig′i·nal

ab′o·rig′i·ne

a·bor′tive

a·bound′

a·bound′ing·ly

a·bout′

a·bove′

ab·rade′

ab·rad′ed

ab·ra′sion

ab·ra′sive

ab′re·ac′tion

a·breast′

a·bridge′

a·bridged′

a·bridg′ment

a·broad′

ab′ro·gate

ab′ro·gat′ed

ab′ro·ga′tion

ab′ro·ga′tive

ab·rupt′

ab·rupt′ly

ab·rupt′ness

ab′scess

ab′scessed

ab·scis′sa

ab·scis′sion

ab·scond′

ab·scond′ed

ab·scond′er

ab′sence

ab′sent

ab′sen·tee′

ab′sen·tee′ism

ab′sent·ly

ab′sinthe

ab′so·lute

ab′so·lute·ly

ab′so·lute·ness

ab′so·lu′tion

ab′so·lut·ism

ab′so·lut·ist

ab·solve′

ab·solved′

ab·sorb′

ab·sorbed′

ab·sorb′en·cy

ab·sorb′ent

ab·sorb′ing·ly

ab·sorp′tion

ab·sorp′tive

ab·stain′

ab·stained′

ab·stain′er

ab·ste′mi·ous

ab·ste′mi·ous·ly

ab·ste′mi·ous·ness

ab·sten′tion

ab′sti·nence

ab′sti·nent

ab′sti·nent·ly

ab′stract

ab·stract′ed

ab·stract′ed·ly

ab·strac′tion

ab·strac′tion·ist

ab′stract·ly

ab·struse′

ab·struse′ness

ab·surd′

ab·surd′i·ty

ab·surd′ly

a·bun′dance

a·bun′dant

a·bun′dant·ly

a·buse′

a·bused′

a·bu′sive

a·bu′sive·ly

a·bu′sive·ness

a·but′

a·but′ment

a·but′tal

a·but′ted

a·but′ter

a·bysm′

a·bys′mal

a·byss′

a·ca′cia

ac′a·dem′ic

a·cad′e·mi′cian

a·cad′e·mies

a·cad′e·my

A·ca′di·an

a·can'thus

ac·cede'

ac·ced'ed

ac·cel'er·an'do

ac·cel'er·ant

ac·cel'er·ate

ac·cel'er·at'ed

ac·cel'er·a'tion

ac·cel'er·a'tive

ac·cel'er·a'tor

ac·cel'er·a·to'ry

ac'cent

ac·cent'ed

ac·cen'tu·ate

ac·cen'tu·at'ed

ac·cen'tu·a'tion

ac·cept'

ac·cept'a·bil'i·ty

ac·cept'a·ble

ac·cept'ance

ac'cep·ta'tion

ac·cept'ed

ac'cess

ac·ces'si·bil'i·ty

ac·ces'si·ble

ac·ces'sion

ac·ces'so·ry

ac'ci·dence

ac'ci·dent

ac'ci·den'tal

ac'ci·den'tal·ly

ac·cip'i·trine

ac·claim'

ac·claimed'

ac'cla·ma'tion

ac·clam'a·to'ry

ac·cli'mate

ac·cli'mat·ed

ac'cli·ma'tion

ac·cli'ma·ti·za'tion

ac·cli'ma·tize

ac·cli'ma·tized

ac·cliv'i·ty

ac'co·lade'

ac·com'mo·date

ac·com'mo·dat'ed

ac·com'mo·dat'ing·ly

ac·com'mo·da'tion

ac·com'mo·da'tive

ac·com'pa·nied

ac·com'pa·ni·ment

ac·com'pa·nist

ac·com'pa·ny

ac·com'plice

ac·com'plish

ac·com'plished

ac·com'plish·ment

ac·cord'

ac·cord'ance

ac·cord'ed

ac·cord'ing·ly

ac·cor'di·on

ac·cost'

ac·cost'ed

ac·count'

ac·count'a·bil'i·ty

ac·count'a·ble

ac·count'an·cy

ac·count'ant

ac·count'ed

ac·cou'tered

ac·cou'ter·ment

ac·cred'it

ac·cred'it·ed

ac·cre'tion

ac·cru'al

ac·crue'

ac·crued'

ac·cu'mu·late

ac·cu'mu·lat'ed

ac·cu'mu·lates

ac·cu'mu·la'tion

ac·cu'mu·la'tive

ac·cu'mu·la'tor

ac'cu·ra·cy

ac'cu·rate

ac'cu·rate·ly

ac'cu·sa'tion

ac·cu'sa·tive

ac·cu'sa·to'ry

ac·cuse'

ac·cused'

ac·cus'er

ac·cus'ing·ly

ac·cus'tom

ac·cus'tomed

ace	ac'o·lyte	ac'ri·mo'ni·ous·ness
a·cerb'	ac'o·nite	ac'ri·mo'ny
a·cer'bic	a'corn	ac'ro·bat
a·cer'bi·ty	a·cous'tic	ac'ro·bat'ic
ac'e·tate	a·cous'ti·cal	ac'ro·bat'i·cal·ly
a·ce'tic	a·cous'ti·cal·ly	ac'ro·bat'ics
ac'e·tone	a·cous'tics	a·crop'o·lis
a·cet'y·lene	ac·quaint'	a·cross'
ache	ac·quaint'ance	a·cros'tic
ached	ac·quaint'ance·ship	act
a·chiev'a·ble	ac·quaint'ed	act'ed
a·chieve'	ac'qui·esce'	ac·tin'ic
a·chieved'	ac'qui·esced'	ac·tin'i·um
a·chieve'ment	ac'qui·es'cence	ac'tion
ach'ro·mat'ic	ac'qui·es'cent	ac'tion·a·ble
ach'ro·mat'i·cal·ly	ac·quire'	ac'ti·vate
a·chro'ma·to'sis	ac·quired'	ac'ti·vat'ed
ac'id	ac·quire'ment	ac'ti·va'tion
a·cid'i·fi·ca'tion	ac·quires'	ac'ti·va'tor
a·cid'i·fi'er	ac'qui·si'tion	ac'tive
a·cid'i·fy	ac·quis'i·tive	ac'tive·ly
a·cid'i·ty	ac·quis'i·tive·ness	ac·tiv'i·ties
ac'i·do'sis	ac·quit'	ac·tiv'i·ty
ac'id·proof'	ac·quit'tal	ac'tiv·ize
a·cid'u·late	ac·quit'ted	ac'tor
a·cid'u·lat'ed	a'cre	ac'tress
a·cid'u·lous	a'cre·age	ac'tu·al
ac·knowl'edge	ac'rid	ac'tu·al'i·ties
ac·knowl'edged	a·crid'i·ty	ac'tu·al'i·ty
ac·knowl'edg·ment	ac'rid·ly	ac'tu·al·ly
ac'me	ac'ri·mo'ni·ous	ac'tu·ar'i·al
ac'ne	ac'ri·mo'ni·ous·ly	ac'tu·ar'y

ac'tu·ate
ac'tu·at'ed
a·cu'i·ty
a·cu'men
a·cute'
a·cute'ly
a·cute'ness
ad'age
a·da'gio
ad'a·mant
ad'a·man'tine
a·dapt'
a·dapt'a·bil'i·ty
a·dapt'a·ble
ad'ap·ta'tion
a·dapt'ed
a·dapt'er
a·dap'tive
add
add'ed
ad·den'da
ad·den'dum
ad'der
ad'dict
ad·dict'ed
ad·dic'tion
ad·di'tion
ad·di'tion·al
ad·di'tion·al·ly
ad'di·tive
ad'dle
ad'dled

ad·dress
ad·dressed'
ad'dress·ee'
Ad·dres'so·graph
ad·duce'
ad·duced'
ad·duct'
ad·duc'tion
ad·duc'tive
ad·duc'tor
ad'e·noid
ad'e·nol'o·gy
ad'e·no'ma
a·dept'
ad'e·qua·cy
ad'e·quate
ad'e·quate·ly
ad'e·quate·ness
ad·here'
ad·hered'
ad·her'ence
ad·her'ent
ad·he'sion
ad·he'sive
ad·he'sive·ness
a·dieu'
ad'i·pose
ad'i·pos'i·ty
ad·ja'cen·cy
ad·ja'cent
ad'jec·ti'val
ad'jec·tive

ad·join'
ad·joined'
ad·journ'
ad·journed'
ad·journ'ment
ad·judge'
ad·judged'
ad·ju'di·cate
ad·ju'di·cat'ed
ad·ju'di·ca'tion
ad·ju'di·ca'tive
ad·ju'di·ca'tor
ad'junct
ad'ju·ra'tion
ad·jur'a·to'ry
ad·jure'
ad·jured'
ad·just'
ad·just'a·ble
ad·just'ed
ad·just'er
ad·just'ment
ad'ju·tan·cy
ad'ju·tant
ad·min'is·ter
ad·min'is·tered
ad·min'is·tra'tion
ad·min'is·tra'tive
ad·min'is·tra'tive·ly
ad·min'is·tra'tor
ad·min'is·tra'trix
ad'mi·ra·ble

ad·mi·ra·bly
ad'mi·ral
ad'mi·ral·ty
ad'mi·ra'tion
ad·mire'
ad·mired'
ad·mis'si·bil'i·ty
ad·mis'si·ble
ad·mis'sion
ad·mit'
ad·mit'tance
ad·mit'ted
ad·mit'ted·ly
ad·mix'ture
ad·mon'ish
ad'mo·ni'tion
ad·mon'i·to'ry
a·do'be
ad'o·les'cence
ad'o·les'cent
a·dopt'
a·dopt'ed
a·dop'tion
a·dop'tive
a·dor'a·ble
ad'o·ra'tion
a·dore'
a·dored'
a·dor'ing·ly
a·dorn'
a·dorned'
a·dorn'ment

ad·re'nal
ad·ren'al·ine
a·drift'
a·droit'
a·droit'ly
a·droit'ness
ad·sorb'
ad·sorp'tion
ad'u·la'tion
ad'u·la·to'ry
a·dult'
a·dul'ter·ant
a·dul'ter·ate
a·dul'ter·at'ed
a·dul'ter·a'tion
a·dul'ter·er
a·dul'ter·ous
a·dul'ter·y
a·dult'hood
ad·um'brate
ad·um'brat·ed
ad'um·bra'tion
ad·vance'
ad·vanced'
ad·vance'ment
ad·van'tage
ad'van·ta'geous
ad'vent
Ad'vent·ist
ad'ven·ti'tious
ad·ven'ture
ad·ven'tur·er

ad·ven'ture·some
ad·ven'tur·ess
ad·ven'tur·ous
ad'verb
ad·ver'bi·al
ad·ver'bi·al·ly
ad'ver·sar'y
ad·ver'sa·tive
ad·verse'
ad·verse'ly
ad·ver'si·ty
ad·vert'
ad'ver·tise
ad·ver'tise·ment
ad'ver·tis'er
ad·vice'
ad·vis'a·bil'i·ty
ad·vis'a·ble
ad·vise'
ad·vised'
ad·vis'ed·ly
ad'vi·see'
ad·vise'ment
ad·vi'so·ry
ad'vo·ca·cy
ad'vo·cate
ad'vo·cat'ed
ad·vow'son
adz
ae'gis
ae·o'li·an
ae'on

a'er·ate

a'er·at'ed

a'er·a'tion

a'er·a'tor

a·e'ri·al

a'er·o·nau'ti·cal

aes·thet'ic

a·far'

af'fa·bil'i·ty

af'fa·ble

af'fa·bly

af·fair'

af·fect'

af'fec·ta'tion

af·fect'ed

af·fect'ed·ly

af·fect'ing·ly

af·fec'tion

af·fec'tion·ate

af·fec'tion·ate·ly

af'fec·tiv'i·ty

af·fi'ance

af·fi'anced

af·fi'ant

af'fi·da'vit

af·fil'i·ate

af·fil'i·at'ed

af·fil'i·a'tion

af·fin'i·ty

af·firm'

af·firm'a·ble

af'fir·ma'tion

af·firm'a·tive

af·firm'a·to'ry

af·firmed'

af·fix'

af·fixed'

af·fla'tus

af·flict'

af·flict'ed

af·flic'tion

af·flic'tive

af'flu·ence

af'flu·ent

af·ford'

af·ford'ed

af·for'est

af·for'est·a'tion

af·fray'

af·fright'

af·fright'ed

af·front'

af·front'ed

af'ghan

a·field'

a·fire'

a·flame'

a·float'

a·foot'

a·fore'said'

a·fore'thought'

a·fore'time'

a·foul'

a·fraid'

a·fresh'

aft'er

aft'er·beat'

aft'er·care'

aft'er·clap'

aft'er·deck'

aft'er-din'ner

aft'er·ef·fect'

aft'er·glow'

aft'er·growth'

aft'er·guard'

aft'er·hatch'

aft'er·hold'

aft'er·im'age

aft'er·life'

aft'er·math

aft'er·most

aft'er·noon'

aft'er·part'

aft'er·taste'

aft'er·thought'

aft'er·time'

aft'er·ward

a·gain'

a·gainst'

a·gape'

ag'ate

ag'ate·ware'

a·ga've

age

aged

age'less

a'gen·cy	ag'i·ta'tor	ai'ler·on
a·gen'da	a·gleam'	ail'ment
a·gen'dum	ag'nate	aim
a'gent	ag·nos'tic	aim'less
a·ger'a·tum	ag·nos'ti·cism	air
ag·glom'er·ate	a·gog'	air'brush'
ag·glom'er·at'ed	ag'o·nize	air'-dry'
ag·glom'er·a'tion	ag'o·nized	aired
ag·glom'er·a'tive	ag'o·niz'ing·ly	air'field'
ag·glu'ti·nate	ag'o·ny	air'foil'
ag·glu'ti·na'tion	a·grar'i·an	air'i·ly
ag·glu'ti·na'tive	a·gree'	air'lin'er
ag'gran·dize	a·gree'a·bil'i·ty	air'mail'
ag·gran'dize·ment	a·gree'a·ble	air'man
ag'gra·vate	a·gree'a·ble·ness	air'plane'
ag'gra·vat'ed	a·greed'	air'port'
ag'gra·vat'ing·ly	a·gree'ment	air'ship'
ag'gra·va'tion	ag'ri·cul'tur·al	air'sick'
ag'gre·gate	ag'ri·cul'ture	air'space'
ag'gre·ga'tion	a·gron'o·my	air'tight'
ag·gres'sion	a·ground'	air'way'
ag·gres'sive	a'gue	air'wor'thy
ag·gres'sor	a·head'	air'y
ag·grieve'	a·hoy'	aisle
ag·grieved'	a·hun'gered	a·jar'
a·ghast'	aid	a·kim'bo
ag'ile	aid'ed	a·kin'
a·gil'i·ty	ai·grette'	al'a·bas'ter
ag'i·o	ai'guil·lette'	a·lac'ri·ty
ag'i·tate	ail	al'a·mo
ag'i·tat'ed	ai·lan'thus	a·larm'
ag'i·ta'tion	ailed	a·larmed'

a·larm′ing·ly	Al·ge′ri·an	al·le′giance
a·larm′ist	a′li·as	al′le·gor′i·cal
a·las′	al′i·bi	al′le·go·rize
al′ba·core	al′i·dade	al′le·go′ry
al′ba·tross	al′ien	al′le·gret′to
al·bi′no	al′ien·a·bil′i·ty	al·le′gro
al′bum	al′ien·a·ble	al′ler·gen
al·bu′min	al′ien·ate	al·ler′gic
al·bu′mi·nous	al′ien·at′ed	al′ler·gy
al′che·mist	al′ien·a′tion	al·le′vi·ate
al′che·my	al′ien·ist	al·le′vi·at′ed
al′co·hol	a·light′	al·le′vi·a′tion
al′co·hol′ic	a·lign′	al′ley
al′co·hol·ism	a·lign′ment	al′ley·way′
al′co·hol·ize	a·like′	al·li′ance
al′cove	al′i·men′ta·ry	al·lied′
al′der	al′i·men·ta′tion	al′li·ga′tor
al′der·man	al′i·mo′ny	al·lit′er·ate
al′der·man′ic	al′i·quant	al·lit′er·a′tion
Al′der·ney	al′i·quot	al·lit′er·a′tive
a′le·a·to′ry	a·live′	al·lit′er·a′tive·ly
a·lem′bic	a·live′ness	al′lo·ca·ble
a·lem′bi·cate	a·liz′a·rin	al′lo·cate
Al′e·mite	al′ka·li	al′lo·cat′ed
a·lert′	al′ka·lin′i·ty	al′lo·ca′tion
a·lert′ly	all	al′lo·cu′tion
a·lert′ness	al·lay′	al′lo·path
ale′wife′	al·layed′	al′lo·path′ic
al′ex·an′drite	al′le·ga′tion	al·lop′a·thy
al·fal′fa	al·lege′	al·lot′
al′ge·bra	al·leged′	al·lot′ment
al′ge·bra′ic	al·leg′ed·ly	al·lot′ted

al·low'

al·low'a·ble

al·low'ance

al·lowed'

al·low'ed·ly

al·loy'

al·loy'age

al·loyed'

all'spice'

al·lude'

al·lud'ed

al·lure'

al·lured'

al·lure'ment

al·lur'ing·ly

al·lu'sion

al·lu'sive

al·lu'sive·ly

al·lu'sive·ness

al·lu'vi·al

al·lu'vi·um

al·ly'

al'ma·nac

al·might'y

al'mond

al'mon·er

al'most

alms

alms'house'

a·lo'di·um

al'oe

a·loft'

a·lo'ha

a·lone'

a·long'

a·long'side'

a·loof'

a·loof'ly

al·o·pe'ci·a

a·loud'

al·pac'a

al'pha·bet

al'pha·bet'ic

al'pha·bet'i·cal

al'pha·bet·ize

al·read'y

al'so

al'tar

al'tar·piece'

al'ter

al'ter·a·ble

al'ter·a'tion

al'ter·a'tive

al'ter·cate

al'ter·ca'tion

al'tered

al'ter·nate

al'ter·nat'ed

al'ter·na'tion

al·ter'na·tive

al'ter·na'tor

al·though'

al'ti·graph

al·tim'e·ter

al'ti·pla'no

al·tis'si·mo

al'ti·tude

al'to

al'to·geth'er

al'tru·ism

al'tru·ist

al'tru·is'tic

al'tru·is'ti·cal·ly

al'um

a·lu'mi·na

a·lu'mi·nate

a·lu'mi·nif'er·ous

a·lu'mi·no'sis

a·lu'mi·num

a·lum'na

a·lum'nae

a·lum'ni

a·lum'nus

al·ve'o·lar

al·ve'o·lus

al'ways

a·lys'sum

a·mal'gam

a·mal'gam·ate

a·mal'gam·at'ed

a·mal'gam·a'tion

a·man'u·en'sis

am'a·ranth

am'a·ran'thine

a·mass'

a·massed'

am'a·teur'

am'a·teur'ish

am'a·teur'ism

am'a·tive

am'a·tive·ness

am'a·to'ry

a·maze'

a·mazed'

a·maze'ment

a·maz'ing·ly

Am'a·zon

Am'a·zo'ni·an

am·bas'sa·dor

am·bas'sa·do'ri·al

am·bas'sa·do'ri·al·ly

am·bas'sa·dress

am'ber

am'ber·gris

am'bi·dex·ter'i·ty

am'bi·dex'trous

am'bi·dex'trous·ly

am'bi·dex'trous·ness

am'bi·ent

am'bi·gu'i·ty

am·big'u·ous

am·big'u·ous·ly

am·big'u·ous·ness

am·bi'tion

am·bi'tious

am·bi'tious·ly

am·biv'a·lence

am·biv'a·lent

am'ble

am·bro'si·a

am·bro'si·al

am·bro'si·al·ly

am'bro·type

am'bu·lance

am'bu·lant

am'bu·la·to'ry

am'bus·cade'

am'bush

a·mel'io·rate

a·mel'io·rat'ed

a·mel'io·ra'tion

a·mel'io·ra'tive

a'men'

a·me'na·bil'i·ty

a·me'na·ble

a·mend'

a·mend'ed

a·mend'ment

a·men'i·ty

A·mer'i·can

A·mer'i·can·i·za'tion

A·mer'i·can·ize

am'e·thyst

a'mi·a·bil'i·ty

a'mi·a·ble

am'i·ca·bil'i·ty

am'i·ca·ble

a·mid'ships

a·midst'

a·miss'

am'i·ty

am'me'ter

am·mo'ni·a

am·mo'ni·um

am'mu·ni'tion

am·ne'si·a

am'nes·ty

a·moe'ba

a·mong'

a·mongst'

a·mor'al

am'o·rous

am'o·rous·ly

am'o·rous·ness

a·mor'phous

a·mor'ti·za'tion

a·mor'tize

a·mor'tized

a·mount'

a·mount'ed

a·mour'

am·per'age

am'pere

am'per·sand

am·phib'i·an

am·phib'i·ous

am·phib'i·ous·ly

am'phi·the'a·ter

am'pho·ra

am'ple

am'pli·fi·ca'tion

am'pli·fied

am'pli·fi'er

am'pli·fy

am'pli·tude

am'ply

am·pul'la

am'pu·tate

am'pu·tat'ed

am'pu·ta'tion

am'pu·ta'tive

am'pu·tee'

a·muck'

am'u·let

a·muse'

a·mused'

a·muse'ment

a·mus'ing·ly

a·nab'o·lism

a·nach'ro·nism

a·nach'ro·nis'tic

a·nach'ro·nous

an'a·con'da

an'a·gram

an'a·lects

an'al·ge'si·a

an'al·ge'sic

an'a·log'i·cal

a·nal'o·gies

a·nal'o·gous

a·nal'o·gous·ly

an'a·logue

a·nal'o·gy

a·nal'y·ses

a·nal'y·sis

an'a·lyst

an'a·lyt'ic

an'a·lyt'i·cal

an'a·lyt'i·cal·ly

an'a·lyze

an'a·lyzed

an'a·lyz'er

an'am·ne'sis

an·ar'chic

an·ar'chi·cal

an'arch·ism

an'arch·ist

an'arch·y

an·as'tig·mat'ic

a·nath'e·ma·tize

an'a·tom'ic

an'a·tom'i·cal

a·nat'o·mist

a·nat'o·mize

a·nat'o·mized

a·nat'o·my

an'ces'tor

an'ces'tors

an·ces'tral

an'ces'try

an'chor

an'chor·age

an'chored

an'cho·rite

an·cho'vy

an'cient

an'cil·lar'y

and

an·dan'te

and'i'ron

an'ec·dot'age

an'ec·dote

a·ne'mi·a

an'e·mom'e·ter

an'e·mom'e·try

a·nem'o·ne

a·nent'

an'er·oid

an'es·the'si·a

an'es·the'si·ol'o·gy

an'es·the'sis

an'es·thet'ic

an'es·thet'i·za'tion

an·es'the·tize

an·es'the·tized

an'eu·rysm

a·new'

an'gel

an·gel'ic

An'ge·lus

an'ger

an'gered

an'gle

an'gled

an'gler

An'gli·can

An'glo-Sax'on

An·go'ra

an'gri·er

an'gri·est

an'gri·ly

an'gry

an'guish

an'guished

an'gu·lar

an'gu·lar'i·ty

an'gu·la'tion

an·hy'drous

an'i·line

an'i·mad·ver'sion

an'i·mal

an'i·mate

an'i·mat'ed

an'i·mat'ed·ly

an'i·ma'tion

an'i·ma'tor

an'i·mism

an'i·mist

an'i·mis'tic

an'i·mos'i·ty

an'i·mus

an'ise

an'ise·root'

an'kle

an'kle·bone'

an'klet

an'ky·lo'sis

an'nal·ist

an'nals

an·neal'

an·nealed'

an·nex'

an'nex·a'tion

an'nex·a'tion·ist

an·nexed'

an·ni'hi·late

an·ni'hi·lat'ed

an·ni'hi·la'tion

an'ni·ver'sa·ry

an'no·tate

an'no·tat'ed

an'no·ta'tion

an·nounce'

an·nounced'

an·nounce'ment

an·nounc'er

an·noy'

an·noy'ance

an·noyed'

an·noy'ing·ly

an'nu·al

an'nu·al·ly

an·nu'i·tant

an·nu'i·ty

an·nul'

an'nu·lar

an·nulled'

an·nul'ment

an·nun'ci·a'tion

an·nun'ci·a'tor

an'ode

an'o·dyne

a·noint'

a·noint'ed

a·nom'a·lies

a·nom'a·lous

a·nom'a·lous·ly

a·nom'a·ly

a·non'

an'o·nym'i·ty

a·non'y·mous

a·non'y·mous·ly

a·noph'e·les

an·oth'er

an'swer

an'swer·a·ble

an'swered

ant

ant·ac'id

an·tag'o·nism

an·tag'o·nist

an·tag'o·nis'tic

an·tag'o·nis'ti·cal·ly

an·tag'o·nize

an·tag'o·nized

ant·arc'tic

an'te

ant'eat'er

an'te·ced'ent

an'te·cham'ber

an'te·date'

an'te·dat'ed

an'te·lope

an'te·na'tal

an·ten'na	an'ti·quar'y	a·part'
an·te'ri·or	an'ti·quat'ed	a·part'ment
an'te·room'	an·tique'	ap'a·thet'ic
an'them	an·tiqued'	ap'a·thet'i·cal·ly
an·thol'o·gies	an·tiq'ui·ty	ap'a·thy
an·thol'o·gist	an'ti·sep'sis	a·pe'ri·ent
an·thol'o·gize	an'ti·sep'tic	a·per'i·tive
an·thol'o·gy	an'ti·sep'ti·cal·ly	ap'er·ture
an'thra·cite	an'ti·so'cial	a'pex
an'thrax	an'ti·tank'	a'pex·es
an'thro·poid	an·tith'e·ses	a·pha'si·a
an'thro·po·log'i·cal	an·tith'e·sis	a'phid
an'thro·pol'o·gy	an'ti·thet'i·cal	aph'o·rism
an'ti·bod'y	an'ti·tox'in	aph'o·ris'tic
an'tic	an'ti·trust'	a'pi·a·rist
an'ti·christ'	ant'ler	a'pi·ar'y
an·tic'i·pate	ant'lered	ap'i·cal
an·tic'i·pat'ed	an'to·nym	ap'i·ces
an·tic'i·pa'tion	an'trum	a·piece'
an·tic'i·pa·to'ry	an'vil	a·poc'a·lypse
an'ti·cli'max	anx·i'e·ty	a·poc'ry·phal
an'ti·cline	anx'ious	ap'o·gee
an'ti·dote	anx'ious·ly	a·pol'o·get'ic
an'ti·gen	an'y	a·pol'o·get'i·cal
an'ti·knock'	an'y·bod'y	a·pol'o·gies
an'ti·mo'ny	an'y·one	a·pol'o·gist
an·tin'o·my	an'y·thing	a·pol'o·gize
an·tip'a·thies	an'y·way	a·pol'o·gized
an·tip'a·thy	an'y·where	a·pol'o·gy
an·tiph'o·nal	a·or'ta	ap'o·plec'tic
an·tip'o·des	a·or'tic	ap'o·plex'y
an'ti·quar'i·an	a·pace'	a·pos'ta·sy

a·pos′tate

a·pos′tle

ap′os·tol′ic

ap′os·tol′i·cal

a·pos′tro·phe

a·pos′tro·phize

a·poth′e·car′y

ap′o·thegm

a·poth′e·o′sis

ap·pall′

ap·palled′

ap·pall′ing·ly

ap′pa·nage

ap′pa·ra′tus

ap′pa·ra′tus·es

ap·par′el

ap·par′eled

ap·par′ent

ap′pa·ri′tion

ap·peal′

ap·pealed′

ap·peal′ing·ly

ap·pear′

ap·pear′ance

ap·peared′

ap·peas′a·ble

ap·pease′

ap·peased′

ap·pease′ment

ap·peas′ing·ly

ap·pel′lant

ap·pel′late

ap′pel·la′tion

ap′pel·lee′

ap·pend′

ap·pend′age

ap′pen·dec′to·my

ap·pend′ed

ap·pen′di·ci′tis

ap·pen′dix

ap·pen′dix·es

ap′per·ceive′

ap′per·ceived′

ap′per·cep′tion

ap′per·cep′tive

ap′per·tain′

ap′per·tained′

ap′pe·tite

ap′pe·tiz′er

ap′pe·tiz′ing·ly

ap·plaud′

ap·plaud′ed

ap·plause′

ap′ple

ap′ple·jack′

ap′ple·nut′

ap′ple·sauce′

ap·pli′ance

ap′pli·ca·bil′i·ty

ap′pli·ca·ble

ap′pli·cant

ap′pli·ca′tion

ap′pli·ca′tor

ap·plied′

ap′pli·qué′

ap·ply′

ap·point′

ap·point′ed

ap·point′ee′

ap·poin′tive

ap·point′ment

ap·por′tion

ap·por′tioned

ap·por′tion·ment

ap′po·site

ap′po·si′tion

ap·prais′al

ap·praise′

ap·praised′

ap·prais′er

ap·prais′ing·ly

ap·pre′ci·a·ble

ap·pre′ci·a·bly

ap·pre′ci·ate

ap·pre′ci·at′ed

ap·pre′ci·a′tion

ap·pre′ci·a′tive

ap·pre′ci·a′tive·ly

ap′pre·hend′

ap′pre·hend′ed

ap′pre·hend′ing·ly

ap′pre·hen′sion

ap′pre·hen′sive

ap′pre·hen′sive·ly

ap′pre·hen′sive·ness

ap·pren′tice

ap·pren'ticed	ap'ti·tude	ar'bi·trat'ed
ap·pren'tice·ship	apt'ly	ar'bi·tra'tion
ap·prise'	apt'ness	ar'bi·tra'tive
ap·prised'	aq'ua·ma·rine'	ar'bi·tra'tor
ap·proach'	aq'ua·relle'	ar'bor
ap·proach'a·ble	a·quar'i·um	ar·bo're·al
ap·proached'	aq'ua·scu'tum	ar·bo're·ous
ap'pro·ba'tion	a·quat'ic	ar·bo·re'tum
ap'pro·ba'tive	aq'ua·tint'	ar·bu'tus
ap'pro·ba'tive·ness	aq'ue·duct	arc
ap·pro'pri·ate	a'que·ous	ar·cade'
ap·pro'pri·at'ed	aq'ui·line	ar·cad'ed
ap·pro'pri·ate·ly	Ar'ab	Ar·ca'di·a
ap·pro'pri·ate·ness	ar'a·besque'	ar·ca'num
ap·pro'pri·a'tion	A·ra'bi·an	arch
ap·prov'al	Ar'a·bic	ar'chae·ol'o·gist
ap·prove'	ar'a·bil'i·ty	ar'chae·ol'o·gy
ap·proved'	Ar'ab·ist	ar·cha'ic
ap·prov'ing·ly	ar'a·ble	arch'an'gel
ap·prox'i·mate	a·rach'nid	arch'an·gel'ic
ap·prox'i·mat'ed	a·rach'noid	arch'bish'op
ap·prox'i·mate·ly	a·rag'o·nite	arch'dea'con
ap·prox'i·ma'tion	Ar'a·ma'ic	arch'di·o·cese
ap·pur'te·nance	ar'ba·lest	arch'du'cal
ap·pur'te·nant	ar'bi·ter	arch'duch'ess
a'pri·cot	ar'bi·tra·ble	arch'duch'y
A'pril	ar'bi·trage	arch'duke'
a'pron	ar·bit'ra·ment	arch'er
ap'ro·pos'	ar'bi·trar'i·ly	arch'er·fish'
apse	ar'bi·trar'i·ness	arch'er·y
ap'sis	ar'bi·trar'y	ar'che·typ'al
apt	ar'bi·trate	ar'che·type

arch'fiend'	ar'gu·men'ta·tive	arm'scye'
ar'chi·pel'a·go	Ar'gy·rol	ar'my
ar'chi·tect	a'ri·a	ar'ni·ca
ar'chi·tec·ton'ic	ar'id	a·ro'ma
ar'chi·tec'tur·al	a·rid'i·ty	ar'o·mat'ic
ar'chi·tec'tur·al·ly	a·right'	a·round'
ar'chi·tec'ture	a·rise'	a·rouse'
ar'chi·trave	a·ris'en	ar·peg'gio
ar'chives	ar'is·toc'ra·cy	ar·raign'
ar'chi·vist	a·ris'to·crat	ar·raigned'
arch'ly	a·ris'to·crat'ic	ar·raign'ment
arch'ness	a·rith'me·tic	ar·range'
arch'way	ar'ith·met'i·cal	ar·ranged'
arc'tic	ark	ar·range'ment
ar'dent	arm	ar·rang'er
ar'dent·ly	ar·ma'da	ar'ras
ar'dor	ar'ma·dil'lo	ar·ray'
ar'du·ous	ar'ma·ment	ar·rayed'
ar'du·ous·ly	ar'ma·ture	ar·rear'age
are	arm'chair	ar·rears'
a're·a	armed	ar·rest'
a·re'na	Ar·me'ni·an	ar·rest'er
ar'gent	arm'ful	ar·rhyth'mic
ar'gen·tif'er·ous	arm'hole'	ar·riv'al
ar'gon	ar'mi·stice	ar·rive'
Ar'go·naut	arm'let	ar·rived'
ar'got	ar'mor	ar'ro·gance
ar'gu·a·ble	ar'mored	ar'ro·gant
ar'gue	ar·mo'ri·al	ar'ro·gant·ly
ar'gued	ar'mor·y	ar'ro·gate
ar'gu·ment	arm'pit'	ar'ro·gat'ed
ar'gu·men·ta'tion	arm'rest'	ar'ro·ga'tion

ar′row	ar·tif′i·cer	a·sep′tic
ar′row·head′	ar′ti·fi′cial	ash
ar′row·head′ed	ar′ti·fi′ci·al′i·ty	a·shamed′
ar′row·wood′	ar′ti·fi′cial·ly	ash′en
ar′row·y	ar·til′ler·ist	ash′es
ar·roy′o	ar·til′ler·y	ash′lar
ar′se·nal	ar′ti·san	a·shore′
ar′se·nate	art′ist	ash′pit′
ar·sen′ic	ar·tis′tic	ash′wort′
ar·sen′i·cal	art′ist·ry	ash′y
ar′se·nide	art′less	A′sian
ar′se·nite	Ar′y·an	A′si·at′ic
ar′son	as	a·side′
ar′son·ist	as′a·fet′i·da	as′i·nine
art	as·bes′tos	as′i·nin′i·ty
ar·te′ri·al	as·cend′	ask
ar′ter·y	as·cend′an·cy	a·skance′
art′ful	as·cend′ant	a·skew′
art′ful·ly	as·cend′er	a·slant′
ar·thrit′ic	as·cen′sion	a·sleep′
ar·thrit′i·cal	as·cent′	asp
ar·thri′tis	as′cer·tain′	as·par′a·gus
ar′thro·plas′ty	as′cer·tain′ment	as′pect
ar′ti·choke	as·cet′ic	as′pen
ar′ti·cle	as·cet′i·cism	as·per′i·ty
ar′ti·cled	as·ci′tes	as·perse′
ar·tic′u·late	a·scor′bic	as·persed′
ar·tic′u·lat′ed	as′cot	as·per′sion
ar·tic′u·la′tion	as·cribe′	as′phalt
ar·tic′u·la′tive	as·cribed′	as·phal′tic
ar′ti·fact	as·crip′tion	as′pho·del
ar′ti·fice	a·sep′sis	as·phyx′i·a

as·phyx′i·ate

as·phyx′i·a′tion

as′pic

as·pir′ant

as′pi·rate

as′pi·rat′ed

as′pi·ra′tion

as′pi·ra′tor

as·pire′

as·pired′

as′pi·rin

as′sa·gai

as·sail′

as·sail′ant

as·sailed′

as·sas′sin

as·sas′si·nate

as·sas′si·nat′ed

as·sas′si·na′tion

as·sault′

as·sault′ed

as·say′

as·sayed′

as·say′er

as·sem′blage

as·sem′ble

as·sem′bled

as·sem′bler

as·sem′bly

as·sent′

as·sent′ed

as·sent′ing·ly

as·sert′

as·sert′ed

as·ser′tion

as·ser′tive

as·ser′tive·ly

as·sess′

as·sess′a·ble

as·sessed′

as·sess′ment

as·ses′sor

as·ses′sor·ship

as′set

as·sev′er·ate

as·sev′er·a′tion

as′si·du′i·ty

as·sid′u·ous

as·sid′u·ous·ly

as·sign′

as·sign′a·ble

as′sig·na′tion

as·signed′

as′sign·ee′

as·sign′ment

as′sign·or′

as·sim′i·la·ble

as·sim′i·late

as·sim′i·lat′ed

as·sim′i·la′tion

as·sim′i·la′tive

as·sim′i·la·to′ry

as·sist′

as·sist′ance

as·sist′ant

as·sist′ed

as·sists′

as·size′

as·so′ci·ate

as·so′ci·at′ed

as·so′ci·a′tion

as·so′ci·a′tive

as′so·nance

as′so·nant

as·sort′

as·sort′ed

as·sort′ment

as·suage′

as·suaged′

as·sum′a·ble

as·sum′a·bly

as·sume′

as·sumed′

as·sum′ed·ly

as·sump′sit

as·sump′tion

as·sur′ance

as·sure′

as·sured′

as·sur′ed·ly

as·sur′ed·ness

as·sur′er

As·syr′i·an

as′ter

as′ter·isk

a·stern′

as'ter·oid	as·tute'ly	a·tone'
as·the'ni·a	as·tute'ness	a·toned'
as·then'ic	a·sun'der	a·tone'ment
asth'ma	a·sy'lum	a'tri·um
asth·mat'ic	a'sym·met'ric	a·tro'cious
as'tig·mat'ic	a'sym·met'ri·cal	a·tro'cious·ly
a·stig'ma·tism	a·sym'me·try	a·troc'i·ty
as·ton'ish	at	at'ro·phied
as·ton'ish·ing·ly	at'a·rax'i·a	at'ro·phy
as·ton'ish·ment	at'a·vism	at'ro·pine
as·tound'	at'a·vis'tic	at·tach'
as·tound'ed	a'the·ism	at·tached'
as·tound'ing·ly	a'the·ist	at·tach'ment
a·strad'dle	a'the·is'tic	at·tack'
as·trag'a·lus	ath'e·nae'um	at·tack'er
as'tra·khan	A·the'ni·an	at·tain'
as'tral	ath'lete	at·tain'a·ble
a·stray'	ath·let'ic	at·tain'der
a·stride'	ath·let'ics	at·tained'
as·trin'gen·cy	a·thwart'	at·tain'ment
as·trin'gent	at'mos·phere	at'tar
as'tro·labe	at'mos·pher'ic	at·tempt'
as·trol'o·ger	at'oll	at·tempt'ed
as·trol'o·gy	at'om	at·tend'
as'tro·nau'tics	at'om·at'ic	at·tend'ance
as·tron'o·mer	a·tom'ic	at·tend'ant
as·tro·nom'i·cal	at'om·is'tic	at·ten'tion
as·tron'o·my	at'om·ize	at·ten'tive
as'tro·phys'i·cal	at'om·ized	at·ten'tive·ly
as'tro·phys'i·cist	at'om·iz'er	at·ten'tive·ness
as'tro·phys'ics	a·ton'al	at·ten'u·ate
as·tute'	a'to·nal'i·ty	at·ten'u·at'ed

at·ten'u·a'tion

at·test'

at'tes·ta'tion

at·tests'

at'tic

at·tire'

at·tired'

at'ti·tude

at'ti·tu'di·nize

at·tor'ney

at·tor'neys

at·tract'

at·tract'ed

at·trac'tion

at·trac'tive

at·trac'tive·ly

at·trib'ute

at·trib'ut·ed

at'tri·bu'tion

at·trib'u·tive

at·tri'tion

at·tune'

at·tuned'

a·twit'ter

a·typ'i·cal

au'burn

auc'tion

auc'tioned

auc'tion·eer'

au·da'cious

au·da'cious·ly

au·dac'i·ty

au'di·bil'i·ty

au'di·ble

au'di·bly

au'di·ence

au'di·o

au'di·om'e·ter

au'dit

au'dit·ed

au·di'tion

au'di·tor

au'di·to'ri·um

au'di·to'ry

au'ger

aught

aug·ment'

aug'men·ta'tion

aug·ment'a·tive

aug·ment'ed

au'gur

au'gured

au'gu·ry

au·gust'

Au'gust

aunt

au'ra

au'ral

au're·ole

au'ri·cle

au·ric'u·lar

au·rif'er·ous

au·ro'ra

au·ro'ral

aus'cul·tate

aus'cul·ta'tion

aus'pice

aus'pic·es

aus·pi'cious

aus·tere'

aus·tere'ly

aus·ter'i·ty

Aus·tral'ian

Aus'tri·an

au·then'tic

au·then'ti·cate

au·then'ti·cat'ed

au·then'ti·ca'tion

au'then·tic'i·ty

au'thor

au·thor'i·tar'i·an

au·thor'i·ta'tive

au·thor'i·ta'tive·ly

au·thor'i·ty

au'thor·i·za'tion

au'thor·ize

au'thor·ized

au'thor·ship

au'to·bi'o·graph'i·cal

au'to·bi·og'ra·phy

au·toch'tho·nous

au'to·clave

au·toc'ra·cy

au'to·crat

au'to·crat'ic

au'to·crat'i·cal·ly

au'to·graph

au'to·in·tox'i·ca'tion

au'to·mat'ic

au·tom'a·tism

au·tom'a·tize

au·tom'a·ton

au'to·mo·bile'

au·ton'o·mize

au·ton'o·mous

au·ton'o·my

au'top·sies

au'top·sy

au'to·sug·ges'tion

au'tumn

au·tum'nal

aux·il'ia·ry

a·vail'

a·vail'a·bil'i·ty

a·vail'a·ble

a·vailed'

av'a·lanche

av'a·rice

av'a·ri'cious

av'a·ri'cious·ly

av'a·tar'

a·venge'

a·venged'

av'e·nue

a·ver'

av'er·age

av'er·aged

a·ver'ment

a·verred'

a·verse'

a·ver'sion

a·vert'

a·vert'ed

a'vi·ar'y

a'vi·a'tion

a'vi·a'tor

av'id

a·vid'i·ty

av'id·ly

av'i·ga'tion

av'o·ca'do

av'o·ca'tion

a·void'

a·void'a·ble

a·void'ed

a·vow'al

a·vow'ed·ly

a·vun'cu·lar

a·wait'

a·wait'ed

a·wake'

a·wak'en

a·wak'ened

a·ward'

a·ward'ed

a·ware'

a·ware'ness

a·wash'

a·way'

awe

awe'some

aw'ful

aw'ful·ly

awk'ward

awk'ward·ly

awk'ward·ness

awl

awn'ing

a·woke'

a·wry'

ax

ax'i·om

ax'i·o·mat'ic

ax'is

ax'le

a·za'le·a

az'i·muth

Az'tec

az'ure

az'u·rite

B

bab'bitt

bab'ble

ba·boon'

ba'by

Bab'y·lo'ni·an

bac'ca·lau're·ate

bac'cha·nal

bac'cha·na'li·an

bach'e·lor

bach'e·lor·hood'

ba·cil'lus

back

back'ache'

back'board'

back'bone'

back'break'er

back'drop'

back'er

back'fire'

back'gam'mon

back'ground'

back'hand'

back'hand'ed

back'lash'

back'log'

back'saw'

back'slide'

back'slid'er

back'spin'

back'stage'

back'stamp'

back'stitch'

back'stop'

back'stroke'

back'track'

back'ward

back'ward·ness

back'wash'

back'wa'ter

back'woods'

ba'con

bac·te'ri·a

bac·te'ri·al

bac·te'ri·cid'al

bac·te'ri·cide

bac·te'ri·o·log'i·cal

bac·te'ri·ol'o·gy

bac·te'ri·um

bad

badge

badg'er

bad'i·nage'

bad'lands'

bad'ly

bad'min·ton

bad'ness

baf'fle

baf'fled

bag

ba·gasse'

bag'a·telle'

bag'gage

bagged

bag'pipe'

bail

bailed

bail'ee'	bal·loon'	bang
bail'iff	bal·loon'ist	bang'board'
bail'i·wick	bal'lot	banged
bail'ment	ball'play'er	bang'le
bait	ball'room'	ban'ish
baize	balm	ban'ish·ment
bake	bal'sa	ban'is·ter
Ba'ke·lite	bal'sam	ban'jo
bak'er	bal'sam·if'er·ous	bank
bak'er·y	bal'us·ter	bank'book'
bal'ance	bal'us·trade'	banked
bal'anced	bam·boo'	bank'er
bal·bo'a	bam·boo'zle	bank'rupt
bal·brig'gan	bam·boo'zled	bank'rupt cy
bal'co·ny	ban	banned
bald	ba'nal	ban'ner
bal'da·chin	ba·nal'i·ty	banns
bal'der·dash	ba·nan'a	ban'quet
bald'ness	band	ban'quet·ed
bal'dric	band'age	ban'shee
bale	ban·dan'na	ban'tam
baled	band'box'	ban'ter
bale'ful	ban·deau'	ban'tered
balk	band'ed	ban'ter·ing·ly
ball	ban'de·role	ban'yan
bal'lad	ban'di·coot	ban'zai'
bal'last	ban'dit	bap'tism
balled	band'mas'ter	bap·tis'mal
bal'le·ri'na	ban'do·leer'	Bap'tist
bal'let	band'stand'	bap·tize'
bal·let'o·mane	ban'dy	bap·tized'
bal·lis'tics	bane'ful	bap·tize'ment

bar	bar'na·cle	base'board'
barb	barn'yard'	based
bar·bar'i·an	bar'o·gram	base'less
bar·bar'ic	bar'o·graph	base'ly
bar'ba·rism	ba·rom'e·ter	base'ment
bar·bar'i·ty	bar'o·met'ric	base'ness
bar'ba·rous	bar'on	bas'er
bar'be·cue	bar'on·age	bas'est
barbed	bar'on·ess	bash'ful
bar'ber	bar'on·et	bas'ic
bar'ber'ry	bar'on·et·cy	bas'i·cal·ly
bar·bette'	ba·ro'ni·al	ba·sil'i·ca
bar'bi·can	bar'o·ny	bas'i·lisk
bard	ba·roque'	ba'sin
bare	bar'rack	ba'sis
bare'back'	bar'ra·cu'da	bask
bared	bar·rage'	bas'ket
bare'faced'	bar'ra·try	bas'ket·ball'
bare'foot'	bar'rel	bas'ket·work'
bare'head'ed	bar'ren	bas'-re·lief'
bare'ly	bar'ren·ness	bass
bare'ness	bar'ri·cade'	bas'si·net'
bar'gain	bar'ri·cad'ed	bas'so
bar'gained	bar'ri·er	bas·soon'
barge	bar'ris·ter	bass'wood'
barge'man	bar'row	bast'ed
bar'i·tone	bar'ter	bas'ti·na'do
bar'i·um	bar'tered	bas'tion
bark	bas'al	bat
bar'ley	ba·salt'	batch
bar'maid'	bas'cule	bath
barn	base	bathe

bathed	bea'dle	be·calm'
bath'er	bead'work'	be·calmed'
bath'house'	bea'gle	be·came'
ba'thos	beak	be·cause'
bath'robe'	beak'er	beck'on
bath'room'	beam	beck'oned
ba·tiste'	beamed	be·cloud'
ba'ton'	bean	be·come'
bat·tal'ion	bear	be·com'ing·ly
bat'ten	bear'a·ble	be·com'ing·ness
bat'tened	beard	bed
bat'ter	beard'ed	be·daub'
bat'tered	bear'er	bed'bug'
bat'ter·y	bear'ish	bed'cham'ber
bat'tle	bear'skin'	bed'clothes'
bat'tled	beast	bed'ded
bat'tle·ment	beast'li·ness	be·deck'
bat'tle·ship'	beast'ly	be·dev'il
bawl	beat	be·dev'iled
bawled	beat'en	bed'fel'low
bay'ber'ry	beat'er	be·diz'en
bay'o·net	be·a·tif'ic	bed'lam
bay'o·net'ed	be·at'i·fi·ca'tion	bed'post'
bay'ou	be·at'i·fy	bed'rid'den
ba·zaar'	beat'ings	bed'rock'
be	be·at'i·tude	bed'roll'
beach	beau'te·ous	bed'room'
beached	beau'ti·ful	bed'side'
beach'comb'er	beau'ti·ful·ly	bed'spread'
bea'con	beau'ti·fy	bed'spring'
bead	beau'ty	bed'stead
bead'ed	bea'ver	bed'time'

bee	be·hav'ior	bell'bird'
beech	be·hav'ior·al	bell'boy'
beef	be·hav'ior·ism	bel'li·cose
beef'steak'	be·head'	bel'li·cos'i·ty
bee'line'	be·head'ings	bel·lig'er·ence
beer	be·held'	bel·lig'er·en·cy
bees'wax'	be·he'moth	bel·lig'er·ent
bee'tle	be·hest'	bel·lig'er·ent·ly
be·fall'	be·hind'	bel'lowed
be·fell'	be·hold'	bel'lows
be·fit'	be·hold'en	be·long'
be·fog'	be·hold'er	be·longed'
be·fore'	be·hoove'	be·long'ings
be·fore'hand'	beige	be·lov'ed
be·friend'	be·jew'el	be·low'
be·fud'dle	be·jew'eled	belt
be·fud'dled	be·la'bor	belt'ed
beg	be·lat'ed	bel've·dere'
be·get'	be·lat'ed·ly	be·moan'
beg'gar	belch	be·moaned'
begged	be·lea'guer	be·mused'
be·gin'	be·lea'guered	bench
be·gone'	bel'fry	bend
be·go'ni·a	Bel'gi·an	bend'ed
be·got'	be·lie'	be·neath'
be·grime'	be·lief'	ben'e·dic'tion
be·guile'	be·liev'a·ble	ben'e·fac'tion
be·guiled'	be·lieve'	ben'e·fac'tor
be'gum	be·lit'tle	ben'e·fac'tress
be·gun'	be·lit'tled	ben'e·fice
be·half'	bell	be·nef'i·cent
be·have'	bel'la·don'na	ben'e·fi'ci·ar'y

ben'e·fit

ben'e·fit'ed

be·nev'o·lence

be·nev'o·lent

be·night'ed

be·nign'

be·nig'nan·cy

be·nig'nant

be·nig'ni·ty

bent

ben'zene

be·queath'

be·quest'

be·rate'

be·rat'ed

be·reave'

be·reaved'

be·reave'ment

ber'ry

berth

ber'yl

be·seech'

be·seeched'

be·seech'ing·ly

be·set'

be·side'

be·sides'

be·siege'

be·sieged'

be·smirch'

be·sot'ted

be·span'gle

be·speak'

Bes'se·mer

best

bes'tial

bes'ti·al'i·ty

be·stow'

be·stowed'

be·stride'

bet

be·take'

be·tide'

be·times'

be·to'ken

be·tray'

be·tray'al

be·tray'er

be·troth'

be·troth'al

bet'ter

bet'tered

bet'ter·ment

be·tween'

be·twixt'

bev'el

bev'eled

bev'er·age

bev'y

be·wail'

be·wailed'

be·ware'

be·wil'der

be·wil'dered

be·wil'der·ing·ly

be·wil'der·ment

be·witch'

be·witch'ing·ly

be·yond'

bez'el

bi·an'nu·al

bi·an'nu·al·ly

bi'as

bi'ased

bi'be·lot'

Bi'ble

Bib'li·cal

bib'li·o·graph'i·cal

bib'li·og'ra·phy

bib'u·lous

bi·cam'er·al

bi·car'bon·ate

bi·cen'te·nar'y

bi'ceps

bi·chlo'ride

bi·chro'mate

bi·cus'pid

bi'cy·cle

bid

bid'der

bide

bi·en'ni·al

bi·en'ni·um

bier

bi·fo'cal

big

big'a·mist	bill'stick'er	birch
big'a·mous	bi'me·tal'lic	bird
big'a·my	bi·met'al·lism	bird'lime'
big'ger	bi·met'al·list	bird'man'
big'gest	bi·month'ly	birth
big'horn'	bin	birth'day'
bight	bi'na·ry	birth'mark'
big'ot	bin·au'ral	birth'place'
big'ot·ed	bind	birth'right'
big'ot·ry	bind'er	bis'cuit
bi'jou	bind'er·y	bi'sect
bi·lat'er·al	bind'ing·ly	bish'op
bile	bind'ings	bish'op·ric
bilge	bind'weed'	bis'muth
bil'i·ar'y	bin'go	bi'son
bi·lin'gual	bin'na·cle	bisque
bil'ious	bin·oc'u·lar	bit
bilk	bi·no'mi·al	bite
bill	bi·og'ra·pher	bit'er
bill'board'	bi'o·graph'ic	bit'ing·ly
billed	bi'o·graph'i·cal	bit'ten
bil'let	bi'o·graph'i·cal·ly	bit'ter
bil'let·ed	bi·og'ra·phy	bit'ter·est
bill'fish'	bi'o·log'i·cal	bit'ter·ly
bill'fold'	bi'o·log'i·cal·ly	bit'tern
bill'head'	bi·ol'o·gist	bit'ter·ness
bil'liards	bi·ol'o·gy	bit'ters
bil'lings	bi'op·sy	bit'ter·weed'
bil'lion	bi·par'tite	bi·tu'men
bil'lion·aire'	bi'ped	bi·tu'mi·nous
bil'low	bi'plane'	biv'ouac
bill'post'er	bi·po'lar	bi·zarre'

black	blan'dish·ing·ly	bleed'er
black'ball'	blan'dish·ment	blem'ish
black'ber'ry	bland'ly	blench
black'bird'	bland·ness	blend
black'board'	blank	blend'ed
black'en	blanked	blend'ings
black'er	blank'er	bless
black'est	blank'est	bless'ed·ness
black'fish'	blan'ket	bless'ings
black'guard	blank'ly	blew
black'head'	blare	blight
black'ish	blared	blight'ed
black'jack'	blar'ney	blimp
black'leg'	blas·pheme'	blind
black'mail'	blas·phemed'	blind'ed
black'mail'er	blas·phem'er	blind'er
black'ness	blas'phe·mous	blind'fold'
black'smith'	blas'phe·my	blind'ly
black'strap'	blast	blind'ness
black'thorn'	blast'ed	blink
blad'der	bla'tant	blinked
blade	blaze	blink'er
blame	blazed	bliss
blamed	blaz'er	bliss'ful
blame'less	bla'zon	bliss'ful·ly
blame'less·ly	bla'zoned	blis'ter
blame'less·ness	bleach	blis'tered
blame'wor'thy	bleached	blis'ter·ing·ly
blanch	bleach'er	blis'ter·y
blanc·mange'	bleak	blithe
bland	bleat	blithe'ly
blan'dish	bleed	blithe'some

bliz′zard	blow	blunt′ness
bloat	blow′er	blur
bloat′ed	blow′fish′	blurb
block	blow′fly′	blurred
block·ade′	blow′gun′	blurt
block·ad′ed	blow′hard′	blush
block·ad′er	blow′hole′	blushed
block′head′	blown	blush′ing·ly
block′house′	blow′off′	blus′ter
blond	blow′out′	blus′tered
blood	blow′pipe′	blus′ter·ing·ly
blood′ed	blow′torch′	blus′ter·y
blood′hound′	blow′y	bo′a
blood′i·est	blub′ber	board
blood′less	bludg′eon	board′ed
blood′let′ting	bludg′eoned	board′er
blood′line′	blue	boast
blood′root′	blue′fish′	boast′ed
blood′shed′	blue′grass′	boast′er
blood′shot′	blue′nose′	boast′ful
blood′stain′	blue′stock′ing	boast′ful·ly
blood′wood′	bluff	boat
blood′y	bluffed	boat′load′
bloom	bluff′er	boat′man′
bloomed	blun′der	boat′swain′
bloom′er	blun′dered	bob′bin
blos′som	blun′der·buss	bob′cat′
blos′somed	blun′der·er	bob′o·link
blot	blun′der·ing·ly	bob′tail′
blotch	blunt	bode
blot′ter	blunt′ed	bod′ice
blouse	blunt′ly	bod′i·ly

bod'kin	bol'stered	bo·ni'to
bod'y	bolt	bon'net
bod'y·guard'	bolt'ed	bon'net·ed
bod'y·mak'er	bolt'head'	bo'nus
bog	bo'lus	bon'y
bo'gey	bomb	boo'by
bog'gle	bom·bard'	boo'dle
bog'gled	bom·bard'ed	book
bo'gus	bom'bard·ier'	book'bind'er
bog'wood'	bom·bard'ment	booked
Bo·he'mi·an	bom'bast	book'ings
boil	bom·bas'tic	book'ish
boiled	bombed	book'keep'er
boil'er	bomb'er	book'keep'ing
bois'ter·ous	bomb'proof'	book'let
bois'ter·ous·ly	bomb'shell'	book'lets
bo'la	bo·nan'za	book'mak'er
bold	bon'bon'	book'man
bold'er	bond	book'mark'
bold'est	bond'age	book'plate'
bold'face'	bond'ed	book'rack'
bold'ly	bond'hold'er	book'rest'
bold'ness	bond'man	book'sell'er
bo·le'ro	bond'slave'	book'shelf
bole'weed'	bonds'man	book'stall'
bo·liv'i·a	bone	book'stand'
bo·li'via'no	boned	book'worm'
boll	bone'fish'	boom
bo'lo	bone'less	boomed
bo·lom'e·ter	bone'set'	boom'er·ang
bol'she·vik	bon'fire'	boon
bol'ster	bon'go	boor

boor'ish

boost

boost'ed

boost'er

boot

boot'black'

boot'ed

boot'ee'

boot'er·y

booth

boot'jack'

boot'leg'

boot'leg'ger

boot'less

boot'strap'

boo'ty

booze

bo·rac'ic

bo'rate

bo'rax

Bor'deaux'

bor'der

bor'de·reau'

bor'dered

bore

bored

bo're·al

bo're·a'lis

bore'dom

bor'er

bore'some

bo'ric

bo'rine

bor'ings

born

bo'ron

bor'ough

bor'row

bor'rowed

bor'row·er

bor'row·ings

borsch

bosk'y

Bos'ni·an

bos'om

boss

bossed

boss'ism

boss'y

bo·tan'ic

bo·tan'i·cal

bot'a·nist

bot'a·nize

bot'a·nized

bot'a·ny

botch

botched

bot'fly'

both

both'er

both'ered

both'er·some

Both'ni·an

bot'tle

bot'tle·bird'

bot'tled

bot'tle·head'

bot'tle·hold'er

bot'tle·neck'

bot'tle·nose'

bot'tom

bot'tom·less

bot'tom·ry

bot'u·lism

bou'doir

bough

boughed

bought

bouil'la·baisse'

bouil'lon'

boul'der

bou'le·vard

bounce

bounced

bounc'er

bound

bound'a·ry

bound'ed

bound'en

bound'er

bound'less

boun'te·ous

boun'te·ous·ly

boun'ti·ful

boun'ty

bou·quet'

bour·geois'	boy'cott	brake'man
bour'geoi'sie'	boy'hood	bram'ble
bourse	boy'ish	bran
bout	boy'ish·ness	branch
bo'va·rysm	brace	branched
bo'vine	braced	branch'ling
bow	brace'let	brand
bow	brack'en	brand'ed
bowd'ler·ize	brack'et	bran'died
bowed	brack'et·ed	bran'dish
bowed	brack'ish	bran'dished
bow'el	brad'awl'	brand'-new'
bow'er	brag	bran'dy
bow'er·bird'	bragged	brash
bow'fin'	brag'ga·do'ci·o	brass
bow'ie	brag'gart	bras'sard
bow'knot'	Brah'man	brass'bound'
bowl	braid	brass'ie
bowled	braid'ed	brass'i·ness
bow'leg'ged	Braille	brass'y
bowl'er	brain	brat
bow'man	brained	brat'ling
bow'shot'	brain'fag'	bra·va'do
bow'sprit	brain'less	brave
bow'string'	brain'sick'	brave'ly
box	brain'work'	brav'er
box'board'	brain'y	brav'er·y
box'car'	braise	brav'est
boxed	braised	bra'vo
box'er	brake	bra·vu'ra
box'wood'	brake'age	brawl
boy	braked	brawled

brawl'er	break'o·ver'	brew'er
brawn	break'-through'	brew'er·y
brawn'y	break'up'	brew'house'
bray	break'wa'ter	bribe
brayed	breast	bribed
braze	breast'band'	brib'er·y
brazed	breast'bone'	bric'-a-brac'
bra'zen	breast'ed	brick
bra'zened	breast'-fed'	brick'bat'
bra'zier	breast'mark'	bricked
bra·zil'ite	breast'pin'	brick'lay'er
bra·zil'wood'	breast'plate'	brick'ma'son
breach	breast'weed'	brick'yard'
breached	breast'work'	brid'al
bread	breath	bride
bread'bas'ket	breathed	bride'groom'
bread'board'	breath'less	brides'maid'
bread'ed	bred	bridge
bread'fruit'	breech	bridged
bread'root'	breed	bridge'head'
bread'stuff'	breed'er	bridge'work'
breadth	breeze	bri'dle
bread'win·ner'	breezed	bri'dled
break	breez'y	brief
break'a·ble	breth'ren	brief'er
break'age	breve	brief'est
break'down'	bre·vet'	brief'ly
break'er	bre'vi·ar'y	brief'ness
break'fast	bre·vier'	bri'er
break'neck'	brev'i·ty	brig
break'off'	brew	bri·gade'
break'out'	brewed	brig'a·dier'

brig'and	bris'tle	broc'a·tel'
brig'and·age	bris'tled	broc'co·li
brig'an·tine	bris'tli·er	bro·chette'
bright	bris'tli·est	bro·chure'
bright'en	bris'tly	bro'gan
bright'er	Bri·tan'ni·a	brogue
bright'est	Bri·tan'nic	broil
bright'ly	Brit'i·cism	broiled
bright'ness	Brit'ish	broil'er
bright'work'	Brit'ish·er	broke
bril'liance	Brit'on	bro'ken
bril'lian·cy	brit'tle	brok'en·ly
bril'liant	brit'tle·ness	bro'ker
bril'lian·tine'	broach	bro'ker·age
bril'liant·ly	broached	bro'mate
bril'liant·ness	broad	bro'mide
brim	broad'ax'	bro·mid'ic
brim'ful'	broad'bill'	bro'mine
brimmed	broad'brim'	bron'chi·al
brim'stone'	broad'cast'	bron·chi'tis
brin'dled	broad'cast'er	bron'cho·scope
brine	broad'en	bron'chus
bring	broad'er	bron'co
brink	broad'est	bronze
brin'y	broad'leaf'	bronzed
bri·oche'	broad'loom'	brooch
bri·quette'	broad'ly	brood
brisk	broad'side'	brood'ed
brisk'en	broad'way'	brood'er
bris'ket	broad'wise'	brood'ling
brisk'ly	bro·cade'	brook
brisk'ness	bro·cad'ed	brook'let

broom	brush'work'	bu·col'ic
broom'weed'	brusque	bud
broom'wood'	bru'tal	bud'ded
broth	bru·tal'i·ty	bud'dy
broth'er	bru'tal·i·za'tion	budge
broth'er·hood	bru'tal·ize	budged
broth'er-in-law'	bru'tal·ized	budg'et
broth'er·li·ness	bru'tal·ly	budg'et·ar'y
broth'er·ly	brute	budg'et·ed
brougham	brut'ish	bud'wood'
brought	brut'ish·ly	bud'worm'
brow	brut'ish·ness	buff
brown	bub'ble	buf'fa·lo
brown'er	bub'bled	buff'er
brown'est	bub'bly	buff'ered
brown'ie	bu·bon'ic	buf'fet
browse	buc'cal	buf·fet'
browsed	buc'ca·neer'	buf'fet·ed
bru'in	buck	buf·foon'
bruise	buck'board'	buf·foon'er·y
bruised	bucked	bug
bruit	buck'et	bug'bear'
brum'ma·gem	buck'et·ed	bugged
brunch	buck'et·ful	bug'gy
bru·net'	buck'le	bu'gle
bru·nette'	buck'led	bu'gler
brunt	buck'ler	bu'gle·weed'
brush	buck'ram	bug'proof'
brushed	buck'saw'	bug'weed'
brush'ful	buck'shot'	build
brush'less	buck'skin'	build'ed
brush'wood'	buck'wheat'	build'er

build'ing

build'ings

built

bulb

bulb'ous

bulge

bulged

bulk

bulk'head'

bulk'i·er

bulk'i·est

bulk'y

bull

bull'doze'

bull'dozed'

bull'doz'er

bul'let

bul'le·tin

bull'fight'

bull'finch'

bull'frog'

bull'head'

bul'lion

bull'ish

bull'ock

bull'weed

bul'ly

bul'ly·rag'

bul'rush'

bul'wark

bum

bum'boat'

bump

bump'er

bump'i·er

bump'i·est

bump'kin

bump'y

bu'na

bunch

bunched

bun'dle

bun'dled

bung

bun'ga·low

bun'gle

bun'gled

bun'gler

bun'ion

bunk'er

bunk'house'

bunt

buoy

buoy'ant

buoy'ant·ly

bur'den

bur'dened

bur'den·some

bu'reau

bu·reauc'ra·cy

bu'reau·crat

bu·rette'

bur'gee

bur'geon

bur'geoned

bur'gess

bur'glar

bur'i·al

bu'rin

bur'lap

bur·lesque'

bur·lesqued'

bur'ly

burn

burned

burn'er

bur'nish

bur'nish·er

burn'out'

burnt

burr

bur'ro

bur'row

bur'rowed

bur'sar

bur·si'tis

burst

bur'y

bus

bus'es

bush

bushed

bush'el

bush'el·er

bush'ings

bus'i·ly

busi′ness

busi′ness·es

busi′ness·like′

bus′kin

bust

bus′tard

bus′tle

bus′tled

bus′y

bus′y·bod′y

but

butch′er

butch′ered

butch′er·y

but′ler

butt

but′ter

but′ter·ball′

but′ter·cup′

but′tered

but′ter·fat′

but′ter·fish′

but′ter·fly′

but′ter·nut′

but′ter·scotch′

but′ter·y

but′ton

but′toned

but′ton·hole′

but′ton·holed′

but′ton·weed′

but′ton·wood′

but′tress

but′tressed

bux′om

buy

buy′er

buzz

buz′zard

buzzed

buzz′er

by

by′gone′

by′pass′

by′path′

by′play′

by′-prod′uct

By·ron′ic

by′stand′er

by′way′

by′word′

C

cab	cac'tus·es	cai'tiff
ca·bal'	ca·dav'er	ca·jole'
cab'bage	ca·dav'er·ous	ca·joled'
cab'in	cad'die	ca·jol'er·y
cab'i·net	ca'dence	cake
ca'ble	ca·den'za	cake'walk'
ca'bled	ca·det'	cal'a·bash
ca'ble·gram	cad'mi·um	cal'a·mine
ca·boose'	Cad'mus	ca·lam'i·tous
cab'ri·o·let'	ca'dre	ca·lam'i·tous·ly
ca·ca'o	ca·du'ce·us	ca·lam'i·ty
cach'a·lot	cad'weed	cal·car'e·ous
cache	Cae·sar'e·an	cal'ci·fi·ca'tion
ca·chet'	cae·su'ra	cal'ci·fy
cach'in·na'tion	ca·fé'	cal'ci·mine
cack'le	caf'e·te'ri·a	cal'cine
cack'led	caf'fe·ine	cal·cined'
ca·coph'o·nous	cage	cal'ci·um
ca·coph'o·ny	caged	cal'cu·late
cac'ti	cairn	cal'cu·lat'ed
cac'toid	cais'son	cal'cu·la'tion
cac'tus	cais'soned	cal'cu·la'tor

cal'dron	calmed	cam'ou·flage
cal'en·dar	calm'er	camp
cal'en·der	calm'est	cam·paign'
cal'en·dered	calm'ly	cam'pa·ni'le
calf	calm'ness	camp'er
calf'skin'	cal'o·mel	camp'fire'
cal'i·ber	ca·lor'ic	cam'phor
cal'i·brate	cal'o·rie	cam'phor·ate
cal'i·brat'ed	cal'u·met	cam'phor·at'ed
cal'i·bra'tion	ca·lum'ni·ate	cam'pus
cal'i·co	ca·lum'ni·at'ed	can
cal'i·per	ca·lum'ni·a'tion	ca·nal'
ca'liph	ca·lum'ni·a'tor	ca·nal'i·za'tion
cal'is·then'ics	cal'um·ny	ca·nar'y
calk	Cal'va·ry	can'can
calked	calved	can'cel
calk'er	ca·lyp'so	can'celed
call	ca'lyx	can'cel·la'tion
cal'la	ca'ma·ra'de·rie	can'cer
call'a·ble	cam'ber	can'cer·ous
called	cam'bi·um	can'cer·weed'
cal'ler	cam'bric	can'de·la'brum
cal·lig'ra·phy	came	can'did
cal·li'o·pe	cam'el	can'di·da·cy
cal·los'i·ty	cam'el·eer'	can'di·date
cal'lous	Cam'e·lot	can'did·ly
cal'loused	Cam'em·bert'	can'died
cal'lous·ly	cam'e·o	can'dle
cal'low	cam'er·a	can'dled
cal'low·ly	cam'er·a·man'	can'dle·fish'
cal'lus	cam'i·sole	can'dle·light'
calm	cam'o·mile	can'dle·nut'

can'dle·stick'
can'dor
can'dy
can'dy·mak'er
cane
cane'brake'
ca'nine
can'is·ter
can'ker
can'kered
can'ker·ous
can'ker·weed'
can'ker·worm'
canned
can'ner
can'ner·y
can'ni·bal
can'ni·bal·ism
can'ni·ly
can'non
can'non·ade'
can'non·eer'
can'ny
ca·noe'
can'on
ca·non'i·cal
ca·non'i·cals
can'on·i·za'tion
can'on·ize
can'o·py
cant
can't

can'ta·loupe
can·tan'ker·ous
can·ta'ta
can·teen'
cant'er
can'tered
can'ti·cle
can'ti·cles
can'ti·le'ver
can'tle
can'to
can'ton
can·ton'ment
can'tor
can'vas
can'vased
can'vass
can'vassed
can'vass·er
can'yon
caou'tchouc
ca'pa·bil'i·ties
ca'pa·bil'i·ty
ca'pa·ble
ca'pa·bly
ca·pa'cious
ca·pac'i·tance
ca·pac'i·tate
ca·pac'i·tat'ed
ca·pac'i·tor
ca·pac'i·ty
cape

ca'per
ca'pered
ca'per·ings
cap'il·lar'i·ty
cap'il·lar'y
cap'i·tal
cap'i·tal·ism
cap'i·tal·ist
cap'i·tal·is'tic
cap'i·tal·ists
cap'i·tal·i·za'tion
cap'i·tal·ize
cap'i·tal·ized
cap'i·tol
ca·pit'u·late
ca·pit'u·lat'ed
ca·pit'u·lates
ca·pit'u·la'tion
ca'pon
capped
ca·price'
ca·pri'cious
cap·size'
cap·sized'
cap'stan
cap'sule
cap'tain
cap'tain·cy
cap'tion
cap'tious
cap'tious·ly
cap'tious·ness

cap'ti·vate

cap'ti·vat·ed

cap'ti·va'tion

cap'tive

cap·tiv'i·ty

cap'ture

cap'tured

car

ca'ra·ba·o

car'a·bi·neer'

car'a·cal

car'a·cole

ca·rafe'

car'a·mel

car'a·mel·ize

car'a·pace

car'at

car'a·van

car'a·van'sa·ry

car'a·vel

car'a·way

car'bide

car'bine

car'bo·hy'drate

car·bol'ic

car'bon

car'bon·ate

car'bon·at'ed

car·bon'ic

car'bon·if'er·ous

car'bon·ize

car'bon·ized

car'bo·run'dum

car'boy

car'bun·cle

car'bu·ret'or

car'cass

car'ci·no'ma

card

card'board'

card'ed

car'di·ac

car'di·gan

car'di·nal

car'di·nal·ate

car'di·o·gram'

car'di·o·graph'

car'di·ol'o·gy

care

cared

ca·reen'

ca·reened'

ca·reer'

care'free'

care'ful

care'ful·ly

care'less

care'less·ly

care'less·ness

ca·ress'

ca·ressed'

ca·ress'ing·ly

car'et

car'fare'

car'go

car'i·bou

car'i·ca·ture

car'i·es

car'il·lon

car'load·ings'

car·min'a·tive

car'mine

car'nage

car'nal

car'nal·ly

car·na'tion

car·nel'ian

car'ni·val

car·niv'o·rous

car'ol

car'oled

car'om

car'omed

ca·rot'id

ca·rous'al

ca·rouse'

ca·roused'

carp

car'pal

car'pen·ter

car'pet

car'pet·ed

car'riage

car'ried

car'ri·er

car'ri·on

car'rot·	cash·ier'	cat'a·lep'sy
car'rou·sel'	cash·iered'	cat'a·lep'tic
car'ry	cash'mere	cat'a·logue
cart	ca·si'no	cat'a·logued
cart'age	cask	ca·tal'pa
cart'ed	cas'ket	ca·tal'y·sis
car'tel	cas·sa'tion	cat'a·lyst
car'ti·lage	cas·sa'va	cat'a·lyt'ic
car'ti·lag'i·nous	cas'se·role	cat'a·lyze
car·tog'ra·phy	cas'si·a	cat'a·mount
car'ton	cas·si'no	cat'a·pult
car·toon'	cas'sock	cat'a·ract
car·touche'	cast	ca·tarrh'
car'tridge	cas'ta·net'	ca·tarrh'al
carve	caste	ca·tas'tro·phe
carved	cast'er	cat'a·stroph'ic
carv'er	cas'ti·gate	cat'a·stroph'i·cal·ly
carv'ings	cas'ti·gat'ed	cat'a·ton'ic
car'y·at'id	cas'ti·ga'tion	Ca·taw'ba
ca·sa'ba	cas'tle	cat'bird'
cas·cade'	cast'off'	cat'boat'
cas·cad'ed	cas'tor	cat'call'
cas·car'a	cas'tra·me·ta'tion	catch
case	cas'u·al	catch'er
ca'se·in	cas'u·al·ly	catch'weed'
case'ment	cas'u·al·ty	catch'word'
case'work'	cas'u·ist	catch'y
cash	cas'u·ist·ry	cat'e·che'sis
cash'book'	ca·tab'o·lism	cat'e·chet'i·cal
cash'box'	cat'a·clysm	cat'e·chism
cashed	cat'a·comb	cat'e·chize
ca·shew'	cat'a·falque	cat'e·gor'i·cal

cat'e·go·rize	cau·sal'i·ty	cease'less
cat'e·go'ry	cau·sa'tion	cease'less·ly
cat'e·nar'y	caus'a·tive	ce'cum
ca'ter	cause	ce'dar
ca'tered	caused	ce'dar·bird'
ca'ter·er	cause'less	cede
cat'er·pil'lar	cau'se·rie'	ced'ed
cat'fish'	cause'way'	ce·dil'la
cat'gut'	caus'tic	ced'ing
ca·thar'sis	cau'ter·i·za'tion	ceil'ings
ca·thar'tic	cau'ter·ize	cel'e·brant
cat'head'	cau'ter·ized	cel'e·brate
ca·the'dral	cau'ter·y	cel'e·brat'ed
cath'e·ter	cau'tion	cel'e·bra'tion
cath'e·ter·ize	cau'tion·ar'y	ce·leb'ri·ty
cath'ode	cau'tioned	ce·ler'i·ty
cath'o·lic	cau'tious	cel'er·y
ca·thol'i·cism	cav'al·cade'	ce·les'ta
cath'o·lic'i·ty	cav'a·lier'	ce·les'tial
ca·thol'i·cize	cav'al·ry	ce·les'tial·ly
cat'kin	ca'va·ti'na	cel'i·ba·cy
cat'like'	cave	cel'i·bate
cat'nip	ca've·at	cell
cat'tail'	cav'ern	cel'lar
cat'tle	cav'ern·ous	cel'lar·er
cat'walk'	cav'i·ar	cel'lar·et'
cau'cus	cav'il	cel'list
cau'cused	cav'i·ty	cel'lo
cau'dal	ca·vort'	cel'lo·phane
caught	cay·enne'	cel'lu·lar
cau'li·flow'er	cease	cel'lu·li'tis
caus'al	ceased	cel'lu·loid

cel'lu·lose

Celt'ic

ce·ment'

ce'men·ta'tion

cem'e·ter'y

cen'a·cle

cen'o·bite

cen'o·taph

cen'ser

cen'sor

cen'sored

cen·so'ri·al

cen·so'ri·ous

cen'sor·ship

cen'sur·a·ble

cen'sure

cen'sured

cen'sus

cent

cen'taur

cen'te·nar'i·an

cen'te·nar'y

cen·ten'ni·al

cen'ter

cen'ter·board'

cen'tered

cen'ter·piece'

cen'ti·grade

cen'ti·me·ter

cen'ti·pede

cen'tral

cen'tral·i·za'tion

cen'tral·ize

cen'tral·ized

cen·trif'u·gal

cen'tri·fuge

cen·trip'e·tal

cen'trist

cen·tu'ri·on

cen'tu·ry

ce·phal'ic

ce·ram'ic

ce're·al

cer'e·bel'lum

cer'e·bral

cer'e·bra'tion

cer'e·brum

cere'ment

cer'e·mo'ni·al

cer'e·mo'ni·al·ly

cer'e·mo'ni·ous

cer'e·mo'ni·ous·ly

cer'e·mo'ni·ous·ness

cer'e·mo'ny

ce·rise'

ce'ri·um

cer'tain

cer'tain·ly

cer'tain·ty

cer·tif'i·cate

cer·tif'i·cat'ed

cer·tif'i·ca'tion

cer'ti·fied

cer'ti·fy

cer'ti·o·ra'ri

cer'ti·tude

cer'vi·cal

cer'vix

ce'si·um

ces·sa'tion

ces'sion

cess'pool'

ces'tus

ce·ta'cean

chafe

chaf'fer

chaf'fered

chaf'finch

chaff'weed'

cha·grin'

cha·grined'

chain

chained

chain'work'

chair

chair'man

chaise

chal·ced'o·ny

cha·let'

chal'ice

chalk

chalk'i·ness

chal'lenge

chal'lenged

cham'ber

cham'bered

cham'ber·lain	chap'lain	char'ter
cham'ber·maid'	chap'let	char'tered
cha·me'le·on	chap'ter	char·treuse'
cham'ois	char	char'y
cham·pagne'	char'ac·ter	chase
cham'per·ty	char'ac·ter·is'tic	chased
cham'pi·on	char'ac·ter·is'ti·cal·ly	chasm
cham'pi·on·ship'	char'ac·ter·i·za'tion	chas'sis
chance	char'ac·ter·ize	chaste
chanced	char'ac·ter·ized	chas'ten
chan'cel	cha·rade'	chas'tened
chan'cel·ler·y	char'coal'	chas'ten·ing·ly
chan'cel·lor	chard	chas·tise'
chan'cer·y	charge	chas·tised'
chan'de·lier'	charge'a·ble	chas'tise·ment
chan'dler	charged	chas'ti·ty
chan'dler·y	charg'er	chas'u·ble
change	char'i·ly	châ·teau'
change'a·ble	char'i·ness	chat'e·laine
changed	char'i·ot	chat'tel
change'less	char'i·ot·eer'	chat'ter
change'ling	char'i·ta·ble	chat'tered
chan'nel	char'i·ta·bly	chat'ter·er
chan'neled	char'i·ty	chat'ty
chant	char'la·tan	chauf·feur'
chant'ed	charm	chau'vin·ism
cha'os	charmed	cheap
cha·ot'ic	charm'ing·ly	cheap'en
cha·ot'i·cal·ly	char'nel	cheap'ened
chap'ar·ral'	charred	cheap'er
chap'el	chart	cheap'est
chap'er·on	chart'ed	cheap'ly

cheap'ness

cheat

cheat'ed

cheat'er

check

check'book'

checked

check'er

check'er·board'

check'ered

check'mate'

check'mat'ed

check'off'

check'rein'

cheek'y

cheer

cheered

cheer'ful

cheer'ful·ly

cheer'ful·ness

cheer'i·ly

cheer'less

cheer'less·ly

cheer'y

cheese

cheese'cake'

cheese'cloth'

chef

chem'i·cal

chem'i·cal·ly

che·mise'

chem'ist

chem'is·try

che·nille'

cher'ish

che·root'

cher'ry

cher'ub

che·ru'bic

cher'u·bim

cher'vil

chess

chess'board'

chess'man

chest

ches'ter·field'

chest'nut

chev'ron

chew

chic

chi·can'er·y

chick'a·dee

chick'en

chick'weed'

chic'le

chic'o·ry

chide

chief

chief'ly

chief'tain

chif'fon

chif'fo·nier'

chig'ger

chil'blain'

child

child'hood

child'ish

child'ish·ly

child'ish·ness

child'less

child'like'

chil'dren

chil'i

chill

chilled

chill'i·er

chill'i·est

chill'ing·ly

chill'y

chime

chimed

chi·me'ra

chi·mer'i·cal

chim'ney

chim'pan·zee'

chin

chi'na

chinch

chin·chil'la

chine

Chi'nese'

chink

chintz

chip

chip'munk

chipped

chip'per

chi·rog'ra·phy

chi·rop'o·dist

chi'ro·prac'tor

chirp

chis'el

chis'eled

chit'chat'

chit'ter·ling

chiv'al·ric

chiv'al·rous

chiv'al·ry

chive

chlo'ral

chlo'rate

chlo'ride

chlo'rin·ate

chlo'rine

chlo'rite

chlo'ro·form

chlo'ro·phyll

chlo·ro'sis

choc'o·late

choice

choir

choir'boy'

choke

chok'er

chol'er

chol'er·a

chol'er·ic

choose

chop

chop'house'

chopped

chop'per

cho·ral'

chord

cho·re'a

cho·re·og'ra·phy

chor'is·ter

chor'tle

cho'rus

chose

cho'sen

chow

chow'der

chrism

chris'ten

Chris'ten·dom

chris'tened

chris'ten·ings

Chris'tian

Chris'ti·an'i·ty

Christ'mas

chro'mate

chro·mat'ics

chrome

chro'mic

chro'mite

chro'mi·um

chro'mo·some

chron'ic

chron'i·cal·ly

chron'i·cle

chron'i·cled

chron'i·cler

chron'i·cles

chron'o·graph

chron'o·log'i·cal

chron'o·log'i·cal·ly

chro·nol'o·gy

chro·nom'e·ter

chron'o·met'ric

chrys'a·lis

chrys·an'the·mum

chrys'o·lite

chub'bi·ness

chub'by

chuck

chuck'le

chuck'led

chuck'le·head'

chuck'ling·ly

chum

chum'my

chump

chunk

chunk'i·ness

chunk'y

church

church'man

churl

churl'ish

churl'ish·ly

churl'ish·ness

churn	cir'cu·lat'ed	cite
churned	cir'cu·la'tion	cit'ed
chute	cir'cu·la·to'ry	cit'i·zen
chut'ney	cir·cum·am'bi·ent	cit'i·zen·ry
chyle	cir·cum'fer·ence	cit'i·zen·ship'
ci·ca'da	cir·cum'fer·en'tial	cit'rate
cic'a·trix	cir'cum·flex	cit'ric
ci'der	cir'cum·lo·cu'tion	cit'ron
ci·gar'	cir'cum·loc'u·to'ry	cit'y
cig'a·rette'	cir'cum·nav'i·gate	civ'ic
cinch	cir'cum·scribe'	civ'il
cinc'ture	cir'cum·scribed'	ci·vil'ian
cinc'tured	cir'cum·spect	ci·vil'i·ty
cin'der	cir'cum·spec'tion	civ'i·li·za'tion
cin'e·ma	cir'cum·spect'ly	civ'i·lize
cin'e·mat'o·graph	cir'cum·spect'ness	civ'i·lized
cin'na·bar	cir'cum·stance	civ'il·ly
cin'na·mon	cir'cum·stanc·es	clack
cinque'foil'	cir'cum·stan'tial	claim
ci'on	cir'cum·stan'ti·al'i·ty	claim'ant
ci'pher	cir'cum·stan'ti·ate	claimed
ci'phered	cir'cum·stan'ti·at'ed	clair·voy'ance
cir'cle	cir'cum·vent'	clair·voy'ant
cir'cled	cir'cum·vent'ed	cla'mant
cir'cuit	cir'cum·ven'tion	clam'bake'
cir·cu'i·tous	cir'cus	clam'ber
cir·cu'i·tous·ly	cir·rho'sis	clam'bered
cir·cu'i·tous·ness	cir·rhot'ic	clam'my
cir'cu·lar	cir'rus	clam'or
cir'cu·lar·i·za'tion	cis'tern	clam'ored
cir'cu·lar·ize	cit'a·del	clam'or·ous
cir'cu·late	ci·ta'tion	clamp

clam'shell'	clas'si·fi·ca'tion	clear'ly
clan	clas'si·fied	clear'ness
clan·des'tine	clas'si·fi'er	cleat
clang	clas'si·fy	cleat'ed
clanged	class'mate'	cleav'age
clang'or	class'room'	cleave
clank	class'work'	cleav'er
clanked	clat'ter	clef
clan'nish	clat'tered	cleft
clan'ship	clause	clem'a·tis
clans'man	claus'tro·pho'bi·a	clem'en·cy
clap	clav'i·chord	clem'ent
clapped	clav'i·cle	clench
clap'per	claw	clere'sto'ry
clap'trap'	clay	cler'gy
claque	clean	cler'gy·man
clar'et	cleaned	cler'i·cal
clar'i·fi·ca'tion	clean'er	cler'i·cal·ism
clar'i·fied	clean'est	clerk
clar'i·fy	clean'li·ness	clev'er
clar'i·net'	clean'ly	clev'er·er
clar'i·on	clean'ness	clev'er·est
clar'i·ty	cleanse	clev'er·ness
clash	cleans'er	clew
clasp	clean'up'	cli·ché'
class	clear	click
clas'sic	clear'ance	cli'ent
clas'si·cal	cleared	cli'en·tele'
clas'si·cal·ism	clear'er	cliff
clas'si·cal·ist	clear'est	cli·mac'ter·ic
clas'si·cal·ly	clear'head'ed	cli·mac'tic
clas'si·cist	clear'ing·house'	cli'mate

cli·mat′ic

cli′max

climb

climbed

climb′er

clinch

clinch′er

cling

cling′ing·ly

clin′ic

clin′i·cal

cli·ni′cian

clink

clinked

clink′er

clip

clip′per

clip′pings

clique

cloak

clock

clock′wise′

clock′work′

clod

clog

cloi′son′né′

clois′ter

clois′tered

clon′ic

close

closed

close′ly

close′ness

clos′er

clos′est

clos′et

clos′et·ed

clo′sure

clot

cloth

clothed

clothes

clothes′pin′

cloth′ier

clot′ted

cloud

cloud′i·er

cloud′i·est

cloud′i·ness

cloud′less

cloud′y

clout

clout′ed

clove

clo′ven

clo′ver

clown

clowned

clown′ish

cloy

cloyed

club

clubbed

club′house′

club′man

cluck

clump

clum′si·er

clum′si·est

clum′si·ly

clum′si·ness

clum′sy

clus′ter

clus′tered

clutch

clut′ter

clut′tered

coach

coach′man

co·ad′ju·tor

co·ag′u·late

co·ag′u·lat′ed

co·ag′u·lates

co·ag′u·la′tion

co·ag′u·la′tive

coal

co′a·lesce′

co′a·lesced′

co′a·les′cence

co′a·les′cent

co′a·li′tion

coal′sack′

coarse

coars′en

coars′ened

coars′er

coars'est

coast

coast'al

coast'er

coast'wise'

coat

coat'ed

coat'ings

co·au'thor

coax

coaxed

co·ax'i·al

coax'ing·ly

co'balt

cob'ble

cob'bled

co'bra

cob'web'

co·caine'

coc'cyx

coch'i·neal'

cock·ade'

cock'a·too'

cock'le

cock'le·shell'

cock'ney

cock'pit'

cock'roach'

cock'sure'

cock'sure'ness

cock'tail'

co'coa

co'co·nut'

co·coon'

co'da

code

cod'ed

co'de·fend'ant

co'de·ine

co'dex

cod'fish'

cod'i·cil

cod'i·fi·ca'tion

cod'i·fy

co'ed'

co'ed'u·ca'tion

co'ef·fi'cient

co·erce'

co·erced'

co·er'cion

co·er'cive

co·e'val

co'ex·ec'u·tor

cof'fee

cof'fer

cof'fin

cog

co'gen·cy

co'gent

cog'i·tate

cog'i·tat'ed

cog'i·ta'tion

cog'i·ta'tive

co'gnac

cog'nate

cog·ni'tion

cog'ni·zance

cog'ni·zant

cog·no'men

co·hab'it

co·here'

co·hered'

co·her'ence

co·her'ent

co·her'ent·ly

co·her'er

co·he'sion

co·he'sive

co'hort

coif

coif·fure'

coign

coil

coiled

coin

coin'age

co'in·cide'

co'in·cid'ed

co·in'ci·dence

co·in'ci·den'tal

coined

coin'er

co'in·sur'ance

co'in·sure'

co'in·sur'er

coke

col'an·der	col·lec'tor·ship	col'or·less
cold	col'lege	co·los'sal
cold'er	col·le'gi·ate	Col·os·se'um
cold'est	col·lide'	co·los'sus
cold'ly	col·lid'ed	col'por'teur
cole'slaw'	col'lie	colt
col'ic	col'lier	col'um·bine
col'i·se'um	col·li'sion	col'umn
co·li'tis	col'lo·ca'tion	co·lum'nar
col·lab'o·rate	col·lo'di·on	co'ma
col·lab'o·rat'ed	col'loid	com'a·tose
col·lab'o·ra'tion	col·loi'dal	comb
col·lapse'	col·lo'qui·al	com'bat
col·lapsed'	col'lo·quy	com'bat·ant
col·laps'i·ble	col'lo·type	com'ba·tive
col'lar	col·lu'sion	com·bat'ive·ness
col'lar·band'	col·lu'sive	combed
col'lar·bone'	co·logne'	com'bi·na'tion
col·late'	co'lon	com'bine
col·lat'ed	colo'nel	com·bined'
col·lat'er·al	co·lo'ni·al	comb'ings
col·la'tion	col'o·nist	com·bust'
col·la'tor	col'o·ni·za'tion	com·bus'ti·ble
col·league'	col'o·nize	com·bus'tion
col'lect	col'o·nized	come
col·lect'ed	col'on·nade'	co·me'di·an
col·lect'i·ble	col'o·ny	com'e·dy
col·lec'tion	col'o·phon	come'li·ness
col·lec'tive	col'or	come'ly
col·lec'tiv·ism	col'or·a'tion	co·mes'ti·ble
col·lec'tiv·ist	col'o·ra·tu'ra	com'et
col·lec'tor	col'ored	com'fit

com'fort

com'fort·a·ble

com'fort·a·bly

com'fort·ed

com'fort·er

com'fort·less

com'ic

com'i·cal

com'ings

com'ma

com·mand'

com'man·dant'

com·mand'ed

com'man·deer'

com·mand'er

com·mand'er·y

com·mand'ing·ly

com·mand'ment

com·man'do

com·mem'o·rate

com·mem'o·rat'ed

com·mem'o·ra'tion

com·mem'o·ra'tive

com·mence'

com·menced'

com·mence'ment

com·mend'

com·mend'a·ble

com'men·da'tion

com·mend'a·to'ry

com·mend'ed

com·men'su·ra·ble

com·men'su·rate

com'ment

com'men·tar'y

com'men·ta'tor

com'ment·ed

com'merce

com·mer'cial

com·mer'cial·ism

com·mer'cial·i·za'tion

com·mer'cial·ize

com·min'a·to'ry

com·min'gle

com·min'gled

com'mi·nute

com'mi·nut'ed

com'mi·nu'tion

com·mis'er·ate

com·mis'er·a'tion

com'mis·sar'

com'mis·sar'i·at

com'mis·sar'y

com·mis'sion

com·mis'sioned

com·mis'sion·er

com·mit'

com·mit'ment

com·mit'ted

com·mit'tee

com·mo'di·ous

com·mod'i·ty

com'mo·dore'

com'mon

com'mon·al·ty

com'mon·er

com'mon·est

com'mon·ly

com'mon·place'

com'mon·wealth'

com·mo'tion

com'mu·nal

com·mune'

com·mu'ni·ca·ble

com·mu'ni·cant

com·mu'ni·cate

com·mu'ni·cat'ed

com·mu'ni·ca'tion

com·mu'ni·ca'tive

com·mun'ion

com·mu'ni·qué'

com'mu·nism

com'mu·nist

com·mu·nis'tic

com·mu'ni·ty

com'mu·ni·za'tion

com'mu·nize

com'mu·ta'tion

com'mu·ta'tor

com·mute'

com·mut'ed

com·mut'er

com·pact'

com·pan'ion

com·pan'ion·a·ble

com·pan'ion·ship

com·pan′ion·way′
com′pa·ny
com′pa·ra·bil′i·ty
com′pa·ra·ble
com·par′a·tive
com·pare′
com·pared′
com·par′i·son
com·part′ment
com′pass
com·pas′sion
com·pas′sion·ate
com·pas′sion·ate·ly
com·pat′i·bil′i·ty
com·pat′i·ble
com·pa′tri·ot
com·peer′
com·pel′
com·pelled′
com·pel′ling·ly
com′pend
com·pen′di·ous
com·pen′di·um
com′pen·sate
com′pen·sat′ed
com′pen·sa′tion
com′pen·sa′tor
com·pen′sa·to′ry
com·pete′
com·pet′ed
com′pe·tence
com′pe·tent

com′pe·tent·ly
com′pe·ti′tion
com·pet′i·tive
com·pet′i·tor
com′pi·la′tion
com·pile′
com·piled′
com·pil′er
com·pla′cence
com·pla′cen·cy
com·pla′cent
com·plain′
com·plain′ant
com·plained′
com·plain′ing·ly
com·plaint′
com·plai′sance
com·plai′sant
com′ple·ment
com′ple·men′tal
com′ple·men′ta·ry
com′ple·ment·ed
com·plete′
com·plet′ed
com·ple′tion
com·plex′
com·plex′ion
com·plex′i·ty
com·pli′ance
com·pli′ant
com′pli·cate
com′pli·cat′ed

com′pli·ca′tion
com·plic′i·ty
com·plied′
com′pli·ment
com′pli·men′ta·ry
com′plin
com·ply′
com·po′nent
com·port′
com·pose′
com·posed′
com·pos′er
com·pos′ite
com·po·si′tion
com·pos′i·tor
com′post
com·po′sure
com′pote
com′pound
com′pre·hend′
com′pre·hend′ed
com′pre·hen′si·bil′i·ty
com′pre·hen′si·ble
com′pre·hen′sion
com′pre·hen′sive
com·press′
com·press′i·bil′i·ty
com·press′ible
com·pres′sion
com·pres′sor
com·prise′
com′pro·mise

com'pro·mis'ing·ly
Comp·tom'e·ter
comp·trol'ler
com·pul'sion
com·pul'sive
com·pul'so·ry
com·punc'tion
com'pu·ta'tion
com·pute'
com·put'ed
com'rade
con·cat'e·na'tion
con'cave
con·cav'i·ty
con·ceal'
con·cealed'
con·ceal'ment
con·cede'
con·ced'ed
con·ceit'
con·ceit'ed
con·ceit'ed·ly
con·ceiv'a·ble
con·ceiv'a·bly
con·ceive'
con·ceived'
con'cen·trate
con'cen·trat'ed
con'cen·tra'tion
con·cen'tric
con'cept
con·cep'tion

con·cep'tu·al
con·cern'
con·cerned'
con'cert
con·cert'ed
con'cer·ti'na
con·ces'sion
con·ces'sion·aire'
conch
con·cil'i·ate
con·cil'i·at'ed
con·cil'i·a'tion
con·cil'i·a·to'ry
con·cise'
con·cise'ness
con'clave
con·clude'
con·clud'ed
con·clu'sion
con·clu'sive
con·clu'sive·ly
con·coct'
con·coct'ed
con·coc'tion
con·com'i·tant
con'cord
con·cord'ance
con'course
con·crete'
con·cur'
con·curred'
con·cur'rence

con·cur'rent
con·cus'sion
con·demn'
con·dem·na'tion
con·dem'na·to'ry
con·demned'
con'den·sa'tion
con·dense'
con·densed'
con·dens'er
con·de·scend'
con·de·scend'ing·ly
con·de·scen'sion
con·dign'
con'di·ment
con·di'tion
con·di'tion·al
con·di'tion·al·ly
con·di'tioned
con·dole'
con·do'lence
con·do·min'i·um
con'do·na'tion
con·done'
con·doned'
con'dor
con·du'cive
con·duct'
con·duct'ed
con·duc'tion
con·duc·tiv'i·ty
con·duc'tor

con'duit

con'dyle

cone

con·fec'tion

con·fec'tion·er

con·fec'tion·er'y

con·fed'er·a·cy

con·fed'er·ate

con·fed'er·a'tion

con·fer'

con'fer·ee'

con'fer·ence

con·ferred'

con·fess'

con·fess'ed·ly

con·fes'sion

con·fes'sion·al

con·fes'sor

con·fide'

con·fid'ed

con'fi·dence

con'fi·dent

con'fi·den'tial

con'fi·den'tial·ly

con'fi·dent·ly

con·fid'ing·ly

con·fig'u·ra'tion

con·fine'

con·fined'

con·fine'ment

con·firm'

con'fir·ma'tion

con·firmed'

con'fis·cate

con'fis·cat'ed

con'fis·ca'tion

con·fis'ca·to'ry

con'fla·gra'tion

con·flict'

con·flict'ed

con·flic'tion

con'flu·ence

con'flu·ent

con·form'

con·form'a·ble

con'for·ma'tion

con·formed'

con·form'er

con·form'i·ty

con·found'

con·found'ed

con'frere

con·front'

con'fron·ta'tion

con·front'ed

con·fuse'

con·fused'

con·fus'ed·ly

con·fus'ing·ly

con·fu'sion

con'fu·ta'tion

con·fute'

con·fut'ed

con·geal'

con·gealed'

con'ge·la'tion

con'ge·ner

con·gen'ial

con·ge'ni·al'i·ty

con·gen'i·tal

con·gest'

con·gest'ed

con·ges'tion

con·glom'er·ate

con·glom'er·a'tion

con·grat'u·late

con·grat'u·lat'ed

con·grat'u·lates

con·grat'u·la'tion

con·grat'u·la·to'ry

con'gre·gate

con'gre·gat'ed

con'gre·ga'tion

con'gre·ga'tion·al

con'gress

con·gres'sion·al

con'gru·ence

con'gru·ent

con·gru'i·ty

con'gru·ous

con'ic

con'i·cal

co'ni·fer

co·nif'er·ous

con·jec'tur·al

con·jec'ture

con·jec'tured
con'ju·gal
con'ju·gate
con'ju·gat'ed
con'ju·ga'tion
con·junc'tion
con·junc'tive
con·junc'ti·vi'tis
con'ju·ra'tion
con·jure'
con·jured'
con'jur·er
con·nect'
con·nect'ed·ly
con·nec'tion
con·nec'tive
con·nec'tor
con·niv'ance
con·nive'
con·nived'
con'nois·seur'
con'no·ta'tion
con·note'
con·not'ed
con·nu'bi·al
con'quer
con'quered
con'quer·or
con'quest
con'san·guin'i·ty
con'science
con'sci·en'tious

con'sci·en'tious·ly
con'scious
con'scious·ly
con'scious·ness
con'script
con·scrip'tion
con'se·crate
con'se·crat'ed
con'se·cra'tion
con'se·cra'tive
con·sec'u·tive
con·sen'sus
con·sent'
con·sent'ed
con'se·quence
con'se·quent
con'se·quen'tial
con'se·quent·ly
con'ser·va'tion
con·serv'a·tism
con·serv'a·tive
con·serv'a·to'ry
con·serve'
con·served'
con·sid'er
con·sid'er·a·ble
con·sid'er·ate
con·sid'er·a'tion
con·sid'ered
con·sign'
con·signed'
con'sign·ee'

con·sign'ment
con·sign'or
con·sist'
con·sist'en·cy
con·sist'ent
con·sis'to·ry
con·so·la'tion
con·sole'
con·soled'
con·sol'i·date
con·sol'i·dat'ed
con·sol'i·da'tion
con·sol'ing·ly
con'sols
con'som·mé'
con'so·nance
con'so·nant
con'so·nan'tal
con·sort'
con·sort'ed
con·spic'u·ous
con·spic'u·ous·ly
con·spir'a·cy
con·spir'a·tor
con·spir'a·to'ri·al
con·spire'
con·spired'
con'sta·ble
con·stab'u·lar'y
con'stan·cy
con'stant
con'stant·ly

con'stel·la'tion

con'ster·na'tion

con'sti·pa'tion

con·stit'u·en·cy

con·stit'u·ent

con'sti·tute

con'sti·tut'ed

con'sti·tu'tion

con'sti·tu'tion·al

con'sti·tu'tion·al'i·ty

con'sti·tu'tion·al·ly

con·strain'

con·strained'

con·straint'

con·strict'

con·strict'ed

con·stric'tion

con·struct'

con·struct'ed

con·struc'tive

con·strue'

con·strued'

con'sul

con'su·lar

con'su·late

con'su·lates

con·sult'

con·sult'ant

con'sul·ta'tion

con·sult'a·tive

con·sult'ed

con·sum'a·ble

con·sume'

con·sumed'

con·sum'er

con'sum·mate

con'sum·ma'tion

con·sump'tion

con·sump'tive

con'tact

con·ta'gion

con·ta'gious

con·tain'

con·tained'

con·tain'er

con·tam'i·nate

con·tam'i·nat'ed

con·tam'i·na'tion

con'tem·plate

con'tem·plat'ed

con'tem·pla'tion

con·tem'pla·tive

con·tem'po·ra'ne·ous

con·tem'po·rar'y

con·tempt'

con·tempt'i·ble

con·temp'tu·ous

con·tend'

con·tend'ed

con·tend'er

con·tent'

con·tent'ed

con·ten'tion

con·ten'tious

con·tent'ment

con'test

con'test·ant

con'tes·ta'tion

con'text

con·tex'tu·al

con·ti·gu'i·ty

con·tig'u·ous

con'ti·nence

con'ti·nent

con'ti·nen'tal

con·tin'gen·cy

con·tin'gent

con·tin'u·al

con·tin'u·al·ly

con·tin'u·ance

con·tin'u·ant

con·tin'u·a'tion

con·tin'ue

con·tin'ued

con'ti·nu'i·ty

con·tin'u·ous

con·tin'u·ous·ly

con·tin'u·um

con·tort'

con·tort'ed

con·tor'tion

con·tor'tion·ist

con'tour

con'tra·band

con'tra·bass'

con'tract

con·tract'ed

con·trac'tile

con·trac'tion

con·trac'tor

con·trac'tu·al

con'tra·dict'

con'tra·dic'tion

con'tra·dic'to·ry

con'tra·dis·tinc'tion

con'tra·in'di·cate

con'tra·in'di·ca'tion

con·tral'to

con·trap'tion

con'tra·ri·ly

con'tra·ri·ness

con'tra·ri·wise'

con'tra·ry

con'trast

con'tra·vene'

con'tra·ven'tion

con·trib'ute

con'tri·bu'tion

con·trib'u·tive

con·trib'u·tor

con·trib'u·to'ry

con'trite

con'trite·ly

con·tri'tion

con·triv'ance

con·trive'

con·trol'

con·trol'la·ble

con·trolled'

con·trol'ler

con'tro·ver'sial

con'tro·ver'sy

con'tro·vert

con'tu·ma'cious

con'tu·ma·cy

con'tu·me'li·ous

con'tu·me'ly

con·tuse'

con·tused'

con·tu'sion

co·nun'drum

con'va·lesce'

con'va·les'cence

con'va·les'cent

con·vec'tion

con·vene'

con·vened'

con·ven'ience

con·ven'ienc·es

con·ven'ient

con·ven'ient·ly

con·vent'

con·ven'tion

con·ven'tion·al

con·ven'tion·al'i·ty

con·ven'tion·al·ize

con·ven'tion·al·ly

con·ven'tu·al

con·ven'tu·al·ly

con·verge'

con·verged'

con·ver'gence

con·ver'gent

con·ver·sant

con'ver·sa'tion

con'ver·sa'tion·al

con'ver·sa'tion·al·ist

con·verse'

con·ver'sion

con·vert'

con·vert'ed

con·vert'i·bil'i·ty

con·vert'i·ble

con'vex

con·vex'i·ty

con·vey'

con·vey'ance

con·veyed'

con·vey'er

con·vict'

con·vict'ed

con·vic'tion

con·vince'

con·vinc'ing·ly

con·viv'i·al

con·viv'i·al'i·ty

con·viv'i·al·ly

con'vo·ca'tion

con·voke'

con·voked'

con'vo·lute

con'vo·lut'ed

con'vo·lu'tion

con·voy'

con·voyed'

con·vulse'

con·vul'sion

con·vul'sive

cook'book'

cook'er

cook'er·y

cook'house'

cool

cooled

cool'er

cool'est

cool'head'ed

cool'house'

coo'lie

cool'ly

cool'ness

coop

coop'er

coop'er·age

co-op'er·ate

co-op'er·at'ed

co-op'er·a'tion

co-op'er·a'tive

co-opt'

co-opt'ed

co-or'di·nate

co-or'di·nat'ed

co-or'di·na'tion

co-or'di·na'tor

coot

co'pal

co·part'ner

co·part'ner·ship

cope

coped

Co·per'ni·can

cop'ied

cop'i·er

cop'ing

co'pi·ous

co'pi·ous·ly

co'pi·ous·ness

cop'per

cop'per·head'

cop'per·plate'

cop'per·smith'

cop'pice

cop'ra

cop'y

cop'y·hold'er

cop'y·ist

cop'y·read'er

cop'y·right'

co'quet·ry

co·quette'

co·quet'tish

cor'a·cle

cor'a·coid

cor'al

cor'al·line

cord

cord'age

cord'ed

cor'dial

cor·dial'i·ty

cor'dial·ly

cord'ite

cor'don

Cor'do·van

cor'du·roy

cord'wood'

core

cored

co're·spond'ent

co'ri·an'der

Co·rin'thi·an

cork

cork'age

cork'screw'

cork'wood'

cor'mo·rant

corn

cor'ne·a

cor'ner

cor'nered

cor'ner·stone'

cor'net

corn'field'

corn'flow'er

cor'nice

corn'stalk'

cor'nu·co'pi·a

cor'ol·lar'y

co·ro'na
cor'o·nar'y
cor'o·na'tion
cor'o·ner
cor'o·net
cor'po·ral
cor'po·rate
cor'po·rate·ly
cor'po·ra'tion
cor'po·ra'tive
cor·po're·al
corps
corpse
cor'pu·lence
cor'pu·lent
cor'pus
cor'pus·cle
cor·pus'cu·lar
cor·ral'
cor·rect'
cor·rect'ed
cor·rec'tion
cor·rec'tion·al
cor·rec'tive
cor·rect'ly
cor·rect'ness
cor·rec'tor
cor're·late
cor're·lat'ed
cor're·la'tion
cor·rel'a·tive
cor're·spond'

cor're·spond'ed
cor're·spond'ence
cor're·spond'ent
cor're·spond'ing·ly
cor're·sponds'
cor'ri·dor
cor·rob'o·rate
cor·rob'o·ra'tion
cor·rob'o·ra'tive
cor·rob'o·ra·to'ry
cor·rode'
cor·rod'ed
cor·ro'si·ble
cor·ro'sion
cor·ro'sive
cor'ru·gate
cor'ru·gat'ed
cor'ru·ga'tion
cor·rupt'
cor·rupt'ed
cor·rupt'i·bil'i·ty
cor·rupt'i·ble
cor·rup'tion
cor·rupt'ly
cor·sage'
cor'sair
corse'let
cor'set
cor·tege'
cor'tex
cor'ti·cal
co·run'dum

cor'us·cate
cor'us·cat'ed
cor'us·ca'tion
cor·vette'
co·ry'za
co·sig'na·to'ry
co·sign'er
cos'i·ly
co'sine
cos·met'ic
cos·me·ti'cian
cos'mic
cos·mog'o·ny
cos·mol'o·gy
cos·mop'o·lis
cos'mo·pol'i·tan
cos·mop'o·lite
cos'mos
Cos'sack
cost
cos'tal
cos'tive
cost'li·ness
cost'ly
cos'tume
cos·tum'er
co'sy
cot
co'te·rie
co·ter'mi·nous
co·til'lion
cot'tage

cot'ter

cot'ton

cot'ton·tail'

cot'ton·wood'

couch

cou'gar

cough

could

coun'cil

coun'ci·lor

coun'sel

coun'seled

count

count'ed

coun'te·nance

count'er

coun'ter·act'

coun'ter·at·tack'

coun'ter·bal'ance

coun'ter·blast'

coun'ter·change'

coun'ter·check'

coun'ter·claim'

coun'ter·clock'wise'

count'ered

coun'ter·feit

coun'ter·feit'er

coun'ter·foil'

coun'ter·ir'ri·tant

coun'ter·mand'

coun'ter·march'

coun'ter·mine'

coun'ter·of·fen'sive

coun'ter·pane'

coun'ter·part'

coun'ter·plot'

coun'ter·point'

coun'ter·shaft'

coun'ter·sign'

coun'ter·sink'

coun'ter·vail'

coun'ter·weight'

count'ess

count'less

coun'try

coun'try·man

coun'try·side'

coun'ty

coup

cou'pé'

cou'ple

cou'pler

cou'plet

cou'pling

cou'pon

cour'age

cou·ra'geous

cour'i·er

course

coursed

cours'er

court

court'ed

cour'te·ous

cour'te·sy

court'house'

cour'ti·er

court'li·ness

court'ly

court'-mar'tial

court'ship

court'yard'

cous'in

cove

cov'e·nant

cov'er

cov'er·age

cov'ered

cov'er·let

cov'ert

cov'et

cov'et·ed

cov'et·ous

cov'ey

cow'ard

cow'ard·ice

cow'ard·ly

cow'bell'

cow'boy'

cow'catch'er

cow'er

cowl

cow'lick'

co-work'er

cow'slip

cox'comb'

cox'swain	crane	craze
coy	craned	cra'zi·er
coy'ly	cra'ni·al	cra'zi·est
coy'ness	cra'ni·om'e·try	cra'zi·ly
coy'ote	cra'ni·ot'o·my	cra'zi·ness
coz'en	cra'ni·um	cra'zy
co'zi·er	crank	creak
co'zi·est	crank'case'	creak'ing·ly
co'zi·ly	cranked	cream
co'zi·ness	crank'i·ly	creamed
co'zy	crank'i·ness	cream'er·y
crab	crank'y	cream'i·er
crack	cran'ny	cream'i·est
cracked	crape	cream'y
crack'er	crash	crease
crack'le	crass	cre·ate'
crack'led	crass'ly	cre·at'ed
cra'dle	crass'ness	cre·a'tion
cra'dled	crate	cre·a'tive
craft	crat'ed	cre·a'tive·ly
craft'i·er	cra'ter	cre·a'tive·ness
craft'i·est	cra·vat'	cre'a·tiv'i·ty
craft'i·ly	crave	cre·a'tor
craft'i·ness	craved	crea'ture
crafts'man	cra'ven	crèche
craft'y	cra'ven·ette'	cre'dence
crag	crav'ings	cre·den'tial
cram	craw'fish'	cre·den'za
crammed	crawl	cred'i·bil'i·ty
cramp	crawled	cred'i·ble
cram'pon	cray'fish'	cred'it
cran'ber'ry	cray'on	cred'it·a·bil'i·ty

cred'it·a·ble

cred'it·ed

cred'i·tor

cre'do

cre·du'li·ty

cred'u·lous

cred'u·lous·ness

creed

creek

creel

creep

creep'er

creep'i·ness

cre'mate

cre'mat·ed

cre·ma'tion

cre'ma·to'ry

Cre·mo'na

cre'ole

cre'o·sote

crepe

crep'i·tant

crep'i·tate

crep'i·ta'tion

cre·scen'do

cres'cent

crest

crest'ed

crest'fall'en

cre'tin

cre'tin·ism

cre'tin·oid

cre'tin·ous

cre·tonne'

cre·vasse'

crev'ice

crew

crew'el

crib

crib'bage

crib'work'

crick'et

crime

crim'i·nal

crim'i·nal'i·ty

crim'i·nal·ly

crim'i·nol'o·gist

crim'i·nol'o·gy

crimp

crim'son

cringe

cringed

crin'kle

crin'kled

crin'o·line

crip'ple

crip'pled

cri'ses

cri'sis

crisp

crisp'er

crisp'est

crisp'ly

crisp'ness

criss'cross'

cri·te'ri·a

cri·te'ri·on

crit'ic

crit'i·cal

crit'i·cal·ly

crit'i·cism

crit'i·cize

crit'i·cized

cri·tique'

croak

croaked

croak'er

croak'ing·ly

croch'et

crock

crock'er·y

croc'o·dile

cro'cus

crook

crook'ed

crook'ed·ness

croon

crooned

croon'er

crop

cro·quet'

cro·quette'

cro'sier

cross

cross'bar'

cross'bow'

cross'bow'man

cross'bred'

cross'cut'

cross'hatch'

cross'ings

cross'o·ver

cross'road'

cross'walk'

cross'wise'

cross'word'

crotch'et

crouch

crouched

croup

crou'pi·er

crow

crow'bar'

crowd

crowd'ed

crown

crowned

crown'work'

cru'cial

cru'cial·ly

cru'ci·ble

cru'ci·fied

cru'ci·fix

cru'ci·fix'ion

cru'ci·form

cru'ci·fy

crude

crud'er

crud'est

cru'di·ty

cru'el

cru'el·ly

cru'el·ty

cru'et

cruise

cruis'er

crul'ler

crumb

crum'ble

crum'bled

crump

crum'pet

crum'ple

crum'pled

crunch

crup'per

cru·sade'

cru·sad'er

cruse

crush

crushed

crush'er

crush'ing·ly

crust

crust'ed

crust'i·er

crust'i·est

crust'y

crutch

crux

cry

cry'o·lite

crypt

cryp'tic

cryp'ti·cal

cryp'ti·cal·ly

cryp'to·gram

cryp'to·graph

cryp·tog'ra·phy

crys'tal

crys'tal·line

crys'tal·li·za'tion

crys'tal·lize

crys'tal·lized

crys'tal·loid

cub

cub'by·hole'

cube

cu'beb

cu'bic

cu'bi·cle

cub'ism

cu'bit

cuck'oo

cu'cum·ber

cud'dle

cud'dled

cudg'el

cudg'eled

cue

cuff

cuffed

cui·rass'	cup'board	cu'ri·ous·ly
cui·sine'	cup'cake'	curl
cu'li·nar'y	cu'pel	curled
cull	cu'pel·la'tion	curl'er
culled	cup'ful	cur'lew
cul'mi·nate	Cu'pid	curl'i·cue
cul'mi·nat'ed	cu·pid'i·ty	curl'y
cul'mi·na'tion	cu'po·la	cur·mudg'eon
cul'pa·bil'i·ty	cupped	cur'rant
cul'pa·ble	cu'pric	cur'ren·cy
cul'prit	cu'prous	cur'rent
cult	cur	cur'rent·ly
cul'ti·vate	cur'a·ble	cur·ric'u·la
cul'ti·vat'ed	cu'ra·çao'	cur·ric'u·lar
cul'ti·va'tion	cu'ra·cy	cur·ric'u·lum
cul'ti·va'tor	cu·ra're	cur'ry
cul'tur·al	cu'rate	curse
cul'tur·al·ly	cur'a·tive	curs'ed
cul'ture	cu·ra'tor	cur'sive
cul'tured	curb	cur'so·ry
cul'vert	curbed	curt
cum'ber	curd	cur·tail'
cum'bered	cure	cur·tailed'
cum'ber·some	cured	cur'tain
cum'brous	cu·ret'tage	cur'te·sy
cum'mer·bund'	cu·rette'	curt'ly
cu'mu·la'tive	cur'few	cur'va·ture
cu'mu·lus	cu'rie	curve
cu·ne'i·form	cu'ri·o	curved
cun'ning	cu'ri·os'i·ties	cur'vi·lin'e·ar
cun'ning·ly	cu'ri·os'i·ty	cush'ion
cup	cu'ri·ous	cush'ioned

cusp

cus'pi·dor

cuss'ed·ness

cus'tard

cus·to'di·al

cus·to'di·an

cus'to·dy

cus'tom

cus'tom·ar'i·ly

cus'tom·ar'y

cus'tom·er

cut

cu·ta'ne·ous

cut'a·way'

cut'back'

cute

cu'ti·cle

cut'lass

cut'ler·y

cut'let

cut'off'

cut'out'

cut'purse'

cut'ter

cut'tings

cut'tle·fish'

cut'weed'

cut'worm

cy'a·nate

cy·an'ic

cy'a·nide

cy'a·nite

cy·an'o·gen

cy'a·no'sis

cyc'la·men

cy'cle

cy'clic

cy'cloid

cy·clom'e·ter

cy'clone

cy·clon'ic

cy'clo·pe'di·a

cy'clo·pe'dic

Cy'clops

cy'clo·ra'ma

cyg'net

cyl'in·der

cy·lin'dric

cy·lin'dri·cal

cym'bal

cyn'ic

cyn'i·cal

cyn'i·cal·ly

cyn'i·cism

cy'no·sure

cy'press

Cy·ril'lic

cyst

cys·ti'tis

cyst'oid

cys'to·lith

czar

Czech

dddddddddddddddd
dddddddddddddddd
dddddddddddddddd
dddddddddddddddd
dddddddddddddddd
dddddddddddddddd

dab'ble	dal'ly	dan'dle
dachs'hund'	dal·ma'tian	dan'dled
da·coit'	dam	dan'druff
dae'dal	dam'age	dan'dy
dae'mon	dam'aged	dan'ger
daf'fo·dil	dam'a·scene'	dan'ger·ous
daft	dam'a·scened'	dan'ger·ous·ly
dag'ger	da·mas'cus	dan'gle
da·guerre'o·type	dam'ask	dan'gled
dahl'ia	dammed	Dan'ish
dai'ly	dam'na·ble	dank
dain'ti·er	dam·na'tion	dap'per
dain'ti·est	damp	dap'ple
dain'ti·ly	damp'en	dap'pled
dain'ti·ness	damp'ened	dare
dain'ty	damp'er	dared
dair'y	damp'est	dar'ing·ly
dair'y·maid'	damp'ness	dark
dair'y·man	dam'sel	dark'en
da'is	dance	dark'er
dai'sy	danc'er	dark'est
dal'li·ance	dan'de·li'on	dark'ly

dark'ness

dar'ling

darned

dart

dart'ed

dash

dash'board'

dashed

dash'ing·ly

das'tard·ly

da'ta

date

dat'ed

da'tive

da'tum

daub

daubed

daugh'ter

daugh'ter-in-law'

daunt

daunt'ed

daunt'less

dau'phin

dav'en·port

dav'it

daw'dle

daw'dled

dawn

dawned

day

day'book'

day'break'

day'dream'

day'light'

day'time'

daz'zle

daz'zled

dea'con

dead

dead'en

dead'ened

dead'fall'

dead'head'

dead'light'

dead'li·ness

dead'lock

dead'ly

deaf

deaf'en

deaf'ened

deaf'en·ing·ly

deaf'er

deaf'est

deal

deal'er

deal'ings

dean

dean'er·y

dear

dear'er

dear'est

dear'ly

dear'ness

dearth

death

death'bed'

death'blow'

death'less

death'like'

death'ly

de·ba'cle

de·bar'

de·bark'

de·barred'

de·base'

de·based'

de·base'ment

de·bat'a·ble

de·bate'

de·bat'ed

de·bat'er

de·bauch'

de·bauched'

de·bauch'er·y

de·ben'ture

de·bil'i·tate

de·bil'i·tat'ed

de·bil'i·ty

deb'it

deb'it·ed

de·bris'

debt

debt'or

de·bunk'

de'but

deb'u·tante'

dec'ade

de·ca'dence

de·ca'dent

de·cal'co·ma'ni·a

de·camp'

de·cant'

de·cant'er

de·cap'i·tate

de·cap'i·ta'tion

de-car'bon·ize

de·cath'lon

de·cay'

de·cayed'

de·cease'

de·ceased'

de·ce'dent

de·ceit'

de·ceit'ful

de·ceit'ful·ness

de·ceive'

de·ceived'

de·cel'er·a'tion

De·cem'ber

de'cen·cy

de·cen'ni·al

de'cent

de'cent·ly

de·cen'tral·i·za'tion

de·cen'tral·ize

de·cep'tion

de·cep'tive

de·cep'tive·ly

de·cep'tive·ness

de·cide'

de·cid'ed·ly

de·cid'u·ous

dec'i·mal

dec'i·mate

dec'i·mat'ed

dec'i·ma'tion

de·ci'pher

de·ci'pher·a·ble

de-ci'phered

de·ci'sion

de·ci'sive

de·ci'sive·ly

de·ci'sive·ness

deck

decked

deck'house'

deck'le

de·claim'

de·claimed'

dec'la·ma'tion

de·clam'a·to'ry

dec'la·ra'tion

de-clar'a·tive

de·clar'a·to'ry

de·clare'

de·clared'

de·clen'sion

dec'li·na'tion

de·cline'

de·clined'

de·cliv'i·ty

de·coc'tion

dé·col'le·tage

dé·col'le·té

de·com'pen·sate

de·com'pen·sa'tion

de'com·pose'

de·com·posed'

de'com·po·si'tion

dec'o·rate

dec'o·rat'ed

dec'o·ra'tion

dec'o·ra'tive

dec'o·ra'tor

dec'o·rous

dec'o·rous·ly

dec'o·rous·ness

de·co'rum

de·coy'

de·crease'

de·creased'

de·creas'ing·ly

de·cree'

de·creed'

de·crep'it

de·crep'i·tude

de·cre'tal

de·cried'

de·cry'

ded'i·cate

ded'i·cat'ed

ded'i·ca'tion

ded'i·ca·to'ry

de·duce'

de·duced'

de·duc'i·ble

de·duct'

de·duct'ed

de·duct'i·ble

de·duc'tion

de·duc'tive·ly

deed

deed'ed

deem

deemed

deep

deep'en

deep'ened

deep'er

deep'est

deep'ly

deep'ness

deer

deer'hound'

deer'skin'

deer'stalk'er

deer'weed'

de·face'

de·faced'

de·fal'cate

de·fal'cat·ed

de'fal·ca'tion

def'a·ma'tion

de·fam'a·to'ry

de·fame'

de·famed'

de·fault'

de·fault'ed

de·fault'er

de·fea'si·ble

de·feat'

de·feat'ed

de·feat'ism

de·fect'

de·fec'tion

de·fec'tive

de·fec'tor

de·fend'

de·fend'ant

de·fend'ed

de·fend'er

de·fense'

de·fen'si·ble

de·fen'sive

de·fen'sive·ly

de·fen'sive·ness

de·fer'

def'er·ence

def'er·en'tial

def'er·en'tial·ly

de·fer'ment

de·fer'ral

de·ferred'

de·fi'ance

de·fi'ant

de·fi'ant·ly

de·fi'cien·cy

de·fi'cient

def'i·cit

def'i·lade'

def'i·lad'ed

de·file'

de·filed'

de·file'ment

de·fin'a·ble

de·fine'

de·fined'

def'i·nite

def'i·nite·ly

def'i·nite·ness

def'i·ni'tion

de·fin'i·tive

de·fin'i·tive·ly

de·fin'i·tive·ness

de·fin'i·tize

de·flate'

de·flat'ed

de·fla'tion

de·fla'tion·ar'y

de·flect'

de·flect'ed

de·flec'tion

de·for'est·a'tion

de·form'

de'for·ma'tion

de·formed'

de·form'i·ty

de·fraud'

de·fraud′ed

de·fray′

de·frayed′

deft

deft′ly

deft′ness

de·funct′

de·fied′

de·fy′

de·gen′er·a·cy

de·gen′er·ate

de·gen′er·at′ed

de·gen·er·a′tion

deg′ra·da′tion

de·grade′

de·grad′ed

de·grad′ing·ly

de·gree′

de·hy′drate

de·hy′drat·ed

de′·i·fi·ca′tion

de′·i·fied

de′·i·fy

deign

deigned

de′ism

de′ist

de′i·ty

de·ject′ed

de·ject′ed·ly

de·jec′tion

de·lay′

de·layed′

de·lec′ta·bil′i·ty

de·lec′ta·ble

de·lec·ta′tion

del′e·gate

del′e·gat′ed

del′e·ga′tion

de·lete′

de·let′ed

del′e·te′ri·ous

del′e·te′ri·ous·ly

de·le′tion

delft′ware′

de·lib′er·ate

de·lib′er·at′ed

de·lib′er·a′tion

de·lib′er·a′tive

del′i·ca·cy

del′i·cate

del′i·cate·ly

del′i·ca·tes′sen

de·li′cious

de·li′cious·ly

de·light′

de·light′ed

de·light′ful

de·light′ful·ly

de·lim′it

de·lim′i·ta′tion

de·lin′e·ate

de·lin′e·at′ed

de·lin′e·a′tion

de·lin′e·a′tive

de·lin′e·a′tor

de·lin′quen·cy

de·lin′quent

del′i·quesce′

del′i·ques′cence

del′i·ques′cent

de·lir′i·ous

de·lir′i·um

de·liv′er

de·liv′er·ance

de·liv′ered

de·liv′er·er

de·liv′er·y

del·phin′i·um

del′ta

del′toid

de·lude′

de·lud′ed

del′uge

del′uged

de·lu′sion

de·lu′sive

de luxe′

delve

de·mag′net·ize

dem′a·gog′ic

dem′a·gogue′

de·mand′

de·mand′ed

de·mand′ing·ly

de′·mar·ca′tion

de·mean'

de·meaned'

de·mean'or

de·ment'ed

de·men'ti·a

de·mer'it

dem'i·god'

de·mil'i·ta·rize

de·mise'

de·mo'bi·li·za'tion

de·mo'bi·lize

de·mo'bi·lized

de·moc'ra·cy

dem'o·crat

dem'o·crat'ic

dem'o·crat'i·cal·ly

de·moc'ra·ti·za'tion

de·moc'ra·tize

de·mol'ish

de·mol'ished

dem'o·li'tion

de'mon

de·mon'e·ti·za'tion

de·mon'e·tize

de'mo·ni'a·cal

de·mon'stra·ble

dem'on·strate

dem'on·strat'ed

dem'on·stra'tion

de·mon'stra·tive

dem'on·stra'tor

de·mor'al·i·za'tion

de·mor'al·ize

de·mor'al·ized

de·mot'ic

de·mount'able

de·mur'

de·mure'

de·mure'ly

de·mur'rage

de·murred'

de·mur'rer

den

de·na'ture

de·na'tured

den·drol'o·gy

de·ni'al

de·nied'

den'i·grate

den'i·zen

de·nom'i·nate

de·nom'i·nat'ed

de·nom'i·na'tion

de·nom'i·na'tion·al

de·nom'i·na'tor

de'no·ta'tion

de·note'

de·not'ed

de·noue'ment

de·nounce'

de·nounced'

dense

dens'er

dens'est

den'si·ty

dent

den'tal

den·tal'gi·a

dent'ed

den'ti·frice

den'tine

den'tist

den'tist·ry

den·ti'tion

den'u·da'tion

de·nude'

de·nun'ci·a'tion

de·nun'ci·a·to'ry

de·ny'

de·o'dor·ant

de·o'dor·ize

de·o'dor·ized

de·part'

de·part'ed

de·part'ment

de'part·men'tal

de'part·men'tal·ize

de·par'ture

de·pend'

de·pend'ed

de·pend'en·cy

de·pend'ent

de·per'son·al·ize

de·pict'

de·pict'ed

de·pic'tion

de·pil'a·to'ry

de·plete'

de·plet'ed

de·ple'tion

de·plor'a·ble

de·plore'

de·plored'

de·ploy'

de·ployed'

de·ploy'ment

de·po'lar·i·za'tion

de·po'lar·ize

de·po'nent

de·pop'u·late

de·pop'u·lat'ed

de·port'

de'por·ta'tion

de·port'ed

de port'ment

de·pose'

de·posed'

de·pos'it

de·pos'i·tar'y

de·pos'it·ed

dep'o·si'tion

de·pos'i·tor

de·pos'i·to'ry

de'pot

dep'ra·va'tion

de·prave'

de·praved'

de·prav'i·ty

dep're·cate

dep're·cat'ed

dep're·ca'tion

dep're·ca·to'ry

de·pre'ci·ate

de·pre'ci·at'ed

de·pre'ci·a'tion

dep're·da'tion

de·press'

de·pres'sant

de·pressed'

de·press'ing·ly

de·pres'sion

de·pres'sive

dep'ri·va'tion

de·prive'

de·prived'

depth

dep'u·ta'tion

de·pute'

de·put'ed

dep'u·tize

dep'u·tized

dep'u·ty

de·rail'

de·railed'

de·rail'ment

de·range'

de·ranged'

de·range'ment

der'by

der'e·lict

der'e·lic'tion

de·ride'

de·rid'ed

de·ri'sion

de·ri'sive

de·riv'a·ble

der'i·va'tion

de·riv'a·tive

de·rive'

de·rived'

der'mal

der'ma·ti'tis

der'ma·tol'o·gy

der'ma·to'sis

der'o·gate

der'o·gat'ed

der'o·ga'tion

de·rog'a·to'ry

der'rick

der'vish

des'cant

de·scend'

de·scend'ant

de·scent'

de·scribe'

de·scribed'

de·scrip'tion

de·scrip'tive

de·scry'

des'e·crate

des'e·crat'ed

des'e·cra'tion

de·sen'si·tize	des'o·lat'ed	de·stroy'er
de·sen'si·tiz'er	des'o·late·ly	de·struct'i·ble
de·sert'	des'o·la'tion	de·struc'tion
de·sert'ed	de·spair'	de·struc'tive
de·sert'er	de·spaired'	des'ue·tude
de·ser'tion	de·spair'ing·ly	des'ul·to'ri·ly
de·serve'	des'per·a'do	des'ul·to'ry
de·served'	des'per·ate	de·tach'
des'ic·cant	des'per·ate·ly	de·tach'a·ble
des'ic·cate	des'per·a'tion	de·tached'
des'ic·cat'ed	des'pi·ca·ble	de·tach'ment
des'ic·ca'tion	de·spise'	de·tail'
des'ic·ca'tive	de·spised'	de·tailed'
de·sid'er·a'ta	de·spite'	de·tain'
de·sid'er·a'tum	de·spoil'	de·tained'
de·sign'	de·spoiled'	de·tect'
des'ig·nate	de·spond'en·cy	de·tect'ed
des'ig·nat'ed	de·spond'ent	de·tec'tion
des'ig·na'tion	de·spond'ing·ly	de·tec'tive
de·signed'	des'pot	de·tec'tor
de·sign'ed·ly	des·pot'ic	de·ten'tion
de·sign'er	des'pot·ism	de·ter'
de·sir'a·bil'i·ty	des'qua·ma'tion	de·ter'gent
de·sir'a·ble	des·sert'	de·te'ri·o·rate
de·sire'	des'ti·na'tion	de·te'ri·o·rat'ed
de·sired'	des'tine	de·te'ri·o·ra'tion
de·sires'	des'tined	de·ter'mi·na·ble
de·sir'ous	des'ti·ny	de·ter'mi·nant
de·sist'	des'ti·tute	de·ter'mi·na'tion
de·sists'	des'ti·tu'tion	de·ter'mi·na'tive
desk	de·stroy'	de·ter'mine
des'o·late	de·stroyed'	de·ter'mined

de·ter'min·ism

de·terred'

de·ter'rent

de·test'

de·test'a·ble

de'tes·ta'tion

de·test'ed

de·throne'

de·throned'

det'o·nate

det'o·nat'ed

det'o·na'tion

det'o·na'tor

de·tour'

de·toured'

de·tract'

de·tract'ed

de·trac'tion

de·trac'tor

det'ri·ment

det'ri·men'tal

de·tri'tus

de·val'u·ate

de·val'u·at'ed

de·val'u·a'tion

dev'as·tate

dev'as·tat'ed

dev'as·tat'ing·ly

dev'as·ta'tion

de·vel'op

de·vel'oped

de·vel'op·ment

de·vel'op·men'tal

de'vi·ate

de'vi·at'ed

de'vi·a'tion

de·vice'

dev'il

dev'il·try

de'vi·ous

de'vi·ous·ness

de·vise'

de·vised'

de·vi'tal·ize

de·void'

de·volve'

de·volved'

de·vote'

de·vot'ed

de·vot'ed·ly

dev'o·tee'

de·vo'tion

de·vo'tion·al

de·vour'

de·voured'

de·vout'ly

dew

dew'y

dex'ter

dex·ter'i·ty

dex'ter·ous

dex'ter·ous·ly

dex'trose

di·a·be'tes

di'a·bet'ic

di'a·bol'ic

di'a·bol'i·cal

di·ac'o·nal

di'a·crit'i·cal

di'a·dem

di·aer'e·sis

di'ag·nose'

di'ag·nosed'

di'ag·no'ses

di'ag·no'sis

di'ag·nos'tic

di'ag·nos·ti'cian

di·ag'o·nal

di·ag'o·nal·ly

di'a·gram

di'al

di'a·lect

di'a·lec'tic

di'aled

di'a·logue

di·al'y·sis

di·am'e·ter

di'a·met'ric

di'a·met'ri·cal·ly

di'a·mond

di'a·pa'son

di'a·per

di·aph'a·nous

di'a·phragm

di'a·rist

di'a·ry

Di·as′po·ra

di·as′to·le

di′as·tol′ic

di′a·ther′mic

di′a·tom

di′a·tom′ic

di′a·tribe

dice

di·chot′o·mous

di·chot′o·my

Dic′ta·phone

dic′tate

dic′tat·ed

dic·ta′tion

dic·ta′tor

dic′ta·to′ri·al

dic′ta·to′ri·al·ly

dic′ta·tor·ship

dic′tion

dic′tion·ar′y

Dic′to·graph

dic′tum

did

di·dac′tic

die

died

die′stock′

di′et

di′e·tar′y

di′e·tet′ics

dif′fer

dif′fered

dif′fer·ence

dif′fer·ent

dif′fer·en′tial

dif′fer·en′ti·ate

dif′fer·en′ti·at′ed

dif′fer·en′ti·a′tion

dif′fi·cult

dif′fi·cul·ty

dif′fi·dence

dif′fi·dent

dif·fract′

dif·frac′tion

dif·fuse′

dif·fused′

dif·fu′sion

dig

di·gest′

di·gest′ed

di·gest′i·ble

di·ges′tion

di·ges′tive

dig′gings

dig′it

dig′i·tal′is

dig′ni·fied

dig′ni·fy

dig′ni·tar′y

dig′ni·ty

di·gress′

di·gres′sion

dike

di·lap′i·date

di·lap′i·dat′ed

di·lap′i·da′tion

dil′a·ta′tion

di·late′

di·lat′ed

di·la′tion

dil′a·to′ry

di·lem′ma

dil′et·tan′te

dil′i·gence

dil′i·gent

dil′i·gent·ly

di·lute′

di·lut′ed

di·lu′tion

dim

dime

di·men′sion

di·men′sion·al

di·min′ish

di·min′u·en′do

dim′i·nu′tion

di·min′u·tive

dim′i·ty

dim′ly

dimmed

dim′mer

dim′mest

dim′ness

dim′ple

dine

dined

din'er

din'gy

din'ner

di'no·saur

dint

di·oc'e·san

di'o·cese

di'o·ra'ma

diph·the'ri·a

diph'thong

di·plo'ma

di·plo'ma·cy

dip'lo·mat

dip'lo·mat'ic

dip'lo·mat'i·cal·ly

di·plo'ma·tist

di·plo'pi·a

dip'per

dip'so·ma'ni·a

dip'so·ma'ni·ac

di·rect'

di·rect'ed

di·rec'tion

di·rec'tion·al

di·rec'tive

di·rect'ly

di·rect'ness

di·rec'tor

di·rec'to·ry

dire'ful

dir'est

dirge

dir'i·gi·ble

dirt

dirt'i·ly

dirt'y

dis'a·bil'i·ty

dis·a'ble

dis·a'bled

dis'a·buse'

dis'ad·van'tage

dis·ad'van·ta'geous

dis'af·fect'ed

dis'af·fec'tion

dis'af·firm'

dis'af·firmed'

dis'a·gree'

dis'a·gree'a·ble

dis'a·gree'ment

dis'al·low'

dis'al·lowed'

dis'ap·pear'

dis'ap·pear'ance

dis'ap·peared'

dis'ap·point'

dis'ap·point'ment

dis'ap·pro·ba'tion

dis'ap·prov'al

dis'ap·prove'

dis·arm'

dis·ar'ma·ment

dis·armed'

dis·arm'ing·ly

dis'ar·range'

dis'ar·ranged'

dis'ar·ray'

dis'ar·tic'u·late

dis'as·so'ci·a'tion

dis·as'ter

dis·as'trous

dis'a·vow'

dis'a·vow'al

dis·band'

dis·band'ed

dis·bar'

dis·bar'ment

dis·barred'

dis'be·lieve'

dis'be·lieved'

dis'be·liev'er

dis'be·liev'ing·ly

dis·burse'

dis·burse'ment

disc

dis'card

dis·card'ed

dis·cern'

dis·cerned'

dis·cern'i·ble

dis·cern'ing·ly

dis·cern'ment

dis·charge'

dis·charged'

dis·ci'ple

dis·ci'ple·ship

dis'ci·pli·nar'y

dis'ci·pline

dis'ci·plined

dis·claim'

dis·claimed'

dis·close'

dis·clo'sure

dis·col'or

dis·col'or·a'tion

dis·col'ored

dis·com'fit

dis·com'fi·ture

dis·com'fort

dis'com·pose'

dis'com·posed'

dis'com·po'sure

dis'con·cert'

dis'con·nect'

dis'con·nect'ed

dis'con'so·late

dis'con·tent'

dis'con·tent'ed

dis'con·tin'u·ance

dis'con·tin'ue

dis'con·tin'ued

dis'cord

dis·cord'ance

dis·cord'ant

dis'count

dis'count·ed

dis·coun'te·nance

dis·cour'age

dis·cour'aged

dis·cour'age·ment

dis·cour'ag·ing·ly

dis·course'

dis·cour'te·ous

dis·cour'te·sy

dis·cov'er

dis·cov'ered

dis·cov'er·er

dis·cov'er·y

dis·cred'it

dis·cred'it·a·ble

dis·cred'it·ed

dis·creet'

dis·crep'an·cy

dis·crete'

dis·cre'tion

dis·cre'tion·ar'y

dis·crim'i·nate

dis·crim'i·nat'ed

dis·crim'i·na'tion

dis·crim'i·na'tive

dis·crim'i·na·to'ry

dis·cur'sive

dis'cus

dis·cuss'

dis·cuss'es

dis·dain'

dis·dained'

dis·dain'ful

dis·ease'

dis·eased'

dis·em'bar·ka'tion

dis'em·bar'rass

dis'em·bod'y

dis'en·chant'

dis'en·gage'

dis'es·tab'lish

dis'es·teem'

dis·fa'vor

dis·fea'ture

dis·fig'ure

dis·fig'ured

dis·fig'ure·ment

dis·fran'chise

dis·gorge'

dis·grace'

dis·grace'ful

dis·grun'tle

dis·guise'

dis·gust'

dis·gust'ed

dis·gust'ed·ly

dis·gust'ing·ly

dish

dis'ha·bille'

dis·har'mo·ny

dis·heart'en

di·shev'el

di·shev'eled

dis·hon'est

dis·hon'est·ly

dis·hon'or

dis·hon'or·a·ble

dis·hon'ored

dis'il·lu'sion

dis·in'cli·na'tion

dis'in·cline'

dis'in·clined'

dis'in·fect'

dis'in·fect'ant

dis·in·gen'u·ous

dis'in·her'it

dis·in'te·grate

dis·in'te·gra'tion

dis·in'ter·est·ed

dis·join'

dis·joined'

dis·join'ings

dis·joint'ed

dis·junc'tion

dis·junc'tive

disk

dis·like'

dis'lo·cate

dis'lo·cat'ed

dis'lo·ca'tion

dis·lodge'

dis·loy'al

dis·loy'al·ty

dis'mal

dis'mal·ly

dis·man'tle

dis·man'tled

dis·mast'

dis·mast'ed

dis·may'

dis·mayed'

dis·mem'ber

dis·mem'bered

dis·mem'ber·ment

dis·miss'

dis·miss'al

dis·mount'

dis·mount'ed

dis'o·be'di·ence

dis'o·be'di·ent

dis'o·bey'

dis'o·beyed'

dis'o·blige'

dis'o·blig'ing·ly

dis·or'der

dis·or'dered

dis·or'der·ly

dis·or'gan·ize

dis·or'gan·ized

dis·own'

dis·par'age

dis·par'age·ment

dis·par'ag·ing·ly

dis'pa·rate

dis·par'i·ty

dis·pas'sion·ate

dis·patch'

dis·patched'

dis·patch'er

dis·pel'

dis·pelled'

dis·pen'sa·ble

dis·pen'sa·ry

dis'pen·sa'tion

dis·pense'

dis·pensed'

dis·per'sal

dis·perse'

dis·persed'

dis·per'sion

dis·pir'it·ed

dis·place'

dis·place'ment

dis·play'

dis·please'

dis·pleas'ure

dis·port'

dis·pos'al

dis·pose'

dis·posed'

dis'po·si'tion

dis'pos·sess'

dis'pos·sessed'

dis·po'sure

dis·praise'

dis·proof'

dis'pro·por'tion

dis'pro·por'tion·ate

dis'pu·ta·ble

dis'pu·tant

dis'pu·ta'tion

dis'pu·ta'tious

dis·pute'

dis·put'ed

dis·qual'i·fi·ca'tion

dis·qual'i·fy

dis·qui'et·ed

dis·qui'e·tude

dis'qui·si'tion

dis're·gard'

dis·re·pair'

dis·rep'u·ta·ble

dis're·pute'

dis're·spect'

dis're·spect'ful

dis·robe'

dis·root'

dis·rupt'

dis·rup'tion

dis·rup'tive

dis'sat·is·fac'tion

dis·sat'is·fied

dis·sect'

dis·sect'ed

dis·sem'ble

dis·sem'i·nate

dis·sem'i·nat'ed

dis·sem'i·na'tion

dis·sen'sion

dis·sent'

dis·sent'er

dis·sen'tient

dis'ser·ta'tion

dis·serv'ice

dis'si·dence

dis'si·dent

dis·sim'i·lar

dis·sim'i·lar'i·ty

dis·sim'u·late

dis·sim'u·lat'ed

dis·sim'u·la'tion

dis'si·pate

dis'si·pat'ed

dis'si·pa'tion

dis·so'ci·ate

dis·so'ci·at'ed

dis·so'ci·a'tion

dis'so·lute

dis'so·lu'tion

dis·solv'a·ble·ness

dis·solve'

dis·solved'

dis'so·nance

dis'so·nant

dis·suade'

dis·sua'sion

dis'taff

dis'tal

dis'tance

dis'tant

dis·taste'

dis·taste'ful

dis·tem'per

dis·tend'

dis·ten'si·ble

dis·till'

dis'til·late

dis'til·la'tion

dis·tilled'

dis·till'er

dis·till'er·y

dis·tinct'

dis·tinc'tion

dis·tinc'tive

dis·tinct'ly

dis·tinct'ness

dis·tin'guish

dis·tin'guished

dis·tort'

dis·tort'ed

dis·tor'tion

dis·tract'

dis·tract'ing·ly

dis·trac'tion

dis·train'

dis·trained'

dis·traught'

dis·tress'

dis·trib'ute

dis'tri·bu'tion

dis·trib'u·tive

dis·trib'u·tor

dis'trict

dis·trust'

dis·trust'ful

dis·turb'

dis·turb'ance

dis·turbed'

dis·turb'er

dis·un'ion

dis'u·nite'	di·vine'ly	dodge
dis·use'	di·vin'i·ty	dodged
ditch	di·vis'i·bil'i·ty	do'do
ditched	di·vis'i·ble	doe
dith'y·ram'bic	di·vi'sion	doe'skin'
dit'to	di·vi'sor	doff
dit'ty	di·vorce'	dog
di·ur'nal	di·vor'cee'	dog'cart'
di'va·gate	di·vorce'ment	doge
di'van	di·vulge'	dog'ged
dive	di·vulged'	dog'ger·el
dived	diz'zi·er	dog'ma
div'er	diz'zi·est	dog·mat'ic
di·verge'	diz'zi·ly	dog'ma·tism
di·verged'	diz'zi·ness	dog'ma·tize
di·ver'gence	diz'zy	dog'trot'
di·ver'gent	do	dog'wood'
di·verg'ing·ly	doc'ile	doi'ly
di·verse'	do·cil'i·ty	do'ings
di·ver'si·fi·ca'tion	dock	dol'drums
di·ver'si·fy	dock'et	dole
di·ver'sion	dock'yard'	doled
di·ver'sion·ar·y	doc'tor	dole'ful
di·ver'si·ty	doc'tor·ate	doll
di·vert'	doc'tri·naire'	dol'lar
di·vest'	doc'tri·nal	dol'man
di·vide'	doc'trine	dol'phin
di·vid'ed	doc'u·ment	dolt
div'i·dend	doc'u·men'ta·ry	do·main'
di·vid'er	doc'u·men·ta'tion	dome
di·vine'	doc'u·ment'ed	domed
di·vined'	dod'der	do·mes'tic

do·mes'ti·cal·ly	door'stop'	dough'y
do·mes'ti·cate	door'way'	dour
do·mes'ti·cat'ed	door'yard'	dove
do'mes·tic'i·ty	dope	dove
dom'i·cile	dor'mant	dove'cot'
dom'i·cil'i·ar'y	dor'mer	dove'tail'
dom'i·nance	dor'mi·to'ry	dow'a·ger
dom'i·nant	dor'mouse'	dow'di·er
dom'i·nate	dor'sal	dow'di·est
dom'i·nat'ed	do'ry	dow'di·ly
dom'i·na'tion	dos'age	dow'dy
dom'i·neer'	dose	dow'el
dom'i·neered'	dos'si·er	dow'eled
dom'i·neer'ing·ly	dot	dow'er
dom'i·nie	dot'age	down
do·min'ion	do'tard	down'cast'
dom'i·no	dote	down'fall'
do'nate	dot'ing·ly	down'heart'ed
do'nat·ed	dot'ted	down'hill'
do·na'tion	dou'ble	down'pour'
don'a·tive	dou'bled	down'right'
done	dou'bly	down'stairs'
don'key	doubt	down'town'
do'nor	doubt'ed	down'ward
doom	doubt'ful	down'y
doomed	doubt'ful·ly	dow'ry
door	doubt'ing·ly	dows'er
door'bell'	doubt'less	dox·ol'o·gy
door'frame'	dough	doze
door'knob'	dough'boy'	doz'en
door'nail'	dough'nut'	drab
door'sill'	dough'ty	drach'ma

draft	dra'per·y	drear'i·er
draft'ed	dras'tic	drear'i·est
draft'ee'	draught	drear'i·ly
draft'i·er	draw	drear'i·ness
draft'i·est	draw'back'	drear'y
draft'i·ly	draw'bar'	dredge
draft'y	draw'bridge'	dredged
drag	draw'ee'	dreg
drag'gle	draw'er	drench
drag'gled	draw'ings	drenched
drag'net'	drawl	dress
drag'on	drawled	dressed
drag'on·fly'	drawn	dress'er
dra·goon'	draw'plate'	dress'ings
dra·gooned'	draw'string'	dress'mak'er
drain	dray	dress'y
drain'age	dray'age	drew
drained	dray'man	drib'ble
drain'er	dread	drib'bled
drake	dread'ed	dried
dra'ma	dread'ful	dri'er
dra·mat'ic	dream	dri'est
dra·mat'i·cal·ly	dreamed	drift
dra·mat'ics	dream'er	drift'wood'
dram'a·tist	dream'i·er	drill
dram'a·ti·za'tion	dream'i·est	drilled
dram'a·tize	dream'i·ly	drill'er
dram'a·tized	dream'i·ness	drink
dram'a·tur'gy	dream'land	drink'a·ble
drank	dream'less	drink'er
drape	dream'like	drip
drap'er	dream'y	drip'pings

drive

driv'el

driv'en

driv'er

drive'way'

driz'zle

driz'zled

droll

droll'er·y

drom'e·dar'y

drone

dron'ing·ly

drool

drool'ings

droop

drop

drop'out'

drop'per

drop'pings

drop'si·cal

drop'sy

dross

drought

drove

drown

drowned

drown'ings

drowse

drow'si·ly

drow'si·ness

drow'sy

drudge

drudg'er·y

drug

drug'gist

drug'store'

dru'id

dru·id'i·cal

drum

drum'head'

drummed

drum'mer

drum'stick'

drunk

drunk'ard

drunk'en

dry

dry'ly

dry'ness

du'al

du'al·ism

du'al·is'tic

du·al'i·ty

du·bi'e·ty

du'bi·ous

du'cal

duc'at

duch'ess

duch'y

duck

duck'ling

duck'pin'

duck'weed'

duct

duc'tile

duc·til'i·ty

dudg'eon

due

du'el

du'el·ist

du·en'na

du·et'

duf'fel

duff'er

dug

du'gong

dug'out'

duke

duke'dom

dul'cet

dul'ci·mer

dull

dull'ard

dull'er

dull'est

dull'ness

du'ly

dumb

dumb'bell'

dum'my

dump

dump'ing

dump'ling

dun

dunce

dune

dun'ga·ree'	du'ress	dwel'lings
dun'geon	dur'ing	dwelt
dun'nage	dusk'y	dwin'dle
dunned	dust	dwin'dled
dupe	dust'ed	dy·nam'ic
du'plex	dust'er	dy'na·mism
du'pli·cate	dust'i·er	dy'na·mite
du'pli·cat'ed	dust'i·est	dy'na·mit'ed
du'pli·ca'tion	dust'y	dy'na·mo
du'pli·ca'tor	du'te·ous	dy'nas·ty
du·plic'i·ty	du'ties	dys'en·ter'y
du'ra·bil'i·ty	du'ti·ful	dys·func'tion
du'ra·ble	du'ty	dys·pep'si·a
du·ral'u·min	dwarf	dys·pep'tic
dur'ance	dwarf'ish	dys'tro·phy
du·ra'tion	dwell	

E

each	ear'shot'	East'er
ea'ger	earth	east'er·ly
ea'ger·ly	earth'en	east'ern
ea'ger·ness	earth'en·ware'	east'ern·er
ea'gle	earth'li·ness	east'ward
ea'glet	earth'ling	east'ward·ly
ear	earth'ly	eas'y
earl	earth'quake'	eas'y·go'ing
earl'dom	earth'ward	eat
ear'li·er	earth'work'	eat'a·ble
ear'li·est	earth'worm'	eat'en
ear'ly	ear'wax'	eat'er
ear'mark'	ear'wig'	eaves'drop'
earn	ease	ebb
earned	eased	ebbed
earn'er	ea'sel	eb'on·ize
ear'nest	ease'ment	eb'on·ized
ear'nest·ly	eas'i·er	eb'on·y
ear'nest·ness	eas'i·est	e·bul'li·ence
earn'ings	eas'i·ly	e·bul'li·ent
ear'ring'	eas'i·ness	eb'ul·li'tion
ear'rings'	east	ec·cen'tric

ec'cen·tric'i·ty	edge'wise'	ef·fec'tu·al
ec'chy·mo'sis	ed'i·bil'i·ty	ef·fec'tu·al·ly
ec·cle'si·as'tic	ed'i·ble	ef·fec'tu·ate
ec·cle'si·as'ti·cal	e'dict	ef·fem'i·na·cy
ech'e·lon	ed'i·fi·ca'tion	ef·fem'i·nate
ech'o	ed'i·fice	ef'fer·ent
ech'oed	ed'i·fied	ef'fer·vesce'
é·clair'	ed'i·fy	ef'fer·ves'cence
é·clat'	ed'it	ef·fer·ves'cent
ec·lec'tic	ed'it·ed	ef·fete'
ec·lec'ti·cism	e·di'tion	ef'fi·ca'cious
e·clipse'	ed'i·tor	ef'fi·ca·cy
ec'logue	ed'i·to'ri·al	ef·fi'cien·cy
e'co·nom'ic	ed'i·to'ri·al·ize	ef·fi'cient
e'co·nom'i·cal	ed'i·to'ri·al·ly	ef'fi·gies
e'co·nom'i·cal·ly	ed'u·ca·ble	ef'fi·gy
e·con'o·mist	ed'u·cate	ef'flo·resce'
e·con'o·mize	ed'u·cat'ed	ef'flo·res'cence
econ'omized	ed'u·ca'tion	ef'flo·res'cent
econ'omy	ed'u·ca'tion·al	ef·flu'vi·a
ec'ru	ed'u·ca'tion·al·ly	ef·flu'vi·um
ec'sta·sy	ed'u·ca'tor	ef'flux
ec·stat'ic	e·duce'	ef'fort
ec·stat'i·cal·ly	eel	ef'fort·less
ec'ze·ma	eel'pot'	ef·fron'ter·y
ed'dy	eel'worm'	ef·ful'gence
e'del·weiss	ee'rie	ef·ful'gent
e·de'ma	ef·face'	ef·fu'sion
edge	ef·face'ment	ef·fu'sive
edged	ef·fect'	ef·fu'sive·ly
edg'er	ef·fect'ed	ef·fu'sive·ness
edge'ways'	ef·fec'tive	e·gal'i·tar'i·an

egg'nog'	e·la'tion	e·lec'trom'e·ter
egg'plant'	el'bow	e·lec'tro·mo'tive
egg'shell'	el'bowed	e·lec'tron
eg'lan·tine	el'bow·room'	e·lec'tron'ic
e'go	eld'er	e·lec'tro·plate'
e'go·cen'tric	el'der·ber'ry	e·lec'tro·pos'i·tive
e'go·cen·tric'i·ty	eld'er·ly	e·lec'tro·scope
e'go·ism	eld'est	e·lec'tro·type
e'go·is'tic	e·lect'	e·lec'tro·typ'er
e'go·tism	e·lect'ed	el'ee·mos'y·nar'y
e'go·tis'tic	e·lec'tion	el'e·gance
e'go·tis'ti·cal	e·lec'tion·eer'	el'e·gant
e·gre'gious	e·lec'tive	el'e·gy
e'gress	e·lec'tor	el'e·ment
e'gret	e·lec'tor·al	el'e·men'tal
E·gyp'tian	e·lec'tor·ate	el'e·men'tal·ly
ei'der	e·lec'tric	el'e·men'ta·ry
ei'ther	e·lec'tri·cal	el'e·phant
e·jac'u·late	e·lec'tri·cal·ly	el'e·phan·ti'a·sis
e·jac'u·la'tion	e·lec'tri'cian	el'e·phan'tine
e·ject'	e·lec'tric'i·ty	el'e·vate
e·jec'tion	e·lec'tri·fi·ca'tion	el'e·vat'ed
e·ject'ment	e·lec'tri·fy	el'e·va'tion
e·jec'tor	e·lec'tro·cute	el'e·va'tor
e·lab'o·rate	e·lec'tro·cu'tion	elf'in
e·lab'o·rate·ly	e·lec'trode	e·lic'it
e·lab'o·ra'tion	e·lec'tro·lier'	e·lic'it·ed
e·lapse'	e·lec'trol'y·sis	e·lide'
e·lapsed'	e·lec'tro·lyt'ic	el'i·gi·bil'i·ty
e·las'tic	e·lec'tro·lyt'i·cal	el'i·gi·ble
e·las'tic'i·ty	e·lec'tro·lyze	e·lim'i·nate
e·lat'ed	e·lec'tro·mag'net	e·lim'i·nat'ed

e·lim'i·na'tion

e·lim'i·na'tive

e·li'sion

e·lite'

e·lix'ir

E·liz'a·be'than

elk

el·lip'sis

el·lips'oid

el·lip'tic

el·lip'ti·cal

elm

el'o·cu'tion

el'o·cu'tion·ist

e·lon'gate

e·lon'gat·ed

e·lon'ga'tion

e·lope'

e·lope'ment

el'o·quence

el'o·quent

el'o·quent·ly

else

else'where

else'wise

e·lu'ci·date

e·lu'ci·dat·ed

e·lu'ci·da'tion

e·lude'

e·lud'ed

e·lu'sive

e·lu'sive·ness

e·lu'so·ry

e·ma'ci·ate

e·ma'ci·at'ed

e·ma'ci·a'tion

em'a·nate

em'a·nat'ed

e·man'ci·pate

e·man'ci·pat'ed

e·man'ci·pa'tion

e·man'ci·pa'tor

e·mas'cu·late

e·mas'cu·la'tion

em·balm'

em·balmed'

em·balm'er

em·bank'ment

em·bar'go

em·bar'goed

em·bark'

em'bar·ka'tion

em·bar'rass

em·bar'rassed

em·bar'rass·ment

em'bas·sy

em·bat'tle

em·bat'tled

em·bel'lish

em·bel'lished

em·bel'lish·ment

em'ber

em·bez'zle

em·bez'zled

em·bez'zle·ment

em·bez'zler

em·bit'ter

em·bit'tered

em·bla'zon

em'blem

em'blem·at'ic

em'blem·at'i·cal

em·bod'ied

em·bod'i·ment

em·bod'y

em·bold'en

em·bold'ened

em'bo·lism

em'bo·lus

em·boss'

em·bossed'

em·brace'

em·braced'

em·bra'sure

em'bro·cate

em'bro·ca'tion

em·broi'der

em·broi'dered

em·broi'der·y

em·broil'

em·broiled'

em'bry·o

em'bry·ol'o·gy

em'bry·on'ic

e·mend'

e'men·da'tion

e·mend'ed

em'er·ald

e·merge'

e·merged'

e·mer'gence

e·mer'gen·cy

e·mer'gent

e·mer'i·tus

em'er·y

e·met'ic

em'i·grant

em'i·grate

em'i·grat'ed

em'i·gra'tion

em'i·nence

em'i·nent

em'is·sar'y

e·mis'sion

e·mit'

e·mit'ted

e·mol'li·ent

e·mol'u·ment

e·mo'tion

e·mo'tion·al

e·mo'tion·al·ly

em·pan'el

em'per·or

em'pha·ses

em'pha·sis

em'pha·size

em'pha·sized

em·phat'ic

em·phat'i·cal·ly

em'pire

em·pir'ic

em·pir'i·cal

em·pir'i·cism

em·place'ment

em·ploy'

em·ployed'

em·ploy'ee

em·ploy'er

em·ploy'ment

em·po'ri·um

em·pow'er

em·pow'ered

em'press

emp'tied

emp'ti·ly

emp'ti·ness

emp'ty

em'py·re'an

e'mu

em'u·late

em'u·lat'ed

em'u·lates

em'u·la'tion

em'u·la'tive

em'u·la·to'ry

em'u·lous

e·mul'si·fi·ca'tion

e·mul'si·fi'er

e·mul'si·fy

e·mul'sion

en·a'ble

en·a'bled

en·act'

en·act'ed

en·act'ment

en·am'el

en·am'eled

en·am'ored

en·camp'

en·camp'ment

en·cap'su·late

en·caus'tic

en'ce·phal'ic

en·ceph'a·li'tis

en·chant'

en·chant'ed

en·chant'ing·ly

en·chant'ment

en·cir'cle

en·cir'cled

en·cir'cle·ment

en'clave

en·close'

en·closed'

en·clo'sure

en·co'mi·a

en·co'mi·as'tic

en·co'mi·um

en·com'pass

en·core'

en·coun'ter

en·coun'tered

en·cour'age

en·cour'aged

en·cour'age·ment

en·cour'ag·ing·ly

en·croach'

en·croached'

en·croach'ment

en·cum'ber

en·cum'bered

en·cum'brance

en·cy'cli·cal

en·cy'clo·pe'di·a

en·cy'clo·pe'dic

en·cyst'

en·cyst'ed

end

en·dan'ger

en·dan'gered

en·dear'

en·deared'

en·deav'or

en·deav'ored

end'ed

en·dem'ic

end'ings

en'dive

end'less

end'less·ly

end'long'

en'do·crine

en'do·cri·nol'o·gy

en'do·derm

en·dog'e·nous

en·dorse'

en·dorse'ment

en·dow'

en·dowed'

en·dow'ment

en·due'

en·dued'

en·dur'a·ble

en·dur'ance

en·dure'

en·dured'

en·dur'ing·ly

end'ways

end'wise

en'e·my

en'er·get'ic

en'er·gize

en'er·gized

en'er·vate

en'er·va'tion

en·fee'ble

en·fee'bled

en'fi·lade'

en·fold'

en·force'

en·force'a·ble

en·forced'

en·force'ment

en·forc'er

en·fran'chise

en·fran'chised

en·gage'

en·gaged'

en·gage'ment

en·gag'ing·ly

en·gen'der

en·gen'dered

en'gine

en'gi·neer'

Eng'lish

Eng'lish·man

en·gorge'

en·gorge'ment

en·grain'

en·grained'

en·grave'

en·graved'

en·grav'er

en·gross'

en·grossed'

en·gross'er

en·gulf'

en·hance'

en·hanced'

en·hance'ment

en·har·mon'ic

e·nig'ma

e'nig·mat'ic

e'nig·mat'i·cal

en·join'

en·joined'

en·joy'

en·joy'a·ble

en·joyed′	en·shrine′	en·thu′si·as′ti·cal·ly
en·joy′ment	en·shrined′	en·tice′
en·large′	en′sign	en·ticed′
en·larged′	en′si·lage	en·tice′ment
en·large′ment	en·slave′	en·tic′ing·ly
en·larg′er	en·slave′ment	en·tire′
en·light′en	en·sue′	en·tire′ly
en·light′ened	en·sued′	en·tire′ty
en·light′en·ing·ly	en·sure′	en·ti′tle
en·light′en·ment	en·sured′	en·ti′tled
en·list′	en·tab′la·ture	en′ti·ty
en·list′ed	en·tail′	en·tomb′
en·list′ment	en·tailed′	en·tombed′
en·liv′en	en·tan′gle	en·tomb′ment
en·liv′ened	en·tan′gled	en′to·mol′o·gist
en·mesh′	en·tan′gle·ment	en′to·mol′o·gy
en′mi·ty	en′ter	en′trails
en·no′ble	en′tered	en′trance
en·no′bled	en′ter·i′tis	en·tranc′ing·ly
e·nor′mi·ty	en′ter·prise	en′trant
e·nor′mous	en′ter·tain′	en·trap′
e·nough′	en′ter·tained′	en·treat′
en·rage′	en′ter·tain′er	en·treat′ed
en·raged′	en′ter·tain′ing·ly	en·treat′y
en·rap′ture	en′ter·tain′ment	en·trench′
en·rap′tured	en·thrall′	en·trust′
en·rich′	en·thralled′	en′try
en·riched′	en·throne′	en′try·way′
en·rich′ment	en·throned′	en·twine′
en·roll′	en·thu′si·asm	e·nu′cle·ate
en·rolled′	en·thu′si·ast	e·nu′cle·a′tion
en·roll′ment	en·thu′si·as′tic	e·nu′mer·ate

e·nu′mer·at′ed

e·nu′mer·a′tion

e·nu′mer·a′tor

e·nun′ci·ate

e·nun′ci·at′ed

e·nun′ci·a′tion

e·nun′ci·a′tor

en·vel′op

en′ve·lope

en·ven′om

en′vi·a·ble

en′vi·ous

en·vi′ron·ment

en·vi′ron·men′tal

en·vi′ron·men′tal·ly

en·vi′rons

en·vis′age

en·vis′aged

en′voy

en′voys

en′vy

en′zyme

e′on

e·phem′er·al

ep′ic

ep′i·cure

ep′i·cu·re′an

ep′i·dem′ic

ep′i·der′mal

ep′i·der′mic

ep′i·der′mis

ep′i·der′moid

ep′i·gas′tric

ep′i·glot′tis

ep′i·gram

ep′i·gram·mat′ic

ep′i·graph

ep′i·lep′sy

ep′i·lep′tic

ep′i·lep′toid

ep′i·logue

e·piph′y·sis

e·pis′co·pa·cy

e·pis′co·pal

e·pis′co·pa′li·an

e·pis′co·pate

ep′i·sode

ep′i·sod′ic

e·pis′te·mol′o·gy

e·pis′tle

e·pis′to·lar′y

e·pis′to·la·to′ry

ep′i·taph

ep′i·tha·la′mi·um

ep′i·the′li·um

ep′i·thet

e·pit′o·me

e·pit′o·mize

ep′i·zo·ot′ic

ep′och

ep′och·al

ep′o·nym

ep·ox′y

eq′ua·ble

eq′ua·bly

e′qual

e′qualed

e·qual′i·tar′i·an

e·qual′i·ty

e′qual·i·za′tion

e′qual·ize

e′qual·ized

e′qual·iz′er

e′qual·ly

e′qua·nim′i·ty

e·quate′

e·quat′ed

e·qua′tion

e·qua′tor

e′qua·to′ri·al

eq′uer·ry

e·ques′tri·an

e·ques′tri·enne′

e′qui·an′gu·lar

e′qui·dis′tance

e′qui·dis′tant

e′qui·lat′er·al

e′qui·lib′ri·um

e′quine

e′qui·noc′tial

e′qui·nox

e·quip′

eq′ui·page

e·quip′ment

e′qui·poise

eq′ui·ta·ble

eq'ui·ta'tion	er·rat'ic	es·pe'cial·ly
eq'ui·ty	er·rat'i·cal·ly	Es'pe·ran'to
e·quiv'a·lence	er·ra'tum	es'pi·o·nage
e·quiv'a·len·cy	erred	es'pla·nade'
e·quiv'a·lent	er·ro'ne·ous	es·pous'al
e·quiv'o·cal	er'ror	es·pouse'
e·quiv'o·cal·ly	erst'while'	es'prit'
e·quiv'o·cate	er'u·dite	es·py'
e·quiv'o·ca'tion	er'u·di'tion	es·quire'
e'ra	e·rupt'	es·say'
e·rad'i·cate	e·rup'tion	es·sayed'
e·rad'i·cat'ed	e·rup'tive	es'say·ist
e·rad'i·ca'tion	er'y·sip'e·las	es'sence
e·rase'	es·ca·lade'	es·sen'tial
e·rased'	es·ca·la'tor	es·sen'tial·ly
e·ras'er	es·ca·pade'	es·tab'lish
e·ra'sure	es·cape'	es·tab'lished
e·rect'	es·cape'ment	es·tab'lish·ment
e·rect'ed	es·cap'ist	es·tate'
e·rec'tile	es·carp'ment	es·teem'
e·rec'tion	es·cheat'	es·teemed'
e·rect'ness	es·chew'	es'ter
erg	es'cort	es·thet'ic
er'go	es·cort'ed	es'ti·ma·ble
er'got	es'cri·toire'	es'ti·mate
er'mine	es'crow'	es'ti·mat'ed
e·rode'	es·cutch'eon	es'ti·ma'tion
e·ro'sion	Es'ki·mo	es'ti·ma'tor
e·rot'ic	e·soph'a·gus	es'ti·vate
err	es'o·ter'ic	es·top'pel
er'rand	es·par'to	es·trange'
er·ra'ta	es·pe'cial	es·tranged'

es·trange'ment

es'tu·ar'y

e·su'ri·ent

etch

etch'er

etch'ings

e·ter'nal

e·ter'nal·ly

e·ter'ni·ty

eth'ane

e'ther

e·the're·al

e·the're·al·ly

eth'i·cal

eth'i·cal·ly

eth'ics

eth·nol'o·gy

eth'yl

e'ti·ol'o·gy

et'i·quette

e'tude

et'y·mo·log'i·cal

et'y·mol'o·gy

eu'ca·lyp'tus

Eu'cha·rist

eu'chre

Eu·clid'e·an

eu·gen'ics

eu'lo·gis'tic

eu'lo·gize

eu'lo·gy

eu'phe·mism

eu'phe·mis'tic

eu·pho'ni·ous

eu'pho·ny

Eur·a'sian

eu·re'ka

Eu'ro·pe'an

Eu·sta'chi·an

eu·tec'tic

eu'tha·na'si·a

e·vac'u·ate

e·vac'u·at'ed

e·vac'u·a'tion

e·vade'

e·vad'ed

e·val'u·ate

e·val'u·a'tion

ev'a·nesce'

ev'a·nes'cence

ev'a·nes'cent

e'van·gel'i·cal

e·van'ge·list

e·vap'o·rate

e·vap'o·rat'ed

e·vap'o·ra'tion

e·vap'o·ra·tor

e·va'sion

e·va'sive

e·va'sive·ly

e·va'sive·ness

e'ven

eve'ning

eve'nings

e'ven·ly

e'ven·ness

e·vent'

e·vent'ful

e·vent'ful·ly

e·ven'tu·al

e·ven'tu·al'i·ty

e·ven'tu·al·ly

e·ven'tu·ate

ev'er

ev'er·glade

ev'er·green'

ev'er·last'ing

ev'er·last'ing·ly

ev'er·y

ev'er·y·bod'y

ev'er·y·day'

ev'er·y·one'

ev'er·y·thing'

ev'er·y·where'

e·vict'

e·vict'ed

e·vic'tion

ev'i·dence

ev'i·dent

ev'i·den'tial

ev'i·den'tial·ly

e'vil

e'vil·ly

e·vince'

e·vinced'

e·vis'cer·ate

ev'o·ca'tion

e·voc'a·tive

e·voke'

e·voked'

ev'o·lu'tion

ev'o·lu'tion·ar'y

ev'o·lu'tion·ist

e·volve'

ewe

ew'er

ex·ac'er·bate

ex·ac'er·ba'tion

ex·act'

ex·act'ed

ex·ac'tion

ex·act'i·tude

ex·act'ly

ex·act'ness

ex·ag'ger·ate

ex·ag'ger·at'ed

ex·ag'ger·a'tion

ex·alt'

ex·al·ta'tion

ex·alt'ed

ex·a'men

ex·am'i·na'tion

ex·am'ine

ex·am'ined

ex·am'in·er

ex·am'ple

ex·as'per·ate

ex·as'per·at'ed

ex·as'per·a'tion

ex'ca·vate

ex'ca·vat'ed

ex'ca·va'tion

ex'ca·va'tor

ex·ceed'

ex·ceed'ed

ex·ceed'ing·ly

ex·cel'

ex·celled'

ex'cel·lence

ex'cel·len·cy

ex'cel·lent

ex·cel'si·or

ex·cept'

ex·cept'ed

ex·cep'tion

ex·cep'tion·al

ex·cep'tion·al·ly

ex·cerpt'

ex·cess'

ex·cess'es

ex·ces'sive

ex·ces'sive·ly

ex·change'

ex·change'a·ble

ex·cheq'uer

ex·cip'i·ent

ex'cise

ex·ci'sion

ex·cit'a·bil'i·ty

ex·cit'a·ble

ex·cit'ant

ex'ci·ta'tion

ex·cite'

ex·cit'ed·ly

ex·cite'ment

ex·claim'

ex·claimed'

ex'cla·ma'tion

ex·clam'a·to'ry

ex·clude'

ex·clud'ed

ex·clu'sion

ex·clu'sive

ex'com·mu'ni·cate

ex'com·mu'ni·ca'tion

ex·co'ri·ate

ex·co'ri·at'ed

ex·co'ri·a'tion

ex·cres'cence

ex·cres'cent

ex·crete'

ex·cret'ed

ex·cre'tion

ex'cre·to'ry

ex·cru'ci·ate

ex·cru'ci·at'ing·ly

ex·cru'ci·a'tion

ex'cul·pate

ex'cul·pat'ed

ex'cul·pa'tion

ex·cur'sion

ex·cus'a·ble

ex·cuse'	ex·haled'	ex·or'bi·tant
ex·cused'	ex·haust'	ex·or'bi·tant·ly
ex·cus'es	ex·haus'tion	ex'or·cise
ex'e·cra·ble	ex·haus'tive	ex'or·cised
ex'e·crate	ex·haust'less	ex'or·cism
ex'e·crat·ed	ex·hib'it	ex·or'di·um
ex'e·cra'tion	ex·hib'it·ed	ex'o·ter'ic
ex·ec'u·tant	ex'hi·bi'tion	ex·ot'ic
ex'e·cute	ex·hib'i·tor	ex·ot'i·cism
ex'e·cut·ed	ex·hil'a·rate	ex·pand'
ex'e·cu'tion	ex·hil'a·rat·ed	ex·pand'ed
ex'e·cu'tion·er	ex·hil'a·ra'tion	ex·panse'
ex·ec'u·tive	ex·hort'	ex·pan'sion
ex·ec'u·tor	ex'hor·ta'tion	ex·pan'sive
ex·ec'u·trix	ex·hort'ed	ex·pa'ti·ate
ex'e·ge'sis	ex·hu·ma'tion	ex·pa'ti·at'ed
ex·em'plar	ex·hume'	ex·pa'tri·ate
ex'em·pla·ry	ex·humed'	ex·pa'tri·a'tion
ex·em'pli·fi·ca'tion	ex'i·gen·cy	ex·pect'
ex·em'pli·fy	ex'i·gent	ex·pect'an·cy
ex·empt'	ex·ig'u·ous	ex·pect'ant
ex·empt'ed	ex'ile	ex'pec·ta'tion
ex·emp'tion	ex'iled	ex·pect'ed
ex'e·qua'tur	ex·ist'	ex·pec'to·rant
ex'er·cise	ex·ist'ed	ex·pec'to·rate
ex'er·cised	ex·ist'ence	ex·pec'to·ra'tion
ex'er·cis'er	ex·ist'ent	ex·pe'di·en·cy
ex·ert'	ex'it	ex·pe'di·ent
ex·ert'ed	ex'o·dus	ex'pe·dite
ex·er'tion	ex·on'er·ate	ex'pe·dit'ed
ex'ha·la'tion	ex·on'er·at·ed	ex'pe·di'tion
ex·hale'	ex·on'er·a'tion	ex'pe·di'tion·ar'y

ex'pe·di'tious

ex'pe·di'tious·ly

ex·pel'

ex·pelled'

ex·pend'

ex·pend'ed

ex·pend'i·ture

ex·pense'

ex·pen'sive·ly

ex·pe'ri·ence

ex·pe'ri·enced

ex·pe'ri·enc·es

ex·per'i·ment

ex·per'i·men'tal

ex·per'i·men'tal·ly

ex·per'i·men·ta'tion

ex·per'i·ment·er

ex·pert'

ex·pert'ly

ex·pert'ness

ex'per'tise'

ex'pi·ate

ex'pi·a'tion

ex'pi·ra'tion

ex·pire'

ex·pired'

ex·plain'

ex·plained'

ex'pla·na'tion

ex·plan'a·to·ry

ex'ple·tive

ex'pli·ca·ble

ex'pli·cate

ex·plic'it

ex·plic'it·ly

ex·plode'

ex·plod'ed

ex'ploit

ex'ploi·ta'tion

ex·ploit'ed

ex'plo·ra'tion

ex·plor'a·to'ry

ex·plore'

ex·plored'

ex·plor'er

ex·plor'ing·ly

ex·plo'sion

ex·plo'sive

ex·po'nent

ex'po·nen'tial

ex·port'

ex'por·ta'tion

ex·pose'

ex·posed'

ex'po·si'tion

ex·pos'i·to'ry

ex·pos'tu·late

ex·pos'tu·lat'ed

ex·pos'tu·la'tion

ex·po'sure

ex·pound'

ex·press'

ex·pres'sion

ex·pres'sive

ex·pres'sive·ly

ex·press'ly

ex·press'man

ex·pro'pri·ate

ex·pro'pri·a'tion

ex·pul'sion

ex·punge'

ex·punged'

ex'pur·gate

ex'pur·gat'ed

ex'pur·ga'tion

ex'qui·site

ex'tant

ex·tem'po·ra'ne·ous

ex·tem'po·rar'y

ex·tem'po·re

ex·tem'po·ri·za'tion

ex·tem'po·rize

ex·tend'

ex·tend'ed

ex·ten'si·ble

ex·ten'sion

ex·ten'sive

ex·tent'

ex·ten'u·ate

ex·ten'u·at'ed

ex·ten'u·a'tion

ex·te'ri·or

ex·ter'mi·nate

ex·ter'mi·nat'ed

ex·ter'mi·na'tion

ex·ter'mi·na'tor

ex·ter'nal

ex·ter'nal·i·za'tion

ex·ter'nal·ly

ex·tinct'

ex·tinc'tion

ex·tin'guish

ex·tin'guished

ex·tin'guish·er

ex'tir·pate

ex'tir·pat'ed

ex'tir·pa'tion

ex·tol'

ex·tolled'

ex·tort'

ex·tort'ed

ex·tor'tion

ex·tor'tion·ate

ex'tra

ex·tract'

ex·tract'ed

ex·trac'tion

ex·trac'tive

ex'tra·cur-
ric'u·lar

ex'tra·dite

ex'tra·dit'ed

ex'tra·di'tion

ex·tra'ne·ous

ex·traor'di·nar'i·ly

ex·traor'di·nar'y

ex·trap'o·late

ex'tra·ter'ri·to'ri·al'i·ty

ex·trav'a·gance

ex·trav'a·gant

ex·trav'a·gan'za

ex·trav'a·sate

ex·trav'a·sa'tion

ex·treme'

ex·trem'ist

ex·trem'i·ty

ex'tri·cate

ex'tri·cat'ed

ex'tri·ca'tion

ex·trin'sic

ex'tro·ver'sion

ex'tro·vert'

ex·trude'

ex·trud'ed

ex·tru'sion

ex·u'ber·ance

ex·u'ber·ant

ex'u·date

ex'u·da'tion

ex·ude'

ex·ud'ed

ex·ult'

ex·ult'ant

ex·ul·ta'tion

ex·ult'ed

ex·ult'ing·ly

eye

eye'ball'

eye'brow'

eye'cup'

eyed

eye'lash'

eye'let

eye'lid'

eye'piece'

eyes

eye'shot'

eye'sight'

eye'strain'

eye'tooth'

eye'wash'

eye'wit'ness

F

Fa'bi·an

fa'ble

fa'bled

fab'ric

fab'ri·cate

fab'ri·cat'ed

fab'ri·ca'tion

fab'u·lous

fa·çade'

face

faced

fac'et

fa·ce'tious

fa'cial

fac'ile

fa·cil'i·tate

fa·cil'i·tat'ed

fa·cil'i·ty

fac'ings

fac·sim'i·le

fact

fac'tion

fac'tion·al

fac'tious

fac·ti'tious

fac'tor

fac'to·ry

fac·to'tum

fac'tu·al

fac'tu·al·ly

fac'ul·ta'tive

fac'ul·ty

fad'dist

fade

fad'ed

fad'ing·ly

Fahr'en·heit

fail

failed

fail'ing·ly

fail'ings

faille

fail'ure

faint

faint'ed

faint'heart'ed

faint'ly

faint'ness

fair

fair'er

fair'est

fair'ly

fair'ness

fair'way'

fair'y

fair'y·land'

faith

faith'ful

faith'less

faith'less·ly

fake

fak'er

fal'con

fall

fal·la'cious

fal'la·cy

fall'en

fal'li·bil'i·ty

fal'li·ble

fal'low

false

false'hood

false'ly

false'ness

fal·set'to

fal'si·fi·ca'tion

fal'si·fi'er

fal'si·fy

fal'si·ty

fal'ter

fal'tered

fal'ter·ing·ly

fame

famed

fa·mil'ial

fa·mil'iar

fa·mil'i·ar'i·ty

fa·mil'iar·ize

fa·mil'iar·ly

fam'i·lies

fam'i·ly

fam'ine

fam'ish

fa'mous

fa'mous·ly

fan

fa·nat'ic

fa·nat'i·cal

fa·nat'i·cism

fan'cied

fan'ci·er

fan'ci·est

fan'ci·ful

fan'cy

fan'fare

fang

fanged

fan'light'

fanned

fan'tail'

fan·ta'sia

fan·tas'tic

fan'ta·sy

far

far'ad

farce

far'cial

far'ci·cal

far'cy

fare

fared

fare'well'

far'fetched'

fa·ri'na

far'i·na'ceous

farm

farmed

farm'er

farm'house'

farm'yard'

far'o

far'ri·er

far'see'ing

far'sight'ed

far'ther

far'thest

far'thing

fas'ci·nate

fas'ci·nat'ed

fas'ci·na'tion

fas'ci·nat'ing·ly

fas'ci·na'tor

fas'cism

fas'cist

fash'ion

fash'ion·a·ble

fash'ioned

fast

fas'ten

fas'tened

fas'ten·ings

fast'er

fast'est

fas·tid'i·ous

fast'ness

fat

fa'tal

fa'tal·ism

fa'tal·ist

fa'tal·is'tic

fa'tal'i·ty

fa'tal·ly

fate	fa'vored	fed'er·al·ize
fat'ed	fa'vor·ite	fed'er·al·ized
fate'ful	fa'vor·it·ism	fed'er·ate
fa'ther	fawn	fed'er·at'ed
fa'thered	fawned	fed'er·a'tion
fa'ther·hood	fe'al·ty	fed'er·a'tive
fa'ther-in-law'	fear	fe·do'ra
fa'ther·land'	feared	fee
fa'ther·less	fear'ful	fee'ble
fa'ther·li·ness	fear'less	fee'ble·ness
fa'ther·ly	fear'less·ly	fee'blest
fath'om	fear'some	fee'bly
fath'omed	fea'si·bil'i·ty	feed
fath'om·less	fea'si·ble	feed'-back'
fa·tigue'	feast	feed'ings
fat'ness	feat	feel
fat'ten	feath'er	feel'er
fat'tened	feath'ered	feel'ing·ly
fat'ter	feath'er·edge'	feel'ings
fat'test	feath'er·weight'	feer
fat'ty	feath'er·y	feered
fa·tu'i·ty	fea'ture	feet
fat'u·ous	fea'tured	feign
fau'cet	fe'brile	feigned
fault	Feb'ru·ar'y	feint
fault'i·ly	fe'cund	feld'spar'
fault'less	fe'cun·date	fe·lic'i·tate
fault'less·ly	fe·cun'di·ty	fe·lic'i·tat'ed
fault'y	fed'er·al	fe·lic'i·ta'tion
fau'na	fed'er·al·ism	fe·lic'i·tous
fa'vor	fed'er·al·ist	fe·lic'i·tous·ly
fa'vor·a·ble	fed'er·al·i·za'tion	fe·lic'i·ty

fe'line	fe·roc'i·ty	fet'id
fel'low	fer'ret	fe'tish
fel'low·ship	fer'ret·ed	fe'tish·ism
fel'on	fer'ric	fet'lock
fe·lo'ni·ous	fer'ro·chrome	fet'ter
fel'o·ny	fer'ro·type	fet'tered
felt	fer'rous	fet'tle
fe·luc'ca	fer'rule	feud
fe'male	fer'ry	feu'dal
fem'i·nine	fer'ry·boat'	feu'dal·ism
fem'i·nin'i·ty	fer'tile	feu'da·to'ry
fem'i·nism	fer·til'i·ty	fe'ver
fem'i·nist	fer'ti·li·za'tion	fe'ver·ish
fem'o·ral	fer'ti·lize	fe'ver·ish·ly
fe'mur	fer'ti·lized	few
fen	fer'ti·liz'er	few'er
fence	fer'ule	few'est
fenc'er	fer'vent	fez
fend	fer'vent·ly	fi·as'co
fend'ed	fer'vid	fi'at
fend'er	fer'vid·ly	fib
fe·nes'trat·ed	fer'vor	fi'ber
fen'es·tra'tion	fes'cue	fi'broid
Fe'ni·an	fes'tal	fib'u·la
fen'nel	fes'ter	fick'le
fe'ral	fes'tered	fic'tion
fer·ment'	fes'ti·val	fic'tion·al
fer'men·ta'tion	fes'tive	fic·ti'tious
fer·ment'ed	fes·tiv'i·ty	fid'dle
fern	fes·toon'	fid'dled
fe·ro'cious	fes·tooned'	fid'dler
fe·ro'cious·ly	fetch	fi·del'i·ty

fidg'et	filed	find
fi·du'ci·ar'y	fil'i·al	find'er
fief	fil'i·bus'ter	find'ings
field	fil'i·gree	fine
field'ed	fil'ings	fined
field'piece'	fill	fine'ly
fiend	filled	fine'ness
fiend'ish	fill'er	fin'er
fiend'ish·ly	fil'let	fin'er·y
fierce	fill'ings	fine'spun'
fierce'ness	film	fi·nesse'
fierc'er	filmed	fin'est
fierc'est	film'y	fin'ger
fi'er·y	fil'ter	fin'gered
fife	fil'tered	fin'ger·print'
fig	filth	fin'i·al
fight	filth'i·er	fi'nis
fig'ment	filth'i·est	fin'ish
fig'u·ra'tion	filth'i·ness	fin'ished
fig'ur·a·tive	filth'y	fin'ish·er
fig'ur·a·tive·ly	fil'trate	fi'nite
fig'ure	fil·tra'tion	fiord
fig'ured	fin	fir
fig'ure·head'	fi'nal	fire
fig'u·rine'	fi'nal·ist	fire'arm'
fil'a·ment	fi·nal'i·ty	fire'boat'
fil'a·ri'a·sis	fi'nal·ly	fire'box'
fil'a·ture	fi·nance'	fire'brand'
fil'bert	fi·nan'cial	fire'break'
filch	fi·nan'cial·ly	fire'brick'
filched	fin'an·cier'	fired
file	finch	fire'fly'

fire′man

fire′place′

fire′proof′

fire′side′

fire′weed′

fire′wood′

fire′works′

fir′kin

firm

fir′ma·ment

firm′er

firm′est

firm′ly

firm′ness

first

first′ly

firth

fis′cal

fish

fish′er·man

fish′er·y

fish′hook′

fish′wife′

fish′y

fis′sile

fis′sion

fis′sure

fist

fist′ic

fist′i·cuffs

fis′tu·la

fit

fit′ful

fit′ful·ly

fit′ness

fit′ted

fit′ter

fit′ting·ly

fit′tings

fix

fix·a′tion

fix′a·tive

fixed

fix′er

fix′ings

fix′i·ty

fix′ture

fiz′zle

fiz′zled

flab′bi·er

flab′bi·est

flab′bi·ness

flab′by

flac′cid

flag

flag′el·lant

flag′el·late

flag′el·la′tion

flag′eo·let′

flag′eo·lets′

fla·gi′tious

flag′on

flag′pole′

fla′grance

fla′grant

fla′grant·ly

flag′ship′

flag′staff′

flag′stone′

flail

flailed

flair

flake

flak′i·ness

flak′y

flam′beau

flam·boy′ant

flame

flamed

fla·men′co

flame′proof′

flam′ing·ly

fla·min′go

flan

flange

flanged

flank

flanked

flan′nel

flan′nel·ette′

flap

flap′jack′

flare

flare′back′

flared

flash

flash'board'

flash'er

flash'i·ly

flash'i·ness

flash'ing·ly

flash'light'

flash'y

flask

flat

flat'-bed'

flat'boat'

flat'fish'

flat'-foot'ed

flat'head'

flat'i'ron

flat'ly

flat'ness

flat'ten

flat'tened

flat'ter

flat'tered

flat'ter·er

flat'ter·ing·ly

flat'ter·y

flat'test

flat'u·lence

flat'u·lent

flat'ware'

flat'wise'

flat'work'

flat'worm'

flaunt

flaunt'ed

flaunt'ing·ly

flau'tist

fla'vor

fla'vored

fla'vor·ings

fla'vors

flaw

flawed

flax

flax'en

flax'seed'

flay

flea

flea'bite'

fleck

fledge

fledg'ling

flee

fleece

fleeced

fleec'i·ness

fleec'y

fleet

fleet'ing·ly

Flem'ish

flesh

flesh'i·ness

flesh'ings

flesh'pot'

flesh'y

Fletch'er·ism

fleur'-de-lis'

flew

flex

flexed

flex'i·bil'i·ty

flex'i·ble

flex'ure

flick

flicked

flick'er

flick'er·ing·ly

fli'er

flight

flight'i·ness

flight'y

flim'si·er

flim'si·est

flim'si·ly

flim'si·ness

flim'sy

flinch

flinched

flinch'ing·ly

fling

flint

flint'i·ness

flint'lock'

flint'y

flip'pan·cy

flip'pant

flip'pant·ly

flip'per

flirt		flor'id·ly		flue	
flir·ta'tion		flor'in		flu'en·cy	
flir·ta'tious		flo'rist		flu'ent	
flirt'ed		floss		flu'ent·ly	
flit		floss'i·er		fluff	
flitch		floss'i·est		fluff'i·ness	
fliv'ver		floss'y		fluff'y	
float		flo·ta'tion		flu'id	
float'ed		flo·til'la		flu'id·ly	
float'er		flot'sam		flu'id·ex'tract	
floc'cu·lence		flounce		flu·id'i·ty	
floc'cu·lent		floun'der		fluke	
flock		floun'dered		flume	
floe		floun'der·ing·ly		flung	
flog		flour		flunk	
flogged		flour'ish		flunked	
flog'gings		flour'ish·ing·ly		flunk'y	
flood		flour'y		flu'o·res'cence	
flood'ed		flout		flu'o·res'cent	
flood'gate'		flout'ed		flu·or'ic	
flood'light'		flow		flu'o·ri·date	
flood'wa'ter		flowed		flu'o·ri·da'tion	
floor		flow'er		flu'o·ride	
floor'walk'er		flow'ered		flu'o·ri·nate	
flop'pi·ness		flow'er·i·ness		flu'o·rine	
flop'py		flow'er·pot'		flu'o·ro·scope	
flo'ral		flow'er·y		flu'or·os'co·py	
Flor'en·tine		flow'ing·ly		flur'ry	
flo'ret		flown		flush	
flo'ri·cul'ture		fluc'tu·ate		flushed	
flor'id		fluc'tu·at'ed		flus'ter	
flo·rid'i·ty		fluc'tu·a'tion		flus'tered	

flute		foe		fond'er	
flut'ed		foe'man		fond'est	
flut'ings		fog		fon'dle	
flut'ist		fog'gi·er		fon'dled	
flut'ter		fog'gi·est		fond'ly	
flut'tered		fog'gy		fond'ness	
flut'ter·ing·ly		fog'horn'		fon·due'	
flut'ter·y		foi'ble		font	
flux		foil		food	
flux'ion		foiled		fool	
fly		foist		fooled	
fly'er		foist'ed		fool'har'di·ness	
fly'leaf'		fold		fool'har'dy	
fly'trap'		fold'ed		fool'ish	
fly'wheel'		fold'er		fool'ish·ly	
foal		fo'li·age		fool'ish·ness	
foaled		fo'li·ate		fool'proof'	
foam		fo'li·a'tion		fools'cap'	
foamed		fo'li·o		foot	
foam'i·er		folk		foot'age	
foam'i·est		folk'way'		foot'ball'	
foam'i·ness		fol'li·cle		foot'board'	
foam'y		fol·lic'u·lar		foot'bridge'	
fob		fol'low		foot'ed	
fobbed		fol'lowed		foot'fall'	
fo'cal		fol'low·er		foot'gear'	
fo'cal·i·za'tion		fol'ly		foot'hill'	
fo'cal·ize		fo·ment'		foot'hold'	
fo'cal·ized		fo'men·ta'tion		foot'ings	
fo'cus		fo·ment'ed		foot'less	
fo'cused		fond		foot'lights'	
fod'der		fon'dant		foot'-loose'	

foot'man		for'ci·ble		fore'mast'	
foot'mark'		ford		fore'most	
foot'note'		ford'ed		fore'name'	
foot'pace'		fore'arm'		fore'noon'	
foot'pad'		fore·bear		fo·ren'sic	
foot'path'		fore·bode'		fore'or·dain'	
foot'print'		fore·bod'ing·ly		fore'or·dained'	
foot'rest'		fore·bod'ings		fore'quar'ter	
foot'sore'		fore·bore'		fore·run'ner	
foot'step'		fore-cast'		fore·saw'	
foot'stool'		fore'cas·tle		fore·see'	
foot'wear'		fore·close'		fore·see'ing·ly	
foot'work'		fore·closed'		fore·shad'ow	
foot'worn'		fore·clo'sure		fore'shore'	
foo'zle		fore'deck'		fore·short'en	
foo'zled		fore·doom'		fore'sight'	
fop'per·y		fore·doomed'		fore'sight'ed·ness	
fop'pish		fore'fa'ther		for'est	
for		fore'fin'ger		fore·stall'	
for'age		fore'foot'		fore·stalled'	
fo·ra'men		fore'front'		for'est·a'tion	
for'as·much'		fore·gone'		for'est·ed	
for'ay		fore'ground'		for'est·er	
for·bear'		fore'hand'ed		for'est·ry	
for·bear'ance		fore'head		fore·taste'	
for·bid'		for'eign		fore·tell'	
for·bid'den		for'eign·er		fore'thought'	
for·bid'ding·ly		for'eign·ism		fore·told'	
force		fore·knowl'edge		for·ev'er	
force'ful		fore'leg'		fore·warn'	
force'meat'		fore'lock'		fore·warned'	
for'ceps		fore'man		fore'wom'an	

fore'word'	for'mat	for'ti·tude
for'feit	for·ma'tion	fort'night
for'feit·ed	form'a·tive	fort'night·ly
for'fei·ture	formed	for'tress
for·gath'er	form'er	for·tu'i·tous
for·gave'	for'mer·ly	for·tu'i·ty
forge	for'mic	for'tu·nate
forged	for'mi·da·ble	for'tune
for'ger	form'less	for'tune·tell'er
for'ger·y	for'mu·la	fo'rum
for·get'	for'mu·lar'y	for'ward
for·get'ful	for'mu·late	for'ward·ed
for·get'ful·ly	for'mu·lat'ed	for'ward·er
for·get'ful·ness	for'mu·la'tion	for'ward·ness
for·give'	for·sake'	fos'sil
for·giv'en	for·sak'en	fos'sil·if'er·ous
for·give'ness	for·sook'	fos'sil·i·za'tion
for·giv'ing·ly	for·sooth'	fos'sil·ize
for·go'	for·swear'	fos'sil·ized
for·got'	for·syth'i·a	fos'ter
for·got'ten	fort	fos'tered
fork	for'ta·lice	fought
forked	forte	foul
for·lorn'	for'te	fou·lard'
form	forth	foul'er
for'mal	forth'com'ing	foul'est
form·al'de·hyde	forth'right'	foul'ly
for'mal·ism	forth'right'ness	foul'ness
for'mal'i·ty	forth'with'	found
for'mal·i·za'tion	for'ti·fi·ca'tion	foun·da'tion
for'mal·ize	for'ti·fy	found'ed
for'mal·ly	for·tis'si·mo	found'er

found'ling

found'lings

found'ry

fount

foun'tain

foun'tain·head'

four'some

four'square'

fourth

fowl

fox

foxes

fox'glove'

fox'i·er

fox'i·est

fox'y

fra'cas

frac'tion

frac'tion·al

frac'tion·al·ly

frac'tion·ate

frac'tion·a'tion

frac'tious

frac'ture

frac'tured

frag'ile

frag'ile·ly

fra·gil'i·ty

frag'ment

frag'men·tar'i·ly

frag'men·tar'y

frag'men·ta'tion

frag'ment·ed

fra'grance

fra'grant

fra'grant·ly

frail

frail'er

frail'est

frail'ty

frame

framed

frame'work'

franc

fran'chise

Fran·cis'can

frank

frank'er

frank'est

frank'furt·er

frank'ly

frank'ness

fran'tic

frap'pé'

fra·ter'nal

fra·ter'nal·ly

fra·ter'ni·ty

frat'er·ni·za'tion

frat'er·nize

frat'er·nized

frat'ri·cid'al

frat'ri·cide

fraud

fraud'u·lent

fraught

fray

fraz'zle

fraz'zled

freak

freak'ish

freck'le

freck'led

free

free'board'

free'born'

free'dom

free'hand'

free'hold'

free'ly

free'man

free'ma'son

free'ma'son·ry

fre'er

fre'est

free'stone'

free'think'er

free'wheel'ing

freeze

freez'er

freight

freight'er

French

fren'zied

fren'zy

fre'quen·cy

fre'quent

fre'quent·ly	fright'en	frond
fres'co	fright'ened	frond'ed
fresh	fright'en·ing·ly	front
fresh'en	fright'ful	front'age
fresh'en·er	fright'ful·ly	fron'tal
fresh'er	fright'ful·ness	front'ed
fresh'est	frig'id	fron·tier'
fresh'ly	Frig'id·aire'	fron'tis·piece
fresh'man	fri·gid'i·ty	frost
fresh'ness	frig'id·ly	frost'bite'
fret	frill	frost'ed
fret'ful	frilled	frost'fish'
fret'ted	frill'i·ness	frost'i·er
fret'work'	frill'y	frost'i·est
fri'a·bil'i·ty	fringe	frost'i·ly
fri'a·ble	fringed	frost'i·ness
fri'ar	frip'per·y	frost'work'
fric'as·see'	frisk	frost'y
fric'tion	frit'ter	froth
fric'tion·al	frit'tered	frothed
Fri'day	fri·vol'i·ty	froth'y
fried	friv'o·lous	fro'ward
friend	friv'o·lous·ly	frown
friend'less	friz'zi·ness	frowned
friend'li·er	friz'zle	frown'ing·ly
friend'li·est	friz'zled	frowz'i·ly
friend'li·ness	frock	frowz'y
friend'ly	frog	froze
friend'ship	frog'fish'	fro'zen
frieze	frol'ic	fruc·tif'er·ous
frig'ate	frol'icked	fruc'ti·fy
fright	from	fru'gal

fru·gal'i·ty	full'er	fun'gus
fru'gal·ly	full'est	fu·nic'u·lar
fruit	full'ness	fun'nel
fruit'er·er	ful'ly	fun'ni·er
fruit'ful	ful'mi·nate	fun'ni·est
fruit'ful·ly	ful'mi·nat'ed	fun'ny
fruit'i·ness	ful'mi·na'tion	fur
fru·i'tion	ful'some	fur'be·low
fruit'less	fum'ble	fur'bish
fruit'less·ly	fum'bling	fu'ri·ous
fruit'less·ness	fume	fu'ri·ous·ly
fruit'worm'	fumed	furl
fruit'y	fu'mi·gate	furled
frump	fu'mi·gat'ed	fur'long
frus'trate	fu'mi·ga'tion	fur'lough
frus·tra'tion	fu'mi·ga'tor	fur'loughed
fry	fun	fur'nace
fry'er	func'tion	fur'nish
fuch'sia	func'tion·al	fur'nished
fud'dle	func'tion·al·ly	fur'nish·ings
fud'dled	func'tion·ar'y	fur'ni·ture
fudge	fund	fu'ror
fu'el	fun'da·men'tal	fur'ri·er
fu'eled	fun'da·men'tal·ly	fur'ri·est
fu·ga'cious	fund'ed	fur'row
fu'gi·tive	fu'ner·al	fur'rowed
fugue	fu·ne're·al	fur'ry
ful'crum	fu·ne're·al·ly	fur'ther
ful·fill'	fun'gi	fur'ther·ance
ful·filled'	fun'gi·ble	fur'ther·more'
ful·fill'ment	fun'gi·cide	fur'thest
full	fun'goid	fur'tive

fur'tive·ly	fu'si·bil'i·ty	fu'tile
fu'run·cle	fu'si·ble	fu'tile·ly
fu'ry	fu'sil·lade'	fu·til'i·ty
furze	fu'sion	fu'ture
fuse	fuss	fu'tur·is'tic
fused	fussed	fu·tu'ri·ty
fu'sel	fuss'i·er	fuzz
fu'se·lage	fuss'y	fuzz'i·ly
fus'es	fus'tian	fuzz'i·ness

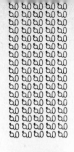

G

gab′ar·dine′	gal′ax·y	gam′bit
ga′ble	gale	gam′ble
gad′fly′	ga·le′na	gam′bled
gad′o·lin′i·um	gall	gam′bler
ga·droon′	gal′lant	gam·boge′
gaff	gal′lant·ry	gam′bol
gag	galled	gam′brel
gage	gal′ler·y	game
gagged	gal′ley	game′ness
gag′gle	Gal′lic	gam′mon
gai′e·ty	gall′ing·ly	gam′ut
gai′ly	gal′li·um	gan′der
gain	gal′lon	gang
gained	gal′lop	ganged
gain′er	gal′lows	gan′gli·a
gain′ful	gall′stone′	gan′gli·on
gain′ful·ly	ga·lore′	gang′plank′
gain′say′	gal′va·nism	gan′grene
gait′ed	gal′va·ni·za′tion	gan′gre·nous
gai′ter	gal′va·nize	gang′ster
ga′la	gal′va·nized	gang′way′
gal′an·tine	gal′va·nom′e·ter	gan′try

gap	gashed	gay'ly
gaped	gas'house'	gay'ness
ga·rage'	gas'ket	gaze
garb	gas'o·line	ga·ze'bo
gar'bage	gasp	ga·zelle'
gar'ble	gas'tight'	ga·zette'
gar'den	gas·tral'gi·a	ga·zet'ted
gar'den·er	gas'tric	gaz'et·teer'
gar·de'ni·a	gas·tri'tis	gear
gar'gle	gas'tro·nom'ic	geared
gar'goyle	gas·tron'o·my	gear'shift'
gar'ish	gate	gei'sha
gar'land	gate'house'	gel'a·tin
gar'lic	gate'post'	ge·lat'i·nize
gar'ment	gate'way'	ge·lat'i·noid
gar'ner	gath'er	ge·lat'i·nous
gar'nered	gath'ered	gem
gar'net	gath'er·er	gen'der
gar'nish	gau'che·rie'	gen'e·a·log'i·cal
gar'nished	gaud'i·er	gen'e·al'o·gist
gar'nish·ee'	gaud'i·est	gen'e·al'o·gy
gar'nish·er	gaud'y	gen'er·al
gar'nish·ment	gauge	gen'er·al·is'si·mo
gar'ni·ture	gauged	gen'er·al·ist
gar'ret	gaunt'let	gen'er·al'i·ty
gar'ri·son	gauze	gen'er·al·i·za'tion
gar'ri·soned	gave	gen'er·al·ize
gar'ru·lous	gav'el	gen'er·al·ized
gar'ter	ga·votte'	gen'er·al·ly
gas	gawk'y	gen'er·al·ship'
gas'e·ous	gay	gen'er·ate
gash	gay'e·ty	gen'er·at'ed

gen′er·a′tion	ge′nus	ges′ture
gen′er·a′tive	ge·od′e·sy	ges′tured
gen′er·a′tor	ge′o·det′ic	get
ge·ner′ic	ge·og′ra·pher	gew′gaw
gen′er·os′i·ty	ge·og′ra·phy	gey′ser
gen′er·ous	ge′o·log′i·cal	ghast′li·ness
gen′er·ous·ly	ge·ol′o·gist	ghast′ly
gen′e·sis	ge·ol′o·gy	gher′kin
ge·net′ics	ge′o·met′ric	ghet′to
ge·ni′al	ge′o·met′ri·cal	ghost
ge′ni·al′i·ty	ge·om′e·try	ghost′li·ness
gen′ial·ly	ge·ra′ni·um	ghost′ly
gen′i·tive	ge′rent	ghoul
gen′ius	ger′i·a·tri′cian	gi′ant
gen·teel′	ger′i·at′rics	gi′ant·ism
gen·teel′ly	germ	gib′ber
gen′tian	Ger′man	gib′ber·ish
gen′tile	ger·mane′	gib′bet
gen·til′i·ty	ger′mi·cide	gib′bon
gen′tle	ger′mi·nal	gibe
gen′tle·man	ger′mi·nant	gib′let
gen′tle·men	ger′mi·nate	gid′di·ly
gen′tle·ness	ger′mi·nat′ed	gid′di·ness
gen′tler	ger′mi·na′tion	gid′dy
gen′tlest	ger′mi·na′tive	gift
gen′tly	ger′und	gift′ed
gen′try	ge·run′di·al	gig
gen′u·flect	ge·run′dive	gi·gan′tic
gen′u·flec′tion	ges′so	gi·gan′ti·cal·ly
gen′u·ine	Ge·stalt′	gi·gan′tism
gen′u·ine·ly	ges·tic′u·late	gig′gle
gen′u·ine·ness	ges·tic′u·la′tion	gig′gled

gild	gla'cier	gleam
gild'ed	glad	gleamed
gild'er	glad'den	glean
gill	glad'dened	glean'er
gill	glade	glean'ings
gilt	glad'i·a'tor	glee'ful
gim'bals	glad'i·a·to'ri·al	glib
gim'crack'	glad'i·o'lus	glib'ly
gim'let	glad'ly	glide
gin	glad'ness	glid'ed
gin'ger	Glad'stone	glid'er
gin'ger·ly	glam'or·ous	glim'mer
ging'ham	glam'our	glim'mered
gin'gi·vi'tis	glance	glim'mer·ings
gi·raffe'	gland	glimpse
gir'an·dole	glan'dered	glimpsed
gird	glan'ders	glint
gird'er	glan'du·lar	glint'ed
gir'dle	glare	gli·o'ma
gir'dled	glared	glis·san'do
gir'dler	glar'ing·ly	glis'ten
girl	glass	glis'tened
girl'hood	glass'ful	glis'ter
girl'ish	glass'house'	glit'ter
girt	glass'i·ly	glit'tered
girth	glass'i·ness	gloat
gist	glass'ware'	gloat'ed
give	glass'y	glob'al
giv'en	glau·co'ma	glob'al·ly
giv'er	glaze	globe
giz'zard	glazed	glob'u·lar
gla'cial	gla'zier	glob'ule

glock'en·spiel'

gloom

gloom'i·ly

gloom'i·ness

glo'ri·fi·ca'tion

glo'ri·fy

glo'ri·ous

glo'ry

gloss

glos'sal

glos'sa·ry

gloss'i·ly

gloss'i·ness

glos·si'tis

gloss'y

glot'tis

glove

glov'er

glow

glowed

glow'er

glow'ered

glow'ing·ly

glow'worm'

glu·ci'num

glu'cose

glue

glued

glue'y

glum

glut

glut'ted

glut'ton

glut'ton·ize

glut'ton·ous

glut'ton·y

glyc'er·in

gnarl

gnarled

gnash

gnashed

gnat

gnath'ic

gnaw

gnawed

gnaw'ings

gneiss

gnome

gno'mic

gno'mon

gnu

go

goad

goal

goat

goat'fish'

goat'herd'

goat'skin'

goat'weed'

gob'ble

gob'bled

gob'let

gob'lin

go'cart'

god

god'child'

god'dess

god'fa'ther

god'head

god'hood

god'less

god'like'

god'li·ness

god'ly

god'moth'er

god'par'ent

god'send'

god'son'

gog'gle

go'ings

goi'ter

gold

gold'en

gold'en·rod'

gold'finch'

gold'smith'

gold'weed'

golf

golf'er

gon'do·la

gon'do·lier'

gone

gong

goo'ber

good

good'-by'

good'ly

good'-na'tured

good'ness

goose

goose'ber'ry

goose'neck'

go'pher

Gor'di·an

gore

gored

gorge

gorged

gor'geous

gor'get

gor'gon

go·ril'la

gos'hawk'

gos'ling

gos'pel

gos'sa·mer

gos'sip

got

Goth'ic

got'ten

gouache

gouge

gouged

gou'lash

gourd

gour'mand

gour'met

gout

gov'ern

gov'ern·ance

gov'erned

gov'ern·ess

gov'ern·ment

gov'ern·men'tal

gov'er·nor

gown

grab

grabbed

grace

grace'ful

grace'less

gra'cious

gra'cious·ly

grack'le

gra·da'tion

grade

grad'ed

gra'di·ent

grad'u·al

grad'u·al·ly

grad'u·ate

grad'u·at'ed

grad'u·a'tion

graft

graft'ed

graft'er

grail

grain

grained

grain'field'

gram'mar

gram·mar'i·an

gram·mat'i·cal

gram·mat'i·cal·ly

gram'pus

gran'a·ry

grand

grand'child'

gran·dee'

gran'deur

grand'fa'ther

gran·dil'o·quence

gran·dil'o·quent

gran'di·ose

grand'ly

grand'moth'er

grand'ness

grand'par'ent

grand'sire'

grand'son'

grand'stand'

grange

gran'ite

gran'it·oid

gra·niv'o·rous

grant

grant'ed

gran'u·lar

gran'u·late

gran'u·lat'ed

gran'u·la'tion

gran'ule

grape

grape'shot'

graph

graph'ic

graph'ics

graph'ite

grap'nel

grap'ple

grap'pled

grasp

grasp'ing·ly

grass

grass'hop'per

grass'plot'

grate

grat'ed

grate'ful

grat'er

grat'i·fi·ca'tion

grat'i·fy

grat'i·fy'ing·ly

grat'i·nate

grat'ings

gra'tis

grat'i·tude

gra·tu'i·tous

gra·tu'i·ty

gra·va'men

grave

grave'dig'ger

grav'el

grav'el·ly

grav'en

grav'er

grav'est

grave'stone'

grave'yard'

grav'i·tate

grav'i·tat'ed

grav'i·ta'tion

grav'i·ta'tion·al

grav'i·ty

gra·vure'

gra'vy

gray

gray'beard'

gray'ish

gray'ness

graze

grazed

gra'zier

grease

greased

grease'wood'

greas'i·er

greas'i·est

greas'i·ly

greas'i·ness

greas'y

great

great'er

great'est

great'ly

great'ness

greed

greed'i·er

greed'i·est

greed'i·ly

greed'i·ness

greed'y

Greek

green

green'back'

green'er

green'er·y

green'est

green'horn'

green'house'

green'ish

green'ness

green'room'

green'stick'

green'sward'

green'wood'

greet

greet'ed

greet'ings

gre·gar'i·ous

Gre·go'ri·an

gre·nade'

gren'a·dier'

gren'a·dine'

grew

grey'hound'

grid

grid'dle

grid'i'ron

grief

griev'ance

grieve

grieved

griev'ous

griev'ous·ly

grif'fin

grill

grilled

grim

gri·mace'

grime

grim'i·er

grim'i·est

grim'i·ly

grim'i·ness

grim'y

grin

grind

grind'er

grind'ing·ly

grind'stone'

grinned

grip

gripe

grip'per

gris'ly

grist

gris'tle

grist'mill'

grit

grit'ti·ness

grit'ty

griz'zle

griz'zled

griz'zly

groan

groaned

groan'ing·ly

gro'cer

gro'cer·y

grog

grog'gy

groin

grom'met

groom

groomed

groove

grooved

grope

grop'ing·ly

gros'beak'

gros'grain'

gross

gross'er

gross'est

gross'ly

gross'ness

gro·tesque'

gro·tesque'ly

grot'to

grouch

grouch'i·ly

grouch'y

ground

ground'ed

ground'less

ground'lings

ground'work'

group

group'ings

grouse

grout

grout'ed

grove

grov'el

grov'eled

grow

grow'er

growl

growled

grown

growth

grub

grubbed

grub'bi·ness

grub'by

grudge

grudg'ing·ly

gru'el

grue'some

gruff

gruff'er

gruff'est

gruff'ly

grum'ble	guile'ful	gun
grum'bled	guile'less	gun'boat'
grump'i·ly	guil'lo·tine	gun'cot'ton
grump'i·ness	guilt	gun'fire'
grump'y	guilt'i·er	gun'lock'
grunt	guilt'i·est	gun'man
grunt'ed	guilt'i·ly	gun'ner
guar'an·tee'	guilt'i·ness	gun'ner·y
guar'an·tor	guilt'y	gun'ny
guar'an·ty	guin'ea	gun'pa'per
guard	guise	gun'pow'der
guard'ed	guis'es	gun'run'ning
guard'i·an	gui·tar'	gun'shot'
guard'i·an·ship'	gulch	gun'smith'
guard'room'	gul'den	gun'stock'
guards'man	gulf	gun'wale
gua'va	gull	gur'gle
gu'ber·na·to'ri·al	gul'let	gu'ru
gudg'eon	gul'li·bil'i·ty	gush
guer'don	gul'li·ble	gush'er
guer·ril'la	gul'ly	gush'y
guess	gulp	gus'set
guess'work'	gum	gust
guest	gum'bo	gus'ta·to'ry
guid'ance	gum'boil'	gust'i·ly
guide	gummed	gus'to
guide'book'	gum·mo'sis	gust'y
guid'ed	gum'my	gut'ter
guide'line'	gump'tion	gut'ter·snipe'
gui'don	gum'shoe'	gut'tur·al
guild	gum'weed'	gut'tur·al·ly
guile	gum'wood'	guy

guz'zle

guz'zled

guz'zler

gym·kha'na

gym·na'si·um

gym'nast

gym·nas'tic

gyn'e·col'o·gist

gyn'e·col'o·gy

gyp'sum

gyp'sy

gy'rate

gy'rat·ed

gy·ra'tion

gy'ra·to'ry

gyr'fal'con

gy'ro

gy'ro·com'pass

gy'ro·scope

gy'ro·stat

gyves

H

hab′er·dash′er	hag′gard	half′heart′ed
hab′er·dash′er·y	hag′gle	half′tone′
ha·bil′i·ment	hag′gled	half′way′
hab′it	hail	half′-wit′ted
hab′it·a·ble	hailed	hal′i·but
hab′i·tat	hail′stone′	hal′ide
hab′i·ta′tion	hail′storm′	hal′ite
hab′it·ed	hair	hal′i·to′sis
ha·bit′u·al	hair′breadth′	hall
ha·bit′u·al·ly	hair′brush′	hall′mark′
ha·bit′u·ate	hair′cut′	hal′low
ha·bit′u·at′ed	hair′line′	hal′lowed
hab′i·tude	hair′pin′	Hal′low·een′
hack′le	hair′split′ter	hal·lu′ci·na′tion
hack′man	hair′spring′	hal·lu′ci·na·to′ry
hack′ney	hair′y	hal·lu′ci·no′sis
hack′neyed	hake	ha′lo
hack saw	ha·la′tion	hal′o·gen
had	hal′berd	halt
had′dock	hal′cy·on	halt′ed
haft	hale	hal′ter
hag	half	halt′ing·ly

halves	hand'some	hard
hal'yard	hand'spring'	hard'en
ham	hand'work'	hard'ened
ham'let	hand'writ'ing	hard'en·er
ham'mer	hand'y	hard'er
ham'mered	hang	hard'est
ham'mer·less	hang'ar	hard'fist'ed
ham'mock	hanged	hard'head'ed
ham'per	hang'er	har'di·hood
ham'pered	hang'ings	har'di·ness
ham'ster	hang'man	hard'ly
ham'string'	han'ker	hard'ness
ham'strung'	han'kered	hard'pan'
hand	han'som	hard'ship
hand'bag'	hap'haz'ard	hard'ware'
hand'ball'	hap'less	har'dy
hand'bill'	hap'loid	hare
hand'book'	hap'pen	hare'brained'
hand'cuff'	hap'pened	hare'lip'
hand'ed	hap'pen·ings	ha'rem
hand'ful	hap'pi·er	hark
hand'i·cap	hap'pi·est	har'le·quin
hand'i·capped	hap'pi·ly	har'le·quin·ade'
hand'i·craft	hap'pi·ness	harm
hand'i·er	hap'py	harmed
hand'i·est	ha·rangue'	harm'ful
hand'i·ly	ha·rangued'	harm'ful·ly
hand'i·ness	har'ass	harm'ful·ness
hand'ker·chief	har'ass·ment	harm'less
han'dle	har'bin·ger	harm'less·ly
han'dled	har'bor	harm'less·ness
hand'rail	har'bored	har·mon'ic

har·mon′i·ca	hasp	hauled
har·mo′ni·ous	has′sock	haunch
har·mo′ni·ous·ly	haste	haunt
har·mo′ni·ous·ness	has′ten	haunt′ed
har·mo′ni·um	has′tened	haunt′ing·ly
har′mo·ni·za′tion	hast′i·er	haut′boy
har′mo·nize	hast′i·est	hau·teur′
har′mo·nized	hast′i·ly	have
har′mo·ny	hast′i·ness	ha′ven
har′ness	hast′y	hav′er·sack
har′nessed	hat	hav′oc
harp	hat′band′	Ha·wai′ian
harp′er	hatch	hawk
harp′ist	hatched	hawk′er
har·poon′	hatch′er·y	hawk′weed′
har·pooned′	hatch′et	hawse
harp′si·chord	hatch′ment	haw′ser
har′ri·er	hatch′way′	haw′thorn
har′row	hate	hay
harsh	hat′ed	hay′cock′
harsh′er	hate′ful	hay′fork′
harsh′est	hate′ful·ly	hay′loft′
harsh′ly	hate′ful·ness	hay′mow′
harsh′ness	hat′pin′	hay′rack′
har′te·beest′	ha′tred	hay′seed′
har′vest	hat′ter	hay′stack′
har′vest·ed	haugh′ti·er	haz′ard
har′vest·er	haugh′ti·est	haz′ard·ed
has	haugh′ti·ly	haz′ard·ous
hash	haugh′ty	haz′ard·ous·ly
hashed	haul	haze
hash′ish	haul′age	ha′zel

ha'zel·nut'

ha'zi·er

ha'zi·est

ha'zi·ly

ha'zi·ness

ha'zy

he

head

head'ache'

head'band'

head'board'

head'cheese'

head'dress'

head'ed

head'er

head'first'

head'fore'most

head'gear'

head'i·ly

head'ings

head'land'

head'less

head'light'

head'line'

head'lock'

head'long

head'mas'ter

head'phone'

head'piece'

head'quar'ters

heads'man

head'spring'

head'stone'

head'strong

head'wa'ter

head'way'

head'work'

head'y

heal

healed

heal'er

health

health'ful

health'ful·ness

health'i·er

health'i·est

health'i·ly

health'y

heap

heaped

hear

heard

hear'er

hear'ings

heark'en

heark'ened

hear'say'

hearse

heart

heart'ache'

heart'beat'

heart'break'

heart'bro'ken

heart'burn'

heart'en

heart'ened

heart'felt'

hearth

hearth'stone'

heart'i·er

heart'i·est

heart'i·ly

heart'less

heart'sick'

heart'sore'

heart'string'

heart'wood'

heart'y

heat

heat'ed

heat'er

heath

hea'then

hea'then·ish

hea'then·ish·ly

heath'er

heat'stroke'

heave

heav'en

heav'en·ly

heav'en·ward

heav'i·er

heav'i·est

heav'i·ly

heav'i·ness

heav'y

He·bra'ic

He'brew

hec'a·tomb

heck'le

heck'led

heck'ler

hec'tic

hec'to·graph

hedge

hedged

hedge'hog'

hedge'row'

he'don·ism

heed

heed'ed

heed'ful·ly

heed'ful·ness

heed'less

heed'less·ness

heel

heft

he·gem'o·ny

he·gi'ra

heif'er

height

height'en

height'ened

hei'nous

heir

heir'ess

heir'loom'

hel'i·cal

hel'i·coid

hel'i·cop'ter

he'li·o·trope

he'li·um

he'lix

helm

hel'met

hel'met·ed

helms'man

help

help'er

help'ful

help'ful·ly

help'ful·ness

help'ing

help'less

help'less·ly

help'less·ness

help'mate'

hem

hem'a·tite

hem'i·cy'cle

hem'i·ple'gi·a

hem'i·sphere

hem'i·spher'i·cal

hem'lock

hemmed

hem'or·rhage

hemp

hemp'en

hem'stitch'

hem'stitched'

hence

hence'forth'

hence'for'ward

hench'man

hen'e·quen

hen'na

he·pat'ic

he·pat'i·ca

hep'a·ti'tis

hep'ta·gon

hep·tam'e·ter

her

her'ald

her'ald·ed

he·ral'dic

her'ald·ry

herb

her·ba'ceous

herb'age

herb'al

her·bar'i·um

her'bi·cide

her·biv'o·rous

Her·cu'le·an

herd

herd'ed

here

here'a·bouts'

here·aft'er

here·by'

he·red'i·ta·bil'i·ty

he·red'i·ta·ble

he·red′i·ta·bly	her′ring	hid
her′e·dit′a·ment	her′ring·bone′	hid′den
he·red′i·tar′y	hers	hide
he·red′i·ty	her·self′	hide′bound′
here′in·aft′er	hes′i·tance	hid′e·ous
here·in′be·fore′	hes′i·tan·cy	hid′e·ous·ly
here·on′	hes′i·tant	hid′e·ous·ness
her′e·sy	hes′i·tate	hi′er·arch′y
her′e·tic	hes′i·tat′ed	hi′er·at′ic
he·ret′i·cal	hes′i·tat′ing·ly	hi′er·o·glyph′ic
here·to′	hes′i·ta′tion	high
here′to·fore′	hes′i·ta′tive·ly	high′born′
here′un·to′	het′er·o·dox	high′boy′
here′up·on′	het′er·o·ge·ne′i·ty	high′er
here·with′	het′er·o·ge′ne·ous	high′est
her′it·a·bil′i·ty	het′er·o·nym′	high′land
her′it·a·ble	heu·ris′tic	high′land·er
her′it·a·bly	hew	high′ly
her′it·age	hewed	high′ness
her·met′ic	hew′er	high′road′
her·met′i·cal·ly	hewn	high′way′
her′mit	hex′a·gon	high′way′man
her′mit·age	hex·ag′o·nal	hike
her′ni·a	hex·am′e·ter	hiked
he′ro	hex·an′gu·lar	hik′er
he·ro′ic	hex′a·pod	hi·lar′i·ous
he·ro′i·cal	hey′day′	hi·lar′i·ty
her′o·ine	hi·a′tus	hill
her′o·ism	hi′ber·nate	hill′i·er
her′on	hi′ber·na′tion	hill′i·est
her′pes	hi·bis′cus	hill′i·ness
her′pe·tol′o·gy	hick′o·ry	hill′ock

hill'side'	hith'er	hoist'way'
hilt	hith'er·to'	ho'kum
him	hive	hold
him·self'	hoar	hold'er
hind	hoard	hold'ings
hin'der	hoard'ed	hole
hin'dered	hoard'er	hol'i·day
hin'drance	hoar'frost'	ho'li·ly
hinge	hoarse	ho'li·ness
hinged	hoars'er	Hol'land
hint	hoars'est	hol'low
hint'ed	hoax	hol'lowed
hin'ter·land'	hob'ble	hol'ly
hip'po·drome	hob'bled	hol'ly·hock
hip'po·pot'a·mus	hob'by	hol'o·caust
hire	hob'gob'lin	hol'o·graph
hired	hob'nail'	hol'o·graph'ic
hire'ling	hob'nailed'	hol'ster
hir'sute	hob'nob'	ho'ly
his	ho'bo	ho'ly·stone'
hiss	hock	hom'age
his·tol'o·gist	hock'ey	home
his·tol'o·gy	hod	home'land'
his·to'ri·an	hoe	home'like'
his·tor'ic	hog	home'li·ness
his·tor'i·cal	hog'back'	home'ly
his'to·ry	hog'fish'	ho'me·o·path'ic
his'tri·on'ic	hog'gish	ho'me·op'a·thy
hit	hogs'head	home'sick'ness
hitch	hog'weed'	home'site'
hitched	hoist	home'spun'
hitch'hike'	hoist'ed	home'stead

home'ward

home'work'

hom'i·cid'al

hom'i·cide

hom'i·let'ics

hom'i·lies

hom'i·ly

hom'i·ny

ho'mo·ge·ne'i·ty

ho'mo·ge'ne·ous

ho'mo·ge'ne·ous·ly

ho·mog'e·nize

ho·mol'o·gous

hom'o·nym

ho·mun'cu·lus

hone

honed

hon'est

hon'est·ly

hon'es·ty

hon'ey

hon'ey·bee'

hon'ey·comb'

hon'ey·dew'

hon'eyed

hon'ey·moon'

hon'ey·suck'le

honk

hon'or

hon'or·a·ble

hon'or·a·bly

hon'o·rar'i·um

hon'or·ar'y

hon'ored

hood

hood'ed

hood'lum

hoo'doo

hood'wink

hoof

hook

hooked

hook'er

hook'worm'

hoop

Hoo'sier

hope

hope'ful

hope'ful·ly

hope'ful·ness

hope'less

hope'less·ly

hope'less·ness

hop'lite

hop'per

hop'scotch'

horde

hore'hound'

ho·ri'zon

hor'i·zon'tal

hor'mone

horn

horn'book'

horned

hor'net

horn'pipe'

ho·rol'o·gy

hor'o·scope

hor·ren'dous

hor'ri·ble

hor'rid

hor'ri·fi·ca'tion

hor'ri·fied

hor'ri·fy

hor'ror

horse

horse'back'

horse chest'nut

horse'hair'

horse'man

horse'man·ship

horse'pow'er

horse'shoe'

horse'weed'

horse'whip'

horse'wom'an

hor'ta·tive

hor'ta·to'ry

hor'ti·cul'ture

hose

ho'sier

ho'sier·y

hos'pice

hos'pi·ta·ble

hos'pi·tal

hos'pi·tal'i·ty

hos'pi·tal·i·za'tion

hos'pi·tal·ize

host

hos'tage

hos'tel

host'ess

hos'tile

hos'tile·ly

hos·til'i·ty

hot

hot'bed'

hot'box'

ho·tel'

hot'head'ed

hot'house'

hot'ly

hot'ness

hot'ter

hot'test

hound

hound'ed

hour

hour'ly

house

housed

house'fly'

house'fur'nish·ings

house'hold

house'hold'er

house'keep'er

house'maid'

house'man

house'moth'er

house'room'

house'wares'

house'warm'ing

house'wife'

house'work'

hov'el

hov'er

hov'ered

hov'er·ing·ly

how

how·ev'er

how'itz·er

howl

how'so·ev'er

hoy'den

hub

hub'bub

huck'le·ber'ry

huck'ster

hud'dle

hud'dled

hue

huff

hug

huge

hug'er

hug'est

Hu'gue·not

hulk

hull

hulled

hum

hu'man

hu·mane'

hu·mane'ly

hu·mane'ness

hu'man·ism

hu'man·ist

hu'man·is'tic

hu·man'i·tar'i·an

hu·man'i·tar'i·an·ism

hu·man'i·ty

hu'man·i·za'tion

hu'man·ize

hu'man·ized

hu'man·kind'

hu'man·ly

hum'ble

hum'bled

hum'ble·ness

hum'bler

hum'blest

hum'bly

hum'bug'

hum'drum'

hu'mer·us

hu'mid

hu·mid'i·fi·ca'tion

hu·mid'i·fied

hu·mid'i·fi'er

hu·mid'i·fy

hu·mid'i·ty

hu'mi·dor

hu·mil′i·ate	hurl	hy′drant
hu·mil′i·at′ed	hurled	hy′drate
hu·mil′i·a′tion	hur′ri·cane	hy·drau′lic
hu·mil′i·ty	hur′ry	hy′dro·car′bon
hummed	hurt	hy′dro·chlo′ric
hum′ming·bird′	hurt′ful	hy′dro·cy·an′ic
hum′mock	hurt′ful·ly	hy′dro·e·lec′tric
hu′mor	hurt′ful·ness	hy′dro·flu·or′ic
hu′mored	hur′tle	hy′dro·foil′
hu′mor·esque′	hur′tled	hy′dro·gen
hu′mor·ist	hus′band	hy·drom′e·ter
hu′mor·ous	hus′band·ry	hy′dro·pho′bi·a
hu′mor·ous·ness	hush	hy′dro·plane
hump	hushed	hy′dro·stat′ics
hu′mus	husk	hy·drox′ide
hunch	husk′i·ly	hy·e′na
hun′dred	husk′i·ness	hy′giene
hun′dred·fold′	hus′ky	hy′gi·en′ic
hun′dredth	hus′sy	hy′gi·en′i·cal·ly
Hun·gar′i·an	hus′tings	hy′gi·en·ist
hun′ger	hus′tle	hy·grom′e·ter
hun′gered	hus′tled	hy′gro·scop′ic
hun′gri·er	hus′tler	hymn
hun′gri·est	hut	hym′nal
hun′gry	hutch	hymn′book′
hunk	hy′a·cinth	hy·per′bo·la
hunt	hy′a·loid	hy·per′bo·le
hunt′ed	hy′brid	hy′per·bol′ic
hunt′er	hy′brid·ism	hy′per·crit′i·cal
hunts′man	hy′brid·i·za′tion	hy′per·e′mi·a
hur′dle	hy′brid·ize	hy′per·o′pi·a
hur′dled	hy·dran′ge·a	hy′per·sen′si·tive

hy′per·thy′roid

hy·per′tro·phy

hy′phen

hy′phen·ate

hy′phen·at′ed

hy′phen·a′tion

hyp·no′sis

hyp·not′ic

hyp′no·tist

hyp′no·tize

hyp′no·tized

hy′po·chon′dri·a

hy′po·chon′dri·ac

hy·poc′ri·sy

hyp′o·crite

hyp′o·crit′i·cal

hy′po·der′mic

hy′po·der′mi·cal·ly

hy·pot′e·nuse

hy·poth′e·cate

hy·poth′e·ca′tion

hy·poth′e·ses

hy·poth′e·sis

hy·poth′e·size

hy′po·thet′i·cal

hy′po·thet′i·cal·ly

hys·te′ri·a

hys·ter′i·cal

hys·ter′ics

hys′ter·oid

I

i·am'bic

I·be'ri·an

i'bex

i'bis

ice

ice'berg'

ice'boat'

ice'box'

ice'break'er

ice'house'

ice'man'

ich·neu'mon

i'chor

ich·thy·ol'o·gy

i'ci·cle

i'ci·er

i'ci·est

i'ci·ly

i'ci·ness

i'con

i'cy

i·de'a

i·de'al

i·de'al·ism

i·de'al·ist

i·de'al·is'tic

i·de'al·i·za'tion

i·de'al·ize

i·de'al·ly

i'de·a'tion

i'de·a'tion·al

i·den'ti·cal

i·den'ti·fi·ca'tion

i·den'ti·fy

i·den'ti·ty

id'e·o·log'i·cal

id'e·ol'o·gy

id'i·o·cy

id'i·om

id'i·o·mat'ic

id'i·o·mat'i·cal·ly

id'i·o·syn'cra·sy

id'i·o·syn·crat'ic

id'i·ot

id'i·ot'ic

id'i·ot'i·cal·ly

i'dle

i'dled

i'dle·ness

i'dler

i'dlest

i'dly

i'dol

i·dol'a·ter

i·dol'a·trize

i·dol'a·trous

i·dol'a·try

i'dol·ize

i'dyl

i·dyl'lic

if

ig'loo

ig'ne·ous

ig·nite'

ig·nit'ed

ig·ni'tion

ig·no′ble	il·lu′mine	im′i·ta′tion
ig′no·min′i·ous	il·lu′mined	im′i·ta′tive
ig′no·min·y	il·lu′sion	im′i·ta′tor
ig′no·ra′mus	il·lu′sive	im·mac′u·late
ig′no·rance	il·lu′so·ry	im·mac′u·late·ly
ig′no·rant	il′lus·trate	im′ma·nent
ig′no·rant·ly	il′lus·trat′ed	im′ma·te′ri·al
ig·nore′	il′lus·tra′tion	im′ma·ture′
ig·nored′	il·lus′tra·tive	im′ma·ture′ly
i·gua′na	il′lus·tra′tor	im′ma·tu′ri·ty
i′lex	il·lus′tri·ous	im·meas′ur·a·ble
Il′i·ad	im′age	im·me′di·a·cy
ilk	im′age·ry	im·me′di·ate
ill	im·ag′i·na·ble	im·me′di·ate·ly
il·le′gal	im·ag′i·nar′y	im·me′di·ate·ness
il·le·gal′i·ty	im·ag′i·na′tion	im′me·mo′ri·al
il·leg′i·ble	im·ag′i·na′tive	im·mense′
il·leg′i·bly	im·ag′ine	im·mense′ly
il′le·git′i·ma·cy	im·ag′ined	im·men′si·ty
il′le·git′i·mate	im·ag′in·ings	im·merse′
il·lib′er·al	i·ma′go	im·mersed′
il·lic′it	i·mam′	im·mer′sion
il·lim′it·a·ble	im′be·cile	im′mi·grant
il·lit′er·a·cy	im′be·cil′i·ty	im′mi·grate
il·lit′er·ate	im·bibe′	im′mi·grat′ed
ill′ness	im·bibed′	im′mi·gra′tion
il·log′i·cal	im·bro′glio	im′mi·nence
il·lu′mi·nant	im·bue′	im′mi·nent
il·lu′mi·nate	im·bued′	im·mo′bile
il·lu′mi·nat′ed	im′i·ta·ble	im′mo·bil′i·ty
il·lu′mi·na′tion	im′i·tate	im·mo′bi·li·za′tion
il·lu′mi·na′tor	im′i·tat′ed	im·mo′bi·lize

im·mod'er·ate

im·mod'est

im'mo·late

im'mo·la'tion

im·mor'al

im'mo·ral'i·ty

im·mor'al·ly

im·mor'tal

im'mor·tal'i·ty

im·mor'tal·ize

im·mor'tal·ly

im'mor·telle'

im·mov'a·bil'i·ty

im·mov'a·ble

im·mov'a·ble·ness

im·mov'a·bly

im·mune'

im·mu'ni·ty

im'mu·ni·za'tion

im'mu·nize

im'mu·nol'o·gy

im·mure'

im'mu·ta·bil'i·ty

im·mu'ta·ble

imp

im'pact

im·pac'tion

im·pair'

im·paired'

im·pair'ment

im·pa'la

im·pale'

im·paled'

im·pale'ment

im·pal'pa·bil'i·ty

im·pal'pa·ble

im·pan'el

im·pan'eled

im·part'

im·part'ed

im·par'tial

im'par·ti·al'i·ty

im·par'tial·ly

im·pass'a·bil'i·ty

im·pass'a·ble

im·passe'

im·pas'sion

im·pas'sioned

im·pas'sive

im·pas'sive·ly

im'pas·siv'i·ty

im·pa'tience

im·pa'tient

im·peach'

im·peach'ment

im·pec'ca·bil'i·ty

im·pec'ca·ble

im'pe·cu'ni·os'i·ty

im'pe·cu'ni·ous

im·ped'ance

im·pede'

im·ped'ed

im·ped'i·ment

im·ped'i·men'ta

im·pel'

im·pelled'

im·pend'

im·pend'ed

im·pen'e·tra·bil'i·ty

im·pen'e·tra·ble

im·pen'i·tent

im·per'a·tive

im'per·cep'ti·ble

im'per·cep'tive

im·per'fect

im'per·fec'tion

im·per'fo·rate

im·pe'ri·al

im·pe'ri·al·ism

im·pe'ri·al·ist

im·pe'ri·al·is'tic

im·pe'ri·ous

im·per'ish·a·ble

im·per'ma·nent

im·per'me·a·ble

im'per·scrip'ti·ble

im·per'son·al

im·per'son·ate

im·per'son·at'ed

im·per'son·a'tion

im·per'ti·nence

im·per'ti·nent

im'per·turb'a·ble

im·per'vi·ous

im'pe·ti'go

im·pet'u·os'i·ty

im·pet′u·ous

im·pet′u·ous·ly

im·pet′u·ous·ness

im′pe·tus

im·pi′e·ty

im·pinge′

im·pinged′

im·pinge′ment

im′pi·ous

im′pi·ous·ly

imp′ish

im·pla′ca·bil′i·ty

im·pla′ca·ble

im·plant′

im·plant′ed

im·plau′si·bil′i·ty

im·plau′si·ble

im′ple·ment

im′ple·ment′ed

im′pli·cate

im′pli·cat′ed

im′pli·ca′tion

im·plic′it

im·plic′it·ly

im·plied′

im′plo·ra′tion

im·plore′

im·plored′

im·plor′ing·ly

im·plo′sion

im·ply′

im′po·lite′

im′po·lite′ly

im′po·lite′ness

im·pol′i·tic

im·pon′der·a·ble

im·port′

im·por′tance

im·por′tant

im′por·ta′tion

im′port′er

im·por′tu·nate

im′por·tune′

im′por·tu′ni·ty

im·pose′

im·posed′

im·pos′ing·ly

im′po·si′tion

im·pos′si·bil′i·ty

im·pos′si·ble

im′post

im·pos′tor

im·pos′ture

im′po·tence

im′po·tent

im·pound′

im·pov′er·ish

im·pov′er·ish·ment

im·pow′er

im·prac′ti·ca·ble

im·prac′ti·cal′i·ty

im′pre·cate

im′pre·ca′tion

im′pre·ca·to′ry

im·preg′na·bil′i·ty

im·preg′na·ble

im·preg′nate

im′preg·na′tion

im′pre·sa′ri·o

im′pre·scrip′ti·ble

im·press′

im·pressed′

im·pres′sion

im·pres′sion·a·ble

im·pres′sion·ism

im·pres′sive

im′pri·ma′tur

im·print′

im·print′ed

im·pris′on

im·pris′oned

im·pris′on·ment

im′prob·a·bil′i·ty

im·prob′a·ble

im·prob′a·bly

im·promp′tu

im·prop′er

im′pro·pri′e·ty

im·prov′a·ble

im·prove′

im·prove′ment

im·prov′i·dence

im·prov′i·dent

im′pro·vi·sa′tion

im′pro·vise

im′pro·vised

im·pru'dence

im·pru'dent

im·pru'dent·ly

im'pu·dence

im'pu·dent

im·pugn'

im·pugn'a·ble

im·pugned'

im·pugn'ment

im'pulse

im·pul'sion

im·pul'sive

im·pu'ni·ty

im·pure'

im·pure'ly

im·pu'ri·ty

im·put'a·ble

im'pu·ta'tion

im·put'a·tive

im·pute'

im·put'ed

in·a·bil'i·ty

in'ac·ces'si·bil'i·ty

in'ac·ces'si·ble

in·ac'cu·ra·cy

in·ac'cu·rate

in·ac'tion

in·ac'ti·vate

in·ac'tive

in·ac·tiv'i·ty

in·ad'e·qua·cy

in·ad'e·quate

in'ad·mis'si·bil'i·ty

in'ad·mis'si·ble

in'ad·vert'ence

in'ad·vert'ent

in'ad·vis'a·bil'i·ty

in'ad·vis'a·ble

in·al'ien·a·ble

in·am'o·ra'ta

in·ane'

in·an'i·mate

in·a·ni'tion

in·an'i·ty

in·ap'pli·ca·ble

in·ap'po·site

in'ap·pro'pri·ate

in·apt'

in·apt'i·tude

in·ar·tic'u·late

in'ar·tis'tic

in'as·much'

in'at·ten'tion

in'at·ten'tive

in'au·di·bil'i·ty

in·au'di·ble

in·au'di·bly

in·au'gu·ral

in·au'gu·rate

in·au'gu·rat'ed

in·au'gu·ra'tion

in'aus·pi'cious

in'board'

in'born'

in'bred'

in·cal'cu·la·ble

in'can·desce'

in'can·des'cence

in'can·des'cent

in'can·ta'tion

in'ca·pa·bil'i·ty

in·ca'pa·ble

in'ca·pac'i·tate

in'ca·pac'i·tat'ed

in'ca·pac'i·ta'tion

in'ca·pac'i·ty

in·car'cer·ate

in·car'cer·at'ed

in·car'cer·a'tion

in·car'nate

in'car·na'tion

in·cen'di·a·rism

in·cen'di·ar'y

in·cense'

in·censed'

in·cen'tive

in·cep'tion

in·cer'ti·tude

in·ces'sant

in·ces'sant·ly

in'cest

in·ces'tu·ous

inch

in·cho'ate

inch'worm'

in'ci·dence

in'ci·dent

in'ci·den'tal

in'ci·den'tal·ly

in·cin'er·ate

in·cin'er·at'ed

in·cin'er·a'tion

in·cin'er·a'tor

in·cip'i·ent

in·cise'

in·cised'

in·ci'sion

in·ci'sive

in·ci'sive·ly

in·ci'sive·ness

in·ci'sor

in'ci·ta'tion

in·cite'

in·cite'ment

in'ci·vil'i·ty

in·clem'en·cy

in·clem'ent

in'cli·na'tion

in·cline'

in·clined'

in·close'

in·closed'

in·clo'sure

in·clude'

in·clud'ed

in·clu'sive

in·clu'sive·ly

in·clu'sive·ness

in·cog'ni·to

in'co·her'ence

in'co·her'ent

in'com·bus'ti·bil'i·ty

in'com·bus'ti·ble

in'come

in'com·men'su·ra·ble

in'com·men'su·rate

in'com·mode'

in'com·mu'ni·ca'do

in·com'pa·ra·ble

in·com'pa·ra·bly

in'com·pat'i·bil'i·ty

in'com·pat'i·ble

in·com'pe·tence

in·com'pe·tent

in·com'pe·tent·ly

in'com·plete'

in'com·pre·hen'si·bil'i·ty

in'com·pre·hen'si·ble

in'com·press'i·bil'i·ty

in'com·press'i·ble

in'con·ceiv'a·bil'i·ty

in'con·ceiv'a·ble

in'con·clu'sive

in'con·clu'sive·ness

in'con·gru'i·ty

in·con'gru·ous

in·con'se·quen'tial

in'con·sid'er·a·ble

in'con·sid'er·ate

in'con·sid'er·ate·ly

in'con·sist'en·cy

in'con·sist'ent

in'con·sol'a·ble

in'con·spic'u·ous

in'con·spic'u·ous·ly

in·con'stan·cy

in·con'stant

in'con·test'a·ble

in·con'ti·nence

in·con'ti·nent

in'con·tro·vert'i·ble

in'con·ven'ience

in'con·ven'ienced

in'con·ven'ient

in'con·ven'ient·ly

in'con·ver'si·bil'i·ty

in'con·vert'i·bil'i·ty

in'con·vert'i·ble

in·cor'po·rate

in·cor'po·rat'ed

in·cor'po·ra'tion

in·cor'po·ra'tor

in·cor·rect'

in·cor'ri·gi·bil'i·ty

in·cor'ri·gi·ble

in'cor·rupt'i·bil'i·ty

in'cor·rupt'i·ble

in·crease'

in·creased'

in·creas'ing·ly

in·cred'i·bil'i·ty

in·cred'i·ble

in·cre·du·li·ty	in·de′cen·cy	in·den′ture
in·cred′u·lous	in·de′cent	in·den′tured
in′cre·ment	in·de′cent·ly	in′de·pend′ence
in′cre·men′tal	in′de·ci′sion	in′de·pend′ent
in·cre′tion	in′de·ci′sive	in′de·scrib′a·ble
in·crim′i·nate	in′de·ci′sive·ly	in′de·struct′i·ble
in·crim′i·nat′ed	in′de·ci′sive·ness	in′de·ter′mi·na·ble
in·crim′i·na′tion	in·dec′o·rous	in′de·ter′mi·nate
in·crim′i·na·to′ry	in′de·co′rum	in′dex
in′crus·ta′tion	in·deed′	in′dexed
in′cu·bate	in′de·fat′i·ga·bil′i·ty	in′dex·er
in′cu·bat′ed	in′de·fat′i·ga·ble	in′dex·es
in′cu·ba′tion	in′de·fea′si·ble	In′di·an
in′cu·ba′tor	in′de·fen′si·ble	in′di·cate
in′cu·bus	in′de·fin′a·ble	in′di·cat′ed
in·cul′cate	in·def′i·nite	in′di·ca′tion
in·cul′cat·ed	in·def′i·nite·ly	in·dic′a·tive
in′cul·ca′tion	in·def′i·nite·ness	in′di·ca′tor
in·cul′pate	in·del′i·bil′i·ty	in′di·ca·to′ry
in·cul′pat·ed	in·del′i·ble	in′di·ces
in′cul·pa′tion	in·del′i·bly	in·di′ci·a
in·cul′pa·to′ry	in·del′i·ca·cy	in·dict′
in·cum′ben·cy	in·del′i·cate	in·dict′a·ble
in·cum′bent	in·del′i·cate·ly	in·dict′ed
in′cu·nab′u·la	in·dem′ni·fi·ca′tion	in·dict′ment
in·cur′	in·dem′ni·fied	in·dif′fer·ence
in·cur′a·ble	in·dem′ni·fy	in·dif′fer·ent
in·cur′a·bly	in·dem′ni·ty	in·dif′fer·ent·ly
in·curred′	in·dent′	in′di·gence
in·cur′sion	in′den·ta′tion	in·dig′e·nous
in·debt′ed	in·dent′ed	in′di·gent
in·debt′ed·ness	in·den′tion	in′di·gest′i·bil′i·ty

in·di·gest'i·ble

in·di·ges'tion

in·dig'nant

in·dig'nant·ly

in·dig·na'tion

in·dig'ni·ty

in'di·go

in·di·rect'

in·di·rec'tion

in·di·rect'ly

in·di·rect'ness

in·dis·creet'

in·dis·creet'ly

in·dis·cre'tion

in·dis·crim'i·nate

in·dis·crim'i·nate·ly

in·dis·pen'sa·bil'i·ty

in·dis·pen'sa·ble

in·dis·pose'

in·dis·posed'

in·dis·po·si'tion

in·dis'pu·ta·ble

in·dis'so·lu·ble

in·dis'so·lu·bly

in·dis·tinct'

in·dis·tinct'ly

in·dis·tin'guish·a·ble

in·dite'

in·dit'ed

in'di·um

in·di·vid'u·al

in·di·vid'u·al·ism

in·di·vid'u·al·ist

in·di·vid'u·al'i·ty

in·di·vid'u·al·ize

in·di·vid'u·al·ly

in·di·vis'i·bil'i·ty

in·di·vis'i·ble

in·doc'tri·nate

in·doc'tri·nat'ed

in·doc'tri·na'tion

in'do·lence

in'do·lent

in'do·lent·ly

in·dom'i·ta·ble

in'doors'

in·dorse'

in·dorsed'

in·dorse'ment

in·dors'er

in·du'bi·ta·ble

in·duce'

in·duced'

in·duce'ment

in·duct'

in·duct'ance

in·duct'ed

in·duc'tion

in·duc'tive

in·duc'tor

in·due'

in·dued'

in·dulge'

in·dul'gence

in·dul'gent

in·dul'gent·ly

in'du·rate

in'du·rat'ed

in·dus'tri·al

in·dus'tri·al·ly

in·dus'tri·al·ism

in·dus'tri·al·ist

in·dus'tri·al·i·za'tion

in·dus'tri·al·ize

in·dus'tri·al·ized

in·dus'tri·ous

in·dus'tri·ous·ly

in·dus'tri·ous·ness

in'dus·try

in·e'bri·ate

in·e'bri·at'ed

in·e'bri·a'tion

in·e'bri·e·ty

in·ed'i·ble

in·ef'fa·ble

in·ef'fa·bly

in·ef·fec'tive

in·ef·fec'tu·al

in·ef·fec'tu·al·ly

in·ef·fi·ca'cious

in·ef·fi'cien·cy

in·ef·fi'cient

in·ef·fi'cient·ly

in·e·las'tic

in·e·las·tic'i·ty

in·el'e·gance

in·el′e·gant

in·el′e·gant·ly

in·el′i·gi·bil′i·ty

in·el′i·gi·ble

in′e·luc′ta·ble

in·ept′

in·ept′i·tude

in′e·qual′i·ty

in·eq′ui·ta·ble

in·eq′ui·ty

in′e·rad′i·ca·ble

in′e·rad′i·ca·bly

in·er′ran·cy

in·er′rant

in·ert′

in·er′tia

in·ert′ly

in·ert′ness

in′es·sen′tial

in·es′ti·ma·ble

in·es′ti·ma·bly

in·ev′i·ta·bil′i·ty

in·ev′i·ta·ble

in·ev′i·ta·bly

in′ex·act′

in′ex·act′i·tude

in′ex·cus′a·ble

in′ex·cus′a·bly

in′ex·haust′i·ble

in′ex·haust′i·bly

in·ex′o·ra·ble

in′ex·pe′di·ence

in′ex·pe′di·en·cy

in′ex·pe′di·ent

in′ex·pen′sive

in′ex·pe′ri·ence

in′ex·pert′

in′ex·pli·ca·ble

in′ex·pli·ca·bly

in′ex·tri·ca·ble

in·fal′li·bil′i·ty

in·fal′li·ble

in′fa·mous

in′fa·my

in′fan·cy

in′fant

in·fan′ti·cide

in′fan·tile

in·fan′ti·lism

in′fan·try

in′fan·try·man

in·farct′

in·farc′tion

in·fat′u·ate

in·fat′u·at′ed

in·fat′u·a′tion

in·fea′si·ble

in·fect′

in·fect′ed

in·fec′tion

in·fec′tious

in·fec′tious·ly

in·fec′tious·ness

in′fe·lic′i·tous

in′fe·lic′i·ty

in·fer′

in′fer·ence

in′fer·en′tial

in·fe′ri·or

in·fe′ri·or′i·ty

in·fer′nal

in·fer′nal·ly

in·fer′no

in·ferred′

in·fer′tile

in′fer·til′i·ty

in·fest′

in′fes·ta′tion

in′fi·del

in′fi·del′i·ty

in′field′

in′field′er

in·fil′trate

in·fil′trat·ed

in′fil·tra′tion

in′fi·nite

in′fin·i·tes′i·mal

in′fin·i·tes′i·mal·ly

in·fin′i·tive

in·fin′i·tude

in·fin′i·ty

in·firm′

in·fir′ma·ry

in·fir′mi·ty

in·flame′

in·flamed′

in·flam′ma·bil′i·ty	in·form′er	in·grat′i·tude
in·flam′ma·ble	in·form′ing·ly	in·gre′di·ent
in·flam′ma·bly	in·frac′tion	in′gress
in′flam·ma′tion	in·fran′gi·ble	in′grown′
in·flam′ma·to′ry	in′fra·red′	in·hab′it
in·flate′	in·fre′quent	in·hab′it·a·ble
in·flat′ed	in·fre′quent·ly	in·hab′it·ance
in·fla′tion	in·fringe′	in·hab′it·ant
in·fla′tion·ar′y	in·fringed′	in·hab′i·ta′tion
in·fla′tion·ist	in·fringe′ment	in·hab′it·ed
in·flect′	in·fu′ri·ate	in′ha·la′tion
in·flect′ed	in·fu′ri·at′ed	in·hale′
in·flec′tion	in·fuse′	in·haled′
in·flex′i·bil′i·ty	in·fused′	in·hal′er
in·flex′i·ble	in·fus′es	in′har·mo′ni·ous
in·flict′	in·fu′sion	in·here′
in·flict′ed	in·gen′ious	in·hered′
in·flic′tion	in·gen′ious·ly	in·her′ence
in′flu·ence	in′ge·nu′i·ty	in·her′ent
in′flu·enced	in·gen′u·ous	in·her′ent·ly
in′flu·en′tial	in·gest′	in·her′it
in′flu·en′tial·ly	in·gest′ed	in·her′it·a·ble
in′flu·en′za	in·ges′tion	in·her′it·ance
in′flux	in·ges′tive	in·her′it·ed
in·form′	in·glo′ri·ous	in·her′i·tor
in·for′mal	in′got	in·hib′it
in′for·mal′i·ty	in·grain′	in·hib′it·ed
in·for′mal·ly	in·grained′	in′hi·bi′tion
in·form′ant	in′grate	in·hib′i·to′ry
in′for·ma′tion	in·gra′ti·ate	in·hos′pi·ta·ble
in·form′a·tive	in·gra′ti·a′tion	in·hos′pi·ta·bly
in·formed′	in·gra′ti·a·to′ry	in·hos′pi·tal′i·ty

in·hu′man

in′hu·mane′

in′hu·man′i·ty

in′hu·ma·tion

in·hume′

in·humed′

in·im′i·cal

in·im′i·ta·ble

in·im′i·ta·bly

in·iq′ui·tous

in·iq′ui·tous·ly

in·iq′ui·ty

in·i′tial

in·i′tialed

in·i′tial·ly

in·i′ti·ate

in·i′ti·at′ed

in·i′ti·a′tion

in·i′ti·a′tive

in·i′ti·a′tor

in·i′ti·a·to′ry

in·ject′

in·ject′ed

in·jec′tion

in·jec′tor

in′ju·di′cious

in′ju·di′cious·ly

in·junc′tion

in·junc′tive

in′jure

in′jured

in·ju′ri·ous

in′ju·ry

in·jus′tice

in·jus′tic·es

ink

inked

ink′horn′

ink′ling

ink′lings

ink′stand′

ink′well′

ink′y

in·laid′

in′land

in·lay′

in·let′

in′mate

in′most

inn

in′nate

in′nate·ly

in′ner

in′ner·most

in′ning

in′nings

inn′keep′er

in′no·cence

in′no·cent

in′no·cent·ly

in·noc′u·ous

in·noc′u·ous·ly

in′no·vate

in′no·va′tion

in′no·va′tive

in′no·va′tor

in′nu·en′do

in·nu′mer·a·ble

in′ob·serv′ant

in·oc′u·late

in·oc′u·lat′ed

in·oc′u·la′tion

in′of·fen′sive

in·op′er·a·ble

in·op′er·a′tive

in·op′por·tune′

in·or′di·nate

in′or·gan′ic

in′pa′tient

in′put′

in′quest

in·qui′e·tude

in·quire′

in·quired′

in·quir′er

in·quires′

in·quir′ies

in·quir′ing·ly

in·quir′y

in′qui·si′tion

in·quis′i·tive

in·quis′i·tor

in·quis′i·to′ri·al

in·road′

in·rush′

in·sane′

in·sane'ly

in·san'i·tar'y

in·san'i·ta'tion

in·san'i·ty

in·sa'ti·a·bil'i·ty

in·sa'ti·a·ble

in·scribe'

in·scribed'

in·scrib'er

in·scrip'tion

in·scru'ta·bil'i·ty

in·scru'ta·ble

in'sect

in·sec'ti·cide

in'sec·tiv'o·rous

in'se·cure'

in'se·cu'ri·ty

in·sen'sate

in·sen'si·bil'i·ty

in·sen'si·ble

in·sen'si·tive

in·sen'si·tive·ness

in·sen'ti·ence

in·sen'ti·ent

in·sep'a·ra·ble

in·sep'a·ra·bly

in·sert'

in·sert'ed

in·ser'tion

in'set'

in'shore'

in'side'

in'sid'er

in·sides'

in·sid'i·ous

in·sid'i·ous·ly

in'sight'

in·sig'ne

in·sig'ni·a

in'sig·nif'i·cance

in'sig·nif'i·cant

in'sig·nif'i·cant·ly

in'sin·cere'

in'sin·cere'ly

in'sin·cer'i·ty

in·sin'u·ate

in·sin'u·at'ed

in·sin'u·at'ing·ly

in·sin'u·a'tion

in·sin'u·a'tive

in·sip'id

in'si·pid'i·ty

in·sip'id·ly

in·sist'

in·sist'ed

in·sist'ence

in·sist'ent

in·sist'ent·ly

in'so·bri'e·ty

in'sole'

in'so·lence

in'so·lent

in'so·lent·ly

in·sol'u·bil'i·ty

in·sol'u·ble

in·solv'a·ble

in·sol'ven·cy

in·sol'vent

in·som'ni·a

in·som'ni·ac

in'so·much'

in·sou'ci·ance

in·sou'ci·ant

in·spect'

in·spect'ed

in·spec'tion

in·spec'tor

in·spec'tor·ate

in'spi·ra'tion

in'spi·ra'tion·al

in'spi·ra'tion·al·ly

in·spir'a·to'ry

in·spire'

in·spired'

in·spir'er

in·spir'ing·ly

in·spir'it·ing·ly

in'sta·bil'i·ty

in·stall'

in'stal·la'tion

in·stalled'

in·stall'ment

in'stance

in'stant

in'stan·ta'ne·ous

in·stan'ter

in′stant·ly	in′stru·men·ta′tion	in·tagl′io
in·state′	in′sub·or′di·nate	in′take′
in·stat′ed	in′sub·or′di·na′tion	in·tan′gi·bil′i·ty
in·stead′	in·suf′fer·a·ble	in·tan′gi·ble
in′step	in′suf·fi′cien·cy	in·tar′si·a
in′sti·gate	in′suf·fi′cient	in′te·ger
in′sti·gat′ed	in′su·lar	in′te·gral
in′sti·ga′tion	in′su·lar′i·ty	in′te·gral·ly
in′sti·ga′tor	in′su·late	in′te·grate
in·still′	in′su·lat′ed	in′te·grat′ed
in·stilled′	in′su·la′tion	in′te·gra′tion
in·stinct′	in′su·la′tor	in·teg′ri·ty
in·stinc′tive	in′su·lin	in·teg′u·ment
in·stinc′tive·ly	in·sult′	in′tel·lect
in·stinc′tu·al	in·sult′ed	in′tel·lec′tu·al
in′sti·tute	in·sult′ing·ly	in′tel·lec′tu·al·ism
in′sti·tut′ed	in·su′per·a·ble	in′tel·lec′tu·al·ize
in′sti·tu′tion	in′sup·port′a·ble	in′tel·lec′tu·al·ly
in′sti·tu′tion·al	in′sup·press′i·ble	in·tel′li·gence
in′sti·tu′tion·al·ize	in·sur′a·bil′i·ty	in·tel′li·gent
in′sti·tu′tion·al·ly	in·sur′a·ble	in·tel′li·gent′si·a
in·struct′	in·sur′ance	in·tel′li·gi·bil′i·ty
in·struct′ed	in·sure′	in·tel′li·gi·ble
in·struc′tion	in·sured′	in·tem′per·ance
in·struc′tion·al	in·sur′er	in·tem′per·ate
in·struc′tive	in·sur′gen·cy	in·tem′per·ate·ly
in·struc′tor	in·sur′gent	in·tend′
in′stru·ment	in′sur·mount′a·ble	in·tend′ant
in′stru·men′tal	in′sur·rec′tion	in·tend′ed
in′stru·men′tal·ist	in′sur·rec′tion·ar′y	in·tense′
in′stru·men′tal′i·ty	in′sur·rec′tion·ist	in·ten′si·fi·ca′tion
in′stru·men′tal·ly	in·tact′	in·ten′si·fi′er

in·ten'si·fy

in·ten'si·ty

in·ten'sive

in·tent'

in·ten'tion

in·ten'tion·al

in·ten'tion·al·ly

in·tent'ly

in·tent'ness

in'ter·act'

in'ter·ac'tion

in'ter·bor'ough

in'ter·breed'

in'ter·cede'

in'ter·ced'ed

in'ter·cept'

in'ter·cept'ed

in'ter·cep'tion

in'ter·cep'tor

in'ter·ces'sion

in'ter·ces'so·ry

in'ter·change'

in'ter·change'a·bil'i·ty

in'ter·change'a·ble

in'ter·col·le'gi·ate

in'ter·com·mu'ni·cate

in'ter·con·nect'

in'ter·cos'tal

in'ter·course

in'ter·de·nom'i·na'tion·al

in'ter·de'part·men'tal

in'ter·de·pend'ence

in'ter·de·pend'ent

in'ter·dict

in'ter·dic'tion

in'ter·est

in'ter·est·ed

in'ter·est·ed·ly

in'ter·est·ing·ly

in'ter·fere'

in'ter·fered'

in'ter·fer'ence

in'ter·fer'ing·ly

in'ter·im

in·te'ri·or

in'ter·ject'

in'ter·ject'ed

in'ter·jec'tion

in'ter·lace'

in'ter·laced'

in'ter·lard'

in'ter·leaf'

in'ter·leave'

in'ter·line'

in'ter·lin'e·al

in'ter·lin'e·ar

in'ter·lin'e·a'tion

in'ter·lined'

in'ter·lock'

in'ter·locked'

in'ter·loc'u·tor

in'ter·loc'u·to'ry

in'ter·lop'er

in'ter·lude

in'ter·mar'riage

in'ter·mar'ry

in'ter·me'di·ar'y

in'ter·me'di·ate

in·ter'ment

in'ter·mez'zo

in·ter'mi·na·ble

in·ter'mi·na·bly

in'ter·min'gle

in'ter·min'gled

in'ter·mis'sion

in'ter·mit'

in'ter·mit'tence

in'ter·mit'tent

in'ter·mit'tent·ly

in'ter·mix'ture

in·tern'

in·ter'nal

in·ter'nal·ly

in'ter·na'tion·al

in'ter·na'tion·al·ize

in'ter·na'tion·al·ly

in'terne

in'ter·ne'cine

in·terned'

in·tern'ment

in'ter·pel'late

in'ter·pel·la'tion

in'ter·plan'e·tar'y

in·ter'po·late

in·ter'po·lat'ed

in·ter'po·la'tion

in·ter·pose'

in·ter·posed'

in·ter·po·si'tion

in·ter·pret

in·ter'pre·ta'tion

in·ter'pre·ta'tive

in·ter'pret·ed

in·ter'pret·er

in'ter·reg'num

in'ter·re·la'tion

in·ter'ro·gate

in·ter'ro·ga'tion

in·ter'rog'a·tive

in·ter'rog'a·to'ry

in'ter·rupt'

in'ter·rupt'ed·ly

in'ter·rup'tion

in'ter·scap'u·lar

in'ter·scho·las'tic

in'ter·sect'

in'ter·sect'ed

in'ter·sperse'

in'ter·spersed'

in'ter·state'

in'ter·stel'lar

in·ter'stice

in·ter'stic·es

in'ter·sti'tial

in'ter·sti'tial·ly

in'ter·twine'

in'ter·twined'

In'ter·type

in'ter·ur'ban

in'ter·val

in'ter·vene'

in'ter·vened'

in'ter·ven'tion

in'ter·ven'tion·ist

in'ter·ver'te·bral

in'ter·view

in'ter·viewed

in'ter·view'er

in'ter·weave'

in'ter·wo'ven

in·tes'ta·cy

in·tes'tate

in·tes'ti·nal

in·tes'tine

in'ti·ma·cy

in'ti·mate

in'ti·mat'ed

in'ti·mate·ly

in'ti·ma'tion

in·tim'i·date

in·tim'i·dat'ed

in·tim'i·da'tion

in'to

in·tol'er·a·ble

in·tol'er·ance

in·tol'er·ant

in'to·na'tion

in·tone'

in·toned'

in·tox'i·cate

in·tox'i·cat'ed

in·tox'i·cat'ing·ly

in·tox'i·ca'tion

in·trac'ta·bil'i·ty

in·trac'ta·ble

in'tra·mu'ral

in·tran'si·gence

in·tran'si·gent

in·tran'si·tive

in'tra·state'

in·trench'ment

in·trep'id

in'tre·pid'i·ty

in·trep'id·ly

in'tri·ca·cies

in'tri·ca·cy

in'tri·cate

in'tri·cate·ly

in·trigue'

in·trigued'

in·trin'sic

in·trin'si·cal

in·trin'si·cal·ly

in'tro·duce'

in'tro·duced'

in'tro·duc'tion

in'tro·duc'to·ry

in·tro'it

in'tro·jec'tion

in'tro·spect'

in'tro·spec'tion

in'tro·spec'tive

in'tro·ver'sion	In·var'	in·ves'tor
in'tro·vert'	in·var'i·a·bil'i·ty	in·vet'er·ate
in'tro·vert'ed	in·var'i·a·ble	in·vid'i·ous
in·trude'	in·var'i·a·ble·ness	in·vid'i·ous·ly
in·trud'ed	in·va'sion	in·vig'i·late
in·trud'er	in·va'sive	in·vig'or·ate
in·tru'sion	in·vec'tive	in·vig'or·at'ed
in·tru'sive	in·veigh'	in·vig'or·at'ing·ly
in·tru'sive·ly	in·vei'gle	in·vig'or·a'tion
in·tu·i'tion	in·vei'gled	in·vig'or·a'tive
in·tu·i'tion·al	in·vent'	in·vin'ci·bil'i·ty
in·tu'i·tive	in·vent'ed	in·vin'ci·ble
in·tu'i·tive·ly	in·ven'tion	in·vi'o·la·bil'i·ty
in·tu·mesce'	in·ven'tive	in·vi'o·la·ble
in·tu·mes'cence	in·ven'tive·ly	in·vi'o·late
in·tu·mes'cent	in·ven'tive·ness	in·vis'i·bil'i·ty
in·unc'tion	in·ven'tor	in·vis'i·ble
in'un·date	in'ven·to'ry	in·vis'i·bly
in'un·dat'ed	in·verse'	in'vi·ta'tion
in'un·da'tion	in·ver'sion	in'vi·ta'tion·al
in·ure'	in·vert'	in·vite'
in·ured'	in·vert'ed	in·vit'ed
in·ur'ed·ness	in·vert'i·ble	in·vit'ing·ly
in·urn'	in·vest'	in'vo·ca'tion
in·vade'	in·vest'ed	in'voice
in·vad'ed	in·ves'ti·gate	in'voiced
in'va·lid	in·ves'ti·gat'ed	in'voic·es
in·val'i·date	in·ves'ti·ga'tion	in·voke'
in·val'i·dat'ed	in·ves'ti·ga'tive	in·voked'
in·val'i·da'tion	in·ves'ti·ga'tor	in·vol'un·tar'i·ly
in'va·lid'i·ty	in·ves'ti·ture	in·vol'un·tar'y
in·val'u·a·ble	in·vest'ment	in'vo·lute

in'vo·lu'tion

in·volve'

in·volved'

in·vul'ner·a·bil'i·ty

in·vul'ner·a·ble

in'ward

in'ward·ly

in'ward·ness

i'o·date

i·od'ic

i'o·dide

i'o·dine

i'o·dize

i·o'do·form

i'on

I·on'ic

i'on·i·za'tion

i'on·ize

i·o'ta

ip'e·cac

I·ra'ni·an

i·ras'ci·bil'i·ty

i·ras'ci·ble

i'rate

i'rate·ly

ire

ir'i·des'cence

ir'i·des'cent

i·rid'i·um

i'ris

I'rish

I'rish·man

i·ri'tis

irk

irked

irk'some

i'ron

i'ron·bound'

i'ron·clad'

i'roned

i·ron'ic

i·ron'i·cal

i·ron'i·cal·ly

i'ron·ings

i'ron·side'

i'ron·ware'

i'ron·weed'

i'ron·wood'

i'ron·work'

i'ron·work'er

i'ro·ny

Ir'o·quois

ir·ra'di·ate

ir·ra'di·at'ed

ir·ra'di·a'tion

ir·ra'tion·al

ir·ra'tion·al'i·ty

ir·ra'tion·al·ly

ir're·claim'a·ble

ir·rec'on·cil'a·ble

ir·rec'on·cil'i·a·bil'i·ty

ir·rec'on·cil'i·a·ble

ir're·cov'er·a·ble

ir're·deem'a·ble

ir're·den'ta

ir're·duc'i·ble

ir·ref'ra·ga·ble

ir're·fran'gi·ble

ir·ref'u·ta·ble

ir·reg'u·lar

ir·reg'u·lar'i·ty

ir·reg'u·lar·ly

ir·rel'e·vance

ir·rel'e·vant

ir're·li'gious

ir're·me'di·a·ble

ir're·mis'si·ble

ir're·mov'a·ble

ir·rep'a·ra·ble

ir're·place'a·ble

ir're·press'i·ble

ir're·proach'a·ble

ir're·sist'i·ble

ir·res'o·lute

ir·res'o·lu'tion

ir're·solv'a·ble

ir're·spec'tive

ir're·spon'si·bil'i·ty

ir're·spon'si·ble

ir're·spon'si·bly

ir're·trace'a·ble

ir're·triev'a·ble

ir·rev'er·ence

ir·rev'er·ent

ir're·vers'i·ble

ir·rev'o·ca·ble

ir'ri·ga·ble	i'so·late	i·tal'i·cize
ir'ri·gate	i'so·lat'ed	itch
ir'ri·gat'ed	i·so·la'tion	itched
ir'ri·ga'tion	i'so·la'tion·ism	itch'i·er
ir'ri·ta·bil'i·ty	i'so·la'tion·ist	itch'i·est
ir'ri·ta·ble	i'so·mer	itch'y
ir'ri·tant	i'so·mer'ic	i'tem
ir'ri·tate	i'so·mor'phic	i'tem·ize
ir'ri·tat'ed	i·sos'ce·les	i'tem·ized
ir'ri·ta'tion	i'so·therm	it'er·ate
ir'ri·ta'tive	i'so·tope	it'er·a'tion
ir·rup'tion	is'su·ance	it'er·a'tive
ir·rup'tive	is'sue	i·tin'er·a·cy
is'chi·um	is'sued	i·tin'er·an·cy
i'sin·glass'	is'sues	i·tin'er·ant
Is'lam	isth'mi·an	i·tin'er·ar'y
is'land	isth'mus	i·tin'er·ate
is'land·er	it	its
isle	I·tal'ian	it·self'
is'let	I·tal'ian·ate	i'vo·ry
i'so·bar	i·tal'ic	i'vy

J

jab′ber	jal′ou·sie	jaun′ty
jab′ber·ing·ly	jam	jave′lin
ja′bot′	jam′bo·ree′	jaw
jack	jammed	jaw′bone′
jack′al	jan′gle	jazz
jack′a·napes′	jan′i·tor	jazz′y
jack′daw′	jan′i·tress	jeal′ous
jack′et	Jan′u·ar′y	jeal′ous·y
jack′et·ed	Ja·pan′	jeer
jack′knife′	Jap′a·nese′	jeered
jack′stone′	ja·panned′	jeer′ing·ly
jack′straw′	jar	Je·ho′vah
jack′weed′	jar′gon	je·june′
Jac·o·be′an	jarred	je·ju′num
jade	jas′mine	jel′lied
jad′ed	jas′per	jel′ly
jade′ite	jaun′dice	jel′ly·fish′
jagged	jaunt	jen′net
jag′uar	jaun′ti·er	jeop′ard·ize
jail	jaun′ti·est	jeop′ard·y
jailed	jaun′ti·ly	jer′e·mi·ad
jail′er	jaun′ti·ness	jerk

157

jerked	jit'ney	jol'li·er
jerk'i·ly	jit'ters	jol'li·est
jer'kin	jit'ter·y	jol'li·fi·ca'tion
jerk'y	job	jol'li·ty
jer'sey	job'ber	jol'ly
jest	jock'ey	jolt
jest'er	jo·cose'	jolt'ed
jest'ing·ly	jo·cose'ly	jon'quil
Jes'u·it	jo·cos'i·ty	jos'tle
Je'sus	joc'u·lar	jos'tled
jet	joc'u·lar'i·ty	jot
jet'sam	joc'u·lar·ly	jot'ted
jet'ti·son	joc'und	jounce
jet'ty	jo·cun'di·ty	jour'nal
jew'el	jodh'purs	jour'nal·ism
jew'eled	jog	jour'nal·ist
jew'el·er	jogged	jour'nal·is'tic
jew'el·ry	jog'gle	jour'nal·ize
Jew'ish	jog'gled	jour'nal·ized
Jew'ry	join	jour'ney
jibe	join'der	jour'neyed
jig	joined	jour'ney·man
jig'ger	join'er	jo'vi·al
jig'gle	join'ings	jo'vi·al'i·ty
jig'gled	joint	jo'vi·al·ly
jig'saw'	joint'ed	jowl
jin'gle	joint'ly	joy
jin'gled	join'ture	joy'ful
jin'go	joist	joy'ful·ly
jin'go·ism	joke	joy'ful·ness
jin·rik'i·sha	jok'er	joy'less
jinx	jok'ing·ly	joy'ous

ju'bi·lance

ju'bi·lant

ju'bi·late

ju'bi·la'tion

ju'bi·lee

Ju'da·ism

judge

judged

judge'ship

judg'ment

ju'di·ca'tive

ju'di·ca·to'ry

ju'di·ca·ture

ju·di'cial

ju·di'cial·ly

ju·di'ci·ar'y

ju·di'cious

jug'gle

jug'gled

jug'gler

jug'u·lar

juice

juic'y

ju'lep

ju'li·enne'

Ju·ly'

jum'ble

jum'bled

jum'bo

jump

jumped

jump'er

junc'tion

junc'ture

June

jun'gle

jun'ior

ju'ni·per

junk

jun'ket

jun'ta

ju'rat

ju·rid'i·cal

ju'ris·con·sult'

ju'ris·dic'tion

ju'ris·pru'dence

ju'rist

ju'ror

ju'ry

ju'ry·man

just

jus'tice

jus·ti'ci·a·ble

jus'ti·fi'a·ble

jus'ti·fi·ca'tion

jus'ti·fi·ca'to·ry

jus'ti·fied

jus'ti·fy

just'ly

just'ness

jut

jute

jut'ted

ju've·nile

ju've·nil'i·ty

jux'ta·po·si'tion

kai′ser	kept	kick′off′
kale	ker′a·tin	kick′shaw′
ka·lei′do·scope	ker′chief	kid
ka·lei′do·scop′ic	ker′nel	kid′nap
kal′so·mine	ker′o·sene′	kid′naped
kan′ga·roo′	ker′sey	kid′ney
ka′o·lin	ketch	kid′skin′
ka′pok	ke·to′sis	kill
kar′ma	ket′tle	killed
kay′ak	key	kill′er
keel	key′board′	kill′ings
keen	keyed	kiln
keen′er	key′hole′	kil′o·cy′cle
keen′est	key′note′	kil′o·gram
keen′ly	key′stone′	kil′o·me′ter
keen′ness	khak′i	kilt
keep	khe·dive′	kilt′ed
keep′er	kib′itz·er	kin
keep′sake′	ki′bosh	kind
keg	kick	kind′er
kelp	kick′back′	kind′est
ken′nel	kick′er	kin′der·gar′ten

160

kin'dle	kite	knock'out'
kin'dled	kith	knoll
kind'li·ness	kit'ten	knot
kind'ly	klep'to·ma'ni·a	knot'hole'
kind'ness	klep'to·ma'ni·ac	knot'ted
kin'dred	knap'sack'	knot'ty
kine	knave	knot'work'
kin'es·thet'ic	knav'er·y	knout
ki·net'ic	knav'ish	know
king	knead	know'a·ble
king'bird'	knead'ed	know'ing·ly
king'bolt'	knee'cap'	know'ing·ness
king'craft	kneel	knowl'edge
king'dom	kneeled	known
king'fish'	knelt	knuck'le
king'fish'er	knew	knuck'led
king'let	knick'ers	knurl
king'li·ness	knick'knack'	knurled
king'ly	knife	knurl'y
king'pin'	knifed	ko'bold
king'ship	knight	ko'dak
kink	knight'ed	kohl'ra'bi
kinked	knight'hood	ko'peck
kink'y	knight'li·ness	Ko·ran'
kin'ship	knight'ly	Ko·re'an
kins'man	knit	ko'sher
ki·osk'	knit'ter	kraft
kip'per	knives	krem'lin
kiss	knob	kryp'ton
kissed	knock	ku·lak'
kitch'en	knock'down'	ky'mo·graph
kitch'en·ette'	knock'er	ky·pho'sis

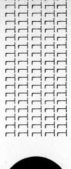

L

la'bel

la'beled

la'bi·al

la'bor

lab'o·ra·to'ry

la'bored

la'bor·er

la·bo'ri·ous

la·bur'num

lab'y·rinth

lab'y·rin'thine

lace

laced

lac'er·ate

lac'er·at'ed

lac'er·a'tion

lac'er·a'tive

lace'wing'

lace'wood'

lace'work'

lach'es

lach'ry·mal

lach'ry·mose

lac'ings

lack

lack'a·dai'si·cal

lack'ey

lack'lus'ter

la·con'ic

lac'quer

lac'quered

la·crosse'

lac'tase

lac'tate

lac·ta'tion

lac'te·al

lac'tic

lac'tose

la·cu'na

la·cu'nae

lad'der

lad'en

la'dle

la'dled

la'dy

la'dy·like'

la'dy·ship

lag

la'ger

lag'gard

lagged

la·goon'

lair

laird

la'i·ty

lake

lamb'doid

lam'bent

lamb'kin

lamb'like'

lam'bre·quin

la'mé'

lame

lamed

lame'ly

lame'ness

la·ment'	land'slip'	large
lam'en·ta·ble	lands'man	large'ly
lam'en·ta'tion	land'ward	large'ness
la·ment'ed	lan'guage	larg'er
lam'i·na	lan'guid	lar'gess
lam'i·nae	lan'guish	larg'est
lam'i·nate	lan'guor	lar'i·at
lam'i·nat'ed	lan'guor·ous	lark
lam'i·na'tion	lank	lark'spur
lamp	lank'er	lar'va
lamp'black'	lank'est	lar'vae
lam·poon'	lank'y	lar'val
lam·pooned'	lan'o·lin	la·ryn'ge·al
lam'prey	lans'downe	lar'yn·gi'tis
lance	lan'tern	lar'ynx
lanc'er	lan'tha·num	las'car
lan'cet	lan'yard	las·civ'i·ous
lan'ci·nate	lap	lash
lan'ci·nat'ed	la·pel'	lashed
lan'ci·na'tion	lap'ful	lash'ings
land	lap'i·dar'y	lass
lan'dau	lap'i·da'tion	las'si·tude
land'ed	lapse	las'so
land'fall'	lapsed	last
land'hold'er	lap'wing'	last'ed
land'la'dy	lar'board	last'ing·ly
land'locked'	lar'ce·nous	last'ly
land'lord'	lar'ce·ny	lasts
land'mark'	larch	Lat'a·ki'a
land'own'er	lard	latch
land'scape	lard'ed	latched
land'slide'	lard'er	latch'key'

latch'string'

late

la·teen'

late'ly

la'ten·cy

late'ness

la'tent

lat'er

lat'er·al

lat'er·al·ly

lat'est

la'tex

lath

lath'er

laths

Lat'in

Lat'in·ism

La·tin'i·ty

Lat'in·i·za'tion

Lat'in·ize

lat'i·tude

lat'i·tu'di·nal

lat'i·tu'di·nar'i·an

lat'ter

lat'ter·most

lat'tice

lat'tice·work'

laud

laud'a·bil'i·ty

laud'a·ble

lau'da·num

lau·da'tion

laud'a·to'ry

laud'ed

laugh

laugh'a·ble

laugh'ing·ly

laugh'ing·stock'

laugh'ter

launch

launch'ings

laun'der

laun'dered

laun'der·ings

laun'dress

laun'dry

laun'dry·man

lau're·ate

lau'rel

la'va

lav'a·liere'

lav'a·to'ry

lav'en·der

lav'ish

lav'ished

lav'ish·ness

law

law'break'er

law'ful

law'ful·ly

law'giv'er

law'less

law'less·ness

law'mak'er

lawn

law'suit'

law'yer

lax

lax'a·tive

lax'i·ty

lax'ly

lax'ness

lay'er

lay'man

laz'a·ret'to

la'zi·er

la'zi·est

la'zi·ly

la'zi·ness

la'zy

leach

leached

lead

lead'en

lead'er

lead'er·ship

leads'man

leaf

leaf'let

league

leagued

leak

leak'age

leak'i·ness

leak'y

lean

leaned	leered	le·git'i·ma·cy
lean'ings	leer'ing·ly	le·git'i·mate
leap	lee'ward	le·git'i·mate·ly
leaped	lee'way'	le·git'i·mate·ness
learn	left	le·git'i·ma'tion
learned	left'-hand'ed	le·git'i·mist
learnt	leg	le·git'i·mize
lease	leg'a·cy	leg'ume
leased	le'gal	le·gu'mi·nous
lease'hold'	le'gal·ism	lei'sure
lease'hold'er	le'gal·is'tic	lei'sure·li·ness
leash	le·gal'i·ty	lei'sure·ly
leashed	le'gal·i·za'tion	lem'mings
least	le'gal·ize	lem'on
leath'er	le'gal·ly	lem'on·ade'
leath'ern	leg'ate	lem'on·weed'
leath'er·oid	leg'a·tee'	le'mur
leath'er·y	le·ga'tion	lend
leave	le·ga'to	length
leav'en	leg'end	length'en
leav'ened	leg'end·ar'y	length'ened
leav'ing	leg'er·de·main'	length'i·er
lec'i·thin	leg'gings	length'i·est
lec'tern	leg'i·bil'i·ty	length'i·ly
lec'ture	leg'i·ble	length'i·ness
lec'tured	le'gion	length'ways
lec'tur·er	le'gion·ar'y	length'wise
ledge	leg'is·late	length'y
ledg'er	leg'is·la'tion	le'ni·ence
leech	leg'is·la'tive	le'ni·en·cy
leek	leg'is·la'tor	le'ni·ent
leer	leg'is·la'ture	le'ni·ent·ly

Len'in·ism	let'tered	li'beled
len'i·tive	let'ter·head'	li'bel·ous
len'i·ty	let'ter·press'	lib'er·al
lens	let'ter·space'	lib'er·al·ism
lent	let'tuce	lib'er·al'i·ty
Lent'en	leu'co·cyte	lib'er·al·i·za'tion
len·tic'u·lar	leu'co·cy·to'sis	lib'er·al·ize
len'til	leu'co·der'ma	lib'er·al·ized
len'toid	leu·ke'mi·a	lib'er·al·ly
le'o·nine	lev'ant	lib'er·ate
leop'ard	lev'ee	lib'er·at'ed
le'o·tard	lev'el	lib'er·a'tion
lep'er	lev'eled	lib'er·a'tor
lep're·chaun'	lev'el·head'ed	lib'er·tar'i·an
lep'ro·sy	le'ver	lib'er·tine
lep'rous	le'ver·age	lib'er·ty
le'sion	lev'i·tate	li·bi'do
less	lev'i·tat'ed	li·brar'i·an
les·see'	lev'i·ta'tion	li'brar'y
less'en	lev'i·ty	li·bret'to
less'ened	lev'u·lose	lice
less'er	lev'y	li'cense
les'son	lex'i·cog'ra·pher	li'cen·see'
les'sor	lex'i·cog'ra·phy	li·cen'ti·ate
lest	lex'i·con	li·cen'tious
let	li'a·bil'i·ty	li·cen'tious·ness
le'thal	li'a·ble	li'chen
le·thar'gic	li·a'na	li'chen·oid
le·thar'gi·cal	li'ar	lic'it
leth'ar·gy	li·ba'tion	lick
let's	li'bel	lic'o·rice
let'ter	li'bel·ant	lic'tor

lie	light'ness	lime'wa·ter
liege	light'ning	lim'i·nal
li'en	light'ship'	lim'it
lieu	light'weight'	lim'it·a·ble
lieu·ten'an·cy	lig'ne·ous	lim'i·ta'tion
lieu·ten'ant	lig'ni·fy	lim'it·ed
life	lig'nite	lim'it·less
life'guard'	lik'a·ble	limn
life'less	like	limned
life'like'	liked	lim·nol'o·gy
life'long'	like'li·er	lim'ou·sine'
life'time'	like'li·est	limp
life'work'	like'li·hood	limped
lift	like'ly	limp'er
lift'ed	lik'en	limp'est
lig'a·ment	like'ness	lim'pet
li'gate	like'wise'	lim'pid
li·ga'tion	lik'ings	lim·pid'i·ty
lig'a·ture	li'lac	lim'pid·ly
lig'a·tured	lil'i·a'ceous	limp'ly
light	lilt	limp'ness
light'ed	lilt'ing·ly	lin'age
light'en	lil'y	lin'den
light'ened	limb	line
light'er	lim'ber	lin'e·age
light'er·age	lim'bo	lin'e·al
light'est	lime	lin'e·al'i·ty
light'face'	lime'kiln'	lin'e·a·ment
light'head'ed	lime'light'	lin'e·ar
light'heart'ed	li'men	lined
light'house'	Lim'er·ick	line'man
light'ly	lime'stone'	lin'en

lin'er	liq'ue·fi'a·ble	lit'er·ate
lines'man	liq'ue·fied	lit'er·a·ture
lin'ger	liq'ue·fy	lith'arge
lin'gered	li'ques'cence	lithe
lin'ge·rie'	li·queur'	lithe'some
lin'ger·ing·ly	liq'uid	lith'i·a
lin'go	liq'ui·date	lith'i·um
lin'gual	liq'ui·dat'ed	lith'o·graph
lin'guist	liq'ui·da'tion	li·thog'ra·pher
lin·guis'tic	liq'ui·da'tor	lith'o·graph'ic
lin·guis'ti·cal·ly	liq'uor	li·thog'ra·phy
lin·guis'tics	li'ra	li·tho'sis
lin'i·ment	lisp	li·thot'o·my
lin'ings	lisped	lit'i·ga·ble
link	lisp'ing·ly	lit'i·gant
link'age	lis'some	lit'i·gate
linked	list	lit'i·gat'ed
Lin·nae'an	list'ed	lit'i·ga'tion
lin'net	lis'ten	li·ti'gious
li·no'le·um	lis'tened	lit'mus
Lin'o·type	lis'ten·er	lit'ter
lin'seed'	list'ings	lit'tered
lint	list'less	lit'tle
lin'tel	lit'a·ny	lit'tlest
li'on	li'ter	lit'to·ral
li'on·ess	lit'er·a·cy	li·tur'gi·cal
li'on·ize	lit'er·al	lit'ur·gist
lip'oid	lit'er·al·ism	lit'ur·gy
li·po'ma	lit'er·al'i·ty	liv'a·ble
liq'ue·fa'cient	lit'er·al·ize	live
liq'ue·fac'tion	lit'er·al·ly	live
liq'ue·fac'tive	lit'er·ar'y	lived

live'li·er	lob'by·ist	lodg'ment
live'li·est	lob'ster	loft
live'li·hood	lo'cal	loft'i·ly
live'li·ness	lo'cal·ism	loft'i·ness
live'long'	lo·cal'i·ty	loft'y
live'ly	lo'cal·i·za'tion	log
liv'er	lo'cal·ize	lo'gan·ber'ry
liv'er·y	lo'cal·ized	log'a·rithm
liv'er·y·man	lo'cal·ly	log'book'
liv'id	lo'cate	loge
li·vid'i·ty	lo'cat·ed	log'ger·heads'
liv'ings	lo·ca'tion	log'gia
liz'ard	lo'ci	log'ic
lla'ma	lock	log'i·cal
lla'no	lock'age	log'i·cal·ly
load	lock'er	lo·gi'cian
load'ed	lock'et	lo·gis'tics
load'ings	lock'jaw'	log'or·rhe'a
loaf	lock'out'	log'o·type
loaf'er	lock'smith'	log'wood'
loam	lock'up'	loin
loan	lo'co·mo'tion	loi'ter
loaned	lo'co·mo'tive	loi'tered
loathe	lo'cus	loi'ter·er
loathed	lo'cust	loll
loath'er	lo·cu'tion	lolled
loath'ful	lode	lol'li·pop
loath'ly	lode'star'	lone
loath'some	lodge	lone'li·ness
lo'bar	lodged	lone'ly
lob'bied	lodg'er	lone'some
lob'by	lodg'ings	lone'some·ly

lone'some·ness	lop'sid'ed	lov'a·ble
long	lo·qua'cious	love
long'boat'	lo·qua'cious·ly	love'less
longed	lo·quac'i·ty	love'li·ness
lon'ger	lord	love'lorn'
long'est	lord'li·ness	love'ly
lon·gev'i·ty	lord'ly	lov'er
long'hand'	lor·do'sis	love'sick'
long'horn'	lord'ship	lov'ing·ly
long'ing·ly	lore	low
long'ings	lor'gnette'	low'born'
lon'gi·tude	lor'ry	low'boy'
lon'gi·tu'di·nal	los'a·ble	low'bred'
long'shore'man	lose	low'er
look	los'er	low'est
look'out'	los'es	low'land
loom	los'ings	low'li·er
loomed	loss	low'li·est
loon	lost	low'li·ness
loon'y	lo'tion	low'ly
loop	lot'ter·y	low'most
loop'hole'	lo'tus	loy'al
loose	loud	loy'al·ism
loose'ly	loud'er	loy'al·ist
loos'en	loud'est	loy'al·ly
loos'ened	loud'ly	loy'al·ty
loose'ness	loud'ness	loz'enge
loos'er	lounge	lu'bri·cant
loos'est	louse	lu'bri·cate
loot	lout	lu'bri·ca'tion
loot'ed	lout'ish	lu'bri·ca'tor
lop	lou'ver	lu·bric'i·ty

lu'cent

lu'cid

lu·cid'i·ty

lu'cid·ly

lu'cid·ness

luck

luck'i·ly

luck'i·ness

luck'less

luck'y

lu'cra·tive

lu'cre

lu'cu·bra'tion

lu'di·crous

lug

lug'gage

lugged

lug'ger

lu·gu'bri·ous

luke'warm'

lull

lull'a·by'

lulled

lum·ba'go

lum'ber

lum'ber·yard'

lu'mi·nar'y

lu'mi·nes'cence

lu'mi·nes'cent

lu'mi·nif'er·ous

lu'mi·nos'i·ty

lu'mi·nous

lump

lump'i·er

lump'i·est

lump'y

lu'na·cy

lu'nar

lu'na·tic

lunch

lunch'eon

lunch'eon·ette'

lunch'room'

lu·nette'

lung

lunge

lunged

lurch

lurched

lurch'ing

lure

lured

lu'rid

lurk

lurked

lus'cious

lush

lust

lus'ter

lust'ful

lust'i·ly

lust'i·ness

lus'trous

lus'trous·ly

lus'trum

lust'y

lute

Lu'ther·an

lux·u'ri·ance

lux·u'ri·ant

lux·u'ri·ate

lux·u'ri·at'ed

lux·u'ri·ous

lux'u·ry

ly·ce'um

lydd'ite

lymph

lym·phat'ic

lymph'oid

lynx

ly'on·naise'

lyre

lyre'bird'

lyr'ic

lyr'i·cal

lyr'i·cism

M

ma·ca′bre	mac′u·late	mag′is·te′ri·al
mac·ad′am	mad	mag′is·tra·cy
mac·ad′am·ize	mad′am	mag′is·tral
mac′a·ro′ni	mad′den·ing·ly	mag′is·trate
mac′a·roon′	mad′der	mag′is·tra·ture
ma·caw′	mad′dest	mag′na·nim′i·ty
mac′er·ate	mad′house′	mag·nan′i·mous
mac′er·at′ed	mad′ly	mag′nate
mac′er·a′tion	mad′man	mag·ne′sia
Mach	mad′ness	mag·ne′si·um
ma·che′te	ma·don′na	mag′net
ma·chic′o·la′tion	mad′ri·gal	mag·net′ic
mach′i·nate	mael′strom	mag·net′i·cal·ly
mach′i·na′tion	maf′fi·a	mag′net·ism
ma·chine′	mag′a·zine′	mag′net·i·za′tion
ma·chined′	ma·gen′ta	mag′net·ize
ma·chin′er·y	mag′got	mag′net·ized
ma·chin′ist	Ma′gi	mag·ne′to
mack′er·el	mag′ic	mag′ni·fi·ca′tion
mac′ro·cosm	mag′i·cal	mag·nif′i·cence
mac′ro·cyte	mag′i·cal·ly	mag·nif′i·cent
ma′cron	ma·gi′cian	mag·nif′i·co

mag'ni·fi'er

mag'ni·fy

mag·nil'o·quent

mag'ni·tude

mag·no'li·a

mag'num

mag'pie

mag'uey

ma·ha·ra'ja

ma·ha·ra'ni

ma·hat'ma

ma·hog'a·ny

maid

maid'en

maid'en·hair'

maid'en·hood

maid'en·ly

maid'serv'ant

mail

mail'a·ble

mail'bag'

mail'box'

mailed

mail'er

mail'ings

maim

maimed

main

main'land'

main'ly

main'mast'

main'sail'

main'sheet'

main'spring'

main'stay'

main·tain'

main·tain'a·ble

main'te·nance

ma·jes'tic

maj'es·ty

ma·jol'i·ca

ma'jor

ma·jor'i·ty

ma·jus'cule

make

make'-be·lieve'

mak'er

make'shift'

mak'ings

mal'a·chite

mal'ad·just'ed

mal'ad·just'ment

mal'a·droit'

mal'a·dy

mal'a·pert

mal'a·prop·ism

mal'ap·ro·pos'

ma·lar'i·a

ma·lar'i·al

mal'as·sim'i·la'tion

Ma·lay'

mal'con·tent'

male

mal'e·dic'tion

mal'e·dic'to·ry

mal'e·fac'tor

ma·lef'i·cence

ma·lef'i·cent

ma·lev'o·lence

ma·lev'o·lent

mal·fea'sance

mal·fea'sor

mal'for·ma'tion

mal·formed'

mal'ice

ma·li'cious

ma·li'cious·ly

ma·li'cious·ness

ma·lign'

ma·lig'nan·cy

ma·lig'nant

ma·lig'nant·ly

ma·ligned'

ma·lig'ni·ty

ma·lign'ly

ma·lin'ger

ma·lin'ger·er

mall

mal'lard

mal'le·a·bil'i·ty

mal'le·a·ble

mal'le·o·lar

mal'le·o·lus

mal'let

mal'low

malm'sey

mal'nu·tri'tion

mal·o'dor·ous

mal'po·si'tion

mal'prac'tice

malt

malt'ase

Mal'tese'

malt'ose

mal·treat'

mal·ver·sa'tion

mam'ba

mam'mal

mam·ma'li·an

mam'ma·ry

mam'mon

mam'moth

man

man'a·cle

man'a·cled

man'age

man'age·a·ble

man'aged

man'age·ment

man'ag·er

man'a·ge'ri·al

man'a·ge'ri·al·ly

man'ag·er·ship'

man'a·tee'

man·da'mus

man'da·rin

man'date

man'dat·ed

man'da·to'ry

man'di·ble

man·dib'u·lar

man'do·lin

man'drake

man'drel

ma·neu'ver

ma·neu'vered

man'ga·nate

man'ga·nese

mange

man'ger

man'gi·ly

man'gi·ness

man'gle

man'gled

man'go

man'grove

man'gy

man'hole'

man'hood

ma'ni·a

ma'ni·ac

ma·ni'a·cal

man'i·cure

man'i·cur'ist

man'i·fest

man'i·fes·ta'tion

man'i·fest·ed

man'i·fes'to

man'i·fold

man'i·fold'ed

man'i·fold'er

man'i·kin

ma·nip'u·late

ma·nip'u·lat'ed

ma·nip'u·lates

ma·nip'u·la'tion

ma·nip'u·la'tive

ma·nip'u·la'tor

ma·nip'u·la·to'ry

man'kind'

man'like'

man'li·ness

man'ly

man'na

man'ner

man'nered

man'ner·ism

man'ner·ly

man'nish

ma·nom'e·ter

man'o·met'ric

man'or

ma·no'ri·al

man'sard

man'serv'ant

man'sion

man'slaugh'ter

man'teau

man'tel

man·til'la

man'tis

man·tis'sa

man'tle	mar'gi·na'li·a	mar'mo·set
man'u·al	mar'gin·al·ly	mar'mot
man'u·al·ly	mar'grave	ma·roon'
man'u·fac'to·ry	mar'i·gold	ma·rooned'
man'u·fac'ture	mar'i·jua'na	mar'plot'
man'u·fac'tured	ma·rim'ba	mar·quee'
man'u·fac'tur·er	ma·ri'na	mar'qui·sette'
man'u·mis'sion	mar'i·nade'	marred
ma·nure'	mar'i·nate	mar'riage
man'u·script	mar'i·nat'ed	mar'riage·a·ble
Manx	ma·rine'	mar'ried
man'y	mar'i·ner	mar'row
Ma'o·ri	mar'i·o·nette'	mar'row·bone'
map	Mar'ist	mar'row·fat'
ma'ple	mar'i·tal	mar'row·y
mapped	mar'i·tal·ly	mar'ry
mar	mar'i·time	Mars
mar'a·bou	mar'jo·ram	mar'shal
mar'a·schi'no	mark	mar'shaled
ma·raud'	marked	marsh'i·ness
ma·raud'er	mark'ed·ly	marsh'mal'low
mar'ble	mark'er	marsh'y
mar'bled	mar'ket	mar·su'pi·al
mar'ca·site	mar'ket·a·bil'i·ty	mart
march	mar'ket·a·ble	mar'ten
march'er	mark'ings	mar'tial
mar'chion·ess	marks'man	mar'tial·ly
mar·co'ni·gram	marks'man·ship	Mar'ti·an
mare	mark'weed'	mar'ti·net'
mar'ga·rine	marl	mar'tin·gale
mar'gin	mar'lin	mar'tyr
mar'gin·al	mar'ma·lade	mar'tyr·dom

mar′tyred	mas′ter·ly	ma·te′ri·al·ized
mar′vel	mas′ter·piece′	ma·te′ri·al·ly
mar′veled	mas′ter·ship	ma·ter′nal
mar′vel·ous	mas′ter·work′	ma·ter′nal·ly
mar′zi·pan	mas′ter·y	ma·ter′ni·ty
mas·car′a	mast′head′	math′e·mat′i·cal
mas′cot	mas′tic	math′e·ma·ti′cian
mas′cu·line	mas′ti·cate	math′e·mat′ics
mas′cu·lin′i·ty	mas′ti·cat′ed	mat′in
mash	mas′ti·ca′tion	mat′i·nee′
mashed	mas′ti·ca′tor	ma′tri·arch
mash′er	mas′ti·ca·to′ry	ma′tri·arch′y
mash′ie	mas′tiff	ma′tri·ces
mask	mas′to·don	ma′tri·cide
masked	mas′toid	ma·tric′u·lant
mask′er	mas′toid·i′tis	ma·tric′u·late
ma′son	mat	ma·tric′u·lat′ed
ma·son′ic	mat′a·dor	ma·tric′u·lates
ma′son·ry	match	ma·tric′u·la′tion
mas′quer·ade′	matched	mat′ri·mo′ni·al
mas′quer·ad′ed	match′less	mat′ri·mo′ni·al·ly
mass	match′less·ly̆	mat′ri·mo′ny
mas′sa·cre	match′mak′er	ma′trix
mas·sage′	match′wood′	ma′tron
mas·seur′	ma·té	ma′tron·li·ness
mas′sive	ma·te′ri·al	ma′tron·ly
mast	ma·te′ri·al·ism	matte
mas′ter	ma·te′ri·al·ist	mat′ted
mas′tered	ma·te′ri·al·is′tic	mat′ter
mas′ter·ful	ma·te′ri·al′i·ty	mat′tered
mas′ter·ful·ly	ma·te′ri·al·i·za′tion	mat′tings
mas′ter·ful·ness	ma·te′ri·al·ize	mat′tock

mat'tress	maze	me·a'tus
mat'u·rate	ma·zur'ka	me·chan'ic
mat'u·rat'ed	me	me·chan'i·cal
mat'u·ra'tion	mead'ow	me·chan'i·cal·ly
ma·tur'a·tive	mead'ow·land'	mech'a·ni'cian
ma·ture'	mea'ger	me·chan'ics
ma·tured'	meal	mech'a·nism
ma·ture'ly	meal'i·er	mech'a·ni·za'tion
ma·ture'ness	meal'i·est	mech'a·nize
ma·tu'ri·ty	meal'time'	med'al
ma·tu'ti·nal	meal'y	med'al·ist
maud'lin	meal'y·mouthed'	me·dal'lion
maul	mean	med'dle
mauled	me·an'der	med'dled
maun'der	mean'ing·ful	med'dle·some
mau'so·le'um	mean'ing·less	me'di·a
mauve	mean'ing·ly	me'di·al
mav'er·ick	mean'ings	me'di·an
ma'vis	mean'ly	me'di·ate
maw	mean'ness	me'di·at'ed
mawk'ish	mean'time'	me'di·a'tion
max'il·lar'y	mean'while'	me'di·a'tive
max'im	mea'sles	me'di·a'tor
max'i·mal	meas'ur·a·ble	med'i·cal
max'i·mize	meas'ur·a·bly	med'i·cal·ly
max'i·mum	meas'ure	me·dic'a·ment
may	meas'ured	med'i·cate
may'be	meas'ure·less	med'i·cat'ed
may'hem	meas'ure·ment	med'i·ca'tion
may'on·naise'	meas'ur·er	med'i·ca'tive
may'or	meat	me·dic'i·nal
may'or·al·ty	meat'cut'ter	me·dic'i·nal·ly

med'i·cine

me'di·e·val

me'di·e·val·ist

me'di·e·val·ly

me'di·o'cre

me'di·oc'ri·ty

med'i·tate

med'i·tat'ed

med'i·ta'tion

med'i·ta'tive

me'di·um

med'lar

me·dul'la

meek

meek'er

meek'est

meek'ly

meek'ness

meer'schaum

meet

meet'ings

meet'ing·house'

meg'a·cy'cle

meg'a·phone

mei·o'sis

mei·ot'ic

mel'an·cho'li·a

mel'an·chol'ic

mel'an·chol'y

mel'a·nism

mel'a·no'sis

meld

mel'io·rate

mel'io·rat'ed

mel'io·ra'tion

mel'io·ra'tive

me·lis'ma

mel'is·mat'ic

mel·lif'lu·ous

mel'low

mel'lowed

mel'low·er

mel'low·est

me·lo'de·on

me·lod'ic

me·lo'di·on

me·lo'di·ous

me·lo'di·ous·ly

mel'o·dra'ma

mel'o·dra·mat'ic

mel'o·dy

mel'on

me'los

melt

melt'ed

melt'ing·ly

mem'ber

mem'ber·ship

mem'brane

mem'bra·nous

me·men'to

mem'oir

mem'o·ra·bil'i·a

mem'o·ra·ble

mem'o·ran'da

mem'o·ran'dum

mem'o·ran'dums

me·mo'ri·al

me·mo'ri·al·i·za'tion

me·mo'ri·al·ize

mem'o·ri·za'tion

mem'o·rize

mem'o·rized

mem'o·ry

men'ace

men'aced

me·nage'

me·nag'er·ie

mend

men·da'cious

men·dac'i·ty

mend'ed

Men·de'li·an

men'di·can·cy

men'di·cant

men'folk'

men·ha'den

me'ni·al

me'ni·al·ly

me·nin'ges

men'in·gi'tis

me·nis'cus

Men'non·ite

men'su·ra'tion

men'su·ra'tive

men'tal

men·tal'i·ty

men'tal·ly

men'thol

men'tion

men'tioned

men'tor

men'u

me·phit'ic

mer'can·tile

mer'ce·nar'y

mer'cer·ize

mer'cer·ized

mer'chan·dise

mer'chan·dis'er

mer'chant

mer'chant·man

mer'ci·ful

mer'ci·less

mer'ci·less·ly

mer·cu'ri·al

mer'cu·ry

mer'cy

mere'ly

mer'est

mer'e·tri'cious

merge

merged

merg'er

me·rid'i·an

me·ringue'

me·ri'no

mer'it

mer'it·ed

mer'i·to'ri·ous

mer'i·to'ri·ous·ly

mer'lin

mer'maid'

mer'ri·er

mer'ri·est

mer'ri·ly

mer'ri·ment

mer'ri·ness

mer'ry

mer'ry·mak'ing

me'sa

mes·cal'

mes·cal'ine

mesh

mesh'work'

mes'mer·ism

mes'on

mess

mes'sage

mes'sen·ger

Mes·si'ah

mess'man

mess'mate'

mes·ti'zo

met'a·bol'ic

me·tab'o·lism

met'a·car'pal

met'a·car'pus

met'al

me·tal'lic

me·tal'li·cal·ly

met'al·loid

met'al·lur'gic

met'al·lur'gi·cal

met'al·lur'gy

met'al·ware'

met'al·work'

met'al·work'er

met'a·mor'phose

met'a·mor'phoses

met'a·mor'pho·sis

met'a·phor

met'a·phor'ic

met'a·phor'i·cal

met'a·phor'i·cal·ly

met'a·phys'i·cal

met'a·phys'i·cal·ly

met'a·phy·si'cian

met'a·phys'ics

me·tas'ta·sis

me·tas'ta·size

met'a·tar'sal

met'a·tar'sus

mete

met'ed

me'te·or

me'te·or'ic

me'te·or·ite

me'te·or·oid'

me'te·or·ol'o·gy

me'ter

me'tered

meth′ane	mi·crom′e·ter	mid′year′
me·thinks′	mi′cron	mien
meth′od	mi′cro·phone	might
me·thod′i·cal	mi′cro·scope	might′i·ly
me·thod′i·cal·ly	mi′cro·scop′ic	might′i·ness
meth′od·ist	mi·cros′co·py	might′y
meth′od·ize	mi′cro·spore	mi′graine
meth′od·ol′o·gy	mi′cro·struc′ture	mi′grant
meth′yl	mi′cro·tome	mi′grate
me·tic′u·lous	mi·crot′o·my	mi′grat·ed
mé·tier′	Mi′das	mi·gra′tion
me·ton′y·my	mid′brain′	mi′gra·to′ry
met′ric	mid′day′	mi·ka′do
met′ri·cal	mid′dle	milch
me·trol′o·gy	mid′dle·man′	mild
met′ro·nome	mid′dle·weight′	mild′er
me·trop′o·lis	midge	mild′est
met′ro·pol′i·tan	midg′et	mil′dew
met′tle	mid′i′ron	mild′ly
met′tled	mid′land	mild′ness
met′tle·some	mid′most	mile
Mex′i·can	mid′night′	mile′age
mez′za·nine	mid′riff	mile′post′
mi·as′ma	mid′ship′man	mil′er
mi·as′mal	mid′ships′	mile′stone′
mi′as·mat′ic	midst	mil′i·tant
mi′ca	mid′stream′	mil′i·ta·rism
mi·ca′ce·ous	mid′sum′mer	mil′i·ta·rist
mi′crobe	mid′way′	mil′i·ta·ris′tic
mi′cro·cosm	mid′week′	mil′i·ta·rize
mi′cro·de·ter′mi·na′tion	mid′wife′	mil′i·tar′y
mi′cro·dis·sec′tion	mid′win′ter	mil′i·tate

mil'i·tat'ed	mim'ic	min'is·try
mi·li'tia	mim'ic·ry	min'i·ver
milk	mi·mo'sa	mink
milk'maid'	min'a·ret'	min'now
milk'man'	min'a·to'ry	mi'nor
milk'weed'	mince	mi·nor'i·ty
milk'y	minced	min'ster
mill	mince'meat'	min'strel
mill'board'	minc'ing·ly	min'strel·sy
milled	mind	mint
mil'le·nar'y	mind'ed	mint'ed
mil·len'ni·al	mind'ful	min'u·end
mil·len'ni·um	mind'less	min'u·et'
mil'le·pede	mine	mi'nus
mill'er	min'er	mi·nus'cule
mil'let	min'er·al	min'ute
mil'line'	min'er·al'o·gy	mi·nute'
mil'li·ner	min'gle	mi·nute'ness
mil'li·ner'y	min'gled	mi·nu'ti·a
mil'lion	min'i·a·ture	mi·nu'ti·ae
mil'lion·aire'	min'i·a·tur·ist	minx
mil'lion·fold'	min'im	mir'a·cle
mil'lionth	min'i·mal	mi·rac'u·lous
mill'pond'	min'i·mi·za'tion	mi·rage'
mill'race'	min'i·mize	mire
mill'stone'	min'i·mum	mired
mill'work'	min'ion	mir'ror
mill'wright'	min'is·ter	mir'rored
Mil·ton'ic	min'is·tered	mirth
mime	min'is·te'ri·al	mirth'ful
mim'e·o·graph'	min'is·te'ri·al·ly	mirth'ful·ly
mi·met'ic	min'is·tra'tion	mirth'less

mis'ad·ven'ture

mis'al·li·ance

mis'an·thrope

mis'an·throp'ic

mis'an·throp'i·cal

mis·an'thro·pism

mis·an'thro·pist

mis·an'thro·py

mis'ap·pli·ca'tion

mis'ap·ply'

mis'ap·pre·hen'sion

mis'ap·pro'pri·ate

mis'ap·pro'pri·a'tion

mis'ar·range'

mis'be·got'ten

mis'be·have'

mis'be·haved'

mis'be·hav'ior

mis'be·liev'er

mis·brand'

mis·cal'cu·late

mis·cal'cu·lat'ed

mis·call'

mis·car'riage

mis·car'ried

mis·car'ry

mis·cast'

mis'ce·ge·na'tion

mis'cel·la'ne·a

mis'cel·la'ne·ous

mis'cel·la'nist

mis'cel·la'ny

mis·chance'

mis'chief

mis'chie·vous

mis'ci·ble

mis'con·ceive'

mis'con·cep'tion

mis'con·duct'

mis'con·struc'tion

mis'con·strue'

mis'count'

mis'cre·ant

mis·cue'

mis·date'

mis·deal'

mis·deed'

mis'de·mean'or

mis'di·rect'

mis'di·rect'ed

mis'di·rec'tion

mis·doubt'

mi'ser

mis'er·a·ble

mi'ser·li·ness

mi'ser·ly

mis'er·y

mis·fea'sance

mis·fire'

mis·fired'

mis·fit'

mis·formed'

mis·for'tune

mis·giv'ings

mis·gov'ern

mis·gov'erned

mis·guide'

mis·guid'ed

mis·hap'

mish'mash'

mis'in·form'

mis'in·formed'

mis'in·ter'pret

mis'in·ter'pre·ta'tion

mis'in·ter'pret·ed

mis·judge'

mis·judged'

mis·laid'

mis·lay'

mis·lead'

mis·lead'ing·ly

mis·like'

mis·liked'

mis·made'

mis·man'age

mis·man'age·ment

mis·mate'

mis·mat'ed

mis·name'

mis·named'

mis·no'mer

mi·sog'y·nist

mis·place'

mis·placed'

mis·print'

mis·pri'sion

mis′pro·nounce′	mis·taught′	mi′tral
mis·pro·nun′ci·a′tion	mis·teach′	mit′ten
mis′quo·ta′tion	mist′i·er	mit′tened
mis·quote′	mist′i·est	mix
mis·read′	mist′i·ly	mixed
mis′re·mem′ber	mist′i·ness	mix′er
mis′re·mem′brance	mis′tle·toe	mix′ture
mis′rep·re·sent′	mis·took′	miz′zen·mast′
mis′rep·re·sen·ta′tion	mis·treat′	mne·mon′ic
mis·rule′	mis·treat′ment	mo′a
miss	mis′tress	moan
mis′sal	mis·tri′al	moaned
missed	mis·trust′	moat
mis·shap′en	mis·trust′ful	mob
mis′sile	mist′y	mob′cap′
mis′sion	mis′un·der·stand′	mo′bile
mis′sion·ar′y	mis′un·der·stand′ings	mo·bil′i·ty
mis′sion·er	mis′un·der·stood′	mo′bi·li·za′tion
mis′sive	mis·us′age	mo′bi·lize
mis·spell′	mis·use′	mo′bi·lized
mis·spelled′	mis·used′	mob·oc′ra·cy
mis·spell′ings	mite	moc′ca·sin
mis·spend′	mi′ter	Mo′cha
mis·spent′	mi′tered	mock
mis·state′	mit′i·ga·ble	mock′er·y
mis·stat′ed	mit′i·gate	mock′ing·ly
mis·state′ment	mit′i·gat′ed	mod′al
mis·step′	mit′i·ga′tion	mo·dal′i·ty
mist	mit′i·ga′tive	mode
mis·take′	mit′i·ga·to′ry	mod′el
mis·tak′en	mi·to′sis	mod′eled
mis·tak′en·ly	mi·tot′ic	mod′er·ate

mod'er·at'ed

mod'er·ate·ly

mod'er·ate·ness

mod'er·a'tion

mod'er·a'tion·ist

mod'er·a'tor

mod'ern

mod'ern·ism

mod'ern·ist

mod'ern·is'tic

mo·der'ni·ty

mod'ern·i·za'tion

mod'ern·ize

mod'ern·ized

mod'est

mod'est·ly

mod'es·ty

mod'i·cum

mod'i·fi·ca'tion

mod'i·fi·ca'tion·ist

mod'i·fied

mod'i·fi'er

mod'i·fy

mod'ish

mod'ish·ly

mod'ish·ness

mod'u·lar

mod'u·late

mod'u·lat'ed

mod'u·la'tion

mod'u·la'tive

mod'u·la'tor

mod'u·la·to'ry

mod'ule

mod'u·lus

mog'a·dore'

Mo·gul'

mo'hair'

Mo·ham'med·an

Mo'hawk

mo'ho

moi'e·ty

moil

moiled

moi·re'

moist

mois'ten

mois'tened

mois'ten·er

mois'ture

mo'lal

mo'lar

mo·lar'i·ty

mo·las'ses

mold

mold'board'

mold'ed

mold'er

mold'ings

mold'y

mole

mo·lec'u·lar

mol'e·cule

mole'hill'

mole'skin'

mo·lest'

mo·les·ta'tion

mo·lest'ed

mol'li·fi·ca'tion

mol'li·fied

mol'li·fy

mol'lusk

mol'ly·cod'dle

molt

molt'ed

mol'ten

mo'ly

mo·lyb'de·num

mo'ment

mo'men·tar'i·ly

mo'men·tar'y

mo'ment·ly

mo·men'tous

mo·men'tum

mon'ad

mo·nad'nock

mon'arch

mo·nar'chi·al

mo·nar'chi·an·ism

mo·nar'chic

mon'arch·ism

mon'arch·ist

mon'arch·is'tic

mon'arch·y

mon'as·te'ri·al

mon'as·te'ri·al·ly

mon'as·ter'y	mon'o·lith'ic	month
mo·nas'tic	mon'o·logue	month'ly
mo·nas'ti·cism	mon'o·ma'ni·a	mon'u·ment
mon'a·tom'ic	mon'o·ma'ni·ac	mon'u·men'tal
Mon'day	mon'o·ma·ni'a·cal	mon'u·men'tal·ly
mo·nel'	mon'o·mor'phic	mood
mon'e·tar'y	mon'o·plane	mood'i·ly
mon'e·ti·za'tion	mon'o·ple'gi·a	mood'i·ness
mon'e·tize	mo·nop'o·lism	mood'y
mon'ey	mo·nop'o·list	moon
mon'eyed	mo·nop'o·lis'tic	moon'beam'
mon'goose	mo·nop'o·lis'ti·cal·ly	moon'faced'
mon'grel	mo·nop'o·li·za'tion	moon'fish'
mon'ism	mo·nop'o·lize	moon'flow'er
mon'i·tor	mo·nop'o·lized	moon'light'
mon'i·tored	mo·nop'o·ly	moon'light'ed
mon'i·to'ri·al	mon'o·rail'	moon'light'er
mon'i·to'ry	mon'o·syl·lab'ic	moon'light'ing
monk	mon'o·syl'la·ble	moon'rise'
mon'key	mon'o·the·ism	moon'shine'
monk'hood	mon'o·the·is'tic	moon'stone'
monk'ish	mon'o·tone	moon'-struck
mon'o·bas'ic	mo·not'o·nous	moor
mon'o·cle	mo·not'o·ny	moor'age
mon'o·cled	mon'o·type	moored
mo·noc'u·lar	mon·ox'ide	moor'ings
mon'o·dy	mon·si'gnor	Moor'ish
mo·nog'a·mous	mon·soon'	moor'land'
mo·nog'a·my	mon'ster	moose
mon'o·gram	mon'strance	moot
mon'o·graph	mon·stros'i·ty	mop
mon'o·lith	mon'strous	mopped

mop'pet

mo·raine'

mor'al

mo·rale'

mor'al·ist

mor'al·is'tic

mo·ral'i·ty

mor'al·i·za'tion

mor'al·ize

mor'al·ized

mor'al·ly

mo·rass'

mor'a·to'ri·um

mo·ray'

mor'bid

mor·bid'i·ty

mor'bid·ly

mor'dant

more

more·o'ver

mo'res

mor'ga·nat'ic

morgue

mor'i·bund

Mor'mon

morn

morn'ing

morn'ings

mo·roc'co

mo'ron

mo·rose'

mo·rose'ly

mor'phine

mor'phin·ism

mor'phin·ize

mor·phol'o·gy

mor'ris

mor'row

mor'sel

mor'tal

mor·tal'i·ty

mor'tal·ly

mor'tar

mor'tar·board'

mort'gage

mort'gaged

mort'ga·gee'

mort'ga·gor'

mor·ti'cian

mor'ti·fi·ca'tion

mor'ti·fied

mor'ti·fy

mor'tise

mort'main

mor'tu·ar'y

mo·sa'ic

Mos'lem

mosque

mos·qui'to

moss

moss'back'

moss'i·ness

moss'y

most

most'ly

mote

mo·tet'

moth

moth'er

moth'er·hood

moth'er-in-law'

moth'er·land'

moth'er·less

moth'er·li·ness

moth'er·ly

moth'er-of-pearl'

mo·tif'

mo'tile

mo'tion

mo'tioned

mo'tion·less

mo'ti·vate

mo'ti·vat'ed

mo'ti·va'tion

mo'ti·va'tion·al

mo'tive

mot'ley

mo'tor

mo'tor·boat'

mo'tor·cy'cle

mo'tored

mo'tor·ist

mo'tor·ize

mo'tor·man

mot'tle

mot'tled

mot'to	mow	mug
mound	mow	mug'gi·ness
mount	mow'er	mug'gy
moun'tain	much	mug'wump'
moun'tain·eer'	mu'ci·lage	mu·lat'to
moun'tain·ous	mu'ci·lag'i·nous	mul'ber'ry
moun'tain·ous·ly	muck	mulch
moun'te·bank	muck'er	mulched
mount'ed	muck'rak'er	mulct
mount'ings	muck'weed'	mulct'ed
mourn	muck'worm'	mule
mourned	mu'coid	mu'le·teer'
mourn'er	mu·co'sa	mu'li·eb'ri·ty
mourn'ful	mu'cous	mul'ish
mouse	mu'cus	mull
mous'er	mud	mulled
mouse'trap'	mud'di·er	mul'let
mousse	mud'di·est	mul'li·ga·taw'ny
mouth	mud'di·ly	mul'lion
mouthed	mud'di·ness	mul'ti·far'i·ous
mouth'ful	mud'dle	mul'ti·fold
mouth'fuls	mud'dled	mul'ti·form
mouth'piece'	mud'dle-head'ed	mul'ti·for'mi·ty
mov'a·bil'i·ty	mud'dy	Mul'ti·graph
mov'a·ble	mud'fish'	Mul'ti·lith'
mov'a·bly	mud'weed'	mul'ti·mil'lion·aire'
move	muff	mul'ti·ped
moved	muf'fin	mul'ti·ple
move'ment	muf'fle	mul'ti·plex
mov'er	muf'fled	mul'ti·pli·cand'
mov'ie	muf'fler	mul'ti·pli·cate
mov'ing·ly	muf'ti	mul'ti·pli·ca'tion

mul'ti·pli·ca'tive	mu'rex	musk
mul'ti·plic'i·ty	mu'ri·at'ic	mus'keg
mul'ti·plied	murk	mus'kel·lunge
mul'ti·pli'er	murk'i·ly	mus'ket
mul'ti·ply	murk'i·ness	mus'ket·eer'
mul'ti·tude	murk'y	mus'ket·ry
mul'ti·tu'di·nous	mur'mur	musk'mel'on
mul'ti·va'lent	mur'mured	musk'rat'
mum'ble	mur'mur·er	mus'lin
mum'bled	mur'mur·ous	muss
mum'mer	mus'ca·dine	mussed
mum'mer·y	mus'cat	mus'sel
mum'mi·fi·ca'tion	mus'ca·tel'	muss'i·er
mum'mi·fied	mus'cle	muss'i·est
mum'mi·fy	mus'cu·lar	muss'y
mum'my	mus'cu·lar'i·ty	must
mumps	mus'cu·lar·ly	mus·tache'
munch	mus'cu·la·ture	mus·ta'chio
munched	muse	mus'tang
mun'dane	mused	mus'tard
mu·nic'i·pal	mu·sette'	mus'ter
mu·nic'i·pal'i·ty	mu·se'um	mus'tered
mu·nic'i·pal·ly	mush	mus'ti·ness
mu·nif'i·cence	mush'room	mus'ty
mu·nif'i·cent	mush'roomed	mu'ta·bil'i·ty
mu'ni·ment	mush'y	mu'ta·ble
mu·ni'tion	mu'sic	mu'tate
mu'ral	mu'si·cal	mu·ta'tion
mur'der	mu'si·cale'	mu'ta·tive
mur'dered	mu'si·cal·ly	mute
mur'der·er	mu·si'cian	mut'ed
mur'der·ous	mu·si'cian·ly	mute'ness

mu'ti·late	muz'zle	mys·te'ri·ous·ly
mu'ti·lat'ed	muz'zled	mys'ter·y
mu'ti·la'tion	my	mys'tic
mu'ti·la'tor	my·col'o·gy	mys'ti·cal
mu'ti·neer'	my·co'sis	mys'ti·cal·ly
mu'ti·nied	my·dri'a·sis	mys'ti·cism
mu'ti·nous	myd'ri·at'ic	mys'ti·fi·ca'tion
mu'ti·ny	my'e·loid	mys'ti·fied
mut'ism	my·o'ma	mys'ti·fy
mut'ter	my·o'pi·a	myth
mut'tered	my·op'ic	myth'i·cal
mut'ter·ings	myr'i·ad	myth'o·log'i·cal
mut'ton	myrrh	my·thol'o·gist
mu'tu·al	myr'tle	my·thol'o·gy
mu'tu·al'i·ty	my·self'	
mu'tu·al·ly	mys·te'ri·ous	

N

na·celle'

na'cre

na'cre·ous

na'dir

nai'ad

nail

nailed

nail'head'

nain'sook

na·ïve'

na·ïve·té'

na'ked

na'ked·ly

na'ked·ness

nam'a·ble

name

named

name'less

name'less·ly

name'ly

name'sake'

nan·keen'

nap

na'per·y

naph'tha

naph'tha·lene

nap'kin

na·po'le·on

Na·po'le·on·a'na

Na·po'le·on'ic

napped

nar·cis'sism

nar·cis'sus

nar·co'sis

nar·cot'ic

nar·cot'i·cism

nar'co·tize

nar'co·tized

nar·rate'

nar·rat'ed

nar·ra'tion

nar'ra·tive

nar·ra'tor

nar'row

nar'rowed

nar'row·er

nar'row·est

nar'row·ly

nar'row·ness

nar'whal

na'sal

na·sal'i·ty

na'sal·ize

na'sal·ly

nas'cent

nas'ti·er

nas'ti·est

nas'ti·ly

nas'ti·ness

nas·tur'tium

nas'ty

na'tal

na·ta'tion

na·ta·to'ri·um

na·ta·to'ry

na'tion

na·tion·al

na·tion·al·ism

na·tion·al·is'tic

na·tion·al'i·ty

na·tion·al·i·za'tion

na·tion·al·ize

na·tion·al·ized

na·tion·al·ly

na'tive

na·tiv'i·ty

nat'u·ral

nat'u·ral·ism

nat'u·ral·ist

nat'u·ral·is'tic

nat'u·ral·i·za'tion

nat'u·ral·ize

nat'u·ral·ized

nat'u·ral·ly

nat'u·ral·ness

na'ture

na'tur·is'tic

naught

naugh'ti·ly

naugh'ti·ness

naugh'ty

nau'se·a

nau'se·ate

nau'se·at'ed

nau'seous

nau'ti·cal

nau'ti·lus

na'val

nave

na'vel

nav'i·ga·ble

nav'i·gate

nav'i·gat'ed

nav'i·ga'tion

nav'i·ga'tion·al

nav'i·ga'tor

na'vy

Naz'a·rene'

neap

Ne·a·pol'i·tan

near

near'by'

neared

near'er

near'est

near'ly

near'ness

near'sight'ed

neat

neat'er

neat'est

neat'herd'

neat'ly

neat'ness

neb'u·la

neb'u·lar

neb'u·los'i·ty

neb'u·lous

neb'u·lous·ly

nec'es·sar'i·ly

nec'es·sar'y

ne·ces'si·tar'i·an

ne·ces'si·tate

ne·ces'si·tat'ed

ne·ces'si·tous

ne·ces'si·ty

neck

neck'band'

neck'cloth'

neck'er·chief

neck'lace

neck'tie'

neck'wear'

nec'ro·log'i·cal

ne·crol'o·gy

nec'ro·man'cy

nec'ro·man'tic

nec'ro·pho'bi·a

ne·crop'o·lis

nec'rop·sy

ne·cro'sis

ne·crot'ic

nec'tar

nec'tar·ine'

need

need'ed

need'ful

need'ful·ly

need'i·er

need'i·est

need'i·ness

nee'dle

nee'dled	neigh'bor·ly	net'ted
nee'dle·ful	nei'ther	net'tings
need'less	nem'a·tode	net'tle
need'less·ly	Nem'e·sis	net'tled
need'less·ness	ne'o·for·ma'tion	net'work'
nee'dle·work'	ne'o·lith'ic	neu'ral
need'y	ne·ol'o·gism	neu·ral'gia
ne·far'i·ous	ne·ol'o·gy	neu'ras·the'ni·a
ne·gate'	ne'on	neu'ras·then'ic
ne·gat'ed	ne'o·phyte	neu·ri'tis
ne·ga'tion	ne'o·plasm	neu·ro'ses
neg'a·tive	ne·pen'the	neu·ro'sis
neg'a·tived	neph'ew	neu·rot'ic
neg'a·tiv·ism	ne·phrec'to·my	neu'ter
neg·lect'	ne·phri'tis	neu'tral
neg·lect'ed	nep'o·tism	neu'tral·ism
neg·lect'ful	nerve	neu'tral·ist
neg'li·gee'	nerve'less	neu·tral'i·ty
neg'li·gence	ner'vous	neu'tral·i·za'tion
neg'li·gent	nerv'ous·ly	neu'tral·ize
neg'li·gi·ble	nerv'ous·ness	neu'tral·ized
ne·go'ti·a·bil'i·ty	nes'ci·ence	neu'tral·iz'er
ne·go'ti·a·ble	nes'ci·ent	neu'tral·ly
ne·go'ti·ate	nest	neu'tron
ne·go'ti·at'ed	nest'ed	nev'er
ne·go'ti·a'tion	nes'tle	nev'er·more'
ne·go'ti·a'tor	nes'tled	nev'er·the·less'
Ne'gro	nest'lings	new
Ne'gro·phile	net	new'com'er
neigh'bor	neth'er	new'el
neigh'bor·hood	neth'er·most	new'er
neigh'bor·li·ness	net'su·ke	new'est

new'fan'gled	niece	nip'ple
new'ly	ni·el'lo	nip'py
new'ness	nig'gard	nir·va'na
news'i·er	nig'gard·li·ness	ni'ter
news'i·est	nig'gard·ly	ni'trate
news'let'ter	nig'gle	ni'tric
news'pa'per	nig'gling·ly	ni'tride
news'reel'	nigh	ni'tri·fi·ca'tion
news'stand'	night	ni'tri·fy
news'y	night'cap'	ni'tro·gen
newt	night'fall'	ni·trog'e·nous
next	night'fish'	ni'tro·glyc'er·in
nex'us	night'gown'	ni'trous
nib'ble	night'hawk'	nit'wit'
nib'bled	night'in·gale	no
nib'lick	night'ly	no·bil'i·ty
nice	night'mare'	no'ble
nice'ly	night'mar'ish	no'ble·man
nice'ness	night'shade'	no'bler
nic'er	night'shirt'	no'blest
nic'est	night'time'	no'bly
ni'ce·ty	night'wear'	no'bod·y
niche	night'work'	noc·tur'nal
nick	night'work'er	noc·tur'nal·ly
nicked	ni'hil·ism	noc'turne
nick'el	ni'hil·ist	nod
nick'el·if'er·ous	ni'hil·is'tic	nod'ded
nick'el·o'de·on	nim'ble	node
nick'name'	nim'bus	nod'ule
nick'named'	nin'com·poop	no·el'
nic'o·tine	nine'pins'	noise
nic'o·tin'ic	nip'per	noise'less

nois'i·er

nois'i·est

nois'i·ly

nois'i·ness

noi'some

nois'y

no'mad

no·mad'ic

no'men·cla'ture

nom'i·nal

nom'i·nal·ism

nom'i·nal·ly

nom'i·nate

nom'i·nat'ed

nom'i·na'tion

nom'i·na·tive

nom'i·nee'

non'a·ge·nar'i·an

non'a·gon

non'ap·pear'ance

non·call'a·ble

nonce

non'cha·lance

non'cha·lant

non'cha·lant·ly

non·com'bat·ant

non'com·mis'sioned

non'com·mit'tal

non'com·mu'ni·cant

non'con·duc'tor

non'con·form'ism

non'con·form'ist

non'con·form'i·ty

non'-co-op'er·a'tion

non'de·script

non·en'ti·ty

non'es·sen'tial

none'such'

non'ex·ist'ence

non·fea'sance

non·fea'sor

non·for'feit·ure

non'in·ter·ven'tion

non'met'al

non'me·tal'lic

non'pa·reil'

non'par·tic'i·pat'ing

non·par'ti·san

non·per'ma·nent

non'plus

non'plused

non·res'i·dence

non·res'i·dent

non're·sist'ance

non're·sist'ant

non'sense

non·sen'si·cal

non'skid'

non'stop'

non'sub·scrib'er

non'suit'

non'sup·port'

non·un'ion

noo'dle

nook

noon

noon'day'

noon'time'

noose

nor

norm

nor'mal

nor·mal'i·ty

nor'mal·ize

nor'mal·ized

nor'mal·ly

Nor'man

nor'ma·tive

Norse

north

north'east'

north'east'er

north'east'er·ly

north'east'ern

north'east'ward

north'east'ward·ly

north'er·ly

north'ern

north'ern·er

north'land

north'ward

north'west'

north'west'er·ly

north'west'ern

Nor·we'gian

nose

nose'band'

nose'bleed'

nose'gay'

nose'piece'

nos'ings

no·sol'o·gy

nos·tal'gi·a

nos·tal'gic

nos'tril

nos'trum

not

no'ta·bil'i·ty

no'ta·ble

no·tar'i·al

no·tar'i·al·ly

no'ta·ry

no·ta'tion

notch

notched

notch'weed'

note

note'book'

not'ed

note'wor'thi·ly

note'wor'thy

noth'ing

noth'ing·ness

no'tice

no'tice·a·ble

no'ticed

no'ti·fi·ca'tion

no'ti·fied

no'ti·fy

no'tion

no·to·ri'e·ty

no·to'ri·ous

no·to'ri·ous·ly

not'with·stand'ing

nou'gat

nou·ga·tine

nought

nou'me·non

noun

nour'ish

nour'ished

nour'ish·ing·ly

nour'ish·ment

nov'el

nov'el·ette'

nov'el·ist

nov'el·ize

no·vel'la

nov'el·ty

No·vem'ber

no·ve'na

nov'ice

no·vi'ti·ate

No'vo·cain'

now

now'a·days'

no'where

nox'ious

nox'ious·ness

noz'zle

nu·ance'

nu'cle·ar

nu'cle·ate

nu'cle·at'ed

nu'cle·a'tion

nu'cle·i

nu·cle'o·lus

nu'cle·us

nude

nudge

nudged

nud'ism

nud'ist

nu'di·ty

nu'ga·to'ry

nug'get

nui'sance

null

nul'li·fi·ca'tion

nul'li·fi·ca'tion·ist

nul'li·fied

nul'li·fy

nul'li·ty

numb

numbed

num'ber

num'bered

num'ber·less

numb'ness

nu'mer·al

nu'mer·ate

nu'mer·a'tion	nursed	nu·tri'tion
nu'mer·a'tor	nurse'maid'	nu·tri'tion·al
nu·mer'ic	nurs'er·y	nu·tri'tion·al·ly
nu·mer'i·cal	nurs'er·y·maid'	nu·tri'tion·ist
nu'mer·ous	nurs'er·y·man	nu·tri'tious
nu'mis·mat'ics	nurs'lings	nu·tri'tious·ly
nu·mis'ma·tist	nur'ture	nu'tri·tive
num'skull'	nur'tured	nu'tri·tive·ly
nun	nut	nut'shell'
nun'ci·a·ture	nut'hatch'	nuz'zle
nun'ci·o	nut'meg	nuz'zled
nun'ner·y	nu'tri·a	nyc'ta·lo'pi·a
nup'tial	nu'tri·ent	nymph
nurse	nu'tri·ment	nys·tag'mus

O

oaf	o·bit'u·ar'y	ob·lique'ness
oak	ob·ject'	ob·liq'ui·ty
oak'en	ob·ject'ed	ob·lit'er·ate
oa'kum	ob·jec'tion	ob·lit'er·at'ed
oar	ob·jec'tion·a·ble	ob·lit'er·a'tion
oar'lock'	ob·jec'tive	ob·liv'i·on
oars'man	ob·jec'tive·ly	ob·liv'i·ous
o·a'sis	ob·jec'tive·ness	ob·liv'i·ous·ly
oat'en	ob'jec·tiv'i·ty	ob·liv'i·ous·ness
oath	ob·jec'tor	ob'long
oat'meal'	ob'jur·gate	ob'lo·quy
ob'bli·ga·to	ob'late	ob·nox'ious
ob'du·ra·cy	ob·la'tion	ob·nox'ious·ly
ob'du·rate	ob'li·gate	o'boe
o·be'di·ence	ob'li·gat'ed	ob·scene'
o·be'di·ent	ob'li·ga'tion	ob·scen'i·ty
o·bei'sance	ob·lig'a·to'ry	ob·scure'
ob'e·lisk	o·blige'	ob·scure'ness
o·bese'	o·bliged'	ob·scu'ri·ty
o·bes'i·ty	o·blig'ing·ly	ob·se'qui·ous
o·bey'	ob·lique'	ob·se'qui·ous·ly
o·beyed'	ob·lique'ly	ob·se'qui·ous·ness

197

ob'se·quy
ob·serv'a·ble
ob·serv'ance
ob·serv'ant
ob'ser·va'tion
ob·serv'a·to'ry
ob·serve'
ob·served'
ob·serv'er
ob·serv'ing·ly
ob·sess'
ob·sessed'
ob·ses'sion
ob·ses'sion·al
ob·ses'sive
ob·sid'i·an
ob'so·les'cence
ob'so·les'cent
ob'so·lete
ob'so·lete·ly
ob'so·lete·ness
ob'sta·cle
ob·stet'ri·cal
ob·ste·tri'cian
ob·stet'rics
ob'sti·na·cy
ob'sti·nate
ob'sti·nate·ly
ob·strep'er·ous
ob·struct'
ob·struct'ed
ob·struc'tion

ob·struc'tion·ism
ob·struc'tion·ist
ob·struc'tive
ob·struc'tor
ob·tain'
ob·tain'a·ble
ob·tained'
ob·trude'
ob·trud'ed
ob·trud'er
ob·tru'sion
ob·tru'sive
ob·tuse'
ob·tuse'ly
ob·tuse'ness
ob'verse
ob'vi·ate
ob'vi·at'ed
ob'vi·a'tion
ob'vi·ous
ob'vi·ous·ly
oc'a·ri'na
oc·ca'sion
oc·ca'sion·al
oc·ca'sion·al·ly
oc·ca'sioned
oc'ci·dent
oc'ci·den'tal
oc'ci·den'tal·ly
oc·cip'i·tal
oc'ci·put
oc·clude'

oc·clud'ed
oc·clu'sion
oc·cult'
oc'cul·ta'tion
oc·cult'ism
oc·cult'ist
oc'cu·pan·cy
oc'cu·pant
oc'cu·pa'tion
oc'cu·pa'tion·al
oc'cu·pa'tion·al·ly
oc'cu·pied
oc'cu·py
oc·cur'
oc·curred'
oc·cur'rence
o'cean
o'ce·an'ic
o'ce·a·nog'ra·phy
o'ce·lot
o'cher
och·loc'ra·cy
oc'ta·gon
oc·tag'o·nal
oc·tag'o·nal·ly
oc·tam'e·ter
oc·tan'gu·lar
oc'tave
oc·ta'vo
oc·tet'
Oc·to'ber
oc'to·ge·nar'i·an

oc'to·pus

oc'u·lar

oc'u·list

odd

odd'er

odd'est

odd'i·ty

odd'ly

odd'ment

odd'ness

ode

o·de'um

o'di·ous

o'di·ous·ly

o'di·ous·ness

o'di·um

o·dom'e·ter

o'dor

o'dor·if'er·ous

o'dor·less

o'dor·ous

oe·nol'o·gy

of

off

of'fal

off'cast'

of·fend'

of·fend'ed

of·fense'

of·fen'sive

of'fer

of'fered

of'fer·ings

of'fer·to'ry

off'hand'

of'fice

of'fi·cer

of·fi'cial

of·fi'cial·ly

of·fi'ci·ate

of·fi'ci·at'ed

of·fi'ci·a'tion

of·fi'cious

of·fi'cious·ly

of·fi'cious·ness

off'ish

off'set'

off'shoot'

off'shore'

of'ten

of'ten·er

of'ten·est

of'ten·times'

o·gee'

o'give

o'gle

o'gled

o'gre

ohm

ohm'age

ohm'me'ter

oil

oiled

oil'er

oil'hole'

oil'i·er

oil'i·est

oil'i·ly

oil'i·ness

oil'man

oil'pa'per

oil'proof'

oil'seed'

oil'skin'

oil'stone'

oil'tight'

oil'y

oint'ment

o·ka'pi

o'kra

old

old'en

old'er

old'est

old'-fash'ioned

old'ish

old'ness

old'ster

o'le·ag'i·nous

o'le·an'der

o'le·ate

o·lec'ra·non

o'le·o

o'le·o·mar'ga·rine

ol·fac'to·ry

ol'i·garch'y

ol'ive	on·tol'o·gy	oph'thal·mol'o·gist
o·me'ga	o'nus	oph'thal·mol'o·gy
om'e·let	on'ward	o'pi·ate
o'men	on'yx	o·pin'ion
o·men'tum	o·öl'o·gy	o·pin'ion·at'ed
om'i·nous	oo'long	o·pin'ion·a'tive
o·mis'sion	ooze	o'pi·um
o·mit'	oozed	o·pos'sum
o·mit'ted	o·pac'i·ty	op·po'nent
om'ni·bus	o'pal	op'por·tune'
om'nip'o·tence	o'pal·esce'	op'por·tun'ism
om·nip'o·tent	o'pal·es'cence	op'por·tu'ni·ty
om'ni·pres'ent	o'pal·es'cent	op·pos'a·ble
om·nis'cience	o·paque'	op·pose'
om·nis'cient	o'pen	op·posed'
om·niv'o·rous	o'pened	op·pos'er
on	o'pen·er	op·pos'ing
on'a·ger	o'pen·ings	op'po·site
once	o'pen·ly	op'po·si'tion
one	o'pen·ness	op·press'
one'ness	o'pen·work'	op·pressed'
on'er·ous	op'er·a	op·pres'sion
one·self'	op'er·a·ble	op·pres'sive
one'time'	op'er·a·logue'	op·pres'sive·ly
on'ion	op'er·ate	op·pres'sive·ness
on'look'er	op'er·at'ed	op·pres'sor
on'ly	op'er·at'ic	op·pro'bri·ous
on'o·mat'o·poe'ia	op'er·at'i·cal·ly	op·pro'bri·ous·ly
on'set'	op'er·a'tion	op·pro'bri·ous·ness
on'slaught'	op'er·a'tive	op·pro'bri·um
on'to	op'er·a'tor	opt
on·tog'e·ny	op'er·et'ta	opt'ed

op'ta·tive

op'tic

op'ti·cal

op·ti'cian

op'tics

op'ti·mism

op'ti·mist

op'ti·mis'tic

op'ti·mis'ti·cal·ly

op'ti·mum

op'tion

op'tion·al

op'tion·al·ly

op·tom'e·trist

op·tom'e·try

op'u·lence

op'u·lent

o'pus

or

or'a·cle

o·rac'u·lar

o·rac'u·lar·ly

o'ral

o'ral·ly

or'ange

o·rang'u·tan'

o·ra'tion

or'a·tor

or'a·tor'i·cal

or'a·to'ri·o

or'a·to'ry

orb

or'bit

or'bit·al

or'bit·ed

or'chard

or'ches·tra

or·ches'tral

or'ches·trate

or'ches·trat'ed

or'ches·tra'tion

or'chid

or'chi·da'ceous

or·dain'

or·dained'

or·deal'

or'der

or'dered

or'der·li·ness

or'der·ly

or'di·nal

or'di·nance

or'di·nar'i·ly

or'di·nar'y

or'di·na'tion

ord'nance

ore

or'gan

or·gan'ic

or·gan'i·cal·ly

or'gan·ism

or'gan·ist

or'gan·i·za'tion

or'gan·i·za'tion·al

or'gan·ize

or'gan·ized

or'gy

o'ri·el

o'ri·ent

o'ri·en'tal

o'ri·en'tal·ism

o'ri·en'tal·ist

o'ri·en'tal·ly

o'ri·en·tate'

o'ri·en·ta'tion

o'ri·ent'ed

or'i·fice

or'i·gin

o·rig'i·nal

o·rig'i·nal'i·ty

o·rig'i·nal·ly

o·rig'i·nate

o·rig'i·nat'ed

o·rig'i·na'tion

o·rig'i·na'tive

o·rig'i·na'tor

o'ri·ole

O·ri'on

or'i·son

or'lop

or'mo·lu

or'na·ment

or'na·men'tal

or'na·men'tal·ly

or'na·men·ta'tion

or·nate'

or·nate'ly	os'se·ous	out'crop'
or'ni·tho·log'i·cal	os'si·fi·ca'tion	out'cry'
or'ni·thol'o·gist	os'si·fied	out·curve'
or'ni·thol'o·gy	os'si·fy	out·dis'tance
o'ro·tund	os·ten'si·ble	out·do'
o'ro·tun'di·ty	os·ten'si·bly	out'doors'
or'phan	os'ten·ta'tion	out'er
or'phan·age	os'ten·ta'tious	out'er·most
or'phaned	os'ten·ta'tious·ly	out·face'
or'phan·hood	os'te·o·path	out'field'
or'phe·um	os'te·op'a·thy	out'fit
or'rer·y	os'tra·cism	out'fit'ter
or'tho·dox	os'tra·cize	out·flank'
or'tho·ëp'y	os'tra·cized	out'flow'
or·thog'ra·phy	os'trich	out·go'
or'tho·pe'dic	o·tal'gi·a	out'growth'
or·thop'tic	oth'er	out'ings
or'to·lan	oth'er·wise'	out·land'ish
os'cil·late	o'ti·ose	out·land'ish·ness
os'cil·lat'ed	ot'ter	out·last'
os'cil·la'tion	Ot'to·man	out'law'
os'cil·la'tor	ought	out'law'ry
os'cil·la·to'ry	ounce	out'lay'
os·cil'lo·scope	our	out'let
os'cu·late	ours	out'lets
os'cu·la'tion	our·selves'	out'line'
os'cu·la·to'ry	oust	out'lined'
o'sier	oust'er	out·live'
os'mi·um	out	out·lived'
os·mo'sis	out'cast'	out·look'
os·mot'ic	out·class'	out'ly'ing
os'prey	out·come'	out'march'

out·mod′ed	ov′en·bird′	o′ver·drawn′
out·num′ber	ov′en·ware′	o′ver·dress′
out′put′	o′ver	o′ver·drew′
out′rage	o′ver·age	o′ver·drive′
out·ra′geous	o′ver·age′	o′ver·driv′en
out·ra′geous·ly	o′ver·alls′	o′ver·due′
out·ra′geous·ness	o′ver·awe′	o′ver·eat′
out·rank′	o′ver·awed′	o′ver·es′ti·mate
out·ranked′	o′ver·bal′ance	o′ver·ex·pose′
out·reach′	o′ver·bear′	o′ver·ex·po′sure
out′rid·er	o′ver·bear′ing·ly	o′ver·flow′
out′rig′ger	o′ver·bid′	o′ver·flow′ing·ly
out′right′	o′ver·board′	o′ver·grown′
out·run′	o′ver·build′	o′ver·hand′
out′set′	o′ver·built′	o′ver·hang′
out′side′	o′ver·bur′den	o′ver·haul′
out′sid′er	o′ver·cap′i·tal·ize	o′ver·head′
out′size′	o′ver·cast′	o′ver·heat′
out′skirt′	o′ver·charge′	o′ver·is′sue
out·stand′ing·ly	o′ver·charged′	o′ver·land′
out·stay′	o′ver·clothes′	o′ver·lap′
out·strip′	o′ver·coat′	o′ver·look′
out·vote′	o′ver·come′	o′ver·lord′
out′ward	o′ver·com′pen·sa′tion	o′ver·ly
out′ward·ly	o′ver·cor·rect′	o′ver·mas′ter·ing·ly
out·wear′	o′ver·count′	o′ver·mod′u·la′tion
out·wit′	o′ver·de·vel′op	o′ver·night′
out·work′	o′ver·do′	o′ver·pass′
o′val	o′ver·done′	o′ver·pay′
o′vate	o′ver·dose′	o′ver·pop′u·la′tion
o·va′tion	o′ver·draft′	o′ver·pow′er
ov′en	o′ver·draw′	o′ver·pow′ered

o'ver·pow'er·ing·ly
o'ver·pro·duc'tion
o'ver·rate'
o'ver·rat'ed
o'ver·reach'
o'ver·ride'
o'ver·ripe'
o'ver·rule'
o'ver·ruled'
o'ver·run'
o'ver·seas'
o'ver·see'
o'ver·se'er
o'ver·sell'
o'ver·shad'ow
o'ver·shad'owed
o'ver·shoe'
o'ver·side'
o'ver·sight'
o'ver·size'
o'ver·spread'
o'ver·state'
o'ver·state'ment
o'ver·stay'
o'ver·step'
o'ver·stock'
o'ver·strain'

o'ver·sub·scribe'
o'ver·sup·ply'
o'vert
o'ver·take'
o'ver·tax'
o'ver·taxed'
o'ver·threw'
o'ver·throw'
o'ver·thrown'
o'ver·time'
o'ver·tone'
o'ver·ture
o'ver·turn'
o'ver·turned'
o'ver·val'ue
o'ver·ween'ing·ly
o'ver·weight'
o'ver·whelm'
o'ver·whelmed'
o'ver·whelm'ing·ly
o'ver·wind'
o'ver·work'
o'ver·worked'
o'ver·wrought'
o'vi·duct
o·vip'a·rous
o'vi·pos'i·tor

o'vule
o'vum
owe
owed
owl
owl'et
owl'ish
own
owned
own'er
own'er·ship
ox
ox'a·late
ox·al'ic
ox'i·da'tion
ox'ide
ox'i·diz'a·ble
ox'i·dize
ox'i·dized
ox'tongue'
ox'y·gen
ox'y·gen·ate
oys'ter
oys'ter·shell'
o'zone
o'zo·nize
o'zo·nized

P

pab'u·lum

pace

pace'mak'er

pac'er

pach'y·derm

pach'y·san'dra

pa·cif'ic

pa·cif'i·cal·ly

pa·cif'i·cate

pac'i·fi·ca'tion

pa·cif'i·ca·to'ry

pac'i·fied

pac'i·fi'er

pac'i·fism

pac'i·fist

pac'i·fy

pack

pack'age

pack'aged

pack'er

pack'et

pack'ings

pack'sack'

pack'sad'dle

pack'thread'

pact

pad

pad'ded

pad'dings

pad'dle

pad'dled

pad'dle·fish'

pad'dock

pad'lock'

pae'an

pa'gan

pa'gan·ism

pa'gan·ize

page

pag'eant

pag'eant·ry

paged

pag'i·na'tion

pa·go'da

paid

pail

pain

pained

pain'ful

pain'kill'er

pain'less

pains'tak'ing·ly

paint

paint'ed

paint'er

paint'ings

paint'pot'

pair

paired

pair'ings

pa·ja'ma

pal'ace

pal'a·din

pal'an·quin'

pal'at·a·bil'i·ty

pal'at·a·ble

pal'a·tal

pal'a·tal·ize

pal'ate

pa·la'tial

pa·la'tial·ly

pa·lat'i·nate

pal'a·tine

pa·lav'er

pale

paled

pa'le·og'ra·phy

pal'er

pal'est

pal'ette

pal'frey

pal'imp·sest

pal'in·drome

pal'ings

pal'i·node

pal'i·sade'

pall

pal·la'di·um

pall'bear'er

palled

pal'let

pal'li·ate

pal'li·at'ed

pal'li·a'tion

pal'li·a'tive

pal'lid

pal·lid'i·ty

pal'lid·ly

pal'li·um

pal'lor

palm

pal'mate

palmed

palm'er

pal·met'to

palm'ist

palm'is·try

pal'pa·bil'i·ty

pal'pa·ble

pal'pate

pal'pat·ed

pal·pa'tion

pal'pa·to'ry

pal'pi·tant

pal'pi·tate

pal'pi·tat'ed

pal'pi·tat'ing·ly

pal'pi·ta'tion

pal'sied

pal'sy

pal'ter

pal'tered

pal'try

pam'pas

pam'per

pam'pered

pam'phlet

pam'phlet·eer'

pam'phlet·ize

pan

pan·a·ce'a

pan·a·ma'

Pan'-A·mer'i·can

Pan'-A·mer'i-
can·ism

pan'cake'

pan'chro·mat'ic

pan'cre·as

pan'cre·at'ic

pan'da

pan·dem'ic

pan'de·mo'ni·um

pan'der

pan'dered

pane

pan'e·gyr'ic

pan'e·gyr'i·cal

pan'e·gy·rize

pan'e·gy·rized

pan'el

pan'eled

pang

Pan'hel·len'ic

pan'ic

pan'icked

pan'ick·y

pan·jan'drum

panned

pan'nier

pan'ni·kin

pan'o·ply

pan'o·ra'ma

pan'o·ram'ic

pan'sy

pant

pan'ta·loon'

pant'ed

pan'the·ism

pan'the·ist

pan'the·is'tic

pan'the·on

pan'ther

pan'to·graph

pan'to·mime

pan'try

pan'try·man

pa'pa·cy

pa'pal

pa·pay'a

pa'per

pa'per·back'

pa'per·board'

pa'pered

pa'per·er

pap'e·terie

pa·poose'

pa·pri'ka

Pap'u·an

pap'ule

pa·py'rus

par

par'a·ble

pa·rab'o·la

par'a·bol'ic

par'a·bol'i·cal

pa·rab'o·loid

par'a·chute

pa·rade'

pa·rad'ed

par'a·digm

par'a·dise

par'a·dox

par'a·dox'i·cal

par·af'fin

par'a·gon

par'a·graph

par'a·graphed

par'a·keet

par'al·lax

par'al·lel

par'al·leled

par'al·lel·ism

par'al·lel'o·gram

pa·ral'y·sis

par'a·lyt'ic

par'a·lyt'i·cal·ly

par'a·lyze

par'a·lyzed

pa·ram'e·ter

par'a·mount

par'a·noi'a

par'a·noi'ac

par'a·noid

par'a·pet

par'a·pher·na'li·a

par'a·phrase

par'a·phrased

par'a·phras'tic

par'a·ple'gi·a

par'a·pleg'ic

par'a·site

par'a·sit'ic

par'a·sit'i·cal

par'a·sit'i·cide

par'a·sit·ism

par'a·sit·ize

par'a·sol

par'a·thy'roid

par'a·ty'phoid

par'a·vane

par'boil'

par'boiled'

par'cel

par'celed

parch

parched

parch'ment

par'don

par'don·a·ble

par'doned

pare

pared

par'e·gor'ic

pa·ren'chy·ma

par'ent

par'ent·age

pa·ren'tal

pa·ren'tal·ly

pa·ren'the·ses

pa·ren'the·sis

pa·ren'the·size

par'en·thet'i·cal

par'en·thet'i·cal·ly

par'ent·hood

pa·re'sis

par·fait'

pa·ri'ah

pa·ri'e·tal

par'ings

par'ish

pa·rish'ion·er

par'i·ty

park

par'ka

parked

park'way'

par'lance

par·lan'do

par'lay

par'ley

par'leyed

par'lia·ment

par'lia·men·tar'i·an

par'lia·men'ta·ri·ly

par'lia·men'ta·ry

par'lor

par'lous

Par'me·san'

Par·nas'sus

pa·ro'chi·al

pa·ro'chi·al·ism

pa·ro'chi·al·ly

par'o·dy

pa·role'

par'o·no·ma'si·a

pa·rot'id

par'ox·ysm

par'ox·ys'mal

par'ox·ys'mal·ly

par·quet'

par'ri·cid'al

par'ri·cid'al·ly

par'ri·cide

par'ried

par'rot

par'rot·ed

par'ry

parse

parsed

par'si·mo'ni·ous

par'si·mo'ny

pars'ley

pars'nip

par'son

par'son·age

part

par·take'

par·tak'er

part'ed

par·terre'

par'the·no·gen'e·sis

Par'the·non

Par'thi·an

par'tial

par'ti·al'i·ty

par'tial·ly

par·tic'i·pant

par·tic'i·pate

par·tic'i·pat'ed

par·tic'i·pa'tion

par·tic'i·pa'tive

par·tic'i·pa'tor

par·tic'i·pi'al

par·ti·cip'i·al·ly

par'ti·ci·ple

par'ti·cle

par·tic'u·lar

par·tic'u·lar'i·ty

par·tic'u·lar·ize

par·tic'u·lar·ized

par·tic'u·lar·ly

part'ings

par'ti·san

par'ti·san·ship'

par·ti'tion

par·ti'tioned

par'ti·tive

part'ner

part'ner·ship

par'tridge

par'ty

par've·nu

pas'chal

pa·sha'

pass

pass'a·ble

pas'sage

pas'sage·way'

pass'book'

passed

pas'sen·ger

pas'sion

pas'sion·ate

pas'sion·ate·ly

Pas'sion·ist

pas'sion·less

pas'sive

pas'sive·ness

pas'siv·ism

pas'siv·ist

pas·siv'i·ty

pass'key'

pass'o·ver

pass'port

pass'word'

past

paste

paste'board'

past'ed

pas·tel'

pas'tern

pas'teur·i·za'tion

pas'teur·ize

pas'teur·ized

pas·tiche'

pas·tille'

pas'time'

past'i·ness

pas'tor

pas'to·ral

pas'to·ral·ly

pas'tor·ate

pas'try

pas'try·man

pas'tur·age

pas'ture

pas'tured

past'y

pat

Pat'a·go'ni·an

patch

patched

patch'ou·li

patch'work'

patch'y

pa·tel'la

pa·tel'lar

pat'ent

pat'ent·a·ble

pat'ent·ed

pat'ent·ee'

pa'ter·fa·mil'i·as

pa·ter'nal

pa·ter'nal·ism

pa·ter'nal·is'tic

pa·ter'nal·ly

pa·ter'ni·ty

path

pa·thet'ic

pa·thet'i·cal·ly

path'less

pa·thol'o·gist

pa·thol'o·gy

pa'thos

path'way'

pa'tience

pa'tient

pat'i·na

pa'ti·o

pat'ness

pat'ois

pa'tri·arch

pa'tri·ar'chal

pa'tri·arch'ate

pa'tri·arch'y

pa·tri'cian

pat'ri·cide

pat'ri·mo'ni·al

pat'ri·mo'ny

pa'tri·ot

pa'tri·ot'ic

pa'tri·ot'i·cal·ly

pa'tri·ot·ism

pa·tris'tic

pa·trol'

pa·trolled'

pa·trol'man

pa'tron

pa'tron·age

pa'tron·ess

pa'tron·ize

pa'tron·ized	pay	peb'bled
pat'ro·nym'ic	pay'a·ble	peb'ble·ware'
pa·troon'	pay'day'	peb'bly
pat'ted	pay'ee'	pe·can'
pat'ten	pay'ees'	pec'ca·dil'lo
pat'ter	pay'er	pec'can·cy
pat'tered	pay'mas'ter	pec'cant
pat'tern	pay'ment	pec'ca·ry
pat'terned	pay'roll'	peck
pau'ci·ty	pea	pec'tase
Paul'ist	peace	pec'tin
paunch	peace'a·ble	pec'to·ral
paunch'i·ness	peace'a·bly	pec'u·late
pau'per	peace'ful	pec'u·lat'ed
pau'per·ism	peace'mak'er	pec'u·la'tion
pau'per·i·za'tion	peach	pec'u·la'tor
pau'per·ize	pea'cock'	pe·cul'iar
pau'per·ized	peak	pe·cu'li·ar'i·ty
pause	peaked	pe·cul'iar·ly
paused	peal	pe·cu'ni·ar'y
pave	pealed	ped'a·gog'ic
paved	pea'nut'	ped'a·gog'i·cal
pave'ment	pear	ped'a·gog'i·cal·ly
pav'er	pearl	ped'a·gogue
pa·vil'lion	pearl'ite	ped'a·go'gy
paw	pearl'y	ped'al
pawed	peas'ant	ped'aled
pawl	peas'ant·ry	ped'ant
pawn	pea'shoot'er	pe·dan'tic
pawn'bro'ker	peat	pe·dan'ti·cal
pawned	pea'vey	pe·dan'ti·cism
pawn'shop'	peb'ble	ped'ant·ry

ped'dle	pelf	pen'e·trat'ed
ped'dled	pel'i·can	pen'e·trat'ing·ly
ped'dler	pe·lisse'	pen'e·tra'tion
ped'es·tal	pel·la'gra	pen'e·tra'tive
pe·des'tri·an	pel'let	pen'guin
pe·des'tri·an·ism	pel·lu'cid	pen'hold'er
pe'di·a·tri'cian	pe·lo'ta	pen'i·cil'lin
pe'di·at'rics	pelt	pen·in'su·la
pe·dic'u·lar	pelt'ed	pen·in'su·lar
pe·dic'u·lo'sis	pel'try	pen'i·tence
ped'i·cure	pel'vic	pen'i·tent
ped'i·gree	pel'vis	pen'i·ten'tial
ped'i·greed	pem'mi·can	pen'i·ten'tial·ly
ped'i·ment	pen	pen'i·ten'tia·ry
pe·dom'e·ter	pe'nal	pen'i·tent·ly
peek	pe'nal·i·za'tion	pen'knife'
peel	pe'nal·ize	pen'man
peeled	pe'nal·ized	pen'man·ship
peel'ings	pen'al·ty	pen'nant
peen	pen'ance	pen'ni·less
peep	pen'chant'	pen'non
peer	pen'cil	pen'ny
peer'age	pen'ciled	pen'ny·roy'al
peered	pend'ant	pen'ny·weight'
peer'less	pend'en·cy	pe·nol'o·gist
pee'vish	pend'ing	pe·nol'o·gy
peg	pen'du·lous	pen'sion
Peg'a·sus	pen'du·lum	pen'sion·ar'y
pegged	pen'e·tra·bil'i·ty	pen'sioned
pe'jo·ra'tive	pen'e·tra·ble	pen'sion·er
pe'koe	pen'e·trant	pen'sive
pe·lag'ic	pen'e·trate	pen'stock'

pent	per·bo'rate	per·en'ni·al·ly
pen'ta·gon	per·cale'	per'fect
pen·tag'o·nal	per·ceiv'a·ble	per·fect'ed
pen·tam'e·ter	per·ceive'	per·fect'i·bil'i·ty
Pen'ta·teuch	per·ceived'	per·fect'i·ble
pen·tath'lon	per cent	per·fec'tion
pen'ta·ton'ic	per·cent'age	per·fec'tion·ism
Pen'te·cost	per·cen'tile	per·fec'tion·ist
pent'house'	per'cept	per'fect·ly
pent·ox'ide	per·cep'ti·bil'i·ty	per·fec'to
pe'nult	per·cep'ti·ble	per·fid'i·ous
pe·nul'ti·mate	per·cep'tion	per'fi·dy
pe·num'bra	per·cep'tive	per'fo·rate
pe·nu'ri·ous	per·cep'tu·al	per'fo·rat'ed
pen'u·ry	per·cep'tu·al·ly	per'fo·ra'tion
pe'on	perch	per'fo·ra'tive
pe'on·age	per·chance'	per'fo·ra'tor
pe'o·ny	per·cip'i·en·cy	per·force'
peo'ple	per·cip'i·ent	per·form'
peo'pled	per'co·late	per·form'a·ble
pep'lum	per'co·la'tion	per·form'ance
pep'per	per'co·la'tor	per·formed'
pep'pered	per·cus'sion	per·form'er
pep'per·i·ness	per·cus'sive	per·fume'
pep'per·mint	per·di'tion	per·fumed'
pep'per·y	per·du'	per·fum'er
pep'sin	per·dur'a·ble	per·fum'er·y
pep'tic	per'e·gri·na'tion	per·func'to·ri·ly
pep'tone	per·emp'to·ri·ly	per·func'to·ri·ness
per'ad·ven'ture	per·emp'to·ri·ness	per·func'to·ry
per·am'bu·late	per·emp'to·ry	per·fuse'
per·am'bu·la'tor	per·en'ni·al	per·fused'

per′go·la

per·haps′

per′i·car′di·al

per′i·car·di′tis

per′i·car′di·um

per′il

per′il·ous

per′il·ous·ly

per·im′e·ter

pe′ri·od

per·i′o·date

pe′ri·od′ic

pe′ri·od′i·cal

pe′ri·od′i·cal·ly

pe′ri·o·dic′i·ty

per′i·os′te·um

per′i·pa·tet′ic

pe·riph′er·al

pe·riph′er·al·ly

pe·riph′er·y

per′i·phras′tic

per′i·scope

per′i·scop′ic

per′ish

per′ish·a·ble

per′ished

per′i·stal′sis

per′i·stal′tic

per′i·stal′ti·cal·ly

per′i·style′

per′i·to·ne′um

per′i·to·ni′tis

per′i·win′kle

per′jure

per′jured

per′jur·er

per·ju′ri·ous·ly

per′ju·ry

perk′y

perm′al·loy′

per′ma·nence

per′ma·nent

per′ma·nent·ly

per·man′ga·nate

per′me·a·bil′i·ty

per′me·a·ble

per′me·ate

per′me·at′ed

per′me·a′tion

per·mis′si·bil′i·ty

per·mis′si·ble

per·mis′sion

per·mis′sive

per·mit′

per·mit′ted

per′mu·ta′tion

per·mute′

per·mut′ed

per·ni′cious

per′o·ra′tion

per·ox′ide

per′pen·dic′u·lar

per′pen·dic′u·lar′i·ty

per′pe·trate

per′pe·trat′ed

per′pe·tra′tion

per′pe·tra′tor

per·pet′u·al

per·pet′u·al·ly

per·pet′u·ate

per·pet′u·at′ed

per·pet′u·a′tion

per·pet′u·a′tor

per′pe·tu′i·ty

per·plex′

per·plexed′

per·plex′ed·ly

per·plex′ing·ly

per·plex′i·ty

per′qui·site

per′qui·si′tion

per′se·cute

per′se·cut′ed

per′se·cu′tion

per′se·cu′tor

per′se·ver′ance

per·sev′er·a′tion

per′se·vere′

per′se·vered′

per′si·flage

per·sim′mon

per·sist′

per·sist′ence

per·sist′en·cy

per·sist′ent

per·sist′ing·ly

per'son

per'son·a·ble

per'son·age

per'son·al

per'son·al'i·ty

per'son·al·ize

per'son·al·ly

per'son·al·ty

per·son'i·fi·ca'tion

per·son'i·fied

per·son'i·fy

per'son·nel'

per·spec'tive

per'spi·ca'cious

per'spi·cac'i·ty

per·spic'u·ous

per'spi·ra'tion

per·spir'a·to·ry

per·spire'

per·spired'

per·suade'

per·suad'ed

per·suad'er

per·sua'sion

per·sua'sive

per·sua'sive·ness

per·sul'phate

pert

per·tain'

per·tained'

per'ti·na'cious

per'ti·nac'i·ty

per'ti·nence

per'ti·nent

per·turb'

per·turb'a·ble

per'tur·ba'tion

per·turbed'

pe·rus'al

pe·ruse'

pe·rused'

Pe·ru'vi·an

per·vade'

per·vad'ed

per·vad'ing·ly

per·va'sion

per·va'sive

per·verse'

per·ver'sion

per·ver'si·ty

per·ver'sive

per·vert'

per·vert'ed

per'vi·ous

pes'si·mism

pes'si·mist

pes'si·mis'tic

pes'si·mis'ti·cal·ly

pest

pes'ter

pes'tered

pest'hole'

pest'house'

pes·tif'er·ous

pes'ti·lence

pes'ti·lent

pes'ti·len'tial

pes'ti·len'tial·ly

pes'tle

pet

pet'al

pe·tard'

pe·tite'

pe·ti'tion

pe·ti'tioned

pe·ti'tion·er

pet'rel

pet'ri·fac'tion

pet'ri·fac'tive

pet'ri·fy

pet'rol

pet'ro·la'tum

pe·tro'le·um

pe·trol'o·gy

pet'ted

pet'ti·coat

pet'ti·er

pet'ti·est

pet'ti·fog'ger

pet'ti·ly

pet'ti·ness

pet'tish

pet'ty

pet'u·lance

pet'u·lant

pe·tu'ni·a

pew	phil'an·throp'i·cal	phon'ic
pew'ter	phi·lan'thro·pist	pho'no·graph
pha'e·ton	phi·lan'thro·py	phos'phate
phag'o·cyte	phil'a·tel'ic	phos'phide
phal'ange	phi·lat'e·list	phos'phite
phal'an·ster'y	phi·lat'e·ly	phos'pho·resce'
pha'lanx	phil'har·mon'ic	phos'pho·res'cence
phan'tasm	phi·lip'pic	phos·phor'ic
phan·tas'ma·go'ri·a	Phil'ip·pine	phos'pho·rous
phan'tom	Phil·is'tine	phos'pho·rus
Phar'aoh	phi·lol'o·gist	pho'to·cop'i·er
phar'ma·ceu'tic	phi·lol'o·gy	pho'to·e·lec'tric
phar'ma·ceu'ti·cal	phi·los'o·pher	pho'to·en·grav'ing
phar'ma·ceu'tics	phil'o·soph'ic	pho'to·gen'ic
phar'ma·cist	phil'o·soph'i·cal	pho'to·graph
phar'ma·col'o·gy	phi·los'o·phize	pho'to·graphed
phar'ma·co·poe'ia	phi·los'o·phy	pho·tog'ra·pher
phar'ma·cy	phil'ter	pho'to·graph'ic
phar'yn·gi'tis	phle·bi'tis	pho·tog'ra·phy
phar'ynx	phle·bot'o·my	pho'to·gra·vure'
phase	phlegm	pho'to·lith'o·graph
phased	phleg·mat'ic	pho'to·mi'cro·graph
pheas'ant	phleg·mat'i·cal·ly	pho'ton
phe'nol	phlo'em	pho'to·play'
phe·nom'e·na	phlox	pho'to·sen'si·tize
phe·nom'e·nal	pho'bi·a	Pho'to·stat
phe·nom'e·nol'o·gy	phoe'nix	pho'to·syn'the·sis
phe·nom'e·non	phone	phrase
phi'al	pho·net'ic	phrased
phi·lan'der	pho·net'i·cal·ly	phra'se·ol'o·gy
phi·lan'der·er	pho·ne·ti'cian	phre·net'ic
phil'an·throp'ic	pho·net'ics	phren'ic

phre·nol'o·gist

phre·nol'o·gy

phthi'sis

phy·lac'ter·y

phys'ic

phys'i·cal

phys'i·cal·ly

phy·si'cian

phys'i·cist

phys'ics

phys'i·og'no·my

phys'i·o·log'i·cal

phys'i·o·log'i·cal·ly

phys'i·ol'o·gy

phy·sique'

pi'a·nis'si·mo

pi·an'ist

pi·a'no

pi·an'o·for'te

pi·az'za

pi'ca

pic'a·resque'

pic'co·lo

pick

pick'ax

picked

pick'er

pick'er·el

pick'et

pick'et·ed

pick'ings

pick'le

pick'led

pick'lock'

pick'pock'et

pick'up'

pic'nic

pic'nick·er

pic'ric

pic'to·graph

pic·to'ri·al

pic·to'ri·al·ly

pic'ture

pic'tured

pic'tur·esque'

pie

pie'bald'

piece

piece'meal'

piece'work'

pie'crust'

pied

pie'plant'

pier

pierce

pierced

pi'e·ty

pig

pi'geon

pi'geon·hole'

pig'fish'

pig'ger·y

pig'gish

pig'head'ed

pig'let

pig'ment

pig'men·tar'y

pig'men·ta'tion

pig'ment·ed

pig'nut'

pig'pen'

pig'skin'

pig'stick'er

pig'sty'

pig'tail'

pig'weed'

pike

pik'er

pike'staff'

pi·las'ter

pil'chard

pile

piled

pile'work'

pile'worm'

pil'fer

pil'fer·age

pil'fered

pil'fer·ings

pil'grim

pil'grim·age

pill

pil'lage

pil'laged

pil'lar

pil'lion

pil'lo·ry

pil'low

pil'low·case'

pil'lowed

pi'lot

pi'lot·ed

pi·men'to

pim'per·nel

pim'ple

pin

pin'a·fore'

pin'cers

pinch

pinched

pin'cush'ion

pine

pine'ap'ple

pined

pin'feath'er

pin'fish'

ping'-pong'

pin'guid

pin'hole'

pin'ion

pink

pink'ish

pink'weed'

pink'wood'

pin'nace

pin'na·cle

pinned

pi'noch'le

pin'prick'

pint

pin'to

pin'weed'

pin'worm'

pi'o·neer'

pi'o·neered'

pi'ous

pi'ous·ly

pip

pip'age

pipe

piped

pipe'line'

pip'er

pipe'stem'

pipe'stone'

pi·pette'

pipe'wood'

pip'ing·ly

pip'ings

pip'it

pip'kin

pip·sis'se·wa

pi'quan·cy

pi'quant

pique

pi·qué'

piqued

pi'ra·cy

pi'rate

pi'rat·ed

pi·rat'ic

pi·rat'i·cal

pi·rogue'

pir'ou·ette'

pir·ou·et'ted

pis'ca·tol'o·gy

pis'ca·to'ri·al

pis'ca·to'ri·al·ly

pis·tach'i·o

pis'tol

pis·tole'

pis'ton

pit

pitch

pitched

pitch'er

pitch'fork'

pit'e·ous

pit'e·ous·ness

pit'fall'

pith

pith'i·ly

pith'i·ness

pith'y

pit'i·a·ble

pit'i·ful

pit'i·less

pit'i·less·ly

pit'i·less·ness

pit'tance

pit'ted

pi·tu'i·tar'y

pit′y		plain′ly		plas′ma	
pit′y·ing·ly		plain′ness		plas′ter	
piv′ot		plaint		plas′tered	
piv′ot·al		plain′tiff		plas′ter·er	
piv′ot·ed		plain′tive		plas′ter·work′	
pla′ca·bil′i·ty		plait		plas′tic	
pla′ca·ble		plait′ed		plas·tic′i·ty	
plac′ard		plait′ings		plas′tron	
pla′cate		plan		plate	
pla′cat·ed		plan·chette′		pla·teau′	
pla′ca·tive·ly		plane		plat′ed	
pla′ca·to′ry		plan′et		plate′hold′er	
place		plan′e·tar′i·an		plate′let	
pla·ce′bo		plan′e·tar′i·um		plat′en	
place′man		plan′e·tar′y		plat′er	
place′ment		plan′et·oid		plat′form′	
pla·cen′ta		plan′gent		plat′i·na	
plac′er		plan′i·sphere		plat′i·nate	
plac′id		plank		plat′ings	
pla·cid′i·ty		planked		pla·tin′ic	
plac′id·ly		plank′ton		plat′i·nize	
plack′et		plan′less		plat′i·noid	
pla′gi·a·rism		planned		plat′i·num	
pla′gi·a·rist		pla′no·graph′ic		plat′i·tude	
pla′gi·a·rize		plant		plat′i·tu′di·nize	
pla′gi·a·ry		plan′tain		plat′i·tu′di-nous	
plague		plan′tar		pla·toon′	
plagued		plan·ta′tion		plat′ter	
plaid		plant′ed		plat′y·pus	
plain		plant′er		plau′dit	
plain′er		plant′ings		plau′si·bil′i·ty	
plain′est		plaque		plau′si·ble	

play	pleat	plinth
play'back'	ple·be'ian	plod
play'bill'	pleb'i·scite	plod'ded
play'boy'	pledge	plod'der
played	pledged	plod'ding·ly
play'er	pledg'ee'	plot
play'ful	pledge'or'	plot'ted
play'ful·ness	pledg'er	plot'ter
play'ground'	pledg'et	plough
play'ings	ple'na·ri·ly	plov'er
play'mate'	ple'na·ry	plow
play'read'er	plen'i·po·ten'ti·ar'y	plow'boy
play'room'	plen'i·tude	plow'ings
play'script'	plen'te·ous	plow'man
play'thing'	plen'ti·ful	plow'share'
play'time'	plen'ty	pluck
play'wright'	ple'num	plucked
pla'za	ple'o·nasm	pluck'i·er
plea	ple'o·nas'tic	pluck'i·est
plead	pleth'o·ra	pluck'i·ly
plead'ed	ple·thor'ic	pluck'i·ness
plead'er	pleu'ra	pluck'y
plead'ing·ly	pleu'ral	plug
plead'ings	pleu'ri·sy	plugged
pleas'ant	plex'us	plum
pleas'ant·ly	pli'a·bil'i·ty	plum'age
pleas'ant·ness	pli'a·ble	plumb
pleas'ant·ry	pli'an·cy	plum·ba'go
please	pli'ant	plum'bate
pleased	pli'ers	plumbed
pleas'ur·a·ble	plight	plumb'er
pleas'ure	plight'ed	plum'bic

plum'bous	plu·to'ni·um	point'less
plume	ply	point'less·ly
plumed	pneu·mat'ic	poise
plum'met	pneu·mat'i·cal·ly	poised
plum'met·ed	pneu·mat'ics	poi'son
plump	pneu·mo'ni·a	poi'soned
plump'er	poach	poi'son·er
plump'est	poach'er	poi'son·ous
plump'ly	pock'et	poke
plump'ness	pock'et·book'	poked
plun'der	pock'et·knife'	pok'er
plun'dered	pock'mark'	poke'weed'
plun'der·er	pod	po'lar
plunge	po·dag'ra	po·lar'i·ty
plunged	po·di'a·try	po'lar·i·za'tion
plung'er	po'di·um	po'lar·ize
plunk	po'em	po'lar·ized
plunked	po'e·sy	po'lar·iz'er
plu'ral	po'et	pole
plu'ral·ism	po'et·as'ter	pole'cat'
plu'ral·ist	po·et'ic	po·lem'ic
plu·ral·is'tic	po·et'i·cal	po·lem'i·cal
plu·ral'i·ty	po'et·ry	po·lem'i·cist
plu'ral·ize	po'i	po·lem'ics
plu'ral·ized	poign'an·cy	pole'star'
plus	poign'ant	po·lice'
plush	poin·ci·an'a	po·liced'
plu·toc'ra·cy	poin·set'ti·a	po·lice'man
plu'to·crat	point	pol'i·cy
plu'to·crat'ic	point'ed	pol'ish
plu'to·crat'i·cal·ly	point'ed·ly	pol'ished
plu·ton'ic	point'er	pol'ish·er

po·lite′	pol′y·gon	pon′der·os′i·ty
po·lite′ly	po·lyg′o·nal	pon′der·ous
po·lite′ness	pol′y·mer′ic	pond′fish′
pol′i·tic	po·lym′er·ism	pond′weed′
po·lit′i·cal	pol′y·mer·i·za′tion	pon·gee′
po·lit′i·cal·ly	pol′y·mer·ize	pon′iard
pol′i·ti′cian	pol′y·no′mi·al	pon′tiff
pol′i·tics	pol′yp	pon·tif′i·cal
pol′ka	po·lyph′o·ny	pon·tif′i·cal·ly
poll	pol′y·syl·lab′ic	pon·tif′i·cate
pol′lard	pol′y·tech′nic	pon·toon′
pol′lard·ed	po·made′	po′ny
polled	po′man·der	poo′dle
pol′len	po·ma′tum	pool
pol′li·nate	pome′gran′ate	pooled
pol′li·na′tion	Pom′er·a′ni·an	pool′room′
pol′li·nif′er·ous	pom′mel	poor
pol·lute′	pom′meled	poor′er
pol·lut′ed	po·mol′o·gy	poor′est
pol·lu′tion	pomp	poor′house′
po′lo	pom′pa·dour	poor′ly
pol′o·naise′	pom′pa·no	poor′ness
po·lo′ni·um	Pom·pe′ian	pop
pol·troon′	pom′pon	pop′corn′
pol′y·an′drous	pom·pos′i·ty	pop′gun′
pol′y·an′dry	pomp′ous	pop′in·jay
pol′y·chrome	pon′cho	pop′lar
pol′y·clin′ic	pond	pop′lin
po·lyg′a·mist	pon′der	pop′o′ver
po·lyg′a·mous	pon′der·a·ble	popped
po·lyg′a·my	pon′dered	pop′pet
pol′y·glot	pon′der·o′sa	pop′py

pop'u·lace	por·ten'tous	pos'si·bil'i·ty
pop'u·lar	por'ter	pos'si·ble
pop'u·lar'i·ty	por'ter·house'	pos'si·bly
pop'u·lar·i·za'tion	port·fo'li·o	pos'sum
pop'u·lar·ize	port'hole'	post
pop'u·lar·ized	por'ti·co	post'age
pop'u·late	por·tiere'	post'al
pop'u·lat'ed	por'tion	post'box'
pop·u·la'tion	por'tioned	post'date'
pop'u·lous	port·man'teau	post'dat'ed
por'ce·lain	por'trait	post'ed
porch	por'trait·ist	post'er
por'cu·pine	por'trai·ture	pos·te'ri·or
pore	por·tray'	pos·ter'i·ty
pored	por·tray'al	pos'tern
por'gy	por·trayed'	post·grad'u·ate
pork	Por'tu·guese	post'haste'
por·nog'ra·phy	por'tu·la'ca	post'hole'
po·ros'i·ty	pose	post'hu·mous
po'rous	posed	pos·til'ion
por'phy·ry	po·si'tion	post'im·pres'sion·ism
por'poise	pos'i·tive	post'ings
por'ridge	pos'i·tiv·ism	post'lude
por'rin·ger	pos'i·tiv·is'tic	post'man
port	pos'i·tron	post·mar'i·tal
port'a·ble	pos'se	post'mark'
por'tage	pos·sess'	post'mas'ter
por'tal	pos·sessed'	post'me·rid'i·an
port·cul'lis	pos·ses'sion	post'mis'tress
por·tend'	pos·ses'sive	post'-mor'tem
por·tend'ed	pos·ses'sor	post·nup'tial
por'tent	pos·ses'sor·ship	post'op'er·a·tive

post'paid'	pot'house'	pow'ered
post·pone'	po'tion	pow'er·ful
post·poned'	pot'latch'	pow'er·ful·ly
post·pone'ment	pot'luck'	pow'er·less
post·pran'di·al	pot'pie'	pow'er·less·ly
post'script	pot'pour'ri'	pow'er·less·ness
pos'tu·lant	pot'sherd'	pow'wow'
pos'tu·late	pot'tage	prac'ti·ca·bil'i·ty
pos'tu·lat'ed	pot'ter	prac'ti·ca·ble
pos'tu·la'tion	pot'ter·y	prac'ti·ca·bly
pos'ture	pouch	prac'ti·cal
pos'tured	poult	prac'ti·cal'i·ty
pos'tur·ings	poul'ter·er	prac'ti·cal·ly
po'sy	poul'tice	prac'tice
pot	poul'ticed	prac'ticed
po·ta·bil'i·ty	poul'try	prac'ti·cum
po'ta·ble	pounce	prac·ti'tion·er
pot'ash'	pounced	prag·mat'ic
po·tas'si·um	pound	prag·mat'i·cal
po·ta'tion	pound'age	prag·mat'i-cal·ly
po·ta'to	pound'cake'	prag'ma·tism
pot'boil'er	pound'ed	prag'ma·tist
po'ten·cy	pound'ings	prai'rie
po'tent	pour	praise
po'ten·tate	poured	praised
po·ten'tial	pout	praise'wor·thy
po·ten'ti·al'i·ty	pout'ed	pra'line
po·ten'tial·ly	pov'er·ty	prance
po·ten'ti·om'e·ter	pow'der	pranced
pot'herb'	pow'dered	pranc'ing·ly
pot'hole'	pow'der·y	prank
pot'hook'	pow'er	prank'ster

prate	pre·cep'tress	pre·cool'
prat'ed	pre·ces'sion	pre·cur'sor
prat'ings	pre·chill'	pre·cur'so·ry
pra·tique'	pre'cinct	pre·da'ceous
prat'tle	pre'ci·os'i·ty	pre·dac'i·ty
prat'tling·ly	pre'cious	pre·date'
prawn	pre'cious·ly	pre·da'tion
pray	prec'i·pice	pred'a·tive
prayed	pre·cip'i·tan·cy	pred'a·tor
prayer	pre·cip'i·tant	pred'a·to'ry
prayer'ful	pre·cip'i·tate	pre'de·cease'
prayer'ful·ly	pre·cip'i·tat'ed	pred'e·ces'sor
preach	pre·cip'i·tate·ly	pre'de·cide'
preached	pre·cip'i·ta'tion	pre·des'ig·nat'ed
preach'er	pre·cip'i·tous	pre'des·ig·na'tion
preach'ment	pré·cis'	pre·des'ti·nar'i·an
preach'y	pre·cise'	pre·des'ti·nar-i·an·ism
pre'ad·o·les'cent	pré·cised'	pre·des'ti·na'tion
pre'am'ble	pre·cise'ly	pre·des'tine
pre'ar·range'	pre·cise'ness	pre·des'tined
pre'ar·range'ment	pre·ci'sion	pre'de·ter'mi·nant
preb'en·dar'y	pre·ci'sion·ist	pre'de·ter'mi·nate
pre·can'celed	pre·clin'i·cal	pre'de·ter'mi·na·tion
pre·car'i·ous	pre·clude'	pre'de·ter'mine
pre·cau'tion	pre·clud'ed	pre'de·ter'mined
pre·cau'tion·ar'y	pre·clu'sion	pre'di·as·tol'ic
pre·cede'	pre·co'cious	pre·dic'a·ment
pre·ced'ed	pre·co'cious·ly	pred'i·cate
pre·ced'ence	pre·coc'i·ty	pred'i·cat'ed
prec'e·dent	pre·con·ceived'	pred'i·ca'tion
pre'cept	pre'con·cep'tion	pred'i·ca'tive
pre·cep'tor	pre·cook'	pre·dict'

pre·dict'a·ble

pre·dict'ed

pre·dic'tion

pre·dic'tion·al

pre·dic'tive

pre'di·gest'

pre'di·gest'ed

pre'di·ges'tion

pre'di·lec'tion

pre'dis·clo'sure

pre'dis·pose'

pre'dis·posed'

pre'dis·po·si'tion

pre·dom'i·nance

pre·dom'i·nant

pre·dom'i·nate

pre·dom'i·nat'ed

pre·dom'i·nate·ly

pre·dom'i·nat'ing·ly

pre·draft'

pre·dry'

pre-em'i·nence

pre-em'i·nent

pre-empt'

pre-empt'ed

pre-emp'tion

pre-emp'tive

preen

preened

pre-es'ti·mate

pre'-ex·ist'

pre'-ex·ist'ent

pref'ace

pref'aced

pre·fash'ion

pref'a·to'ry

pre'fect

pre'fec·ture

pre·fer'

pref'er·a·ble

pref'er·a·bly

pref'er·ence

pref'er·en'tial

pref'er·en'tial·ly

pre·fer'ment

pre·ferred'

pre·fig'ure

pre·fig'ured

pre'fix

pre'fix·al

pre·fixed'

pre·form'

pre·formed'

pre·gath'er

preg'nan·cy

preg'nant

pre·har'vest

pre·hen'sile

pre'hen·sil'i·ty

pre'his·tor'ic

pre'im·ag'ine

pre'in·au'gu·ral

pre'in·cline'

pre'in·clined'

pre·in'ven·to'ry

pre·judge'

pre·judged'

prej'u·diced

prej'u·di'cial

prej'u·di'cial·ly

prel'a·cy

prel'ate

pre·lim'i·nar'y

pre·lit'er·ate

prel'ude

pre'ma·ter'ni·ty

pre'ma·ture'

pre·med'i·cal

pre·med'i·tate

pre·med'i-tat'ed

pre·med·i·ta'tion

pre'mi·er

prem'ise

prem'is·es

pre'mi·um

pre'mo·ni'tion

pre·mon'i·to'ry

pre·na'tal

pre·na'tal·ly

pre·oc'cu·pa'tion

pre·oc'cu·pied

pre·oc'cu·py

pre·op'er·a·tive

pre'or·dain'

pre'or·dained'

pre·paid'

prep'a·ra'tion

pre·par'a·tive

pre·par'a·to'ry

pre·pare'

pre·pared'

pre·par'ed·ness

pre·pay'

pre·pay'ment

pre·pense'

pre·pon'der·ance

pre·pon'der·ant

pre·pon'der·ate

pre·pon'der·at'ing·ly

prep'o·si'tion

prep'o·si'tion·al

pre'pos·sess'

pre'pos·ses'sion

pre·pos'ter·ous

pre·print'·

pre're·lease'

pre·req'ui·site

pre·rog'a·tive

pre·sage'

pre·saged'

pres'by·ter

Pres'by·te'ri·an

pres'by·ter'y

pre'sci·ence

pre'sci·ent

pre·scribe'

pre·scribed'

pre·scrip'tion

pre·scrip'tive

pres'ence

pres'ent

pre·sent'a·bil'i·ty

pre·sent'a·ble

pres'en·ta'tion

pre·sent'ed

pre·sen'ti·ment

pres'ent·ly

pre·sent'ment

pres'er·va'tion

pre·serv'a·tive

pre·serve'

pre·serv'er

pre·side'

pre·sid'ed

pres'i·den·cy

pres'i·dent

pres'i·den'tial

press

press'board'

pressed

pres'sings

press'man

press'room'

pres'sure

press'work'

pres'ti·dig'i·ta'tor

pres·tige'

pres·tig'i·ous

pres'to

pre·sum'a·ble

pre·sume'

pre·sumed'

pre·sum'ed·ly

pre·sump'tion

pre·sump'tive

pre·sump'tu·ous

pre'sup·pose'

pre'sys·tol'ic

pre·tend'

pre·tend'ed

pre·tend'er

pre·tense'

pre·ten'sion

pre·ten'tious

pre·ten'tious·ly

pre·ten'tious·ness

pret'er·it

pre'ter·mit'

pre'ter·mit'ted

pre'ter·nat'u·ral

pre'text

pret'ti·er

pret'ti·est

pret'ti·ly

pret'ti·ness

pret'ty

pret'zel

pre·vail'

pre·vailed'

pre·vail'ing·ly

prev'a·lence

prev'a·lent

prev′a·lent·ly

pre·var′i·cate

pre·var′i·cat′ed

pre·var′i·ca′tion

pre·var′i·ca′tor

pre·vent′

pre·vent′a·bil′i·ty

pre·vent′a·ble

pre·vent′ed

pre·ven′tion

pre·ven′tive

pre′view′

pre′vi·ous

pre·vi′sion

pre·vo·ca′tion·al

prey

price

priced

price′less

prick

pricked

prick′le

prick′led

prick′li·ness

prick′ly

pride

pride′ful

priest

priest′ess

priest′hood

priest′ly

prig′gish

prim

pri′ma·cy

pri′mal

pri′ma·ri·ly

pri′ma·ry

pri′mate

pri′mate·ship

prime

primed

prim′er

pri·me′val

prim′i·tive

prim′i·tiv·ism

prim′ly

prim′ness

pri′mo·gen′i·ture

pri·mor′di·al

prim′rose′

prince

prince′li·ness

prince′ling

prince′ly

prin′ces

prin′cess

prin′ci·pal

prin′ci·pal′i·ty

prin′ci·pal·ly

prin′ci·ple

prin′ci·pled

print

print′a·ble

print′ed

print′er

print′er·y

print′ings

pri′or

pri·or′i·ty

pri′o·ry

prism

pris·mat′ic

pris′on

pris′on·er

pris′tine

pri′va·cy

pri′vate

pri′va·teer′

pri′vate·ly

pri′vate·ness

pri·va′tion

priv′et

priv′i·lege

priv′i·ly

priv′i·ty

priv′y

prize

prized

prob′a·bil′i·ty

prob′a·ble

prob′a·bly

pro′bate

pro·ba′tion

pro·ba′tion·ar′y

probe

prob′i·ty

prob'lem

prob'lem·at'ic

pro·bos'cis

pro·ce'dur·al

pro·ce'dure

pro·ceed'

pro·ceed'ed

pro·ceed'ings

proc'ess

proc'essed

proc'ess·es

pro·ces'sion

pro·ces'sion·al

pro·claim'

pro·claimed'

proc'la·ma'tion

pro·cliv'i·ty

pro·con'sul

pro·cras'ti·nate

pro·cras'ti·nat'ed

pro·cras'ti·na'tion

pro·cras'ti·na'tor

pro·cre·a'tion

pro·cre·a'tive

proc'tor

pro·cur'a·ble

proc'u·ra'tion

proc'u·ra'tor

pro·cure'

pro·cured'

pro·cure'ment

prod

prod'ded

prod'i·gal

prod'i·gal'i·ty

prod'i·gal·ly

pro·di'gious

pro·di'gious·ly

prod'i·gy

pro·duce'

pro·duced'

pro·duc'er

prod'uct

pro·duc'tion

pro·duc'tive

pro'duc·tiv'i·ty

pro'em

prof'a·na'tion

pro·fan'a·to'ry

pro·fane'

pro·faned'

pro·fan'i·ty

pro·fess'

pro·fessed'

pro·fess'ed·ly

pro·fes'sion

pro·fes'sion·al

pro·fes'sion·al·ism

pro·fes'sion·al·ize

pro·fes'sion·al·ly

pro·fes'sor

pro'fes·so'ri·al

pro·fes'sor·ship

prof'fer

prof'fered

pro·fi'cien·cy

pro·fi'cient

pro·fi'cient·ly

pro'file

prof'it

prof'it·a·ble

prof'it·a·bly

prof'it·ed

prof'it·eer'

prof'it·less

prof'li·ga·cy

prof'li·gate

pro·found'

pro·found'ness

pro·fun'di·ty

pro·fuse'

pro·fuse'ly

pro·fuse'ness

pro·fu'sion

pro·gen'i·tor

prog'e·ny

prog·no'sis

prog·nos'tic

prog·nos'ti·cate

prog·nos'ti-
cat'ed

prog·nos'ti-
,ca'tion

pro'gram

pro'gramed

pro·gress'

pro·gressed'

pro·gres'sion

pro·gres′sive	pro·mis′cu·ous·ly	pro·nounce′ment
pro·hib′it	pro·mis′cu·ous·ness	pro·nun′ci·a′tion
pro·hib′it·ed	prom′ise	proof
pro′hi·bi′tion	prom′ised	proofed
pro′hi·bi′tion·ist	prom′is·ing·ly	prop
pro·hib′i·tive	prom′is·so′ry	prop′a·gan′da
pro·hib′i·to′ry	prom′on·to′ry	prop′a·gan′dist
pro·ject′	pro·mote′	prop′a·gate
pro·ject′ed	pro·mot′ed	prop′a·gat′ed
pro·jec′tile	pro·mot′er	prop′a·ga′tion
pro·jec′tion	pro·mo′tion	pro·pel′
pro·jec′tive	pro·mo′tion·al	pro·pel′lant
pro·jec′tor	prompt	pro·pelled′
pro′le·tar′i·an	prompt′ed	pro·pel′ler
pro′le·tar′i·at	prompt′er	pro·pen′si·ty
pro·lif′er·ate	prompt′est	prop′er
pro·lif′er·a′tion	promp′ti·tude	prop′er·ly
pro·lif′ic	prompt′ly	prop′er·ty
pro·lif′i·ca′tion	prompt′ness	proph′e·cy
pro·lix′	pro·mul′gate	proph′e·sied
pro·lix′i·ty	pro·mul′gat·ed	proph′e·sy
pro′logue	pro′mul·ga′tion	proph′et
pro·long′	pro′nate	pro·phet′ic
pro·lon′gate	pro·na′tion	pro·phet′i·cal·ly
pro′lon·ga′tion	prone	pro′phy·lac′tic
pro·longed′	prong	pro′phy·lax′is
prom′e·nade′	prong′horn′	pro·pin′qui·ty
prom′e·nad′ed	pro·nom′i·nal	pro·pi′ti·ate
prom′i·nence	pro′noun	pro·pi′ti·at′ed
prom′i·nent	pro·nounce′	pro·pi′ti·a′tion
prom′is·cu′i·ty	pro·nounce′a·ble	pro·pi′ti·a·to′ry
pro·mis′cu·ous	pro·nounced′	pro·pi′tious

pro·po'nent	pro·scribe'	pros·tra'tion
pro·por'tion	pro·scribed'	pros'y
pro·por'tion·a·ble	pro·scrip'tion	pro·tag'o·nist
pro·por'tion·al	prose	pro'te·an
pro·por'tion·al·ly	pros'e·cute	pro·tect'
pro·por'tion·ate	pros'e·cut·ed	pro·tect'ed
pro·por'tion·ate·ly	pros'e·cu'tion	pro·tect'ing·ly
pro·por'tioned	pros'e·cu'tor	pro·tec'tion
pro·pos'al	pros'e·lyte	pro·tec'tion·ism
pro·pose'	pros'e·lyt'ed	pro·tec'tion·ist
pro·posed'	pros'e·lyt·ize	pro·tec'tive
prop'o·si'tion	pros'e·lyt·iz'er	pro·tec'tive·ly
pro·pound'	pros'i·er	pro·tec'tive·ness
pro·pound'ed	pros'i·est	pro·tec'tor
pro·pri'e·tar'y	pros'i·fy	pro·tec'tor·ate
pro·pri'e·tor	pros'i·ly	pro'té·gé
pro·pri'e·to'ri·al	pros'i·ness	pro'te·in
pro·pri'e·to'ri·al·ly	pros'o·dy	pro·test'
pro·pri'e·tor·ship'	pros'pect	prot'es·tant
pro·pri'e·to'ry	pros'pect·ed	prot'es·ta'tion
pro·pri'e·ty	pro·spec'tive	pro·test'ed
pro·pul'sion	pros'pec·tor	pro·test'ing·ly
pro·pul'sive	pro·spec'tus	pro·thon'o·tar'y
pro'rate'	pros'per	pro'to·col
pro'rat'ed	pros'pered	pro'ton
pro·ra'tion	pros·per'i·ty	pro'to·plasm
pro'ro·ga'tion	pros'per·ous	pro'to·type
pro·rogue'	pros'per·ous·ly	pro·tox'ide
pro·rogued'	pros'the·sis	Pro'to·zo'a
pro·sa'ic	pros·thet'ic	pro·tract'
pro·sa'i·cal·ly	pros'trate	pro·tract'ed
pro·sce'ni·um	pros'trat·ed	pro·trac'tile

pro·trac'tion

pro·trac'tive

pro·trac'tor

pro·trude'

pro·trud'ed

pro·tru'sion

pro·tru'sive

pro·tu'ber·ance

pro·tu'ber·ant

proud

proud'er

proud'est

proud'ly

prov'a·ble

prove

proved

prov'en

prov'e·nance

Prov'en·çal'

prov'en·der

prov'erb

pro·ver'bi·al

pro·ver'bi·al·ly

pro·vide'

pro·vid'ed

prov'i·dence

prov'i·dent

prov'i·den'tial

prov'i·den'tial·ly

pro·vid'er

prov'ince

pro·vin'cial

pro·vin'cial·ism

pro·vin'ci·al'i·ty

pro·vin'cial·ly

pro·vi'sion

pro·vi'sion·al

pro·vi'sion·al·ly

pro·vi'so

pro·vi'so·ry

prov'o·ca'tion

pro·voc'a·tive

pro·voke'

pro·voked'

pro·vok'ing·ly

prov'ost

prow

prow'ess

prowl

prowled

prowl'er

prox'i·mal

prox'i·mal·ly

prox'i·mate

prox·im'i·ty

prox'i·mo

prox'y

prude

pru'dence

pru'dent

pru·den'tial

pru·den'tial·ly

pru'dent·ly

prud'er·y

prud'ish

prune

pruned

pru'ri·ence

pru'ri·ent

pru·ri'tus

Prus'sian

pry

pry'ing·ly

psalm

psalm'book'

psalm'ist

psal'mo·dist

psal'mo·dy

psal'ter

pseu'do·nym

pso·ri'a·sis

psy'chi·at'ric

psy'chi·at'ri·cal·ly

psy·chi'a·trist

psy·chi'a·try

psy'chic

psy'chi·cal

psy'chi·cal·ly

psy'cho·a·nal'y·sis

psy'cho·bi·ol'o·gy

psy'cho·dy·nam'ics

psy'cho·gen'e·sis

psy'cho·ge·net'ic

psy'cho·log'i·cal

psy·chol'o·gist

psy·chol'o·gy

psy'cho·path'ic

psy'cho·pa·thol'o·gy

psy·chop'a·thy

psy·cho'sis

psy·chot'ic

Ptol'e·ma'ic

pto'maine

pub'lic

pub'li·ca'tion

pub'li·cist

pub·lic'i·ty

pub'lic·ly

pub'lish

pub'lished

pub'lish·er

puce

puck

puck'er

puck'ered

pud'dings

pud'dle

pud'dled

pud'dler

pu'den·cy

pudg'i·ness

pudg'y

pueb'lo

pu'er·ile

pu'er·il'i·ty

puff

puf'fin

puff'i·ness

puff'y

pug

pu'gil·ism

pu'gil·ist

pu'gil·is'tic

pug·na'cious·ly

pug·nac'i·ty

pu'is·sance

pu'is·sant

pul'chri·tude

pul'chri·tu'di·nous

pul'ing

pul'ing·ly

pull

pulled

pul'let

pul'ley

Pull'man

pul'lu·late

pul'mo·nar'y

Pul'mo'tor

pulp

pulp'i·er

pulp'i·est

pulp'i·ness

pul'pit

pul'pit·eer'

pulp'y

pul'sate

pul'sat·ed

pul·sa'tion

pul·sa'tor

pul'sa·to'ry

pulse

pul'ver·i·za'tion

pul'ver·ize

pul'ver·iz'er

pum'ice

pump

pum'per·nick'el

pump'kin

pun

punch

punched

pun'cheon

punch'ings

punc·til'i·o

punc·til'i·ous

punc·til'i·ous·ly

punc·til'i·ous·ness

punc'tu·al

punc'tu·al'i·ty

punc'tu·al·ly

punc'tu·ate

punc'tu·at'ed

punc'tu·a'tion

punc'ture

punc'tured

pun'dit

pung

pun'gen·cy

pun'gent

pu'ni·ness

pun'ish

pun'ish·a·ble	pur'ist	pur'sy
pun'ished	Pu'ri·tan	pu'ru·lence
pun'ish·ment	pu'ri·tan'ic	pu'ru·len·cy
pu'ni·tive	pu'ri·tan'i·cal	pu'ru·lent
punk	Pu'ri·tan·ism	pur·vey'
punt	pu'ri·ty	pur·vey'ance
pu'ny	purl	pur·vey'or
pup	pur'lieu	pur'view
pu'pa	pur·loin'	pus
pu'pae	pur'ple	push
pu'pil	pur'plish	push'cart'
pup'pet	pur·port'	push'er
pup'pet·eer'	pur·port'ed	pu'sil·la·nim'i·ty
pup'pet·ry	pur'pose	pu'sil·lan'i·mous
pup'py	pur'pose·ful	puss'y·foot'
pur'blind'	pur'pose·ful·ly	pus'tu·lant
pur'chase	pur'pose·ful·ness	pus'tu·lar
pur'chased	pur'pose·less	pus'tu·late
pur'chas·er	pur'pose·ly	pus'tu·la'tion
pure	pur'pos·ive	pus'tule
pure'ly	purr	put
pur'er	purred	pu'ta·tive
pur'est	purse	pu'tre·fac'tion
pur'ga·tive	pursed	pu'tre·fac'tive
pur'ga·to'ry	purs'er	pu'tre·fied
purge	purs'lane	pu'tre·fy
purged	pur·su'ance	pu·tres'cence
pu'ri·fi·ca'tion	pur·su'ant	pu·tres'cent
pu'ri·fied	pur·sue'	pu'trid
pu'ri·fi'er	pur·sued'	putt
pu'ri·fy	pur·suit'	putt'ee
pur'ism	pur'sui·vant	putt'er

put′ty		py′lon		py·ri′tes	
puz′zle		py·lo′rus		py·rog′ra·phy	
puz′zled		py′or·rhe′a		py′ro·ma′ni·a	
puz′zler		pyr′a·mid		py·rom′e·ter	
puz′zles		py·ram′i·dal		py′ro·tech′nics	
py·e′mi·a		pyre		py·rox′y·lin	
pyg′my		py′rex		Pyr′rhic	
py·ja′ma		py·rex′i·a		py′thon	

Q

quack

quack'er·y

quad

quad'ran'gle

quad·ran'gu·lar

quad'rant

quad'rat

quad·rat'ic

quad·rat'ics

quad'ra·ture

quad·ren'ni·al

quad·ren'ni·al·ly

quad·ren'ni·um

quad'ri·lat'er·al

qua·drille'

quad'ri·par'tite

quad'ru·ped

quad·ru'ple

quad·ru·plet

quad·ru·plex

quad·ru'pli·cate

quaff

quag'mire'

qua'hog

quail

quailed

quaint

quaint'ly

quaint'ness

quake

quaked

quak'er

quak'ing·ly

qual'i·fi·ca'tion

qual'i·fied

qual'i·fi'er

qual'i·fy

qual'i·ta'tive

qual'i·ties

qual'i·ty

qualm

quan'da·ry

quan'ti·ta'tive

quan'ti·ties

quan'ti·ty

quan'tum

quar'an·tine

quar'an·tined

quar'rel

quar'reled

quar'rel·some

quar'ri·er

quar'ry

quar'ry·man

quart

quar'tan

quar'ter

quar'ter·back'

quar'tered

quar'ter·ings

quar'ter·ly

quar'ter·mas'ter

quar'ter·saw'

quar·tet'

quar'tile

quar'to

235

quartz

quash

qua'si

qua·ter'na·ry

quat'rain

quat're·foil'

qua'ver

qua'vered

qua'ver·ing·ly

quay

quay'age

quea'sy

queen

queen'ly

queer

queer'er

queer'est

quell

quelled

quench

quenched

quench'less

que'ried

quer'u·lous

que'ry

quest

quest'ing·ly

ques'tion

ques'tion·a·ble

ques'tion·er

ques'tion·ing·ly

ques'tion·naire'

queue

quib'ble

quick

quick'en

quick'ened

quick'er

quick'est

quick'lime'

quick'ly

quick'ness

quick'sand'

quick'sil'ver

quick'step'

quid'di·ty

qui·es'cence

qui'et

qui'et·ed

qui'et·ly

qui'et·ness

qui'e·tude

qui·e'tus

quill

quilled

quill'work'

quilt

quilt'ed

quince

qui'nine

quin·quen'ni·al

quin'tal

quint·es'sence

quin'tes·sen'tial

quin·tet'

quin'tu·plet

quip

qui'pu

quire

quirk

quirt

quit

quit'claim'

quite

quit'rent'

quit'tance

quit'ter

quiv'er

quiv'ered

quiv'er·ing·ly

quix·ot'ic

quiz

quiz'zi·cal

quoin

quoit

quon'dam

quo'rum

quo'ta

quot'a·ble

quo·ta'tion

quote

quot'ed

quoth

quo·tid'i·an

quo'tient

quot'ing

R

rab'bet	rac'y	ra'di·o·pho'to·graph
rab·bin'i·cal	ra'di·al	ra'di·o·scope'
rab'bit	ra'di·al·ly	ra'di·o·sen'si·tive
rab'bit·ry	ra'di·ance	ra'di·o·tel'e·gram
rab'ble	ra'di·ant	rad'ish
rab'id	ra'di·ant·ly	ra'di·um
rab'id·ly	ra'di·ate	ra'di·us
ra'bi·es	ra'di·at'ed	ra'di·us·es
rac·coon'	ra'di·a'tion	ra'dix
race	ra'di·a'tor	ra'don
raced	rad'i·cal	raf'fi·a
rac'er	rad'i·cal·ism	raf'fle
race'way'	rad'i·cal·ly	raf'fled
ra·chit'ic	ra·dic'u·lar	raft
ra·chi'tis	ra'di·i	raft'er
ra'cial	ra'di·o	rafts'man
ra'cial·ly	ra'di·o·ac'tive	rag
rac'i·ly	ra'di·o·ac·tiv'i·ty	rag'a·muf'fin
rac'i·ness	ra'di·o·gram'	rage
rack	ra'di·o·graph'	raged
rack'et	ra'di·om'e·ter	rag'ged
rac'on·teur'	ra'di·o·phone'	rag'lan

ra·gout'	ram	ranked
rag'pick'er	ram'ble	ran'kle
rag'time'	ram'bled	ran'kled
rag'weed'	ram'bler	rank'ling·ly
raid	ram·bunc'tious	ran'sack
rail	ram'e·kin	ran'som
rail'bird'	ram'i·fi·ca'tion	ran'somed
railed	ram'i·fied	rant
rail'head'	ram'i·fy	rant'ed
rail'ing·ly	rammed	rant'ing·ly
rail'ings	ram'mer	ra·pa'cious
rail'ler·y	ramp	ra·pac'i·ty
rail'road'	ram'page	rap'id
rail'road'er	ramp'ant	ra·pid'i·ty
rail'way'	ram'part	rap'id·ly
rai'ment	ram'rod'	ra'pi·er
rain	ram'shack'le	rap'ine
rain'bow'	ranch	rap·port'
rain'coat'	ranch'er	rap·scal'lion
rained	ran·che'ro	rapt
rain'fall'	ranch'man	rap·to'ri·al
rain'spout'	ran'cho	rap'ture
rain'storm'	ran'cid	rap'tur·ous
rain'y	ran·cid'i·ty	rap'tur·ous·ly
raise	ran'cid·ly	rap'tur·ous·ness
raised	ran'cor	rare
rai'sin	ran'cor·ous	rar'e·fac'tion
ra'ja	ran'dom	rar'e·fy
rake	range	rare'ly
rak'ish	ranged	rare'ness
ral'lied	rang'er	rar'er
ral'ly	rank	rar'est

rar'i·ty

ras'cal

ras·cal'i·ty

ras'cal·ly

rash

rash'er

rash'est

rash'ly

rash'ness

rasp

rasp'ber'ry

rasped

rasp'ing·ly

rat

rat'a·ble

ratch'et

rate

rat'ed

rath'er

raths'kel'ler

rat'i·fi·ca'tion

rat'i·fied

rat'i·fy

rat'ings

ra'tio

ra'ti·oc'i·na'tion

ra'ti·oc'i·na'tive

ra'tion

ra'tion·al

ra'tion·al·ism

ra'tion·al·ist

ra'tion·al·is'tic

ra'tion·al·i·za'tion

ra'tion·al·ize

ra'tion·al·ized

ra'tion·al·ly

ra'tioned

rat'line

rat·tan'

rat'ter

rat'tle

rat'tle·brain'

rat'tle·brained'

rat'tled

rat'tle·head'ed

rat'tler

rat'tle·snake'

rat'tlings

rat'tly

rau'cous

rav'age

rav'aged

rave

raved

rav'el

rav'eled

ra'ven

rav'en·ous

rav'en·ous·ly

rav'en·ous·ness

ra'vi'gote'

ra·vine'

rav'ings

ra·vi·o'li

rav'ish

rav'ished

rav'ish·er

rav'ish·ing·ly

rav'ish·ment

raw

raw'boned'

raw'er

raw'est

raw'hide'

raw'ness

ray

ray'less

ray'on

raze

razed

ra'zor

ra'zor·back'

ra'zor·edge'

reach

reached

reach'ings

re·act'

re·act'ance

re·ac'tion

re·ac'tion·ar'y

re·ac'ti·vate

re'ac·ti·va'tion

read

read'a·bil'i·ty

read'a·ble

read'er

read'i·ly

read'i·ness

read'ings

re'ad·just'

re'ad·just'a·ble

re'ad·just'ment

re'ad·mis'sion

re'ad·mit'

read'y

re'af·firm'

re'af·fir·ma'tion

re·a'gent

re'al

re'a·lign'

re'al·ism

re'al·ist

re'al·is'tic

re'al·is'ti·cal·ly

re·al'i·ty

re'al·iz'a·ble

re'al·i·za'tion

re'al·ize

re'al·ized

re'al·ly

realm

re'al·tor

re'al·ty

ream

reamed

ream'er

re·an'i·mate

reap

reap'er

re'ap·pear'

re'ap·pear'ance

re'ap·point'

re'ap·point'ment

rear

reared

re·ar'gue

re·arm'

re·ar'ma·ment

re·armed'

rear'most

re'ar·range'

re'ar·range'ment

rear'ward

rea'son

rea'son·a·ble

rea'son·a·ble·ness

rea'son·a·bly

rea'soned

re'as·sem'ble

re'as·sert'

re'as·sert'ed

re'as·sign'

re'as·sume'

re'as·sur'ance

re'as·sure'

re'as·sured'

re'bate

re'bat·ed

re·bel'

re·belled'

re·bel'lion

re·bel'lious

re·bind'

re·birth'

re·born'

re·bound'

re·buff'

re·buffed'

re·build'

re·built'

re·buke'

re·buked'

re·buk'ing·ly

re'bus

re·but'

re·but'tal

re·but'ted

re·but'ter

re·cal'ci·trance

re·cal'ci·trant

re·call'

re·called'

re·cant'

re'can·ta'tion

re·cant'ed

re·cap'i·tal·ize

re'ca·pit'u·late

re'ca·pit'u·lat'ed

re'ca·pit'u·la'tion

re'ca·pit'u·la·to'ry

re·cap'ture

re·cast'

re·cede'

re·ced'ed

re·ceipt'

re·ceipt'ed

re·ceiv'a·ble

re·ceiv'a·bles

re·ceive'

re·ceived'

re·ceiv'er

re·ceiv'er·ship

re'cent

re'cent·ly

re·cep'ta·cle

re·cep'tion

re·cep'tion·ist

re·cep'tive

re·cep'tive·ly

re·cep'tive·ness

re'cep·tiv'i·ty

re·cep'tor

re·cess'

re·cessed'

re·cess'es

re·ces'sion

re·ces'sion·al

re·ces'sive

re·charge'

re·charged'

re·cher'ché'

re·cid'i·vism

re·cid'i·vist

rec'i·pe

re·cip'i·ent

re·cip'ro·cal

re·cip'ro·cal·ly

re·cip'ro·cate

re·cip'ro·cat'ed

re·cip'ro·ca'tion

re·cip'ro·ca'tive

re·cip'ro·ca'tor

rec'i·proc'i·ty

re·cit'al

re·cit'al·ist

rec'i·ta'tion

rec'i·ta·tive'

re·cite'

re·cit'ed

reck

reck'less

reck'less·ly

reck'less·ness

reck'on

reck'oned

reck'on·er

reck'on·ings

re·claim'

re·claim'a·ble

re·claimed'

rec'la·ma'tion

re·cline'

re·clined'

re·cluse'

rec'og·ni'tion

rec'og·niz'a·ble

re·cog'ni·zance

rec'og·nize

rec'og·nized

re·coil'

re·coiled'

rec'ol·lect'

rec'ol·lect'ed

rec'ol·lec'tion

re'com·mence'

rec'om·mend'

rec'om·men·da'tion

rec'om·mend'a·to'ry

rec'om·mend'ed

re'com·mit'

rec'om·pen'sa·ble

rec'om·pense

rec'om·pensed

rec'on·cil'a·ble

rec'on·cile

rec'on·ciled

rec'on·cile'ment

rec'on·cil'i·a'tion

rec'on·cil'i·a·to'ry

rec'on·dite

rec'on·nais·sance

rec'on·noi'ter

rec'on·noi'tered

re·con'quer

re'con·sid'er

re'con·sti·tute

re'con·struct'

re'con·struct'ed

re'con·struc'tion	rec'tan'gle	red'dened
re'con·struc'tive	rec·tan'gu·lar	red'der
re·con'vert	rec·tan'gu·lar'i·ty	red'dest
re'con·vey'	rec'ti·fi'a·ble	red'dish
re·cord'	rec'ti·fi·ca'tion	re·deal'
re·cord'ed	rec'ti·fied	re·deem'
re·cord'er	rec'ti·fi'er	re·deem'a·bil'i·ty
re·cord'ings	rec'ti·fy	re·deem'a·ble
re·count'	rec'ti·lin'e·ar	re·deemed'
re·count'ed	rec'ti·tude	re·deem'er
re·coup'	rec'tor	re·demp'tion
re·couped'	rec'tor·ate	Re·demp'tor·ist
re·coup'ment	rec·to'ri·al	re·demp'to·ry
re·course'	rec'to·ry	re'de·ter'mine
re·cov'er	re·cum'ben·cy	re'de·vel'op
re·cov'er·a·ble	re·cum'bent	re'di·rect'
re·cov'er·y	re·cu'per·ate	re'di·rect'ed
rec're·ant	re·cu'per·at'ed	re'dis'count
re'-cre·ate'	re·cu'per·a'tion	re'dis·cov'er
rec're·a'tion	re·cu'per·a'tive	re'dis·trib'ute
rec're·a'tion·al	re·cu'per·a·to'ry	re'dis·tri·bu'tion
re·crim'i·nate	re·cur'	re·dis'trict
re·crim'i·na'tion	re·curred'	red'ness
re·crim'i·na'tive	re·cur'rence	red'o·lence
re·crim'i·na·to'ry	re·cur'rent	red'o·lent
re'cru·des'cence	re·cur'rent·ly	re·dou'ble
re'cru·des'cent	rec'u·sant	re·doubt'
re·cruit'	red	re·doubt'a·ble
re·cruit'ed	red'bird'	re·dound'
re·cruit'ment	red'breast'	re·draft'
re'crys·tal·li·za'tion	red'bud'	re·dress'
re'crys'tal·lize	red'den	re·dressed'

re·duce′	re′-en·force′	re·flec′tion
re·duced′	re′-en·force′ment	re·flec′tive
re·duc′er	re′-en·gage′	re·flec′tor
re·duc′i·ble	re′-en·grave′	re′flex
re·duc′tion	re′-en·list′	re·flex′ive
re·dun′dance	re-en′ter	re′flux
re·dun′dan·cy	re-en′trance	re′for·est·a′tion
re·dun′dant	re-en′try	re·form′
re·dun′dant·ly	re′-es·tab′lish	ref′or·ma′tion
re·du′pli·cate	re′-ex·am′i·na′tion	re·form′a·tive
re·du′pli·cat′ed	re′-ex·am′ine	re·form′a·to′ry
re·du·pli·ca′tion	re′-ex·port′	re·formed′
red′wood′	re′-ex·por·ta′tion	re·form′er
re-ech′o	re·fec′to·ry	re·fract′
re-ech′oed	re·fer′	re·fract′ed
reed	ref′er·a·ble	re·frac′tion
reed′bird′	ref′er·ee′	re·frac′tion·ist
reed′i·ness	ref′er·ence	re·frac′tive
re-ed′it	ref′er·en′dum	re′frac·tiv′i·ty
re-ed′u·cate	re·ferred′	re·frac′tor
re′-ed·u·ca′tion	re·fig′ure	re·frac′to·ry
reed′y	re′fill	re·frain′
reef	re′fi·nance′	re·frained′
reef′er	re·fine′	re·fresh′
reek	re·fined′	re·freshed′
reek′ing·ly	re·fine′ment	re·fresh′er
reel	re·fin′er	re·fresh′ing·ly
re′-e·lect′	re·fin′er·y	re·fresh′ment
re′-em·bark′	re·fit′	re·frig′er·ant
re′-em·bar·ka′tion	re·flect′	re·frig′er·ate
re′-em·ploy′	re·flect′ed	re·frig′er·at′ed
re′-en·act′	re·flect′ing·ly	re·frig′er·a′tion

re·frig'er·a'tive

re·frig'er·a'tor

ref'uge

ref'u·gee'

re·ful'gence

re·ful'gent

re·fund'

re·fund'ed

re·fur'nish

re·fus'al

re·fuse'

re·fused'

ref'u·ta'tion

re·fute'

re·fut'ed

re·gain'

re·gained'

re'gal

re·gale'

re·galed'

re·gale'ment

re·ga'li·a

re·gal'i·ty

re'gal·ly

re·gard'

re·gard'ed

re·gard'ful

re·gard'less

re·gat'ta

re'ge·la'tion

re'gen·cy

re·gen'er·a·cy

re·gen'er·ate

re·gen'er·at'ed

re·gen'er·a'tion

re·gen'er·a'tive

re·gen'er·a'tor

re'gent

reg'i·cid'al

reg'i·cide

re·gime'

reg'i·men

reg'i·ment

reg'i·men'tal

reg'i·men'tals

reg'i·men·ta'tion

reg'i·ment'ed

re'gion

re'gion·al

re'gion·al·ism

re'gion·al·ize

re'gion·al·ly

reg'is·ter

reg'is·tered

reg'is·trar

reg'is·tra'tion

reg'is·try

re'gress

re·gres'sion

re·gres'sive

re·gret'

re·gret'ful

re·gret'ful·ly

re·gret'ful·ness

re·gret'ta·ble

re·gret'ted

reg'u·lar

reg'u·lar'i·ty

reg'u·lar·i·za'tion

reg'u·lar·ize

reg'u·late

reg'u·lat'ed

reg'u·lates

reg'u·la'tion

reg'u·la'tor

re·gur'gi·tate

re·gur'gi·tat'ed

re·gur'gi·ta'tion

re'ha·bil'i·tate

re'ha·bil'i·tat'ed

re'ha·bil'i·ta'tion

re·hash'

re·hears'al

re·hearse'

re·hearsed'

re·heat'

reign

reigned

re'im·burse'

re'im·bursed'

re'im·port'

re'im·por·ta'tion

rein

re'in·car'nate

re'in·car·na'tion

rein'deer'

reined

re'in·force'

re'in·forced'

re'in·sert'

re'in·stall'

re'in·state'

re'in·stat·ed

re'in·state'ment

re'in·sur'ance

re'in·sure'

re·in'te·grate

re'in·tro·duce'

re'in·vest'

re'in·vig'o·rate

re·is'sue

re·it'er·ate

re·it'er·at'ed

re·it'er·a'tion

re·it'er·a'tive

re·ject'

re·ject'ed

re·jec'tion

re·joice'

re·joiced'

re·joic'es

re·joic'ing·ly

re·join'

re·join'der

re·ju've·nate

re·ju've·nat'ed

re·ju've·na'tion

re·ju've·na'tive

re·ju've·nes'cence

re·ju've·nes'cent

re·kin'dle

re·lapse'

re·lapsed'

re·late'

re·lat'ed

re·la'tion

re·la'tion·al

re·la'tion·ship

rel'a·tive

rel'a·tive·ly

rel'a·tiv·ism

rel'a·tiv'i·ty

re·la'tor

re·lax'

re·lax·a'tion

re·laxed'

re·lax'es

re·lay'

re·layed'

re·lease'

re·leased'

rel'e·gate

rel'e·gat'ed

rel'e·ga'tion

re·lent'

re·lent'ed

re·lent'ing·ly

re·lent'less

rel'e·vance

rel'e·van·cy

rel'e·vant

re·li'a·bil'i·ty

re·li'a·ble

re·li'ant

rel'ic

re·lief'

re·lieve'

re·lieved'

re·li'gion

re·li'gious

re·li'gious·ly

re·lin'quish

re·lin'quished

re·lin'quish·ment

rel'i·quar'y

rel'ish

rel'ished

re·live'

re·load'

re·lo'cate

re·lo'cat·ed

re·lo·ca'tion

re·lo'ca·tor

re·lu'cent

re·luc'tance

re·luc'tant

re·luc'tant·ly

re·ly'

re·main'

re·main'der

re·mained'

re·make'

re·mand'

re·mand'ed

re·mark'

re·mark'a·ble

re·mar'ried

re·mar'ry

re·me'di·a·ble

re·me'di·al

rem'e·died

rem'e·dy

re·mem'ber

re·mem'bered

re·mem'brance

re·mind'

re·mind'ed

re·mind'er

re·mind'ful

re·mind'ing·ly

rem'i·nis'cence

rem'i·nis'cent

re·miss'

re·mis'sion

re·mit'

re·mit'tal

re·mit'tance

re·mit'ted

re·mit'tent

re·mit'ter

rem'nant

re·mod'el

re·mon'e·ti·za'tion

re·mon'e·tize

re·mon'strance

re·mon'strant

re·mon'strate

re·mon'strat·ed

re·mon'strat·ing·ly

re'mon·stra'tion

re'mon'stra·tive·

re·morse'

re·morse'ful

re·morse'ful·ly

re·morse'less

re·mote'

re·mote'ness

re·mot'er

re·mot'est

re·mount'

re·mov'a·bil'i·ty

re·mov'a·ble

re·mov'al

re·move'

re·moved'

re·moves'

re·mu'ner·ate

re·mu'ner·at'ed

re·mu'ner·a'tion

re·mu'ner·a'tive

ren'ais·sance'

re'nal

re·nas'cent

rend

ren'der

ren'dered

ren'der·ings

ren'dez·vous

ren·di'tion

ren'e·gade

re·nege'

re'ne·go'ti·ate

re·new'

re·new'a·ble

re·new'al

re·newed'

ren'net

re·nom'i·nate

re·nom'i·na'tion

re·nounce'

re·nounced'

ren'o·vate

ren'o·vat'ed

ren'o·va'tion

re·nown'

re·nowned'

rent

rent'al

rent'ed

re·num'ber

re·nun'ci·a'tion

re·nun'ci·a'tive

re·nun'ci·a·to'ry

re·o'pen

re·or'der

re'or·gan·i·za'tion

re·or'gan·ize

re·o'ri·ent

re·paid'

re·paint'

re·pair'

re·paired'

re·pair'er

rep'a·ra·ble

rep'a·ra'tion

re·par'a·tive

rep'ar·tee'

re·past'

re·pa'tri·ate

re·pay'

re·pay'ment

re·peal'

re·pealed'

re·peal'er

re·peat'

re·peat'ed·ly

re·peat'er

re·pel'

re·pelled'

re·pel'lence

re·pel'len·cy

re·pel'lent

re·pel'ling·ly

re·pent'

re·pent'ance

re·pent'ed

re'per·cus'sion

re'per·cus'sive

rep'er·toire

rep'er·to'ry

rep'e·tend

rep'e·ti'tion

rep'e·ti'tious

re·pet'i·tive

re·phrase'

re·pine'

re·pined'

re·place'

re·placed'

re·place'ment

re·plant'

re·plen'ish

re·plen'ished

re·plen'ish·ment

re·plete'

re·ple'tion

re·plev'in

rep'li·ca

rep'li·ca'tion

re·plied'

re·ply'

re·port'

re·port'ed

re·port'er

re·pose'

re·posed'

re·pose'ful

re·pos'i·to'ry

re'pos·sess'

re'pos·sessed'

rep're·hend'

rep're·hen'si·ble

rep're·hen'sion

rep're·hen'sive

rep're·sent'

rep're·sen·ta'tion

rep're·sent'a·tive

rep're·sent'ed

re·press'

re·pres'sion

re·pres'sive

re·prieve'

re·prieved'

rep'ri·mand

rep'ri·mand'ed

rep'ri·mand'ing·ly

re'print'

re·print'ed

re·pris'al

re·prise'

re·proach'

re·proached'

re·proach'ful

re·proach'ful·ly

re·proach'ful·ness

rep'ro·bate

rep'ro·ba'tion

re'pro·duce'

re'pro·duc'er

re'pro·duc'tion

re'pro·duc'tive

re·proof'

re·prove'

re·proved'

re·prov'ing·ly

rep'tile

rep·til'i·an

re·pub'lic

re·pub'li·can

re·pub'li·can·ism

re·pub'li·can·ize

re·pub'lish

re·pu'di·ate

re·pu'di·a'tion

re·pug'nance

re·pug'nant

re·pulse'

re·pulsed'

re·pul'sion

re·pul'sive

re·pul'sive·ness

re·pur'chase

rep'u·ta·ble

rep'u·ta'tion

re·pute'

re·put'ed

re·put'ed·ly

re·quest'

re'qui·em

re·quire'

re·quired'

re·quire'ment

req'ui·site

req'ui·si'tion

re·quit'al

re·quite'

re·quit'ed

rere'dos

re·run'

re·sale'

re·scind'

re·scind'ed

re·scis'sion

re·score'

res'cue

res'cued

re·search'

re·search'er

re·sec'tion

re·sem'blance

re·sem'ble

re·sem'bled

re·sent'

re·sent'ed

re·sent'ful

re·sent'ful·ness

re·sent'ment

res'er·va'tion

res'er·va'tion·ist

re·serve'

re·served'

re·serv'ist

res'er·voir

re·set'

re·set'tle

re·set'tle·ment

re·ship'

re·ship'ment

re·side'

re·sid'ed

res'i·dence

res'i·den·cy

res'i·dent

res'i·den'tial

re·sid'u·al

re·sid'u·ar'y

res'i·due

re·sid'u·um

re·sign'

res'ig·na'tion

re·signed'

re·sign'ed·ly

re·sil'i·en·cy

re·sil'i·ent

res'in

res'in·ous

re·sist'

re·sist'ance

re·sist'ant

re·sist'i·ble

re·sis'tive

re'sis·tiv'i·ty

re·sist'less

re·sol'u·ble

res'o·lute

res'o·lute·ness

res'o·lu'tion

re·solv'a·ble

re·solve'

re·solved'

re·sol'vent

res'o·nance

res'o·nant

res'o·nate

res'o·na'tor

re·sort'

re·sort'ed

re·sound'

re·sound'ed

re·sound'ing·ly

re·source'

re·source'ful

re·source'ful·ness

re·spect'

re·spect'a·bil'i·ty

re·spect'a·ble

re·spect'ed

re·spect'er

re·spect'ful

re·spec'tive

re·spec'tive·ly

re·spell'

re·spir'a·ble

res'pi·ra'tion

res'pi·ra'tor

re·spir'a·to'ry

re·spire'

re·spired'

res'pite

re·splend'ence

re·splend'en·cy

re·splend'ent

re·spond'

re·spond'ed

re·spond'ent

re·sponse'

re·spon'si·bil'i·ties

re·spon'si·bil'i·ty

re·spon'si·ble

re·spon'sive

re·spon'sive·ness

rest

re·state'

re·state'ment

res'tau·rant

res'tau·ra·teur'

rest'ed

rest'ful

rest'ful·ly

rest'ful·ness

res'ti·tu'tion

res'tive

res'tive·ly

res'tive·ness

rest'less

rest'less·ness

re·stock'

res'to·ra'tion

re·stor'a·tive

re·store'

re·stored'

re·strain'

re·strained'

re·strain'ed·ly

re·strain'ing·ly

re·straint'

re·strict'

re·strict'ed

re·stric'tion

re·stric'tive

re·sult'

re·sult'ant

re·sum'a·ble

re·sume'

re·sumed'

re·sump'tion

re·sur'gence

re·sur'gent

res'ur·rect'

res'ur·rect'ed

res'ur·rec'tion

re·sus'ci·tate

re·sus'ci·tat'ed

re·sus'ci·ta'tion

re·sus'ci·ta'tive

re·sus'ci·ta'tor

re'tail

re'tailed

re'tail·er

re·tain'

re·tained'

re·tain'er

re·take'

re·tal'i·ate

re·tal'i·at'ed

re·tal'i·a'tion

re·tal'i·a'tion·ist

re·tal'i·a'tive

re·tal'i·a·to'ry

re·tard'

re'tar·da'tion

re·tard'ed

re·tard'er

retch

retched

re·tell'

re·tell'ings

re·ten'tion

re·ten'tive

re'ten·tiv'i·ty

ret'i·cence

ret'i·cent

ret'i·cent·ly

ret'i·cle

re·tic'u·lar

re·tic'u·late

re·tic'u·lat'ed

re·tic'u·la'tion

ret'i·cule

ret'i·na

ret'i·nal

ret'i·ni'tis

ret'i·nue

re·tire'

re·tired'

re·tire'ment

re·tir'ing·ly

re·told'

re·tort'

re·tort'ed

re·touch'

re·touch'er

re·trace'

re·trace'a·ble

re·tract'

re·tract'ed

re·trac'tile

re·trac'tion

re·trac'tive

re·trac'tor

re-tread'

re·treat'

re·treat'ed

re·trench'

re·trenched'

re·trench'ment

re·tri'al

ret'ri·bu'tion

re·trib'u·tive

re·triev'al

re·trieve'

re·trieved'

re·triev'er

ret'ro·ac'tive

ret'ro·ac·tiv'i·ty

ret'ro·cede'

ret'ro·ces'sion

ret'ro·ces'sive

ret'ro·flex

ret'ro·flex'ion

ret'ro·grade

ret'ro·grad'ed

ret'ro·gress

ret'ro·gres'sion

ret'ro·gres'sive

ret'ro·spect

ret'ro·spec'tion

ret'ro·spec'tive

ret'ro·ver'sion

re·turn'

re·turn'a·ble

re·turned'

re·un'ion

re'u·nite'

re-use'

re-used'

re·vac'ci·nate

re·val'i·date

re·val'or·ize

re·val'u·a'tion

re·val'ue

re·vamp'

re·veal'

re·vealed'

re·veal'ing·ly

re·veal'ment

rev'eil·le

rev'el

rev'e·la'tion

rev'e·la·to'ry

rev'eled

rev'el·er

rev′el·ry

re·venge′

re·venged′

re·venge′ful

rev′e·nue

re·ver′ber·ant

re·ver′ber·ate

re·ver′ber·at′ed

re·ver′ber·a′tion

re·ver′ber·a′tive

re·ver′ber·a′tor

re·ver′ber·a·to′ry

re·vere′

re·vered′

rev′er·ence

rev′er·end

rev′er·ent

rev′er·en′tial

rev′er·ie

re·ver′sal

re·verse′

re·versed′

re·vers′i·bil′i·ty

re·vers′i·ble

re·ver′sion

re·ver′sion·ar′y

re·vert′

re·vert′ed

re·vert′i·ble

re·vest′

re·vet′

re·vet′ment

re·vict′ual

re·view′

re·viewed′

re·view′er

re·vile′

re·viled′

re·vile′ment

re·vil′ing·ly

re·vin′di·cate

re·vise′

re·vised′

re·vis′er

re·vi′sion

re·vi′sion·ism

re·vi′sion·ist

re·vis′it

re·viv′al

re·viv′al·ism

re·viv′al·ist

re·vive′

re·vived′

re·viv′i·fi·ca′tion

re·viv′i·fi′er

re·viv′i·fy

rev′o·ca′tion

re·vok′a·ble

re·voke′

re·voked′

re·volt′

re·volt′ed

re·volt′ing·ly

rev′o·lu′tion

rev′o·lu′tion·ar′y

rev′o·lu′tion·ist

rev′o·lu′tion·ize

rev′o·lu′tion·ized

re·volve′

re·volved′

re·volv′er

re·vue′

re·vul′sion

re·vul′sive

re·ward′

re·ward′ed

re·ward′ing·ly

re·wind′

re·wire′

re·word′

re·worked′

re·write′

re·writ′ten

rhap·sod′ic

rhap′so·dist

rhap′so·dize

rhap′so·dized

rhap′so·dy

rhe′ni·um

rhe′o·stat

rhe′sus

rhet′o·ric

rhe·tor′i·cal

rhet′o·ri′cian

rheum

rheu·mat′ic

rheu'ma·tism	rich'ness	right'eous
rheu'ma·toid	rich'weed'	right'eous·ly
rheum'y	rick'ets	right'eous·ness
rhine'stone'	ric'o·chet'	right'ful
rhi·ni'tis	rid'dance	right'ful·ly
rhi·noc'er·os	rid'den	right'ly
rhi·nol'o·gy	rid'dle	right'ness
rhi'no·scope	ride	rig'id
rhi·nos'co·py	rid'er	ri·gid'i·ty
rhi'zome	rid'er·less	rig'id·ly
rho'di·um	ridge	rig'id·ness
rhom'boid	ridged	rig'or
rhom'bus	rid'i·cule	rig'or·ous
rhu'barb	rid'i·culed	rig'or·ous·ly
rhyme	ri·dic'u·lous	rile
rhymed	ri·dic'u·lous·ly	riled
rhythm	ri·dot'to	rill
rhyth'mic	rife	rim
rhyth'mi·cal	rif'fle	rime
Ri·al'to	rif'fled	rind
ri'ant	riff'raff'	ring
rib	ri'fle	ring'bolt'
rib'ald	ri'fled	ring'bone'
rib'ald·ry	ri'fle·man	ringed
ribbed	ri'flings	ring'er
rib'bon	rift	ring'ing·ly
rice	rig	ring'lead'er
rich	rig'a·doon'	ring'let
rich'er	rigged	ring'let·ed
rich'es	rig'ger	ring'mas'ter
rich'est	right	ring'side'
rich'ly	right'ed	ring'worm'

rink		rite		roared	
rinse		rit'u·al		roar'ings	
rinsed		rit'u·al·ism		roast	
ri'ot		rit'u·al·ist		roast'ed	
ri'ot·ed		rit'u·al·is'tic		roast'er	
ri'ot·er		rit'u·al·ly		rob	
ri'ot·ous		ri'val		robbed	
ri'ot·ous·ly		ri'valed		rob'ber	
ri'ot·ous·ness		ri'val·ry		rob'ber·y	
rip		rive		robe	
ri·par'i·an		riv'er		robed	
ripe		riv'er·side'		rob'in	
ripe'ly		riv'et		ro'bot	
rip'en		riv'et·ed		ro·bust'	
rip'ened		riv'et·er		ro·bust'ly	
rip'er		riv'u·let		ro·bust'ness	
rip'est		roach		rock	
ri·poste'		road		rock'er	
rip'ple		road'a·bil'i·ty		rock'et	
rip'pled		road'bed'		rock'fish'	
rip'pling·ly		road'house'		rock'weed'	
rip'ply		road'man		rock'work'	
rip'rap'		road'side'		rock'y	
rise		road'stead		ro·co'co	
ris'en		road'ster		rod	
ris'er		road'way'		ro'dent	
ris'i·bil'i·ty		road'weed'		ro'de·o	
ris'i·ble		roam		rod'man	
ris'ings		roamed		roe	
risk		roam'er		roent'gen	
risked		roam'ings		rogue	
risk'y		roar		ro'guer·y	

ro'guish	room'i·ness	ro'tat·ed
ro'guish·ly	room'mate'	ro·ta'tion
ro'guish·ness	room'y	ro·ta'tion·al
roil	roost	ro'ta·tive
roiled	roost'er	ro'ta·tor
roist'er	root	ro'ta·to'ry
roll	root'ed	rote
rolled	root'er	ro'te·none
roll'er	root'let	ro'to·gra·vure'
roll'mop'	root'worm'	ro'tor
ro·maine'	rope	rot'ten
Ro'man	rope'danc'er	rot'ten·ness
ro·mance'	rope'mak'er	rot'ter
Ro'man·esque'	rope'work'	ro·tund'
ro·man'tic	ro·quet'	ro·tun'da
ro·man'ti·cal·ly	ro·sa'ceous	ro·tun'di·ty
ro·man'ti·cism	ro'sa·ry	rouge
ro·man'ti·cist	rose	rouged
ro·man'ti·cize	ro'se·ate	rough
romp	rose'mar'y	rough'age
romp'ers	ro·sette'	rough'cast'
ron'deau	rose'wood'	rough'dry'
ron'do	ros'i·ly	rough'en
roof	ros'in	rough'ened
roof'er	ros'i·ness	rough'er
roof'less	ros'ter	rough'est
roof'tree'	ros'trum	rough'hew'
rook'er·y	ros'y	rough'hewn'
room	rot	rough'house'
roomed	Ro·tar'i·an	rough'ish
room'er	ro'ta·ry	rough'ly
room'ful	ro'tate	rough'neck'

rough'ness	row	ru'bri·ca'tor
rough'rid'er	row	ru'by
rou·lade'	row'boat	ruch'ing
rou·leau'	row'dy	ruck'sack'
rou·lette'	rowed	ruck'us
round	row'el	rud'der
round'a·bout'	row'eled	rud'der·post'
round'ed	row'en	rud'di·er
roun'de·lay	row'er	rud'di·est
round'er	row'lock	rud'di·ly
round'est	roy'al	rud'di·ness
round'fish'	roy'al·ism	rud'dy
round'house'	roy'al·ist	rude
round'ish	roy'al·ly	rude'ly
round'ly	roy'al·ty	rude'ness
round'ness	rub	rud'er
rounds'man	rubbed	rud'est
round'worm'	rub'ber	ru'di·ment
rouse	rub'ber·ize	ru'di·men'tal
roused	rub'ber·ized	ru'di·men'ta·ry
rous'ing·ly	rub'ber·y	rue
roust'a·bout'	rub'bings	rued
rout	rub'bish	rue'ful
route	rub'ble	ruff
rout'ed	rub'down'	ruf'fi·an
rout'ed	ru·be·fa'cient	ruf'fi·an·ism
rou·tine'	ru'be·fac'tion	ruf'fle
rou·tin'i·za'tion	ru·be'o·la	ruf'fled
rou·tin'ize	ru'bi·cund	Rug'by
rov'er	ru·bid'i·um	rug'ged
rov'ing·ly	ru'ble	rug'ged·ness
rov'ings	ru'bric	ru'gose

ru·gos′i·ty	rum′ple	rus′set
ru′in	rum′pled	Rus′sian
ru′in·a′tion	rum′pus	rust
ru′ined	run	rust′ed
ru′in·ous	run′a·bout′	rus′tic
rule	run′a·gate	rus′ti·cate
ruled	rune	rus′ti·cat′ed
rul′er	rung	rus′ti·ca′tion
rul′ings	ru′nic	rus′ti·cism
rum	run′ner	rus·tic′i·ty
rum′ble	run′off′	rus′tic·ly
rum′bled	runt	rust′i·er
rum′bling·ly	run′way′	rust′i·est
rum′blings	ru·pee′	rus′tle
ru′mi·nant	rup′ture	rus′tled
ru′mi·nate	rup′tured	rus′tler
ru′mi·nat′ed	ru′ral	rus′tling·ly
ru′mi·nat′ing·ly	ru′ral·ism	rus′tlings
ru′mi·na′tion	ru′ral·i·za′tion	rust′proof′
ru′mi·na′tive	ru′ral·ize	rust′y
rum′mage	ru′ral·ly	rut
rum′maged	ruse	ru′ta·ba′ga
rum′my	rush	ruth
ru′mor	rush′ing·ly	ru·the′ni·um
ru′mored	rush′light′	ruth′less
rump	rusk	rye

S

Sab′ba·tar′i·an	sa′cred	sad′ly
Sab′bath	sa′cred·ly	sad′ness
sab·bat′i·cal	sa′cred·ness	sa·fa′ri
sab′ba·tine	sac′ri·fice	safe
sa′ber	sac′ri·ficed	safe′guard′
sa′ble	sac′ri·fi′cial	safe′keep′ing
sab′o·tage′	sac′ri·lege	safe′ly
sac′cha·rine	sac′ri·le′gious	safe′ness
sac′er·do′tal	sac′ris·tan	saf′er
sa′chem	sac′ris·ty	saf′est
sa·chet′	sac′ro·sanct	safe′ty
sack′but	sa′crum	saf′fron
sack′cloth′	sad	sag
sacked	sad′der	sa′ga
sack′ful	sad′dest	sa·ga′cious
sa′cral	sad′dle	sa·ga′cious·ly
sac′ra·ment	sad′dle·back′	sa·gac′i·ty
sac′ra·men′tal	sad′dle·bag′	sag′a·more
sac′ra·men′tal·ism	sad′dled	sage
sac′ra·men′tal·ist	sad′dler	sagged
sac′ra·men′tal·ly	sad′dler·y	sag′it·tal
sac′ra·men·tar′i·an	sad′i′ron	sa′go

257

sa'hib

said

sail

sail'boat'

sailed

sail'fish'

sail'ings

sail'or

saint

saint'ed

saint'hood

saint'li·ness

saint'ly

sake

sa'ker

sa·laam'

sal'a·bil'i·ty

sal'a·ble

sa·la'cious

sa·la'cious·ly

sa·la'cious·ness

sal'ad

sal'a·man'der

sal'a·ried

sal'a·ry

sale

sal'e·ra'tus

sales'man

sales'man·ship

sales'peo'ple

sales'per'son

sales'room'

sales'wom'an

sal'i·cyl'ic

sa'li·ence

sa'li·ent

sa·lif'er·ous

sa'line

sa·li'va

sal'i·vant

sal'i·vate

sal'i·va'tion

sal'low

sal'low·er

sal'low·est

sal'ly

salm'on

sa·loon'

sal'si·fy

salt

sal'ta·to'ry

salt'cel'lar

salt'ed

salt'i·er

salt'i·est

salt'pe'ter

salt'y

sa·lu'bri·ous

sa·lu'bri·ty

sal'u·tar'y

sal'u·ta'tion

sa·lu'ta·to'ri·an

sa·lu'ta·to'ry

sa·lute'

sa·lut'ed

sal'vage

sal'vaged

sal·va'tion

salve

salved

sal'ver

sal'vo

Sa·mar'i·tan

sa·ma'ri·um

same

same'ness

sam'ite

Sa·mo'an

sam'o·var

sam'pan

sam'ple

sam'pled

sam'pler

sam'plings

sam'u·rai

san'a·tive

san'a·to'ri·um

san'a·to'ry

sanc'ti·fi·ca'tion

sanc'ti·fied

sanc'ti·fy

sanc'ti·mo'ni·ous

sanc'ti·mo'ni·ous·ly

sanc'ti·mo'ni·ous·ness

sanc'tion

sanc'tioned

sanc'ti·tude	san'guine	sar'do·nyx
sanc'ti·ty	san'i·tar'i·um	sar·gas'so
sanc'tu·ar'y	san'i·tar'y	sa'ri
sanc'tum	san'i·ta'tion	sa·rong'
sand	san'i·ty	sar'sa·pa·ril'la
san'dal	sank	sar·to'ri·al
san'dal·wood'	San'skrit	sash
sand'bag'	sap	sas'sa·fras
sand'bank'	sa'pi·ence	sat
sand'blast'	sa'pi·ent	Sa'tan
sand'box'	sap'lings	sa·tan'ic
sand'bur'	sa·pon'i·fi·ca'tion	satch'el
sand'ed	sa·pon'i·fy	sate
sand'er	sap'per	sat'ed
sand'fish'	sap'phire	sa·teen'
sand'flow'er	sap'pi·er	sat'el·lite
sand'i·ness	sap'pi·est	sa'ti·ate
sand'man'	sap'py	sa'ti·at'ed
sand'pa'per	sap'wood'	sa'ti·a'tion
sand'pip'er	sar'a·band	sa·ti'e·ty
sand'stone'	Sar'a·cen	sat'in
sand'storm'	sar'casm	sat'i·nette'
sand'wich	sar·cas'tic	sat'ire
sand'wiched	sar·cas'ti·cal·ly	sa·tir'ic
sand'worm'	sar·co'ma	sa·tir'i·cal
sand'y	sar·co'ma·ta	sa·tir'i·cal·ly
sane	sar'co·phag'ic	sat'i·rist
sane'ly	sar·coph'a·gus	sat'i·rize
san'er	sar·dine'	sat'i·rized
san'est	Sar·din'i·an	sat'is·fac'tion
sang	sar·don'ic	sat'is·fac'to·ri·ly
san'gui·nar'y	sar·don'i·cal·ly	sat'is·fac'to·ry

sat'is·fied	sav'a·ble	sca'lar
sat'is·fy	sav'age	scald
sat'is·fy'ing·ly	sav'age·ly	scald'ed
sa'trap	sav'age·ry	scale
sat'u·rate	sa·van'na	scaled
sat'u·rat'ed	sa·vant'	sca·lene'
sat'u·ra'tion	save	scal'er
Sat'ur·day	saved	scal'lion
Sat'urn	sav'ings	scal'lop
sat'ur·nine	sav'ior	scalp
sat'yr	sa'vor	scalped
sat'yr·esque'	sa'vor·less	scal'pel
sauce	sa'vor·y	scalp'er
sauce'boat'	saw	scal'y
sauce'dish'	saw'dust'	scamp
sauce'pan'	sawed	scamped
sau'cer	saw'fish'	scam'per
sau'cer·like'	saw'fly'	scam'pered
sau'ci·er	saw'horse'	scan
sau'ci·est	saw'mill'	scan'dal
sau'ci·ly	saw'yer	scan'dal·i·za'tion
sau'cy	Sax'on	scan'dal·ize
saun'ter	say	scan'dal·ized
saun'tered	say'ings	scan'dal·ous
saun'ter·er	says	scan'dal·ous·ly
saun'ter·ing·ly	scab	Scan'di·na'vi·a
saun'ter·ings	scab'bard	scan'di·um
sau'ri·an	scab'by	scanned
sau'sage	sca'bi·es	scan'ner
sau·té'	sca'bi·ous	scan'sion
sau·téed'	sca'brous	scan·so'ri·al
sau·terne'	scaf'fold	scant

scant'ed

scant'i·ly

scant'i·ness

scant'lings

scant'y

scape'goat'

scape'grace'

scap'u·la

scap'u·lar

scar

scar'ab

scarce

scarce'ly

scarc'er

scarc'est

scar'ci·ty

scare

scared

scarf

scar'i·fi·ca'tion

scar'i·fied

scar'i·fi'er

scar'i·fy

scar'la·ti'na

scar'let

scarred

scathed

scathe'less

scath'ing

scath'ing·ly

scat'ter

scat'ter·brain'

scat'tered

scat'ter·ing·ly

scat'ter·ings

scav'en·ger

sce·na'ri·o

scen'er·y

scene'shift'er

sce'nic

sce'ni·cal

scent

scent'ed

scent'less

scent'wood'

scep'ter

scep'tered

sched'ule

sched'uled

sche·mat'ic

sche·mat'i·cal·ly

sche'ma·tize

sche'ma·tized

scheme

schemed

schem'er

schem'ing·ly

scher·zan'do

scher'zo

schism

schis·mat'ic

schis·mat'i·cal

schist

schiz'oid

schiz'o·phre'ni·a

schiz'o·phren'ic

schnapps

schnau'zer

schnit'zel

schol'ar

schol'ar·ly

schol'ar·ship

scho·las'tic

scho·las'ti·cal

scho·las'ti·cal·ly

scho·las'ti·cism

scho'li·ast

scho'li·um

school

school'book'

schooled

school'house'

school'man

school'mas'ter

schoon'er

schot'tische

sci·at'ic

sci·at'i·ca

sci'ence

sci'en·tif'ic

sci'en·tif'i·cal·ly

sci'en·tist

scim'i·tar

scin·til'la

scin'til·lant

scin'til·late

scin′til·lat′ed	score	scrab′blings
scin′til·lat′ing·ly	scored	scrag′gy
scin′til·la′tion	scor′er	scram′ble
sci′on	scor′ings	scram′bled
scis′sors	scorn	scram′blings
scle·ri′tis	scorned	scrap
scle·ro′sis	scorn′er	scrap′book′
scle·rot′ic	scorn′ful	scrape
scle′ro·ti′tis	scorn′ful·ly	scraped
scle·rot′o·my	scor′pi·on	scrap′er
scoff	Scot	scrap′ing·ly
scoffed	Scotch	scrap′ings
scoff′er	Scotch′man	scrap′man
scoff′ing·ly	Scots′man	scrap′pi·er
scoff′law′	Scot′tish	scrap′pi·est
scold	scoun′drel	scrap′ple
scold′ed	scoun′drel·ly	scrap′py
scold′ing·ly	scour	scratch
scold′ings	scoured	scratched
sco′li·o′sis	scour′er	scratch′i·ness
sconce	scourge	scratch′ings
scone	scourged	scratch′y
scoop	scourg′ing·ly	scrawl
scooped	scour′ings	scrawled
scoop′ing·ly	scout	scrawl′ings
scoot	scout′ed	scraw′ni·ly
scoot′er	scow	scraw′ni·ness
scope	scowl	scraw′ny
scorch	scowled	scream
scorched	scowl′ing·ly	screamed
scorch′er	scrab′ble	scream′ing·ly
scorch′ing·ly	scrab′bled	screech

screeched	scrip'ture	scru'ti·ny
screech'i·er	scrive'ner	scud
screech'i·est	scrod	scud'ded
screech'y	scrof'u·la	scuff
screed	scrof'u·lous	scuffed
screen	scroll	scuf'fle
screened	scrolled	scuf'fled
screen'ings	scroll'work'	scuf'fling·ly
screen'play'	scroug'er	scuf'flings
screw	scrounge	scull
screw'driv'er	scrub	sculled
screwed	scrub'bed	scull'er
scrib'ble	scrub'bi·er	scul'ler·y
scrib'bled	scrub'bi·est	scul'lion
scrib'bler	scrub'bings	scul'pin
scrib'bling·ly	scrub'by	sculp'tor
scrib'blings	scrub'land'	sculp'tur·al
scribe	scruff	sculp'ture
scrib'er	scrum'mage	sculp'tur·esque'
scrim	scrump'tious	scum
scrim'mage	scrunch	scum'my
scrimp	scrunched	scup'per
scrimped	scru'ple	scup'per·nong
scrimp'i·ly	scru'pled	scurf
scrimp'i·ness	scru'pu·los'i·ty	scur·ril'i·ty
scrimp'ing·ly	scru'pu·lous	scur'ril·ous
scrim'shaw'	scru'pu·lous·ly	scur'ril·ous·ly
scrip	scru'pu·lous·ness	scur'ril·ous·ness
script	scru'ti·ni·za'tion	scur'ry
scrip'tur·al	scru'ti·nize	scur'vy
scrip'tur·al·ism	scru'ti·nized	scut'tle
scrip'tur·al·ist	scru'ti·niz'ing·ly	scut'tled

scut'tle·ful	sea'sick'ness	sec're·tar'i·al
scu'tum	sea'side'	sec're·tar'i·at
scythe	sea'son	sec're·tar'y
sea	sea'son·a·ble	se·crete'
sea'board'	sea'son·al	se·cret'ed
sea'coast'	sea'son·al·ly	se·cre'tion
sea'far'er	sea'soned	se·cre'tive
sea'fowl'	sea'son·ings	se·cre'tive·ly
sea'go'ing	seat	se·cre'tive·ness
seal	seat'ed	se'cret·ly
sealed	sea'ward	se·cre'to·ry
seal'er	sea'wor'thi·ness	sect
seal'skin'	sea'wor'thy	sec·tar'i·an
seam	se·ba'ceous	sec·tar'i·an·ism
sea'man	se'cant	sec'ta·ry
sea'man·like'	se·cede'	sec'tion
sea'man·ship	se·ced'ed	sec'tion·al
seamed	se·ces'sion	sec'tion·al·ism
seam'stress	se·ces'sion·ism	sec'tion·al·ize
seam'y	se·ces'sion·ist	sec'tion·al·ized
sea'plane'	se·clude'	sec'tion·al·ly
sea'port'	se·clud'ed	sec'tor
sear	se·clu'sion	sec'u·lar
search	sec'ond	sec'u·lar·ism
searched	sec'ond·ar'i·ly	sec'u·lar·ist
search'er	sec'ond·ar'y	sec'u·lar'i·ty
search'ing·ly	sec'ond·ed	sec'u·lar·i·za'tion
search'light'	sec'ond·er	sec'u·lar·ize
seared	sec'ond·hand'	sec'u·lar·ized
sea'scape	sec'ond·ly	sec'u·lar·iz'er
sea'shore'	se'cre·cy	se·cure'
sea'sick'	se'cret	se·cured'

se·cure'ly

se·cu'ri·ty

se·dan'

se·date'

se·date'ly

se·date'ness

se·da'tion

sed'a·tive

sed'en·tar'y

sedge

sed'i·ment

sed'i·men'tal

sed'i·men'ta·ry

sed'i·men·ta'tion

se·di'tion

se·di'tious

se·di'tious·ly

se·di'tious·ness

se·duce'

se·duced'

se·duc'er

se·duc'i·ble

se·duc'tion

se·duc'tive

se·duc'tive·ly

se·duc'tive·ness

sed'u·lous

sed'u·lous·ly

sed'u·lous·ness

se'dum

see

seed

seed'ed

seed'i·er

seed'i·est

seed'i·ness

seed'less

seed'less·ness

seed'lings

seed'y

seek

seek'er

seem

seemed

seem'ing·ly

seem'ly

seen

seep

seep'age

seep'weed'

se'er

seer'ess

seer'suck'er

see'saw'

seethe

seethed

seg'ment

seg·men'tal

seg'men·tar'y

seg'men·ta'tion

seg're·gate

seg're·gat'ed

seg're·ga'tion

seg're·ga'tion·ist

se'gui·dil'la

seine

seis'mic

seis'mo·graph

seis·mol'o·gy

seiz'a·ble

seize

seized

sei'zure

sel'dom

se·lect'

se·lect'ed

se·lec'tion

se·lec'tive

se·lec'tiv'i·ty

se·lect'man

se·lect'men

se·lec'tor

sel'e·nate

se·le'nic

sel'e·nide

sel'e·nite

se·le'ni·um

self

self'-as·ser'tion

self'-as·ser'tive

self'-as·sured'

self'-cen'tered

self'-col'ored

self'-com·mand'

self'-com·pla'cent

self'-com·posed'

self'-con·ceit'

self'-con·cern'

self'-con'fi·dence

self'-con'scious

self'-con'scious·ness

self'-con·tained'

self'-con'tra·dic'tion

self'-con·trol'

self'-cov'ered

self'-de·ceit'

self'-de·fense'

self'-de·ni'al

self'-de·struc'tion

self'-de·ter'mi·na'tion

self'-de·ter'mined

self'-dis'ci·pline

self'-dis·trust'

self'-ed'u·cat'ed

self'-ef·face'ment

self'-ef·fac'ing·ly

self'-es·teem'

self'-ev'i·dent

self'-ex·am'i·na'tion

self'-ex'e·cut'ing

self'-ex·plain'ing

self'-ex·plan'a·to'ry

self'-ex·pres'sion

self'-for·get'ful

self'-gov'erned

self'-gov'ern·ment

self'-help'

self'-im·por'tance

self'-im·prove'ment

self'-in·duced'

self'-in·duc'tance

self'-in·dul'gent

self'-in'ter·est

self'ish

self'ish·ly

self'ish·ness

self'-knowl'edge

self'less

self'-lim'it·ed

self'-liq'ui·dat'ing

self'-love'

self'-made'

self'-mas'ter·y

self'-o·pin'ion·at'ed

self'-pos·sessed'

self'-pos·ses'sion

self'-pres'er·va'tion

self'-pro·pel'ling

self'-rat'ing

self'-read'ing

self'-re·al'i·za'tion

self'-re·gard'

self'-reg'is·ter·ing

self'-re·li'ance

self'-re·li'ant

self'-re·nun'ci·a'tion

self'-re·proach'

self'-re·proach'ful

self'-re·proach'ing·ly

self'-re·spect'

self'-re·straint'

self'-right'eous

self'-right'eous·ness

self'-sac'ri·fice

self'-sac'ri·fic'ing·ly

self'same'

self'-sat'is·fied

self'-seek'er

self'-serv'ice

self'-start'er

self'-stud'y

self'-styled'

self'-suf·fi'cien·cy

self'-suf·fi'cient

self'-sup·port'

self'-sur·ren'der

self'-sus·tain'ing

self'-un'der·stand'ing

self'-will'

self'-willed'

self'-wind'ing

sell

sell'er

sell'out'

Selt'zer

sel'vage

se·man'tic

sem'a·phore

sem'blance

se·mes'ter

sem'i·cir'cle

sem'i·cir'cu·lar

sem'i·civ'i·lized

sem'i·co'lon

sem'i·con'scious

sem'i·de·tached'

sem'i·fi'nal

sem'i·fi'nal·ist

sem'i·fin'ished

sem'i·month'ly

sem'i·nar'

sem'i·nar'i·an

sem'i·nar'y

Sem'i·nole

sem'i·per'me·a·ble

sem'i·pre'cious

sem'i·se'ri·ous

sem'i·skilled'

Sem'ite

Se·mit'ic

Sem'i·tism

sem'i·tone'

sem'i·week'ly

sem'o·li'na

sem'pi·ter'nal

sen'ate

sen'a·tor

sen'a·to'ri·al

sen'a·to'ri·al·ly

sen'a·tor·ship'

send

send'er

Sen'e·ca

se·nes'cence

se·nes'cent

sen'es·chal

se'nile

se·nil'i·ty

sen'ior

sen·ior'i·ty

sen'na

sen'nit

sen'sate

sen·sa'tion

sen·sa'tion·al

sen·sa'tion·al·ism

sen·sa'tion·al·ly

sense

sense'less

sense'less·ly

sense'less·ness

sen'si·bil'i·ty

sen'si·ble

sen'si·tive

sen'si·tive·ly

sen'si·tive·ness

sen'si·tiv'i·ty

sen'si·ti·za'tion

sen'si·tize

sen'si·tized

sen'si·tiz'er

sen'si·tom'e·ter

sen·so'ri·um

sen'so·ry

sen'su·al

sen'su·al·ism

sen'su·al·ist

sen'su·al·is'tic

sen'su·al'i·ty

sen'su·al·i·za'tion

sen'su·al·ize

sen'su·al·ized

sen'su·al·ly

sen'su·ous

sen'su·ous·ly

sen'su·ous·ness

sen'tence

sen'tenced

sen·ten'tious

sen·ten'tious·ly

sen·ten'tious·ness

sen'ti·ence

sen'ti·en·cy

sen'ti·ment

sen'ti·men'tal

sen'ti·men'tal·ism

sen'ti·men'tal·ist

sen'ti·men·tal'i·ty

sen'ti·men'tal·ize

sen'ti·men'tal·ized

sen'ti·nel

sen'try

sep'a·ra·bil'i·ty

sep'a·ra·ble

sep'a·rate

sep'a·rat'ed

sep'a·rate·ly

sep'a·ra'tion

sep'a·ra'tion·ist	Se·quoi'a	se'ri·ous·ness
sep'a·ra·tism	se·ragl'io	ser'mon
sep'a·ra'tist	se·ra'pe	ser'mon·ize
sep'a·ra'tive	ser'aph	ser'mon·ized
sep'a·ra'tor	se·raph'ic	se'rous
sep'a·ra·to'ry	se·raph'i·cal	ser'pent
se'pi·a	ser'a·phim	ser'pen·tine
se'poy	Ser'bi·an	ser·pig'i·nous
sep'sis	sere	ser'rate
Sep·tem'ber	ser'e·nade'	ser·ra'tion
sep·ten'ni·al	ser'e·nad'ed	ser'ried
sep·tet'	ser'e·nad'er	se'rum
sep'tic	ser'e·na'ta	serv'ant
sep'ti·ce'mi·a	ser'en·dip'i·ty	serve
Sep'tu·a·gint	se·rene'	served
sep'tum	se·rene'ly	serv'er
sep'ul·cher	se·rene'ness	serv'ice
se·pul'chral	se·ren'i·ty	serv'ice·a·bil'i·ty
se·pul'tur·al	serf	serv'ice·a·ble
sep'ul·ture	serf'dom	serv'ice·a·bly
se'quel	serge	serv'iced
se·que'la	ser'geant	Serv'i·dor
se·que'lae	se'ri·al	ser'vile
se'quence	se'ri·al·i·za'tion	ser·vil'i·ty
se·quen'tial	se'ri·al·ize	serv'ings
se·quen'tial·ly	se'ri·al·ly	ser'vi·tor
se·ques'ter	se'ri·a'tim	ser'vi·tude
se·ques'tered	ser'i·cul'ture	ser'vo·mech'-a·nism
se·ques'trate	se'ries	ser'vo·mo'tor
se·ques'trat·ed	ser'if	ses'a·me
se'ques·tra'tion	se'ri·ous	ses'qui·sul'phide
se'quin	se'ri·ous·ly	ses'sion

ses'terce	sex·tet'	shak'en
ses·tet'	sex'ton	shak'er
set	sex'tu·ple	Shake·spear'e·an
set'back'	sex·tu'pli·cate	shake'-up'
set'off'	shab'bi·ly	shak'i·er
set·tee'	shab'bi·ness	shak'i·est
set'ter	shab'by	shak'i·ly
set'tings	shack	shak'i·ness
set'tle	shack'le	shak'o
set'tled	shack'led	shak'y
set'tle·ment	shade	shale
set'tler	shad'ed	shall
sev'er	shad'i·er	shal'lop
sev'er·a·ble	shad'i·est	shal·lot'
sev'er·al	shad'i·ly	shal'low
sev'er·al·ly	shad'i·ness	shal'lowed
sev'er·al·ty	shad'ings	shal'low·er
sev'er·ance	shad'ow	shal'low·est
sev'er·a'tion	shad'owed	shal'low·ly
se·vere'	shad'ow·less	shal'low·ness
sev'ered	shad'ow·y	sham
se·vere'ly	shad'y	sha'man
se·ver'er	shaft	sham'ble
se·ver'est	shag	sham'bled
se·ver'i·ty	shag'bark'	sham'bling·ly
sew	shag'gi·er	shame
sew'age	shag'gi·est	shamed
sewed	shag'gi·ly	shame'faced'
sew'er	shag'gy	shame·fac'ed·ly
sew'er·age	sha·green'	shame'ful
sewn	shake	shame'ful·ly
sex'tant	shake'down'	shame'ful·ness

shame'less·ly	sharp'ness	sheep'skin'
shame'less·ness	sharp'shoot'er	sheer
shammed	sharp'-wit'ted	sheer'er
sham'mer	shas'tra	sheer'est
sham·poo'	shat'ter	sheer'ly
sham·pooed'	shat'tered	sheet
sham'rock	shat'ter·ing·ly	sheet'ed
shan'dy·gaff	shat'ter·proof'	sheet'ings
shang·hai'	shave	sheet'ways'
shang·haied'	shaved	sheet'wise'
shank	shav'er	sheet'work'
shan't	shave'tail'	shek'el
shan'ty	shav'ings	shel'drake'
shape	shaw	shelf
shaped	shawl	shell
shape'less	she	shel·lac'
shape'less·ly	sheaf	shell'back'
shape'less·ness	shear	shell'burst'
shape'li·ness	sheared	shelled
shape'ly	shear'ings	shell'fish'
shard	shears	shell'proof'
share	sheathe	shell'work'
shared	sheathed	shel'ter
share'hold'er	sheaves	shel'tered
shark	shed	shel'ter·ing·ly
sharp	sheen	shel'ter·less
sharp'en	sheep	shelve
sharp'ened	sheep'herd'er	shelved
sharp'en·er	sheep'ish	shelves
sharp'er	sheep'ish·ly	shep'herd
sharp'est	sheep'ish·ness	shep'herd·ed
sharp'ly	sheep'man	shep'herd·ess

Sher'a·ton

sher'bet

sher'iff

Sher'pa

sher'ry

Shet'land

shew'bread'

shib'bo·leth

shied

shield

shield'ed

shift

shift'ed

shift'i·er

shift'i·est

shift'i·ly

shift'i·ness

shift'less

shift'y

shil·le'lagh

shil'lings

shim

shimmed

shim'mer

shim'mered

shim'mer·ing·ly

shim'mer·y

shin

shin'bone'

shine

shin'er

shin'gle

shin'gled

shin'i·ly

shin'i·ness

shin'ing·ly

shin'ny

shin'plas'ter

Shin'to'

Shin'to·ism

Shin'to·ist

Shin'to·is'tic

shin'y

ship

ship'board'

ship'build'er

ship'load'

ship'mas'ter

ship'mate'

ship'ment

ship'own'er

ship'per

ship'shape'

ship'worm'

ship'wreck'

ship'wright'

ship'yard'

shire

shirk

shirked

shirk'er

shirr

shirred

shirt

shirt'ings

shirt'less

shiv'er

shiv'ered

shiv'er·ing·ly

shiv'er·ings

shoal

shoal'ness

shock

shocked

shock'ing·ly

shod

shod'di·er

shod'di·est

shod'dy

shoe

shoe'horn'

shoe'lace'

shoe'less

shoe'mak'er

shoe'man

shoes

shoe'string'

sho'gun'

shook

shoot

shoot'er

shoot'ings

shop

shop'keep'er

shop'lift'er

shop'man

shop'per	should	shrewd
shop'work'	shoul'der	shrewd'er
shop'worn'	shoul'dered	shrewd'est
shore	shout	shrewd'ly
shored	shout'ed	shrewd'ness
shorn	shove	shriek
short	shoved	shrieked
short'age	shov'el	shrift
short'bread'	shov'eled	shrike
short'cake'	shov'el·head'	shrill
short'change'	show	shrilled
short'com'ings	show'boat'	shrill'er
short'en	show'down'	shrill'est
short'ened	showed	shrill'ness
short'en·ing	show'er	shrill'y
short'er	show'ered	shrimp
short'est	show'i·er	shrimp'er
short'fall'	show'i·est	shrine
short'hand'	show'i·ly	Shrin'er
short'hand'ed	show'i·ness	shrink
short'horn'	show'ings	shrink'age
short'ish	show'man	shrink'er
short'leaf'	show'man·ship	shrink'ing·ly
short'-lived'	shown	shrive
short'ly	show'room'	shriv'el
short'ness	show'y	shriv'eled
short'-range'	shrank	shriv'en
short'sight'ed	shrap'nel	shroud
short'-time'	shred	shroud'ed
shot	shred'ded	shrub
shot'gun'	shred'der	shrub'ber·y
shot'ted	shrew	shrub'wood'

shrug	sib'yl	siege
shrugged	sib'yl·line	si·en'na
shrunk	Si·cil'i·an	si·er'ra
shrunk'en	sick	si·es'ta
shuck	sick'bed'	sieve
shucked	sick'en	sift
shud'der	sick'ened	sift'age
shud'dered	sick'en·ing·ly	sift'ed
shud'der·ing·ly	sick'er	sift'ings
shud'der·ings	sick'est	sigh
shuf'fle	sick'le	sighed
shuf'fled	sick'li·er	sigh'ing·ly
shuf'fling·ly	sick'li·est	sigh'ings
shuf'flings	sick'li·ness	sight
shun	sick'ly	sight'ed
shunt	sick'ness	sight'ings
shunt'ed	sick'room'	sight'less
shut	side	sight'li·ness
shut'off'	side'board'	sight'ly
shut'ter	side'car'	sig'ma
shut'tered	sid'ed	sign
shut'tle	side'long'	sig'nal
shut'tled	side'piece'	sig'naled
shy	si·de're·al	sig'nal·ize
shy'ly	sid'er·ite	sig'nal·ized
shy'ness	side'split'ting	sig'nal·ly
shy'ster	side'walk'	sig'na·to'ry
Si'a·mese'	side'ways'	sig'na·ture
sib'i·lance	side'wise'	sign'board'
sib'i·lant	sid'ings	signed
sib'i·late	si'dle	sign'er
sib'ling	si'dled	sig'net

sig·nif′i·cance	sil′li·est	sim·plic′i·ty
sig·nif′i·cant	sil′li·ness	sim′pli·fi·ca′tion
sig·nif′i·cant·ly	sil′ly	sim′pli·fied
sig′ni·fi·ca′tion	si′lo	sim′pli·fy
sig′ni·fied	silt	sim′ply
sig′ni·fy	sil·ta′tion	sim′u·la′crum
sign′post′	silt′ed	sim′u·late
sign′writ′er	sil′van	sim′u·la′tion
si′lage	sil′ver	si′mul·ta′ne·ous
si′lence	sil′vered	si·mul·ta′ne·ous·ly
si′lenced	sil′ver·smith′	sin
si′lenc·er	sil′ver·ware′	since
si′lent	sil′ver·y	sin·cere′
si′lent·ly	sim′i·an	sin·cere′ly
si′lent·ness	sim′i·lar	sin·cere′ness
si′lex	sim′i·lar′i·ty	sin·cer′er
sil′hou·ette′	sim′i·lar·ly	sin·cer′est
sil′i·ca	sim′i·le	sin·cer′i·ty
sil′i·cate	si·mil′i·tude	sine
sil′i·con	sim′mer	si′ne·cure
sil′i·co′sis	sim′mered	sin′ew
silk	sim′mer·ing·ly	sin′ew·y
silk′en	sim′o·ny	sin′ful
silk′i·er	si·moon′	sin′ful·ly
silk′i·est	sim′per	sin′ful·ness
silk′i·ly	sim′pered	sing
silk′i·ness	sim′per·ing·ly	sing′a·ble
silk′weed′	sim′ple	singe
silk′worm′	sim′pler	singed
silk′y	sim′plest	sing′er
sil′la·bub	sim′ple·ton	sin′gle
sil′li·er	sim′plex	sin′gled

sin'gle·ness	sip'per	siz'es
sin'gle·ton	sir	siz'ings
sin'gly	sir·dar'	siz'zle
sin'gu·lar	sire	siz'zled
sin'gu·lar'i·ty	sired	siz'zling·ly
sin'gu·lar·ly	si'ren	skate
sin'is·ter	sir'loin'	skat'ed
sin'is·tral	si·roc'co	skat'er
sink	sir'up	skein
sink'age	sir'up·y	skel'e·tal
sink'er	si'sal	skel'e·ton
sink'hole'	sis'kin	skel'e·ton·ize
sink'ings	sis'si·fied	skel'e·ton·ized
sink'less	sis'sy	skep'tic
sin'less	sis'ter	skep'ti·cal
sin'less·ly	sis'ter·hood	skep'ti·cal·ly
sin'less·ness	sis'ter-in-law'	skep'ti·cism
sinned	sis'ter·ly	sketch
sin'ner	Sis'tine	sketched
Sin'o·log'i·cal	sis'trum	sketch'i·ly
Si·nol'o·gist	sit	sketch'i·ness
Sin'o·logue	site	sketch'y
Sin'o·phile	sit'ter	skew
sin'ter	sit'tings	skewed
sin'u·os'i·ty	sit'u·ate	skew'er
sin'u·ous	sit'u·at'ed	skew'ered
si'nus·i'tis	sit'u·a'tion	skew'ings
Sioux	sixth	ski
sip	siz'a·ble	ski'a·gram
si'phon	size	ski'a·graph
si'phoned	sized	ski·am'e·try
sipped	siz'er	skid

skid'ded	skir'mished	sky'writ'ing
skied	skir'mish·er	slab
skiff	skir'mish·ing·ly	slack
ski·jor'ing	skirt	slacked
skill	skirt'ed	slack'en
skilled	skirt'ings	slack'ened
skil'let	skit	slack'er
skill'ful	skit'ter	slack'est
skill'ful·ly	skit'tish	slack'ness
skill'ful·ness	skit'tish·ly	slag
skim	skit'tish·ness	slain
skimmed	skit'tles	slake
skim'mer	skive	slaked
skim'ming·ly	skived	slam
skimp	skiv'er	slammed
skimped	skiv'ings	slan'der
skimp'i·ness	skoal	slan'dered
skimp'y	skulk	slan'der·er
skin	skulked	slan'der·ing·ly
skin'flint'	skull	slan'der·ous
skink'er	skunk	slan'der·ous·ly
skinned	skunk'weed'	slan'der·ous·ness
skin'ner	sky	slang
skin'ni·er	sky'lark'	slang'y
skin'ni·est	sky'larked'	slank
skin'ny	sky'light'	slant
skin'worm'	sky'rock'et	slant'ed
skip	sky'scape	slant'ing·ly
skipped	sky'scrap'er	slant'ways'
skip'per	sky'shine'	slant'wise'
skip'ping·ly	sky'ward	slap
skir'mish	sky'writ'er	slap'dash'

slap'stick'	sleek'er	slick'est
slash	sleek'est	slid
slashed	sleek'ly	slide
slash'er	sleek'ness	sli'er
slash'ing·ly	sleep	sli'est
slash'ings	sleep'er	slight
slate	sleep'i·er	slight'ed
slat'er	sleep'i·est	slight'er
slat'ted	sleep'i·ly	slight'est
slat'tern	sleep'i·ness	slight'ing·ly
slat'tern·ly	sleep'less	slight'ly
slaugh'ter	sleep'less·ness	slight'ness
slaugh'tered	sleep'y	slim
slaugh'ter·er	sleet	slime
slaugh'ter·house'	sleeve	slim'i·er
slave	sleigh	slim'i·est
slaved	sleight	slim'i·ly
slav'er	slen'der	slim'i·ness
slav'er·y	slen'der·er	slim'mer
slav'ish	slen'der·est	slim'mest
slav'ish·ly	slen'der·ness	slim'ness
slav'ish·ness	slept	slim'y
slaw	sleuth	sling
slay	sleuthed	slink
slay'er	sleuth'hound'	slink'i·er
slay'ings	slew	slink'i·est
sleave	slewed	slink'y
slea'zi·ness	slice	slip
slea'zy	sliced	slip'case'
sled	slic'er	slip'knot'
sledge	slick	slip'page
sleek	slick'er	slipped

slip'per

slip'per·i·ness

slip'per·y

slip'shod'

slit

slith'er

slith'ered

slit'ter

sliv'er

sliv'ered

sliv'er·y

slob

slob'ber

sloe

sloe'ber'ry

slog

slo'gan

slo'gan·eer'

slogged

sloop

slop

slope

sloped

slop'ing·ly

slopped

slop'py

slosh

sloshed

slot

sloth

sloth'ful

sloth'ful·ly

sloth'ful·ness

slot'ted

slouch

slouched

slouch'i·ly

slouch'i·ness

slouch'ing·ly

slough

slough

sloughed

slov'en

slov'en·li·ness

slov'en·ly

slow

slowed

slow'er

slow'est

slow'go'ing

slow'ly

slow'poke'

sloyd

slub

slubbed

sludge

slug

slug'gard

slug'gard·ly

slugged

slug'ger

slug'gish

slug'gish·ly

slug'gish·ness

sluice

sluiced

sluice'way'

sluic'ings

slum

slum'ber

slum'bered

slum'ber·er

slum'ber·ing·ly

slum'ber·land'

slum'ber·ous

slump

slumped

slung

slur

slurred

slur'ring·ly

slur'ry

slush

slush'i·ly

slush'i·ness

slush'y

slut'tish

sly

sly'boots'

sly'ly

sly'ness

smack

smacked

smack'ing·ly

small

small'er

small'est	smil'ing·ly	smooth'ing·ly
small'ness	smirch	smooth'ly
small'pox'	smirched	smooth'ness
smart	smirk	smote
smart'ed	smirked	smoth'er
smart'en	smirk'ing·ly	smoth'ered
smart'ened	smirk'ish	smoth'er·ing·ly
smart'er	smite	smudge
smart'est	smith	smudged
smart'ing·ly	Smith·so'ni·an	smudg'i·ly
smart'ly	smith'y	smudg'i·ness
smart'ness	smit'ten	smudg'y
smash	smock	smug
smash'up'	smoke	smug'gle
smat'ter	smoked	smug'gled
smat'ter·ings	smoke'house'	smug'gler
smear	smoke'less	smug'ly
smeared	smoke'proof'	smug'ness
smear'i·er	smok'er	smut
smear'i·est	smoke'stack'	smut'ted
smear'i·ness	smoke'wood'	smut'ti·er
smear'y	smok'i·er	smut'ti·est
smell	smok'i·est	smut'ti·ly
smelled	smok'i·ness	smut'ti·ness
smelt	smok'y	smut'ty
smelt'ed	smol'der	snack
smelt'er	smol'dered	snaf'fle
smelt'er·y	smooth	sna·fu'
smidg'en	smooth'bore'	snag
smi'lax	smoothed	snag'ged
smile	smooth'er	snag'gled
smiled	smooth'est	snail

snake	snatch'y	snip'pet
snake'bird'	snath	snip'pi·er
snaked	sneak	snip'pi·est
snake'like'	sneaked	snip'pi·ness
snake'stone'	sneak'er	snip'py
snake'weed'	sneak'i·er	sniv'el
snake'wood'	sneak'i·est	sniv'eled
snak'i·er	sneak'ing·ly	sniv'el·er
snak'i·est	sneak'y	sniv'el·ings
snak'i·ly	sneer	snob
snak'i·ness	sneered	snob'ber·y
snak'y	sneer'ing·ly	snob'bish
snap	sneeze	snob'bish·ly
snap'drag'on	sneezed	snob'bish·ness
snapped	sneeze'weed'	snood
snap'per	snick'er	snook'er
snap'pi·er	snick'ered	snoop
snap'pi·est	snick'er·ing·ly	snoop'er
snap'ping·ly	snick'er·ings	snoot
snap'pish	sniff	snooze
snap'py	sniffed	snore
snap'shot'	sniff'i·ly	snored
snap'weed'	sniff'i·ness	snor'ing·ly
snare	sniff'ing·ly	snor'ings
snared	sniff'ings	snor'kel
snarl	snif'fle	snort
snarled	snif'fled	snort'ing·ly
snarl'ing·ly	sniff'y	snort'ings
snarl'y	snig'ger·ing·ly	snout
snatch	snip	snow
snatched	snipe	snow'ball'
snatch'ing·ly	snipped	snow'bell'

snow'ber'ry	snuf'flings	so'ber·ly
snow'bird'	snug	so'ber·sides'
snow'bound'	snug'ger	so·bri'e·ty
snow'bush'	snug'ger·y	so'bri·quet
snow'cap'	snug'gest	soc'age
snow'drift'	snug'gle	soc'cer
snow'drop'	snug'gled	so'cia·bil'i·ty
snowed	snug'ly	so'cia·ble
snow'fall'	snug'ness	so'cia·bly
snow'flake'	so	so'cial
snow'flow'er	soak	so'cial·ism
snow'i·er	soaked	so'cial·ist
snow'i·est	soap	so'cial·is'tic
snow'plow'	soap'box'	so'cial·i·za'tion
snow'shed'	soaped	so'cial·ize
snow'shoe'	soap'i·ness	so'cial·ized
snow'slide	soap'root'	so'cial·iz'er
snow'slip	soap'stone'	so·ci'e·tal
snow'storm	soap'suds'	so·ci'e·tar'i·an
snow'worm'	soap'y	so·ci'e·tar'i·an·ism
snow'y	soar	so·ci'e·ty
snub	soared	so'ci·o·log'i·cal
snubbed	soar'ing·ly	so'ci·o·log'i·cal·ly
snub'ber	sob	so'ci·ol'o·gist
snub'bing·ly	sobbed	so'ci·ol'o·gy
snub'bings	sob'bing·ly	sock
snuff	so·be'it	sock'et
snuffed	so'ber	sock'et·ed
snuff'er	so'bered	So·crat'ic
snuf'fle	so'ber·er	sod
snuf'fled	so'ber·est	so'da
snuf'fling·ly	so'ber·ing·ly	so·dal'i·ty

sod'den

so·di·um

so'fa

soft

sof'ten

sof'tened

sof'ten·er

soft'er

soft'est

soft'ly

soft'ness

soft'wood'

sog'gi·ly

sog'gi·ness

sog'gy

soil

soiled

so·journ'

so·journed'

so·journ'er

sol'ace

sol'aced

so'lar

so·lar'i·um

sold

sol'der

sol'dered

sol'dier

sol'diered

sol'dier·ly

sol'dier·y

sole

sol'e·cism

soled

sole'ly

sol'emn

so·lem'ni·ty

sol'em·ni·za'tion

sol'em·nize

sol'em·nized

sol'emn·ly

so'le·noid

so'le·noi'dal

sole'print'

sol'fe·ri'no

so·lic'it

so·lic'i·ta'tion

so·lic'it·ed

so·lic'i·tor

so·lic'it·ous

so·lic'i·tude

sol'id

sol'i·dar'i·ty

so·lid'i·fi'a·ble·ness

so·lid'i·fi·ca'tion

so·lid'i·fy

so·lid'i·ty

sol'id·ly

so·lil'o·quize

so·lil'o·quized

so·lil'o·quy

sol'i·taire'

sol'i·tar'i·ly

sol'i·tar'y

sol'i·tude

so'lo

so'loed

so'lo·ist

sol'stice

sol'u·bil'i·ty

sol'u·ble

sol'ute

so·lu'tion

solv'a·ble

sol'vate

sol·va'tion

solve

solved

sol'ven·cy

sol'vent

so·mat'ic

so'ma·tol'o·gy

som'ber

som·bre'ro

some

some'bod'y

some'how

some'one'

som'er·sault

some'thing

some'time'

some'what'

some'where'

som·nam'bu·lism

som·nam'bu·list

som'no·lent

son	so·phis'tic	sort
so'nant	so·phis'ti·cal	sort'ed
so·na'ta	so·phis'ti·cate	sort'er
so·na'ti·na	so·phis'ti·cat'ed	sor'tie
song	so·phis'ti·ca'tion	sor'ti·lege
song'bird'	soph'ist·ry	sos'te·nu'to
song'book'	soph'o·more	sot
song'ful	soph'o·mor'ic	sot'tish
song'ful·ness	soph'o·mor'i·cal	sot'tish·ness
song'ster	so'po·rif'ic	sou·brette'
son'ic	so·pra·ni'no	souf'flé'
son'-in-law'	so·pra'no	sought
son'net	sor'cer·er	soul
son'net·eer'	sor'cer·ess	soul'ful
so·nor'i·ty	sor'cer·y	soul'ful·ly
so·no'rous	sor'did	soul'ful·ness
soon	sor'did·ness	soul'less
soon'er	sore	soul'less·ly
soon'est	sore'head'	soul'less·ness
soot	sore'ly	sound
soot'ed	sore'ness	sound'ed
soothe	sor'ghum	sound'er
soothed	so·ror'i·ty	sound'est
sooth'ing·ly	so·ro'sis	sound'ing·ly
sooth'say'er	sor'rel	sound'ings
soot'i·er	sor'ri·er	sound'less
soot'i·est	sor'ri·est	sound'less·ly
soot'i·ly	sor'row	sound'less·ness
soot'y	sor'rowed	sound'ly
sop	sor'row·ful	sound'ness
soph'ism	sor'row·ful·ly	sound'proof'
soph'ist	sor'ry	soup

soup'bone'	sowed	spare'rib'
sour	sow'er	spar'ing·ly
source	sow'ings	spark
soured	soy	spark'ed
sour'er	soy'bean'	spar'kle
sour'est	spa	spar'kled
souse	space	spar'kler
soused	spaced	spar'kling·ly
sou·tane'	spac'ings	sparred
south	spa'cious	spar'ring·ly
south'east'	spa'cious·ly	spar'row
south'east'er	spa'cious·ness	sparse
south'east'er·ly	spade	sparse'ly
south'east'ern	spad'ed	sparse'ness
south'er·ly	spade'fish'	spars'er
south'ern	spade'work'	spars'est
south'ern·er	spa·ghet'ti	spar'si·ty
south'ern·most	spal·peen'	Spar'tan
south'ward	span	spasm
south'west'	span'drel	spas·mod'ic
south'west'er	span'gle	spas·mod'i·cal
south'west'er·ly	span'gled	spas·mod'i·cal·ly
sou've·nir'	Span'iard	spas'tic
sov'er·eign	span'iel	spas'ti·cal·ly
sov'er·eign·ty	Span'ish	spas·tic'i·ty
so'vi·et'	spank	spat
so'vi·et'ism	spanked	spat'ter
so'vi·et'i·za'tion	spank'ing·ly	spat'tered
so'vi·et'ize	spank'ings	spat'ter·ing·ly
so'vi·et·ol'o·gist	span'ner	spat'ter·ings
sow	spare	spat'ter·proof'
sow	spared	spat'ter·work'

spat'u·la	specked	speed'i·ly
spat'u·late	speck'le	speed'i·ness
spav'ined	speck'led	speed'ing·ly
spawn	spec'ta·cle	speed·om'e·ter
spawned	spec'ta·cles	speed'way'
speak	spec·tac'u·lar	speed'y
speak'er	spec·tac'u·lar·ly	spe'le·ol'o·gist
spear	spec·ta'tor	spe'le·ol'o·gy
speared	spec'ter	spell
spear'fish'	spec'tral	spell'bind'er
spear'head'	spec·trom'e·ter	spell'bound'
spear'mint'	spec'tro·scope	spelled
spear'wood'	spec'trum	spell'er
spe'cial	spec'u·late	spell'ings
spe'cial·ist	spec'u·lat'ed	spel'ter
spe'cial·i·za'tion	spec'u·la'tion	Spen·ce'ri·an
spe'cial·ize	spec'u·la'tive	spend
spe'cial·ized	spec'u·la'tive·ly	spend'er
spe'cial·ly	spec'u·la'tive·ness	spend'ings
spe'cial·ty	spec'u·la'tor	spend'thrift'
spe'cie	spec'u·la·to'ry	spent
spe'cies	spec'u·lum	sper'ma·ce'ti
spe·cif'ic	speech	spew
spe·cif'i·cal·ly	speech'less	spewed
spec'i·fi·ca'tion	speech'less·ly	sphag'num
spec'i·fied	speech'less·ness	sphere
spec'i·fy	speed	spher'i·cal
spec'i·men	speed'boat'	spher'i·cal·ly
spe'cious	speed'ed	sphe·ric'i·ty
spe'cious·ly	speed'er	sphe'roid
spe'cious·ness	speed'i·er	sphinx
speck	speed'i·est	spice

spiced	spin'y	splash'ings
spic'i·ly	spi'ral	splash'y
spic'i·ness	spi'raled	splat'ter
spic'y	spi'ral·ly	splat'ter·work'
spi'der	spire	splayed
spi'der·y	spired	splay'foot'
spied	spir'it	spleen
spig'ot	spir'it·ed	splen'did
spike	spir'it·ed·ly	splen'did·ly
spiked	spir'it·u·al	splen'dor
spik'y	spir'it·u·al·ism	splen'dor·ous
spile	spir'it·u·al·ist	sple·net'ic
spiled	spir'it·u·al·is'tic	splen'i·tive
spill	spir'it·u·al'i·ty	splice
spilled	spir'it·u·al·ize	spliced
spill'way'	spir'it·u·al·ized	splic'er
spin	spir'it·u·al·ly	splic'ings
spin'ach	spir'it·u·ous	splint
spi'nal	spi'ro·chete	splint'ed
spin'dle	spit	splin'ter
spine	spit'ball'	splin'tered
spine'less	spite	splin'ter·proof'
spin'et	spite'ful	split
spin'i·er	spite'ful·ly	split'tings
spin'i·est	spite'ful·ness	split'worm'
spin'na·ker	spit'fire'	splotch
spin'ner	spit·toon'	splotched
spin'ner·et	splash	splotch'y
spin'ney	splashed	splurge
spin'ning·ly	splash'i·er	splurged
spin'ster	splash'i·est	splut'ter
spin'ster·hood	splash'ing·ly	splut'tered

spoil	spooled	spout'ings
spoil'age	spoon	sprain
spoiled	spoon'bill'	sprained
spoils'man	spooned	sprang
spoil'sport'	spoon'er·ism	sprat
spoke	spoon'ful	sprawl
spo'ken	spoon'fuls	sprawled
spoke'shave'	spoor	sprawl'ing·ly
spokes'man	spo·rad'ic	spray
spo'li·a'tion	spore	sprayed
spo'li·a'tive	sport	spray'er
spo'li·a·to'ry	sport'ed	spread
spon'dee	spor'tive	spread'er
sponge	spor'tive·ly	spread'ing·ly
sponge'cake'	spor'tive·ness	spree
sponged	sports'man	sprig
spong'er	sports'man·ship	spright'li·er
spon'gi·er	sports'wear'	spright'li·est
spon'gi·est	sport'y	spright'li·ness
spong'ings	spot	spright'ly
spon'gy	spot'less	spring
spon'sor	spot'less·ly	spring'board'
spon'sor·ship	spot'less·ness	spring'bok'
spon'ta·ne'i·ty	spot'light'	spring'fish'
spon·ta'ne·ous	spot'ted	spring'i·ly
spon·ta'ne·ous·ly	spot'ter	spring'i·ness
spon·ta'ne·ous·ness	spot'ti·er	spring'ing·ly
spoof	spot'ti·est	spring'time'
spook	spot'ty	spring'wood'
spook'i·ness	spouse	spring'y
spook'y	spout	sprin'kle
spool	spout'ed	sprin'kled

sprin'kler	spurt'ed	squashed
sprin'kling·ly	sput'nik	squat
sprin'klings	sput'ter	squat'ted
sprint	sput'tered	squat'ter
sprint'er	sput'ter·ing·ly	squaw
sprite	sput'ter·ings	squaw'fish'
sprit'sail'	spu'tum	squawk
sprock'et	spy	squeak
sprout	spy'glass'	squeal
sprout'ed	squab	squealed
sprout'ling	squab'ble	squeam'ish
spruce	squab'bled	squee'gee
spruc'er	squab'bling·ly	squeeze
spruc'est	squab'blings	squeezed
sprung	squad	squelch
spry	squad'ron	squelched
spud	squal'id	squelch'ing·ly
spume	squa·lid'i·ty	squib
spumed	squal'id·ly	squid
spu·mo'ne	squall	squig'gle
spun	squalled	squig'gly
spunk	squall'ings	squint
spunk'i·er	squall'y	squint'ed
spunk'i·est	squal'or	squint'ing·ly
spunk'y	squan'der	squire
spur	squan'dered	squirm
spu'ri·ous	square	squirmed
spu'ri·ous·ly	squared	squirm'ing·ly
spurn	square'head'	squirm'ings
spurned	square'ly	squir'rel
spurred	square'ness	squir'rel·fish'
spurt	squash	squir'rel·proof'

squirt	stag'nat·ed	stamped
stab	stag·na'tion	stam·pede'
stabbed	staid	stam·ped'ed
stab'bing·ly	stain	stamp'er
stab'bings	stained	stamp'ings
sta·bil'i·ty	stain'less	stance
sta'bi·li·za'tion	stair	stanch
sta'bi·lize	stair'case'	stan'chion
sta'bi·lized	stair'way'	stand
sta'bi·liz'er	stake	stand'ard
sta'ble	staked	stand'ard·i·za'-
stac·ca'to	sta·lac'tite	tion
stack	sta·lag'mite	stand'ard·ize
sta'di·a	stale	stand'ings
sta'di·um	stale'mate'	stand'off'
staff	stal'er	stand'pipe'
stag	stal'est	stand'point'
stage	stalk	stand'still'
stage'coach'	stalked	stank
stage'craft'	stalk'er	stan'nate
staged	stalk'ing·ly	stan'nic
stage'hand'	stall	stan'nous
stag'er	stalled	stan'za
stage'wor'thy	stal'lion	sta'ple
stag'ger	stal'wart	sta'pled
stag'gered	sta'men	sta'pler
stag'ger·ing·ly	stam'i·na	star
stag'horn'	stam'mer	star'board
stag'hound'	stam'mered	starch
stag'hunt'	stam'mer·er	starched
stag'nant	stam'mer·ing·ly	starch'y
stag'nate	stamp	stare
		stared

star'fish'	states'man·like'	steak
star'gaz'er	stat'ic	steal
star'ing·ly	sta'tion	stealth
stark	sta'tion·ar'y	stealth'i·er
star'less	sta'tioned	stealth'i·est
star'let	sta'tion·er	stealth'i·ly
star'light'	sta'tion·er'y	steam
star'like'	stat'ism	steam'boat'
star'lings	stat'ist	steamed
starred	sta·tis'ti·cal	steam'er
star'ri·er	sta·tis'ti·cal·ly	steam'i·er
star'ri·est	stat'is·ti'cian	steam'i·est
star'ry	sta·tis'tics	steam'i·ness
start	stat'u·ar'y	steam'ship'
start'ed	stat'ue	steam'y
start'er	stat'u·esque'	ste'a·tite
star'tle	stat'u·ette'	steel
star'tled	stat'ure	steel'head'
star'tling·ly	sta'tus	steel'work'
star·va'tion	stat'ute	steel'yard
starve	stat'u·to'ry	steep
starved	stave	steep'er
starve'ling	stay	steep'est
state	stayed	stee'ple
stat'ed	stead	stee'ple·chase'
state'hood	stead'fast	steer
State'house'	stead'fast·ly	steer'age
state'li·ness	stead'fast·ness	steered
state'ly	stead'i·er	steer'ing
state'ment	stead'i·est	steers'man
state'room'	stead'i·ly	stein
states'man	stead'y	stel'lar

stem	stern'er	stiff'est
stemmed	stern'est	stiff'ness
stench	stern'ly	sti'fle
sten'cil	stern'ness	sti'fled
sten'ciled	stern'post'	sti'fling·ly
ste·nog'ra·pher	ster'num	stig'ma
sten'o·graph'ic	ster'nu·ta'tion	stig·mat'a
ste·nog'ra·phy	ster'to·rous	stig·mat'ic
ste·no'sis	stet	stig'ma·tism
sten·to'ri·an	steth'o·scope	stig'ma·ti·za'tion
step	ste've·dore'	stig'ma·tize
step'child'	stew	stig'ma·tized
step'daugh'ter	stew'ard	stile
step'lad'der	stew'ard·ess	sti·let'to
step'moth'er	stewed	still
steppe	stick	still'born'
stepped	stick'er	stilled
step'sis'ter	stick'ful	still'er
step'son'	stick'i·er	still'est
ster'e·o	stick'i·est	still'ness
ster'e·o·phon'ic	stick'i·ly	still'room'
ster'e·op'ti·con	stick'i·ness	still'y
ster'e·o·scope'	stick'le·back'	stilt
ster'e·o·scop'ic	stick'ler	stilt'ed
ster'ile	stick'pin'	stim'u·lant
ste·ril'i·ty	stick'weed'	stim'u·late
ster'i·li·za'tion	stick'y	stim'u·lat'ed
ster'i·lize	stiff	stim'u·lat'ing·ly
ster'i·lized	stiff'en	stim'u·la'tion
ster'i·liz'er	stiff'ened	stim'u·lus
ster'ling	stiff'en·er	sting
stern	stiff'er	sting'er

sting'fish'	stir'rings	stodg'i·er
stin'gi·er	stir'rup	stodg'i·est
stin'gi·est	stitch	stodg'y
sting'ing·ly	stitched	sto'gy
stin'gy	stitch'er	sto'ic
stink	stitch'ings	sto'i·cal
stink'bug'	stitch'work'	sto'i·cal·ly
stink'er	sti'ver	sto'i·cism
stink'ing·ly	sto'a	stoke
stink'pot'	stoat	stoked
stink'weed'	stock	stoke'hold'
stink'wood'	stock·ade'	stok'er
stint	stock·ad'ed	stole
stint'ed	stock'breed'er	sto'len
stint'ing·ly	stock'bro'ker	stol'id
stipe	stocked	stol·id'i·ty
sti'pend	stock'fish'	stol'id·ly
sti·pen'di·ar'y	stock'hold'er	stom'ach
sti·pen'di·um	stock'house'	stom'ach·ful
stip'ple	stock'i·ness	sto·mach'ic
stip'pled	stock'i·net'	stone
stip'plings	stock'ings	stone'boat'
stip'u·late	stock'job'ber	stoned
stip'u·lat'ed	stock'keep'er	stone'fish'
stip'u·lates	stock'mak'er	stone'ma'son
stip'u·la'tion	stock'man	stone'ware'
stip'u·la·to'ry	stock'own'er	stone'weed'
stir	stock'pile'	stone'wood'
stir'pes	stock'pot'	stone'work'
stirps	stock'tak'er	stone'yard'
stirred	stock'y	ston'i·er
stir'ring·ly	stock'yard'	ston'i·est

ston'i·ly

ston'y

stood

stool

stoop

stooped

stoop'ing·ly

stop

stop'cock'

stope

stop'gap'

stop'o'ver

stop'page

stopped

stop'per

stop'pered

stop'ple

stor'age

store

stored

store'house'

store'keep'er

store'room'

sto'ried

stork

storm

storm'bound'

stormed

storm'i·er

storm'i·est

storm'ing·ly

storm'y

sto'ry

sto'ry·tell'er

stoup

stout

stout'er

stout'est

stout'heart'ed

stout'ly

stout'ness

stove

stow

stow'age

stra·bis'mus

strad'dle

strad'dled

strad'dling·ly

strafe

strag'gle

strag'gled

strag'gler

strag'gling·ly

straight

straight'edge'

straight'en

straight'ened

straight'er

straight'est

straight'for'ward

straight'for'ward·ly

straight'for'ward·ness

straight'way'

straight'ways'

strain

strained

strain'er

strain'ing·ly

strain'ings

strait

strait'en

strait'ened

strait'er

strait'est

strake

strand

strand'ed

strange

strange'lings

strange'ly

strange'ness

stran'ger

strang'est

stran'gle

stran'gled

stran'gler

stran'gles

stran'gling·ly

stran'glings

stran'gu·late

stran'gu·lat'ed

stran'gu·la'tion

strap

strap'less

strap·pa'do

strapped

strap'pings

stra'ta

strat'a·gem

stra·te'gic

stra·te'gi·cal

strat'e·gist

strat'e·gy

strat'i·fi·ca'tion

strat'i·fied

strat'i·fy

strat'o·sphere

stra'tum

straw

straw'ber'ry

straw'flow'er

stray

strayed

streak

streaked

streak'i·er

streak'i·est

streak'y

stream

streamed

stream'er

stream'ing·ly

stream'line'

stream'way'

street

strength

strength'en

strength'ened

strength'en·er

stren'u·ous

stren'u·ous·ly

stren'u·ous·ness

stress

stressed

stress'ful

stretch

stretched

stretch'er

stretch'er·man

stretch'-out'

strew

strewed

strewn

stri'ate

stri'at·ed

stri·a'tion

strick'en

strict

strict'ly

strict'ness

stric'ture

stride

stri'dent

stri'dent·ly

strid'ing·ly

strid'u·lous

strife

strig'il

strike

strike'break'er

strik'er

strik'ing·ly

string

stringed

strin'gen·cy

strin'gent

strin'gent·ly

string'er

string'i·er

string'i·est

string'piece'

string'y

strip

stripe

striped

strip'lings

strip'per

strip'pings

strive

striv'en

strob'o·scope

strode

stroke

stroked

strok'ings

stroll

strolled

stroll'er

strong

strong'box'

strong'er

strong'est

strong'hold'	stub'born	stump
strong'ly	stub'by	stump'age
stron'ti·um	stuc'co	stumped
strop	stuck	stump'i·er
stro'phe	stud	stump'i·est
stroph'ic	stud'book'	stump'y
strove	stud'ded	stun
struck	stu'dent	stung
struc'tur·al	stud'fish'	stunk
struc'tur·al·ly	stud'horse'	stunned
struc'ture	stud'ied	stun'ner
struc'tured	stu'di·o	stun'ning·ly
stru'del	stu'di·ous	stunt
strug'gle	stu'di·ous·ly	stunt'ed
strug'gled	stu'di·ous·ness	stu'pe·fa'cient
strug'gler	stud'work'	stu'pe·fac'tion
strug'gling·ly	stud'y	stu'pe·fied
strug'glings	stuff	stu'pe·fy
strum	stuffed	stu·pen'dous
strummed	stuff'er	stu'pid
strung	stuff'ings	stu·pid'i·ty
strut	stuff'i·er	stu'pid·ly
strut'ted	stuff'i·est	stu'por
strut'ter	stuff'i·ly	stu'por·ous
strut'ting·ly	stuff'i·ness	stur'di·ly
strut'tings	stuff'y	stur'di·ness
strych'nine	stul'ti·fi·ca'tion	stur'dy
stub	stul'ti·fied	stur'geon
stubbed	stul'ti·fy	stut'ter
stub'bi·ness	stum'ble	stut'tered
stub'ble	stum'bled	stut'ter·er
stub'bly	stum'bling·ly	stut'ter·ing·ly

sty	sub·arc'tic	sub·ject'ed
Styg'i·an	sub'a·tom'ic	sub·jec'tion
style	sub·cal'i·ber	sub·jec'tive
style'book'	sub'cap'tion	sub·jec'tive·ly
styled	sub'cel'lar	sub·jec'tive·ness
styl'ings	sub'class'	sub·jec'tiv·ism
styl'ish	sub'com·mit'tee	sub'jec·tiv'i·ty
styl'ish·ness	sub·con'scious	sub·join'
styl'ist	sub·con'scious·ly	sub·join'der
sty·lis'tic	sub·con'scious·ness	sub·joined'
sty·lis'ti·cal·ly	sub'con·stel·la'tion	sub'ju·gate
styl'ize	sub·con'ti·nent	sub'ju·gat'ed
styl'ized	sub·con'tract	sub'ju·ga'tion
sty'lo·graph	sub'con·tract'ed	sub·junc'tive
sty'lo·graph'ic	sub'con·trac'tor	sub·king'dom
sty'lus	sub'cu·ta'ne·ous	sub'lap·sar'i·an
sty'mie	sub·dea'con	sub'lease'
styp'tic	sub'di·vide'	sub'les·see'
Styx	sub'di·vid'ed	sub·les'sor
su'a·bil'i·ty	sub'di·vi'sion	sub·let'
su'a·ble	sub·due'	sub'li·mate
sua'sion	sub·dued'	sub'li·mat'ed
suave	sub·du'ing·ly	sub'li·ma'tion
suave'ly	sub·ed'i·tor	sub·lime'
suave'ness	sub·fam'i·ly	sub·limed'
suav'i·ty	sub'foun·da'tion	sub·lim'er
sub'a·cute'	sub'grade'	sub·lim'est
sub'a·dult'	sub'group'	sub·lim'i·nal
sub·a'gent	sub'head'	sub·lim'i·ty
sub·al'tern	sub·head'ings	sub'lu·nar'y
sub'a·quat'ic	sub·hu'man	sub'lux·a'tion
sub·a'que·ous	sub'ject	sub·mar'gin·al

sub'ma·rine'	sub·poe'na	sub·stan'ti·at'ed
sub'ma·rin'er	sub·poe'naed	sub·stan'ti·a'tion
sub·merge'	sub·ro·ga'tion	sub'stan·tive
sub·merged'	sub·scribe'	sub'sta'tion
sub·mer'gence	sub·scribed'	sub'sti·tute
sub·mers'i·ble	sub·scrib'er	sub'sti·tut'ed
sub·mer'sion	sub'script	sub'sti·tu'tion
sub·me'ter·ing	sub·scrip'tion	sub·stra'tum
sub·mis'sion	sub'se·quent	sub·struc'ture
sub·mis'sive	sub'se·quent·ly	sub·sur'face
sub·mis'sive·ly	sub·serve'	sub·tan'gent
sub·mis'sive·ness	sub·served'	sub·ten'ant
sub·mit'	sub·ser'vi·ence	sub·tend'
sub·mit'tal	sub·ser'vi·en·cy	sub·tend'ed
sub·mit'ted	sub·ser'vi·ent	sub'ter·fuge
sub·mit'ting·ly	sub·side'	sub'ter·ra'ne·an
sub·nor'mal	sub·sid'ed	sub'ter·ra'ne·ous
sub'nor·mal'i·ty	sub·sid'ence	sub'ti'tle
sub'o·ce·an'ic	sub·sid'i·ar'y	sub'tle
sub·or'der	sub'si·dize	sub'tler
sub·or'di·nate	sub'si·dized	sub'tlest
sub·or'di·nat'ed	sub'si·dy	sub'tle·ty
sub·or'di·nat'ing·ly	sub·sist'	sub'tly
sub·or'di·na'tion	sub·sist'ed	sub·tract'
sub·or'di·na'tive	sub·sist'ence	sub·tract'ed
sub·orn'	sub'soil'	sub·trac'tion
sub'or·na'tion	sub'spe'cies	sub'tra·hend'
sub·orned'	sub'stance	sub·treas'ur·y
sub·orn'er	sub·stand'ard	sub·trop'i·cal
sub·phy'lum	sub·stan'tial	sub'urb
sub'plinth'	sub·stan'tial·ly	sub·ur'ban
sub'plot'	sub·stan'ti·ate	sub·ur'ban·ite

sub·ven'tion	suc'tion	suf·fused'
sub·ver'sion	sud'den	suf·fu'sion
sub·ver'sive	sud'den·ly	sug'ar
sub·vert'	sud'den·ness	sug'ared
sub·vert'ed	su·dor·if'er·ous	sug'ar·plum'
sub'way'	su·dor·if'ic	sug'ar·y
suc·ceed'	suds	sug·gest'
suc·ceed'ed	sue	sug·gest'ed
suc·ceed'ing·ly	sued	sug·gest'i·bil'i·ty
suc·cess'	suède	sug·gest'i·ble
suc·cess'ful	su'et	sug·ges'tion
suc·cess'ful·ly	suf'fer	sug·ges'tive
suc·ces'sion	suf'fer·a·ble	sug·ges'tive·ness
suc·ces'sive	suf'fer·ance	su'i·cid'al
suc·ces'sor	suf'fered	su'i·cid'al·ly
suc·cinct'	suf'fer·er	su'i·cide
suc·cinct'ly	suf'fer·ing·ly	suit
suc'cor	suf'fer·ings	suit'a·bil'i·ty
suc'cored	suf·fice'	suit'a·ble
suc'co·tash	suf·ficed'	suit'case'
suc'cu·lence	suf·fi'cien·cy	suite
suc'cu·lent	suf·fi'cient	suit'ed
suc'cu·lent·ly	suf'fix	suit'ing·ly
suc·cumb'	suf'fo·cate	suit'ings
suc·cumbed'	suf'fo·cat'ed	suit'or
such	suf'fo·cat'ing·ly	sulk
suck	suf'fo·ca'tion	sulked
sucked	suf'fo·ca'tive	sulk'i·er
suck'er	suf'fra·gan	sulk'i·est
suck'le	suf'frage	sulk'i·ly
suck'led	suf'fra·gist	sulk'i·ness
suck'lings	suf·fuse'	sulk'y

sul'len	sump	sun'rise'
sul'len·ly	sump'ter	sun'room'
sul'len·ness	sump'tu·ar'y	sun'set'
sul'lied	sump'tu·ous	sun'shade'
sul'ly	sump'tu·ous·ly	sun'shine'
sul'phate	sump'tu·ous·ness	sun'shin'y
sul'phide	sun	sun'spot'
sul'phite	sun'beam'	sun'stone'
sul'phur	sun'bon'net	sun'stroke'
sul·phu'ric	sun'burn'	sun'ward
sul'phu·rous	sun'burned	sup
sul'tan	sun'burst'	su'per·a·ble
sul·tan'a	sun'dae	su'per·a·bun'dance
sul'tan·ate	Sun'day	su'per·a·bun'dant
sul'tri·er	sun'der	su'per·an'nu·ate
sul'tri·est	sun'der·ance	su'per·an'nu·at'ed
sul'try	sun'dered	su'per·an'nu·a'tion
sum	sun'di'al	su·perb'
su'mac	sun'dry	su'per·cal'en·der
sum'ma·ri·ly	sun'fish'	su'per·cal'en-dered
sum'ma·ri·ness	sun'flow'er	su'per·car'go
sum'ma·rize	sun'glass'	su'per·charg'er
sum'ma·rized	sun'glow'	su'per·cil'i·ous
sum'ma·ry	sunk	su'per·cil'i·ous·ly
sum·ma'tion	sunk'en	su'per·cil'i·ous·ness
summed	sun'less	su'per·con·duc'-tance
sum'mer	sun'light'	su'per·con'duc-tiv'i·ty
sum'mered	sun'lit'	su'per·con·duc'-tor
sum'mer·y	sunned	su'per·cool'
sum'mit	sun'ni·ness	su'per·dread'-nought'
sum'mon	sun'ny	su'per·em'i·nence
sum'moned	sun'proof'	su'per·em'i·nent

su·per·er'o·ga'tion	su·per'nal·ly	su·pine'ness
su'per·fam'i·ly	su'per·nat'u·ral	sup'per
su'per·fi'cial	su'per·nat'u·ral·ly	sup·plant'
su'per·fi'ci·al'i·ty	su'per·nat'u·ral·ism	sup·plant'ed
su'per·fi'cial·ly	su'per·nat'u·ral·ist	sup'ple
su'per·fine'	su'per·nor'mal	sup'ple·ment
su'per·flu'i·ty	su'per·nu'mer·ar'y	sup'ple·men'tal
su·per'flu·ous	su'per·po·si'tion	sup'ple·men'ta·ry
su·per'flu·ous·ly	su'per·sat'u·rate	sup'ple·men·ta'tion
su·per'flu·ous·ness	su'per·sat'u·rat'ed	sup'ple·ment'ed
su'per·heat'	su'per·sat'u·ra'tion	sup'pli·ant
su'per·heat'ed	su'per·scribe'	sup'pli·cant
su'per·het'er·o·dyne'	su'per·scribed'	sup'pli·cate
su'per·hu'man	su'per·scrip tion	sup'pli·cat'ed
su'per·hu'man·ly	su'per·sede'	sup'pli·cat'ing·ly
su'per·im·pose'	su'per·sed'ed	sup'pli·ca'tion
su'per·im·posed'	su'per·ses'sion	sup'pli·ca·to'ry
su'per·im'po·si'tion	su'per·son'ic	sup·plied'
su'per·im·po'sure	su'per·sti'tion	sup·pli'er
su'per·in·duce'	su'per·sti'tious	sup·ply'
su'per·in·duced'	su'per·sti'tious·ly	sup·port'
su'per·in·tend'	su'per·stra'tum	sup·port'ed
su'per·in·tend'ed	su'per·struc'ture	sup·port'er
su'per·in·tend'ence	su'per·tax'	sup·pose'
su'per·in·tend'en·cy	su'per·vene'	sup·posed'
su'per·in·tend'ent	su'per·vened'	sup·pos'ed·ly
su·pe'ri·or	su'per·vise'	sup'po·si'tion
su·pe'ri·or'i·ty	su'per·vised'	sup·pos'i·ti'tious
su·per'la·tive	su'per·vi'sion	sup·pos'i·ti'tious·ly
su·per'la·tive·ly	su'per·vi'sor	sup·press'
su'per·man'	su'per·vi'so·ry	sup·pressed'
su·per'nal	su·pine'	sup·pres'sion

sup·pres'sive	sur'li·ness	sur·round'ings
sup'pu·rate	sur'ly	sur'tax'
sup'pu·rat'ed	sur·mise'	sur'tout'
sup'pu·ra'tion	sur·mised'	sur·veil'lance
sup'pu·ra'tive	sur·mount'	sur·vey'
su·prem'a·cy	sur·mount'ed	sur·veyed'
su·preme'	sur'name'	sur·vey'or
su·preme'ly	sur'named'	sur·viv'al
sur'base'	sur·pass'	sur·viv'al·ism
sur·cease'	sur·passed'	sur·vive'
sur·charge'	sur·pass'ing·ly	sur·vived'
sur·charged'	sur'plice	sur·vi'vor
sur'cin'gle	sur'pliced	sur·vi'vor·ship
surd	sur'plus	sus·cep'ti·bil'i·ty
sure	sur'plus·age	sus·cep'ti·ble
sure'ly	sur·prise'	sus·cep'ti·bly
sure'ness	sur·prised'	sus·pect'
sure'ty	sur·pris'ed·ly	sus·pect'ed
sure'ty·ship	sur·pris'ing·ly	sus·pend'
surf	sur're·but'tal	sus·pend'ed
sur'face	sur're·but'ter	sus·pend'ers
sur'faced	sur're·join'der	sus·pense'
sur'fac·ings	sur·ren'der	sus·pense'ful
sur'feit	sur·ren'dered	sus·pen'sion
sur'feit·ed	sur'rep·ti'tious	sus·pen'sive
surge	sur'rep·ti'tious·ly	sus·pen'sive·ly
surged	sur'rep·ti'tious·ness	sus·pen'sive·ness
sur'geon	sur'rey	sus·pi'cion
sur'ger·y	sur'ro·gate	sus·pi'cious
sur'gi·cal	sur'ro·ga'tion	sus·pi'cious·ly
sur'li·er	sur·round'	sus·pi'cious·ness
sur'li·est	sur·round'ed	sus·pire'

sus·tain′	swal′low-tailed′	sweat′box′
sus·tained′	swa′mi	sweat′er
sus·tain′ed·ly	swamp	sweat′i·er
sus·tain′ing·ly	swamped	sweat′i·est
sus′te·nance	swan	sweat′i·ly
sus·ten·tac′u·lar	swan′herd′	sweat′i·ness
sus′ten·ta′tion	swank	sweat′shop
su′sur·ra′tion	swank′i·er	sweat′y
sut′ler	swank′i·est	Swed′ish
sut·tee′	swank′y	sweep
su′ture	swans′down′	sweep′er
su′tured	swap	sweep′ing·ly
su′ze·rain	swapped	sweep′ings
su′ze·rain·ty	sward	sweep′stake′
svelte	swarm	sweet
swab	swarmed	sweet′bread′
swabbed	swart	sweet′bri′er
swad′dle	swarth′y	sweet′en
swad′dled	swash	sweet′ened
swad′dling	swas′ti·ka	sweet′en·er
swad′dlings	swat	sweet′en·ings
swag	swatch	sweet′heart′
swage	swath	sweet′ish
swaged	swathe	sweet′ish·ly
swag′ger	swat′ter	sweet′ly
swag′gered	sway	sweet′meat′
swag′ger·ing·ly	swayed	sweet′ness
Swa·hi′li	sway′ing·ly	sweet′root′
swain	swear	sweet′shop′
swal′low	swear′ing·ly	sweet′wa′ter
swal′lowed	sweat	sweet′weed′
swal′low·er	sweat′band′	sweet′wood′

swell	swipe	sworn
swelled	swiped	swung
swell'er	swirl	swum
swell'fish	swirled	syb'a·rite
swell'ings	swirl'ing·ly	syc'a·more
swel'ter	swish	syc'o·phan·cy
swel'tered	swished	syc'o·phant
swel'ter·ing·ly	Swiss	syc'o·phan'tic
swept	switch	syl'la·bi
swerve	switch'board'	syl·lab'ic
swerved	switched	syl·lab'i·cate
swift	switch'gear'	syl·lab'i·cat'ed
swift'er	switch'keep'er	syl·lab'i·ca'tion
swift'est	switch'man	syl·lab'i·fi·ca'tion
swift'ly	switch'tail'	syl·lab'i·fy
swift'ness	switch'yard'	syl'la·ble
swig	swiv'el	syl'la·bus
swigged	swiv'eled	syl'la·bus·es
swill	swol'len	syl'lo·gism
swilled	swoon	syl'lo·gis'tic
swim	swooned	syl'lo·gize
swim'mer	swoon'ing·ly	sylph
swim'ming·ly	swoop	syl'van
swin'dle	swooped	sym'bi·o'sis
swin'dled	sword	sym'bi·ot'ic
swin'dler	sword'bill'	sym'bol
swine	sword'fish'	sym·bol'ic
swine'herd'	sword'play'	sym·bol'i·cal
swing	swords'man	sym·bol'i·cal·ly
swing'ing·ly	sword'stick'	sym'bol·ism
swin'ish	sword'tail'	sym'bol·ist
swink	swore	sym'bol·i·za'tion

sym'bol·ize	syn'chro·nize	syn·o'vi·al
sym'bol·ized	syn'chro·nized	syn'o·vi'tis
sym·met'ri·cal	syn'chro·nous	syn·tac'ti·cal
sym'me·try	syn'co·pate	syn'tax
sym'pa·thec'to·my	syn'co·pat'ed	syn'the·ses
sym'pa·thet'ic	syn'co·pa'tion	syn'the·sis
sym'pa·thet'i·cal·ly	syn'co·pe	syn'the·size
sym'pa·thize	syn'cre·tism	syn'the·sized
sym'pa·thized	syn'dic	syn·thet'ic
sym'pa·thiz'er	syn'di·cal	syn·thet'i·cal·ly
sym'pa·thiz'ing·ly	syn'di·cal·ism	syr'inge
sym'pa·thy	syn'di·cal·ize	syr'up
sym·phon'ic	syn'di·cate	sys'tem
sym'pho·ny	syn'di·cat'ed	sys'tem·at'ic
sym'phy·sis	syn'di·ca'tion	sys'tem·a·ti·za'tion
sym·po'si·um	syn'drome	sys'tem·a·tize
symp'tom	syn·ec'do·che	sys'tem·a·tized
symp'to·mat'ic	syn'od	sys'tem·a·tiz'er
symp'tom·a·tol'o·gy	syn'od·ist	sys'tem·a·tol'o·gy
syn'a·gogue	syn'o·nym	sys·tem'ic
syn·apse'	syn·on'y·mous	sys·tem'i·cal·ly
syn·ap'sis	syn·op'ses	sys'to·le
syn'chro·nism	syn·op'sis	sys·tol'ic
syn'chro·ni·za'tion	syn·op'tic	syz'y·gy

T

tab	tab'u·late	tac'ti·cal
tab'ard	tab'u·lat'ed	tac·ti'cian
ta·bas'co	tab'u·la'tion	tac'tics
tab'er·nac'le	tab'u·la'tor	tac'tile
tab'er·nac'led	ta·chis'to·scope	tact'less
ta'bes	ta·chom'e·ter	tact'less·ly
tab'la·ture	ta·chyg'ra·pher	tact'less·ness
ta'ble	ta·chyg'ra·phy	tad'pole'
ta'bleau	tac'it	taf'fe·ta
ta'ble·cloth'	tac'it·ly	taff'rail
ta'bled	tac'i·turn	taf'fy
ta'ble·maid'	tac'i·tur'ni·ty	tag
ta'ble·man	tack	tag'board'
ta'ble·spoon'	tacked	tagged
tab'let	tack'le	Ta·hi'ti·an
ta'ble·ware'	tack'led	tail
tab'loid	tack'ler	tail'board'
ta·boo'	tack'y	tailed
ta'bor	tact	tail'first'
tab'o·ret	tact'ful	tail'ings
ta·bu'	tact'ful·ly	tail'less
tab'u·lar	tact'ful·ness	tai'lor

tai'lored	tal'lowed	tan'gent
tail'piece'	tal'low·i·ness	tan·gen'tial
tail'race'	tal'low·root'	tan·gen'ti·al'i·ty
tail'stock'	tal'low·wood'	tan'ge·rine'
taint	tal'low·y	tan'gi·ble
taint'ed	tal'ly	tan'gi·bly
take	tal'ly·ho'	tan'gle
take'down'	tal'ly·man	tan'gled
tak'en	Tal'mud	tan'gle·root'
tak'er	Tal·mud'ic	tan'gling·ly
tak'ing·ly	tal'on	tan'go
tak'ing·ness	tal'oned	tang'y
tak'ings	tam'a·rack	tank
talc	tam'a·rind	tank'age
tal'cum	tam'bour	tank'ard
tale	tam'bou·rine'	tanked
tale'bear'er	tame	tank'er
tal'ent	tamed	tan'nage
tal'ent·ed	tame'ness	tanned
tal'i·pes	tam'er	tan'ner
tal'is·man	tam'est	tan'ner·y
tal'is·man'ic	Tam'il	tan'nic
talk	Tam'ma·ny	tan'nin
talk'a·tive	tamp'er	tan'nings
talked	tam'pered	tan'sy
talk'er	tam'per·proof'	tan'ta·li·za'tion
tall	tam'pon	tan'ta·lize
tall'er	tan	tan'ta·lized
tall'est	tan'a·ger	tan'ta·lum
tall'ish	tan'bark'	tan'ta·lus
tall'ness	tan'dem	tan'ta·mount'
tal'low	tang	tan'trum

tan·vat	tar'di·ness	taste
tan'wood'	tar'dy	tast'ed
tap	tare	taste'ful
tape	tar'flow'er	taste'ful·ly
taped	targe	taste'ful·ness
tape'line'	tar'get	taste'less
tape'man	tar'iff	taste'less·ly
ta'per	tar'la·tan	taste'less·ness
ta'pered	tar'nish	tast'er
ta'per·ing·ly	tar'nished	tast'i·er
tap'es·try	tar'ot	tast'i·est
tape'worm'	tar·pau'lin	tast'i·ly
tap'hole'	tar'pon	tast'ing·ly
tap'house'	tar'ra·gon	tast'ings
tap'i·o'ca	tarred	tast'y
ta'pir	tar'ried	Ta'tar
tap'per	tar'ry	tat'ter
tap'pet	tar'ry·ing·ly	tat'tered
tap'pings	tart	tat'ting
tap'room'	tar'tan	tat'tle
tap'root'	tar'tar	tat'tled
tap'ster	tart'let	tat'tler
tar	tart'ness	tat·too'
tar'an·tel'la	tar'trate	tat·tooed'
ta·ran'tu·la	tar'weed'	tat·too'er
tar'board'	task	taught
tar·boosh'	task'mas'ter	taunt
tar'brush'	task'mis'tress	taunt'ed
tar'bush'	task'work'	taunt'ing·ly
tar'di·er	Tas·ma'ni·an	taupe
tar'di·est	tas'sel	tau'rine
tar'di·ly	tas'seled	taut

taut'en	teach'er·age	tech'ni·cal·ly
taut'ened	teach'ing·ly	tech·ni'cian
tau'to·log'i·cal	teach'ings	tech·nique'
tau·tol'o·gy	tea'cup'	tech·noc'ra·cy
tav'ern	teak	tech'no·crat
taw'dri·er	tea'ket'tle	tech'no·log'i·cal
taw'dri·est	teal	tech·nol'o·gy
taw'dri·ly	team	te'di·ous
taw'dri·ness	teamed	te'di·ous·ly
taw'dry	team'mate'	te'di·ous·ness
taw'ny	team'ster	te'di·um
tax	team'work'	tee
tax'a·ble	tea'pot'	teed
tax·a'tion	tear	teem
taxed	tear	teemed
tax'es	tear'ful	teem'ing·ly
tax'i	tear'ful·ly	tee'ter
tax'i·cab'	tear'ful·ness	tee'ter·board'
tax'i·der'mist	tear'less	tee'tered
tax'i·der'my	tear'less·ly	teeth
tax'i·me'ter	tea'room'	tee·to'tal
tax'ing·ly	tear'stain'	tee·to'tal·er
tax·on'o·my	tear'y	tee·to'tal·ly
tax'paid'	tease	tel·au'to·graph
tax'pay'er	teased	tel'e·cast
tea	teas'er	tel'e·com·mu'ni·ca'tion
tea'ber'ry	teas'ing·ly	tel'e·gram
tea'cart'	tea'spoon'	tel'e·graph
teach	tea'spoon·ful	te·leg'ra·pher
teach'a·bil'i·ty	tea'tast'er	tel'e·graph'ic
teach'a·ble	tech'ni·cal	te·leg'ra·phy
teach'er	tech'ni·cal'i·ty	tel'e·ol'o·gy

tel′e·path′ic	tem′pered	ten′ant
te·lep′a·thy	tem′pest	ten′ant·a·ble
tel′e·phone	tem·pes′tu·ous	ten′ant·ed
tel′e·phon′ic	tem·pes′tu·ous·ly	ten′ant·less
te·leph′o·ny	tem·pes′tu·ous·ness	ten′ant·ry
tel′e·pho′to	tem′plate	tend
tel′e·scope	tem′ple	tend′ed
tel′e·scop′ic	tem′pled	tend′en·cy
tel′e·type	tem′po	tend′er
tel′e·type′set′ter	tem′po·ral	ten′dered
tel′e·type′writ′er	tem′po·ral·ty	ten′der·er
tel′e·vise	tem′po·rar′i·ly	ten′der·est
tel′e·vised	tem′po·rar′y	ten′der·foot′
tel′e·vi′sion	tem′po·ri·za′tion	ten′der·loin′
tel′ford	tem′po·rize	ten′der·ly
tell	tem′po·rized	ten′der·ness
tell′er	tem′po·riz′er	ten′don
tell′ing·ly	tem′po·riz′ing·ly	ten′dril
tell′ings	tempt	Ten′e·brae
tell′tale′	temp·ta′tion	ten′e·brous
tel·lu′ri·um	tempt′ed	ten′e·ment
tel′pher	tempt′er	ten′et
tel′pher·age	tempt′ing·ly	ten′nis
te·mer′i·ty	tempt′ing·ness	ten′on
tem′per	tempt′ress	ten′or
tem′per·a·ment	ten′a·bil′i·ty	ten′pins′
tem′per·a·men′tal	ten′a·ble	tense
tem′per·a·men′tal·ly	te·na′cious	tense′ly
tem′per·ance	te·na′cious·ly	tense′ness
tem′per·ate	te·na′cious·ness	tens′er
tem′per·ate·ly	te·nac′i·ty	tens′est
tem′per·a·ture	ten′an·cy	ten′sile

ten'sion	ter'mite	ters'est
ten'sor	term'less	ter'tian
tent	tern	ter'ti·ar'y
ten'ta·cle	ter'na·ry	tes'sel·late
ten'ta·tive	ter'race	tes'sel·lat'ed
ten'ter·er	ter'raced	tes'sel·la'tion
ten'ter·hooks'	ter·rain'	test
ten·u'i·ty	ter'ra·pin	tes'ta·ment
ten'u·ous	ter·raz'zo	tes'ta·men'ta·ry
ten'u·ous·ly	ter·res'tri·al	tes·ta'tor
ten'ure	ter'ri·ble	test'ed
te'pee	ter'ri·bly	tes'ter
tep'id	ter'ri·er	tes'ti·fied
te·pid'i·ty	ter·rif'ic	tes'ti·fy
tep'id·ly	ter·rif'i·cal·ly	tes'ti·mo'ni·al
ter'a·tol'o·gy	ter'ri·fied	tes'ti·mo'ny
ter·cen'te·nar'y	ter'ri·fy	test'ing·ly
te·re'do	ter'ri·fy'ing·ly	test'ings
ter'gi·ver·sate'	ter·rine'	tes'ty
term	ter'ri·to'ri·al	tet'a·nus
ter'ma·gant	ter'ri·to'ri·al'i·ty	teth'er
termed	ter'ri·to'ry	teth'ered
ter'mi·na·ble	ter'ror	tet'ra·gon
ter'mi·nal	ter'ror·ism	te·trag'o·nal
ter'mi·nate	ter'ror·ist	te·tral'o·gy
ter'mi·nat'ed	ter'ror·is'tic	te·tram'e·ter
ter'mi·na'tion	ter'ror·i·za'tion	te'trarch
ter'mi·na'tive	ter'ror·ize	te·trig'id
ter'mi·no·log'i·cal	ter'ror·ized	Tex'an
ter'mi·no·log'i·cal·ly	terse	tex'as
ter'mi·nol'o·gy	terse'ness	text
ter'mi·nus	ters'er	text'book'

tex'tile	the·at'ri·cal·ly	the'o·ry
tex'tu·al	the·at'ri·cals	the'o·soph'ic
tex'tu·al·ism	thee	the'o·soph'i·cal
tex'tu·al·ist	theft	the'o·soph'i·cal·ly
tex'tu·al·ly	their	the·os'o·phism
tex'tur·al	theirs	the·os'o·phist
tex'tur·al·ly	the'ism	the·os'o·phy
tex'ture	the'ist	ther'a·peu'tic
tex'tured	the·is'tic	ther'a·peu'ti·cal
tha·las'sic	them	ther'a·peu'ti·cal·ly
thal'li·um	the·mat'ic	ther'a·py
than	the·mat'i·cal	there
than'a·top'sis	theme	there'a·bouts'
thane	them·selves'	there'a·bove'
thank	then	there·aft'er
thanked	thence	there·at'
thank'ful	thence'forth'	there·by'
thank'ful·ly	thence'for'ward	there'fore
thank'ful·ness	the·oc'ra·cy	there·from'
thank'less	the·od'o·lite	there·in'
thank'less·ly	the'o·lo'gi·an	there'in·aft'er
thanks·giv'ing	the'o·log'i·cal	there·in'be·fore'
that	the'o·log'i·cal·ly	there·of'
thatch	the·ol'o·gy	there·on'
thatched	the'o·rem	there·to'
thau'ma·tur'gist	the'o·ret'ic	there'to·fore'
thau'ma·tur'gy	the'o·ret'i·cal	there·un'der
thaw	the'o·ret'i·cal·ly	there'un·to'
the'a·ter	the'o·rist	there'up·on'
the·at'ri·cal	the'o·rize	there·with'
the·at'ri·cal·ism	the'o·rized	ther'mal
the·at'ri·cal'i·ty	the'o·riz'er	therm'i'on

therm′i·on′ic	thigh	thorn
ther′mite	thill	thorn′bush′
ther′mo·e·lec′tric	thim′ble	thorned
ther·mom′e·ter	thim′ble·ful	thorn′i·er
ther′mo·met′ric	thim′ble·rig′ger	thorn′i·est
ther′mo·met′ri·cal	thin	thorn′y
ther′mo·met′ri·cal·ly	thing	thor′ough
ther′mo·stat	things	thor′ough·bred′
the·sau′rus	think	thor′ough·fare′
these	think′a·ble	thor′ough·go′ing
the′ses	think′er	thor′ough·ly
the′sis	think′ing·ly	thor′ough·ness
thew	thinks	those
they	thin′ly	thou
thick	thin′ner	though
thick′en	thin′ness	thought
thick′ened	thin′nest	thought′ful
thick′en·er	third	thought′ful·ly
thick′er	thirst	thought′ful·ness
thick′est	thirst′ed	thought′less
thick′et	thirst′i·ly	thought′less·ly
thick′et·ed	thirst′i·ness	thought′less·ness
thick′head′ed	thirst′ing·ly	thou′sand
thick′ly	thirst′y	thou′sand·fold′
thick′ness	this	thou′sandth
thick′set′	this′tle	thrall
thick′-skinned′	thith′er	thrall′dom
thick′-wit′ted	thole	thrash
thief	thong	thrashed
thiev′er·y	tho·rac′ic	thrash′er
thiev′ing·ly	tho′rax	thrash′ings
thiev′ish	tho′ri·um	thra·son′i·cal

thread	thrips	thrown
thread'bare'	thrive	throw'off'
thread'ed	thriv'ing·ly	thrum
thread'weed'	throat	thrummed
thread'worm'	throat'ed	thrush
thread'y	throat'i·er	thrust
threat	throat'i·est	thud
threat'en	throat'i·ly	thud'ded
threat'ened	throat'i·ness	thud'ding·ly
threat'en·ing·ly	throat'root'	thug
three	throat'wort'	thug'ger·y
three'some	throat'y	thu'li·um
thren'o·dy	throb	thumb
thre'nos	throbbed	thumbed
thresh	throb'bing·ly	thumb'mark'
threshed	throes	thumb'nail'
thresh'er	throm·bo'sis	thumb'piece'
thresh'old	throm'bus	thumb'print'
threw	throne	thump
thrice	throne'less	thumped
thrift	throne'like'	thump'ing·ly
thrift'i·er	throng	thump'ings
thrift'i·est	thronged	thun'der
thrift'i·ly	throng'ing·ly	thun'der·bird'
thrift'i·ness	throt'tle	thun'der·bolt'
thrift'less	throt'tled	thun'dered
thrift'less·ly	throt'tling·ly	thun'der·fish'
thrift'less·ness	through	thun'der·head'
thrift'y	through·out'	thun'der·ing
thrill	throw	thun'der·ing·ly
thrilled	throw'back'	thun'der·ings
thrill'ing·ly	throw'er	thun'der·ous

thun'der·show'er	tick'lish·ness	tight'en·ing
thun'der·struck'	tid'al	tight'er
thun'der·y	tid'bit'	tight'est
thun'drous	tide	tight'fist'ed
thu'ri·ble	tid'ed	tight'ly
Thurs'day	tide'race'	tight'rope'
thus	tide'wa'ter	tight'wad'
thwack	tide'way'	til'bu·ry
thwacked	ti'died	til'de
thwack'ing·ly	ti'di·er	tile
thwart	ti'di·est	tiled
thwart'ed	ti'di·ly	tile'fish'
thwart'ing·ly	ti'di·ness	til'er
thy	ti'dings	tile'root'
thyme	ti'dy	till
thy'mus	tie	till'a·ble
thy'roid	tie'back'	till'age
thy·self'	tied	tilled
ti·ar'a	tier	till'er
tib'i·a	tiered	tilt
tick	tiff	tilt'ed
ticked	tif'fa·ny	tilth
tick'er	tiffed	tilt'yard'
tick'et	tif'fin	tim'bale
tick'et·ed	ti'ger	tim'ber
tick'ings	ti'ger·ish	tim'bered
tick'le	ti'ger·like'	tim'ber·land'
tick'led	ti'ger·wood'	tim'ber·wood'
tick'ler	tight	tim'ber·work'
tick'ling·ly	tight'en	time
tick'lish	tight'ened	timed
tick'lish·ly	tight'en·er	time'keep'er

time′less	tink′er	tip′sy
time′less·ly	tink′ered	tip′toe′
time′less·ness	tin′kle	tip′toed′
time′li·ness	tin′kled	tip′toe′ing·ly
time′ly	tin′kling·ly	tip′top′
time′piece′	tin′klings	ti′rade
tim′er	tinned	tire
time′serv′ing	tin′ni·er	tired
time′ta′ble	tin′ni·est	tire′less
tim′id	tin′ni·ly	tire′less·ly
ti·mid′i·ty	tin′ni·ness	tire′less·ness
tim′id·ly	tin·ni′tus	tire′some
tim′ings	tin′ny	tire′some·ly
tim′or·ous	tin′sel	tire′some·ness
tim′or·ous·ly	tin′seled	tir′ing·ly
tin	tin′smith′	tis′sue
tinct	tint	tis′sued
tinct′ed	tint′ed	tis′sues
tinc′ture	tin′tin·nab′u·la′tion	Ti′tan
tinc′tured	tin′type′	ti·tan′ic
tin′der	tin′ware′	ti·tan·if′er·ous
tin′der·box′	tin′work′	ti·ta′ni·um
tine	ti′ny	tit′bit′
tined	tip	tith′a·ble
tine′weed′	tipped	tithe
tinge	tip′pet	tithed
tinged	tip′ple	tith′ings
tin′gle	tip′pled	ti′tian
tin′gled	tip′pler	tit′il·late
tin′gling·ly	tip′si·er	tit′il·lat′ed
tin′glings	tip′si·est	tit′il·lat′ing·ly
tin′horn′	tip′ster	tit′il·la′tion

tit'il·la'tive	to·bog'ganed	tol'er·ance
tit'i·vate	toc·ca'ta	tol'er·ant
tit'i·vat'ed	toc'sin	tol'er·ate
tit'i·va'tion	to·day'	tol'er·at'ed
ti'tle	tod'dle	tol'er·a'tion
ti'tled	tod'dled	tol'er·a'tion·ism
ti'tle·hold'er	tod'dler	tol'er·a'tive
tit'mouse'	tod'dy	toll
ti'trate	toe	tolled
ti'trat·ed	toe'cap'	toll'gate'
ti·tra'tion	toed	toll'house'
tit'ter	toe'nail'	tom'a·hawk
tit'tered	toe'plate'	to·ma'to
tit'ter·ingly	tof'fee	tomb
tit'ter·ings	to'ga	tombed
tit'tle	to·geth'er	tom'bo·la
tit'tup	to·geth'er·ness	tom'boy'
tit'u·lar	tog'gle	tomb'stone'
tit'u·lar·ly	tog'gled	tom'cat'
tit'u·lar'y	toil	tom'cod'
to	toiled	tome
toad	toil'er	tom'fool'
toad'fish'	toi'let	tom'fool'er·y
toad'root'	toi'let·ry	tom'fool'ish·ness
toad'stone'	toi'let·ware'	to·mor'row
toad'stool'	toil'ing·ly	ton
toad'y	To·kay'	ton'al
toast	to'ken	ton'al·ist
toast'ed	to'kened	to·nal'i·ty
toast'er	told	tone
to·bac'co	tol'er·a·ble	toned
to·bog'gan	tol'er·a·bly	tone'less

tongs	tooth'less·ness	top'side'
tongue	tooth'pick'	top'stone'
tongued	tooth'some	toque
ton'ic	too'tle	torch
ton'i·cal·ly	too'tled	torch'light'
to·nic'i·ty	top	torch'weed'
to·night'	to'paz	torch'wood'
ton'ka	top'coat'	tore
ton'nage	top'er	tor'e·a·dor'
ton·neau'	to'pi·a·rist	tor·ment'
ton'sil	to'pi·ar'y	tor·ment'ed
ton'sil·li'tis	top'ic	tor·ment'ing·ly
ton·so'ri·al	top'i·cal	tor·men'tor
ton'sure	top'knot'	tor·na'do
ton'tine	top'less	tor·pe'do
too	top'loft'y	tor·pe'doed
took	top'man	tor'pid
tool	top'mast'	tor·pid'i·ty
tool'box'	top'most	tor'pid·ly
tooled	to·pog'ra·pher	tor'por
tool'ings	top'o·graph'ic	torque
tool'mak'er	top'o·graph'i·cal	tor'rent
tool'room'	top'o·graph'i·cal·ly	tor·ren'tial
tool'smith'	to·pog'ra·phy	tor·ren'tial·ly
toot	topped	tor'rid
toot'ed	top'per	tor·rid'i·ty
tooth	top'piece'	tor'rid·ly
tooth'ache'	top'ping·ly	tor'sion
tooth'brush'	top'pings	tor'sion·al
toothed	top'ple	tor'so
tooth'less	top'pled	tort
tooth'less·ly	top'sail'	tor'toise

tor'tu·os'i·ty	tot'tered	tou'sle
tor'tu·ous	tot'ter·ing·ly	tou'sled
tor'tu·ous·ly	tot'ter·ings	tout
tor'tu·ous·ness	tot'ter·y	tout'ed
tor'ture	tou·can'	to·va'rish
tor'tured	touch	tow
tor'tur·er	touch'a·ble	tow'age
tor'tur·ing·ly	touch'down'	to'ward
tor'tur·ous	touched	to'wards
tor'tur·ous·ly	touch'hole'	tow'boat'
To'ry	touch'i·er	towed
toss	touch'i·est	tow'el
tossed	touch'i·ly	tow'el·ings
toss'ing·ly	touch'i·ness	tow'er
toss'ings	touch'ing·ly	tow'ered
toss'up'	touch'stone'	tow'er·ing·ly
to'tal	touch'wood'	tow'er·man
to'taled	touch'y	tow'head'
to·tal'i·tar'i·an	tough	tow'line'
to·tal'i·tar'i·an·ism	tough'en	town
to·tal'i·ty	tough'ened	town'folk'
to'tal·i·za'tion	tough'er	town'ship
to'tal·i·za'tor	tough'est	towns'man
to'tal·ize	tou·pee'	town'wear'
to'tal·ized	tour	tow'path'
to'tal·iz'er	toured	tow'rope'
to'tal·ly	tour'ism	tox·e'mi·a
tote	tour'ist	tox'ic
tot'ed	tour'ma·line	tox·ic'i·ty
to'tem	tour'na·ment	tox'i·co·log'i·cal
toth'er	tour'ney	tox'i·col'o·gist
tot'ter	tour'ni·quet	tox'i·col'o·gy

tox′i·co′sis	trac′tive	trained
tox′oid	trac′tor	train′er
toy	trac′tor·ize	train′ful
toyed	trade	train′load′
toy′ing·ly	trad′ed	train′man
toy′man	trad′er	trait
toy′shop′	trades′man	trai′tor
trace	tra·di′tion	trai′tor·ous
trace′a·ble	tra·di′tion·al	trai′tor·ous·ly
traced	tra·di′tion·al·ism	tra·jec′to·ry
trac′er	tra·di′tion·al·ly	tram
trac′er·y	tra·duce′	tram′car′
tra′che·a	tra·duced′	tram′mel
tra′che·al	tra·duc′er	tram′meled
tra·cho′ma	tra·duc′ing·ly	tram′mel·ing·ly
trac′ings	traf′fic	tra·mon′tane
track	traf′ficked	tramp
track′age	trag′a·canth	tramped
tracked	tra·ge′di·an	tram′ple
track′er	tra·ge′di·enne′	tram′pled
track′lay′er	trag′e·dy	tram′po·lin
track′less	trag′ic	tram′road′
track′man	trag′i·cal	tram′way′
track′mas′ter	trag′i·cal·ly	trance
tract	trag′i·com′e·dy	trance′like′
trac′ta·bil′i·ty	tra′gus	tran′quil
trac′ta·ble	trail	tran′quil·i·za′tion
trac′ta·bly	trailed	tran′quil·ize
trac·tar′i·an	trail′er	tran′quil·ized
trac′tate	trail′ing·ly	tran′quil·iz′er
trac′tile	train	tran′quil·iz′ing·ly
trac′tion	train′band′	tran·quil′li·ty

tran'quil·ly

trans·act'

trans·act'ed

trans·ac'tion

trans·al'pine

trans·at·lan'tic

tran·scend'

tran·scend'ed

tran·scend'ence

tran·scend'en·cy

tran·scend'ent

tran'scen·den'tal

tran'scen·den'tal·ism

tran'scen·den'tal·ist

trans'con·ti·nen'tal

tran·scribe'

tran·scribed'

tran·scrib'er

tran'script

tran·scrip'tion

trans·duc'er

trans·duc'tion

tran'sept

trans·fer'

trans·fer'a·bil'i·ty

trans·fer'a·ble

trans·fer'al

trans·fer'ence

trans'ferred'

trans·fer'rer

trans·fig'u·ra'tion

trans·fig'ure

trans·fig'ured

trans·fig'ure·ment

trans·fix'

trans·fixed'

trans·form'

trans'for·ma'tion

trans·formed'

trans·form'er

trans·form'ing·ly

trans·fuse'

trans·fused'

trans·fu'sion

trans·fu'sions

trans·gress'

trans·gressed'

trans·gress'ing·ly

trans·gres'sion

trans·gres'sor

tran'sient

tran·sis'tor

tran·sis'tor·ize

trans'it

tran·si'tion

tran·si'tion·al

tran·si'tion·al·ly

tran'si·tive

tran'si·tive·ly

tran'si·tive·ness

tran'si·to'ry

trans·lat'a·ble

trans·late'

trans·lat'ed

trans·la'tion

trans·la'tor

trans·la'to·ry

trans·lit'er·ate

trans·lu'cence

trans·lu'cen·cy

trans·lu'cent

trans·lu'cent·ly

trans'ma·rine'

trans·mi'grant

trans'mi·gra'tion

trans·mis'si·ble

trans·mis'sion

trans·mit'

trans·mit'tal

trans·mit'ted

trans·mit'ter

trans·mog'ri·fi·ca-
tion

trans·mog'ri·fied

trans·mog'ri·fy

trans·mut'a·ble

trans'mu·ta'tion

trans·mute'

trans·mut'ed

tran'som

trans'pa·cif'ic

trans·par'en·cy

trans·par'ent

tran'spi·ra'tion

tran·spir'a·to'ry

tran·spire'

tran·spired'

trans·plant′	trau′ma·ta	treas′ur·y
trans′plan·ta′tion	trau·mat′ic	treat
trans·plant′ed	trau·mat′i·cal·ly	treat′ed
trans·port′	trau′ma·tism	trea′tise
trans′por·ta′tion	trau′ma·tize	treat′ment
trans·port′ed	trav′ail	trea′ty
trans·port′ing·ly	trav′el	tre′ble
trans·pos′al	trav′eled	tre′bled
trans·pose′	trav′el·er	tree
trans·posed′	trav′e·logue	treed
trans′po·si′tion	trav′ers·a·ble	tree′nail′
trans·ship′	trav′ers·al	trek
trans·ship′ment	trav′erse	trekked
tran′sub·stan′ti·a′tion	trav′ersed	trel′lis
trans·ver′sal	trav′er·tine	trel′lised
trans·verse′	trav′es·ty	trem′ble
trap	trawl	trem′bled
trap door	trawl′er	trem′bling·ly
tra·peze′	tray	trem′blings
tra·pe′zi·um	treach′er·ous	tre·men′dous
trap′e·zoid	treach′er·ous·ly	tre·men′dous·ly
trapped	treach′er·ous·ness	tre′mo·lan′do
trap′per	treach′er·y	trem′o·lo
trap′pings	trea′cle	trem′or
Trap′pist	tread	trem′u·lous
trap′rock′	trea′dle	trem′u·lous·ly
trap′shoot′ing	tread′mill′	trem′u·lous·ness
trash	trea′son	trench
trash′i·er	trea′son·a·ble	trench′an·cy
trash′i·est	treas′ure	trench′ant
trash′y	treas′ured	trench′ant·ly
trau′ma	treas′ur·er	trench′er

trench'er·man	trice	trig
trend	tri'ceps	trig'ger
trend'ed	tri·chi'na	trig'gered
tre·pan'	trich'i·no'sis	trig'ger·fish'
tre·phine'	tri·chot'o·my	tri'glyph
tre·phined'	trick	trig'o·no·met'- ric
trep'i·da'tion	tricked	trig'o·no·met'- ri·cal
tres'pass	trick'er·y	trig'o·nom'- e·try
tres'passed	trick'i·er	tri·lem'ma
tres'pass·er	trick'i·est	tri·lin'gual
tress	trick'i·ly	trill
tres'tle	trick'i·ness	trilled
tres'tle·work'	trick'le	tril'lion
tri'ad	trick'led	Tril'li·um
tri·ad'ic	trick'ling·ly	tri'lo·bite
tri'al	trick'lings	tril'o·gy
tri'an'gle	trick'ster	trim
tri·an'gu·lar	trick'sy	trimmed
tri·an'gu·lar'i·ty	trick'y	trim'mer
tri·an'gu·late	tri'col'or	trim'mings
tri·an'gu·lat'ed	tri'corn	trim'ness
tri·an'gu·la'tion	tri'cot	tri·month'ly
trib'al	tri'cy·cle	trin'i·ty
trib'al·ism	tri'dent	trin'ket
tri·bas'ic	tried	tri·no'mi·al
tribe	tri·en'ni·al	tri'o
tribes'man	tri·en'ni·al·ly	tri'ode
trib'u·la'tion	tri'fle	tri'o·let
tri·bu'nal	tri'fled	trip
trib'une	tri'fler	tri·par'tite
trib'u·tar'y	tri'fling·ly	tripe
trib'ute	tri'flings	triph'thong

tri'ple

tri'pled

tri'plet

tri'plex

trip'li·cate

trip'li·cat'ed

trip'li·ca'tion

tri'ply

tri'pod

tripped

trip'per

trip'ping·ly

trip'tych

tri'reme

tri'sect'

tri'sect'ed

tri·sec'tion

tri·sec'tor

tris·kel'i·on

tris'yl·lab'ic

trite

trite'ly

trite'ness

Tri'ton

tri'tone'

trit'u·rate

trit'u·rat'ed

trit'u·ra'tion

tri'umph

tri·um'phal

tri·um'phant

tri'umphed

tri'umph·ing·ly

tri·um'vir

tri·um'vi·rate

tri'une

tri·va'lent

triv'et

triv'i·a

triv'i·al

triv'i·al'i·ty

triv'i·al·ly

tro·cha'ic

tro'che

troi'ka

troll

trolled

trol'ley

trom'bone

troop

trooped

troop'er

troop'ship'

trope

tro'phy

trop'ic

trop'i·cal

trop'i·cal·ly

tro'pism

trop'ist

tro·pol'o·gy

trop'o·pause

trop'o·sphere

trot

troth

trot'line'

trot'ted

trot'ter

trou'ba·dour

trou'ble

trou'bled

trou'ble·some

trou'ble·some·ly

trou'ble·some·ness

trou'bling·ly

trou'blous

trough

trough'like'

trounce

trounced

trounc'ings

troupe

troup'er

trou'sers

trous'seau'

trout

trout'let

trout'ling

trow'el

trow'eled

troy

tru'an·cy

tru'ant

tru'ant·ism

truce

tru'cial

truck	trun'cat·ed	tub
truck'age	trun·ca'tion	tu'ba
trucked	trun'cheon	tubbed
truck'er	trun'dle	tub'bi·er
truck'le	trun'dled	tub'bi·est
truck'led	trunk	tub'bings
truck'ling·ly	trun'nion	tub'by
truck'man	truss	tube
truc'u·lence	trussed	tu'ber
truc'u·lent	truss'ings	tu'ber·cle
trudge	trust	tu·ber'cu·lar
trudged	trus·tee'	tu·ber'cu·lin
trudg'en	trus·tee'ship	tu·ber'cu·lo'sis
true	trust'ful	tu·ber'cu·lous
trued	trust'ful·ly	tu'ber·os'i·ty
true'love'	trust'ful·ness	tu'ber·ous
true'ness	trust'i·er	tub'ings
truf'fle	trust'i·est	tu'bu·lar
truf'fled	trust'ing·ly	tu'bu·la'tion
tru'ism	trust'wor'thi·ness	tuck
tru'ly	trust'wor'thy	tucked
trump	trust'y	Tu'dor
trumped	truth	Tues'day
trump'er·y	truth'ful	tuft
trum'pet	truth'ful·ly	tuft'ed
trum'pet·ed	truth'ful·ness	tuft'ings
trum'pet·er	try	tug
trum'pet·ings	try'ing·ly	tug'boat'
trum'pet·like'	try'sail'	tugged
trum'pet·weed'	tryst	tug'ging·ly
trum'pet·wood'	tryst'ed	tug'gings
trun'cate	tset'se	tu·i'tion

tu'la·re'mi·a

tu'lip

tu'lip·wood'

tulle

tum'ble

tum'bled

tum'bler

tum'ble·weed'

tum'bling·ly

tum'brel

tu'me·fac'tion

tu'me·fied

tu'me·fy

tu'mid

tu·mid'i·ty

tu'mor

tu'mor·ous

tu'mult

tu·mul'tu·ous

tu·mul'tu·ous·ly

tu·mul'tu·ous·ness

tu'mu·lus

tun

tu'na

tun'dra

tune

tuned

tune'ful

tune'less

tune'less·ly

tune'less·ness

tun'er

tung'sten

tu'nic

tun'ings

Tu·ni'sian

tun'nel

tun'neled

tun'ny

tu'pe·lo

tur'ban

tur'bid

tur·bid'i·ty

tur'bid·ly

tur'bi·nate

tur'bine

tur'bot

tur'bu·lence

tur'bu·lent

tur'bu·lent·ly

tu·reen'

turf

turfed

turf'man

tur'gid

tur·gid'i·ty

tur'gid·ly

Turk

tur'key

Turk'ish

tur'mer·ic

tur'moil

turn

turn'buck'le

turn'coat'

turn'cock'

turned

turn'er

turn'ings

tur'nip

turn'key'

turn'off'

turn'out'

turn'o'ver

turn'pike'

turn'spit'

turn'stile'

tur'pen·tine

tur'pi·tude

tur'quoise

tur'ret

tur'ret·ed

tur'tle

Tus'can

tusk

tusked

tus'sle

tus'sled

tus'sock

tu'te·lage

tu'te·lar'y

tu'tor

tu'tored

tu·to'ri·al

tux·e'do

twad'dle

twad'dled	twin'klings	ty'phoid	
twain	twirl	ty·phoi'dal	
twang	twirled	ty·phoon'	
twanged	twist	ty'phous	
tweak	twist'ed	ty'phus	
tweaked	twist'er	typ'i·cal	
tweed	twist'ings	typ'i·cal·ly	
tweez'ers	twit	typ'i·fi·ca'tion	
twice	twitch	typ'i·fy	
twid'dle	twitched	typ'ings	
twid'dled	twit'ted	typ'ist	
twig	twit'ter	ty·pog'ra·pher	
twi'light'	twit'tered	ty'po·graph'ic	
twill	twit'ter·ing·ly	ty·pog'ra·phy	
twilled	twit'ter·ings	ty·poth'e·tae	
twin	two	ty·ran'ni·cal	
twin'born'	two'fold'	ty·ran'ni·cide	
twine	two'some	tyr'an·nize	
twined	ty·coon'	tyr'an·nized	
twinge	type	tyr'an·niz'ing·ly	
twinged	typed	tyr'an·nous	
twin'kle	type'set'ter	tyr'an·ny	
twin'kled	type'writ'er	ty'rant	
twin'kling·ly	type'writ·ten	ty'ro	

U

u·biq'ui·tous
u·biq'ui·tous·ly
u·biq'ui·ty
ud'der
ug'li·er
ug'li·est
ug'li·ness
ug'ly
uh'lan
u·kase'
u'ku·le'le
ul'cer
ul'cer·ate
ul'cer·at'ed
ul'cer·a'tion
ul'cer·a'tive
ul'cer·ous
ul'cer·ous·ly
ul'na
ul'nar
ul'ster
ul·te'ri·or

ul'ti·mate
ul'ti·mate·ly
ul'ti·ma'tum
ul'ti·mo
ul'tra·ism
ul'tra·le·gal'i·ty
ul'tra·ma·rine'
ul'tra·mi'cro·scope
ul'tra·mod'ern
ul'tra·mon'tane
ul'tra·na'tion·al·ism
ul'tra·na'tion·al·ist
ul'tra·red'
ul'tra·son'ic
ul'tra·vi'o·let
ul'u·late
ul'u·lat'ed
ul'u·la'tion
um'ber
um'bra
um'brage
um·bra'geous

um·brel'la
um'laut
um'pire
um'pired
un·a'ble
un'a·bridged'
un'ac·cent'ed
un'ac·cept'a·ble
un'ac·com'mo·dat'ing
un'ac·com'pa·nied
un'ac·count'a·ble
un'ac·cus'tomed
un'ac·quaint'ed
un'a·dorned'
un'a·dul'ter·at'ed
un'af·fect'ed
un'al·loyed'
un·al'ter·a·ble
un·al'tered
un'-A·mer'i·can
un·a'mi·a·ble
u·nan'i·mous

327

un·an'swer·a·ble

un'ap·peas'a·ble

un'ap·proach'a·ble

un'ap·pro'pri·at'ed

un'ap·prov'ing·ly

un·armed'

un'a·shamed'

un·asked'

un'as·sail'a·ble

un'as·signed'

un'as·sim'i·lat'ed

un'as·sist'ed

un'as·sum'ing·ly

un'at·tached'

un'at·tain'a·ble

un'at·tempt'ed

un'at·trac'tive·ly

un·au'thor·ized

un'a·vail'a·ble

un'a·vail'ing·ly

un'a·void'a·ble

un'a·ware'

un·bal'anced

un·bal'last·ed

un·bar'

un·barred'

un·bear'a·bly

un·beat'a·ble

un'be·com'ing·ly

un'be·fit'ting·ly

un'be·known'

un'be·knownst'

unbe·lief'

un'be·liev'a·ble

un'be·liev'er

un'be·liev'ing·ly

un'be·liev'ing·ness

un·bend'

un·bend'ing·ly

un·bi'ased

un·bid'den

un·bind'

un·blem'ished

un·blessed'

un·blocked'

un·blush'ing·ly

un·bolt'

un·bolt'ed

un·born'

un·bos'om

un·bos'omed

un·bound'

un·bound'ed

un·bowed'

un·break'a·ble

un·bri'dled

un·bro'ken

un·buck'le

un·bur'den

un·bur'dened

un·burned'

un·busi'ness·like'

un·but'ton

un·but'toned

un·cage'

un·can'ny

un·cap'ti·vat'ed

un·car'pet·ed

un·cat'a·logued

un·ceas'ing·ly

un'cer·e·mo'ni·ous

un·cer'tain

un·cer'tain·ly

un·cer'tain·ness

un·cer'tain·ty

un·chal'lenged

un·change'a·ble

un·change'a·bly

un·chang'ing·ly

un·char'i·ta·ble

un·chid'ing·ly

un·chris'tened

un·chris'tian

un'ci·al

un·civ'il

un·civ'i·lized

un·clad'

un·claimed'

un·clasp'

un'cle

un·clean'

un·clean'ly

un·closed'

un·clothe'

un·coil'

un'col·lect'ed

un·colt'

un·com'fort·a·ble

un·com'fort·a·ble·ness

un·com'mon

un·com·mu'ni·ca'tive

un·com'pa·nied

un·com'pro·mis'ing

un'con·cerned'

un'con·di'tion·al

un'con·di'tion·al'i·ty

un'con·fined'

un'con·firmed'

un'con·form'i·ty

un'con·gen'ial

un·con'quer·a·ble

un·con'quered

un·con'scion·a·ble

un·con'scious

un·con'scious·ly

un·con'scious·ness

un·con'se·crat'ed

un'con·se·quen'tial

un'con·se·quen'tial·ly

un'con·sid'er·ate·ly

un'con·sid'ered

un'con·sti·tu'tion·al

un'con·sti·tu'tion·al·ly

un'con·strained'

un'con·strain'ed·ly

un'con·tam'i·nat'ed

un'con·tra·dic'to·ry

un'con·trol'la·ble

un'con·trolled'

un'con·ven'tion·al

un'con·ven'tion·al·ly

un'con·vert'ed

un'con·vinced'

un'con·vinc'ing·ly

un'co·op'er·a'tive

un·cork'

un·corked'

un'cor·rect'ed

un'cor·rupt'ed

un·count'a·ble

un·count'ed

un·cou'ple

un·cou'pled

un·couth'

un·couth'ness

un·cov'er

un·cov'ered

un·cowed'

un·creased'

un·crit'i·cal

un·crit'i·ciz'ing·ly

un·crowd'ed

un·crowned'

unc'tion

unc'tu·ous

un·cul'ti·vat'ed

un·cul'tured

un·curbed'

un·curl'

un·cut'

un·dam'aged

un·damped'

un·dashed'

un·dat'ed

un·daunt'ed

un'de·ceive'

un'de·ceived'

un'de·cid'ed

un'de·ci'pher·a·ble

un'de·ci'phered

un·dec'o·rous

un'de·feat'ed

un'de·fend'ed

un'de·filed'

un'de·fin'a·ble

un'de·liv'er·a·ble

un'dem·o·crat'ic

un'de·mon'stra·tive

un'de·ni'a·ble

un'de·pend'a·ble

un'de·pos'it·ed

un'der

un'der·age'

un'der·arm'

un'der·bid'

un'der·bod'y

un'der·brush'

un'der·buy'

un'der·cap'i·tal·i·za'tion

un'der·cap'i·tal·ize

un'der·car'riage

un'der·charge'

un'der·charged'

un'der·class'man

un'der·clothes'

un'der·coat'

un'der·con·sump'tion

un'der·cov'er

un'der·cur'rent

un'der·cut'

un'der·done'

un'der·dose'

un'der·es'ti·mate

un'der·ex·pose'

un'der·feed'

un'der·foot'

un'der·gar'ment

un'der·glaze'

un'der·go'

un'der·grad'u·ate

un'der·ground'

un'der·growth'

un'der·hand'ed

un'der·hand'ed·ly

un'der·hand'ed·ness

un'der·hung'

un'der·laid'

un'der·lay'

un'der·lie'

un'der·line'

un'der·lined'

un'der·lings

un'der·manned'

un'der·mine'

un'der·mined'

un'der·neath'

un'der·nour'ish

un'der·nour'ished

un'der·nour'ish·ment

un'der·pass'

un'der·pin'nings

un'der·priv'i·leged

un'der·pro·duc'tion

un'der·quote'

un'der·rate'

un'der·rat'ed

un'der·score'

un'der·scored'

un'der·sec're·tar'y

un'der·sell'

un'der·shirt'

un'der·shot'

un'der·signed'

un'der·sized'

un'der·skirt'

un'der·slung'

un'der·sparred'

un'der·stand'

un'der·stand'ing·ly

un'der·stand'ings

un'der·state'

un'der·state'ment

un'der·stood'

un'der·stud'y

un'der·take'

un'der·tak'en

un'der·tak'er

un'der·tak'ings

un'der·things'

un'der·tone'

un'der·took'

un'der·tow'

un'der·turn'

un'der·val'ue

un'der·wa'ter

un'der·wear'

un'der·weight'

un'der·world'

un'der·write'

un'der·writ'er

un'de·scrib'a·ble

un'de·served'

un'de·sir'a·ble

un'de·sired'

un'de·stroyed'

un'de·tect'ed

un'de·ter'mined

un'de·vel'oped

un'di·ag·nosed'

un'di·a·pered

un'di·gest'ed

un·dig'ni·fied

un'di·lut'ed

un'di·min'ished

un·dimmed'

un'di·rect'ed

un·dis'ci·plined

un'dis·closed'

un'dis·cov'ered

un'dis·crim'i·nat'ing·ly

un'dis·guised'

un'dis·tin'guished

un'dis·trib'ut·ed

un'di·vid'ed

un·do'

un'do·mes'ti·cat'ed

un·done'

un·doubt'ed

un·doubt'ed·ly

un'dra·mat'i·cal·ly

un·draped'

un·drawn'

un·dress'

un·dressed'

un·drink'a·ble

un·due'

un'du·lant

un'du·late

un'du·lat'ed

un'du·la'tion

un·du'ly

un·du'ti·ful

un·dy'ing·ly

un·earned'

un·earth'

un·earthed'

un·earth'ly

un·eas'i·er

un·eas'i·est

un·eas'i·ly

un·eas'i·ness

un·eas'y

un·eat'a·ble

un·ed'u·ca·ble

un·ed'u·cat'ed

un'em·bar'rassed

un'em·bit'tered

un'em·broi'dered

un'e·mo'tion·al

un'em·ploy'a·ble

un'em·ploy'a·ble·ness

un'em·ployed'

un'em·ploy'ment

un'en·cum'bered

un'en·dan'gered

un·end'ing

un'en·dorsed'

un'en·dur'a·ble

un'en·force'a·ble

un'en·gaged'

un'en·graved'

un'en·grossed'

un'en·larged'

un'en·light'ened

un'en·slaved'

un'en'tered

un'en'ter·pris'ing

un'en·ter·tain'ing

un'en·thu'si·as'tic

un'en·thu'si·as'ti·cal·ly

un·en'vi·a·ble

un·en'vi·a·bly

un·en'vied

un·e'qual

un·e'qual·a·ble

un·e'qualed

un·e'qual·ize

un·e'qual·ized

un·e'qual·ly

un·e'quipped'

un·e·quiv'o·cal

un·e·rad'i·cat'ed

un·e·ras'a·ble

un·e·rased'

un·err'ing

un·err'ing·ly

un·es·sen'tial

un·es'ti·mat'ed

un·eth'i·cal

un·eth'i·cal·ly

un·e'ven

un·e'ven·ly

un'e·vent'ful

un'e·vent'ful·ly

un'ex·am'pled

un'ex·celled'

un'ex·cep'tion·a·ble

un'ex·cep'tion·al

un'ex·cit'a·ble

un'ex·cit'ing

un'ex·cused'

un'ex'e·cut'ed

un'ex·haust'ed

un'ex·pect'ed

un'ex·pect'ed·ly

un'ex·pect'ed·ness

un'ex·plain'a·ble

un'ex·plained'

un'ex·ploit'ed

un'ex·posed'

un'ex·pressed'

un'ex·press'i·ble

un·ex'pur·gat'ed

un·ex·tin'guished

un·ex'tri·cat·ed

un·fad'ed

un·fad'ing·ly

un·fail'ing·ly

un·fair'

un·fair'ly

un·fair'ness

un·faith'ful

un·faith'ful·ly

un·faith'ful·ness

un·fal'ter·ing

un'fa·mil'iar

un·farmed'

un·fash'ion·a·ble

un·fash'ion·a·bly

un·fas'ten

un·fas'tened

un·fa'ther·ly

un·fath'om·a·ble

un·fath'omed

un'fa·tigue'a·ble

un'fa·tigued'

un·fa'vor·able

un·fa'vor·a·bly

un·fear'ing·ly

un·fea'si·ble

un·fea'si·bly

un·fed'

un·feel'ing·ly

un·feigned'

un·felt'

un·fem'i·nine

un·fenced'

un'fe·nes'trat·ed

un·fer·ment'ed

un·fer'ti·lized

un·fet'ter

un·fet'tered

un·filed'

un·fil'i·al

un·fil'i·al·ly

un·fill'a·ble

un·fil'tered

un·fin'ished

un·fit'

un·fit'ting·ly

un·flag'ging·ly

un·flat'ter·ing·ly

un·flick'er·ing·ly

un·flinch'ing·ly

un·flinch'ing·ness

un·flood'ed

un·flur'ried

un·flus'tered

un·fo'cused

un·fold'

un·fold'ed

un·forced'

un'fore·see'a·ble

un'fore·seen'

un'fore·tell'a·ble

un·for'feit·ed

un·for·get'ta·ble

un'for·get'ting·ly

un'for·giv'a·ble

un'for·giv'en

un'for·giv'ing·ly

un'for·giv'ing·ness

un·for·got'ten

un·for'mal·ized

un·formed'

un·for'ti·fied

un·for'tu·nate

un·for'tu·nate·ly

un·found'ed

un·frayed'

un'fre·quent'ed

un·friend'ed

un·friend'li·ness

un·friend'ly

un·frock'

un·frocked'

un·fru'gal

un·fruit'ful

un·fu'eled

un'ful·filled'

un·fund'ed	un·grudg'ing·ly	un·heed'ing·ly
un·fun'ny	un·guard'ed	un·help'ful
un·fur'bished	un·guard'ed·ly	un·her'ald·ed
un·furl'	un'guent	un'he·ro'ic
un·furled'	un·guid'ed	un·hes'i·tat'ing
un·fur'nished	un·gummed'	un·hes'i·tat'ing·ly
un·gain'li·ness	un·hack'neyed	un·hin'dered
un·gain'ly	un·hal'lowed	un·hinge'
un·gal'lant	un·ham'pered	un·hinged'
un·gar'land·ed	un·hand'i·ness	un·hitch'
un·gar'nished	un·hand'some	un·hitched'
un·gen'er·ous	un·hand'y	un·ho'li·ness
un·gen'tle	un·hanged'	un·ho'ly
un·gen'tle·man·ly	un·hap'pi·er	un·home'like'
un·ger'mi·nat'ed	un·hap'pi·est	un·hon'ored
un·gift'ed	un·hap'pi·ly	un·hook'
un·girt'	un·hap'pi·ness	un·hooked'
un·glazed'	un·hap'py	un·hoped'
un·glo'ri·ous	un·hard'ened	un·horse'
un·gloved'	un·harmed'	un·hum'bled
un·god'li·ness	un·har'ness	un·hu'mor·ous
un·god'ly	un·har'nessed	un·hurt'
un·gov'ern·a·ble	un·har'vest·ed	un'hy·gi·en'ic
un·gov'ern·a·bly	un·hatched'	un·hy'phen·at'ed
un·gra'cious	un·healed'	u'ni·corn
un·gra'cious·ly	un·health'ful	u'ni·cy'cle
un·grad'ed	un·health'ful·ness	un'i·den'ti·fi'a·ble
un'gram·mat'i·cal	un·health'y	un'i·den'ti·fied
un·grate'ful	un·heard'	u'ni·fi·ca'tion
un·grate'ful·ly	un·heat'ed	u'ni·fied
un·grate'ful·ness	un·heed'ed	u'ni·form
un·ground'ed	un·heed'ful·ly	u'ni·formed

u'ni·form'i·ty

u'ni·fy

u'ni·lat'er·al

u'ni·lat'er·al·ly

un'il·lu'mi·nat'ing

un'im·ag'i·na·ble

un'im·ag'i·na'tive

un'im·paired'

un'im·peach'a·ble

un'im·ped'ed

un'im·por'tant

un'im·por'tant·ly

un'im·pos'ing

un'im·pressed'

un'im·pres'sion·a·ble

un'im·pres'sive

un'im·proved'

un'in·cor'po·rat'ed

un'in·dem'ni·fied

un·in'dexed

un'in·dict'ed

un·in'flu·enced

un'in·formed'

un'in·hab'it·a·ble

un'in·hab'it·ed

un'in·hib'it·ed

un·in'jured

un·inked'

un'in·scribed'

un'in·spired'

un'in·spir'ing·ly

un'in·struct'ed

un'in·struc'tive

un·in'su·lat'ed

un'in·sur'a·ble

un'in·sured'

un·in'te·grat'ed

un'in·tel'li·gent

un'in·tel'li·gi·ble

un'in·tend'ed

un'in·ten'tion·al

un'in·ten'tion·al·ly

un·in'ter·est·ed

un·in'ter·est·ed·ly

un·in'ter·est·ing·ly

un'in·ter·mit'ting·ly

un'in·ter·rupt'ed·ly

un·in'ti·mat'ed

un'in·tim'i·dat'ed

un'in·tox'i·cat'ed

un'in·vad'ed

un'in·ven'tive

un'in·vig'o·rat'ed

un'in·vit'ing·ly

un'ion

un'ion·ism

un'ion·ist

un'ion·i·za'tion

un'ion·ize

un'ion·ized

u·nique'

u·nique'ly

u·nique'ness

un'ir·ra'di·at'ed

u'ni·son

un·is'sued

u'nit

U'ni·tar'i·an

U'ni·tar'i·an·ism

u'ni·tar'y

u·nite'

u·nit'ed

u·nit'ed·ly

u'ni·ty

u'ni·ver'sal

U'ni·ver'sal·ist

u'ni·ver·sal'i·ty

u'ni·ver'sal·ly

u'ni·verse

u'ni·ver'si·ty

un·jok'ing·ly

un·just'

un·jus'ti·fi'a·ble

un·jus'ti·fi'a·bly

un·jus'ti·fied

un·just'ly

un·kempt'

un·killed'

un·kind'

un·kind'li·ness

un·kind'ly

un·know'a·ble

un·know'ing·ly

un·known'

un·la'beled

un·lace'

un·laced'

un·la'dy·like'

un'la·ment'ed

un·lashed'

un·latch'

un·law'ful

un·law'ful·ly

un·law'ful·ness

un·lead'ed

un·learn'

un·leash'

un·leashed'

un·leav'ened

un·less'

un·let'tered

un·lib'er·at·ed

un·li'censed

un·light'ed

un·lik'a·ble

un·like'

un·like'li·hood

un·like'ly

un·lim'ber

un·lim'bered

un·lim'it·ed

un·lined'

un·list'ed

un·load'

un·load'ed

un·lo'cal·ized

un·lock'

un·locked'

un·looked'

un·loos'en

un·loved'

un·lov'ing·ly

un·luck'i·ly

un·luck'y

un·made'

un·mag'ni·fied

un·maid'en·ly

un·mail'a·ble

un·make'

un·man'

un·man'age·a·ble

un·man'li·ness

un·man'ly

un·manned'

un·man'ner·li·ness

un·man'ner·ly

un·marked'

un·mar'riage·a·ble

un·mar'ried

un·mask'

un·masked'

un·matched'

un·meas'ur·a·ble

un·meas'ured

un·men'tion·a·ble

un·men'tioned

un·mer'ci·ful

un·mer'ci·ful·ly

un·mer'it·ed

un·me'tered

un·mind'ful

un'mis·tak'a·ble

un·mit'i·gat'ed

un·mixed'

un'mo·lest'ed

un·moored'

un·mort'gaged

un·mo'ti·vat'ed

un·mount'ed

un·moved'

un·mov'ing·ly

un·named'

un·nat'u·ral

un·nat'u·ral·ly

un·nav'i·ga·ble

un·nec'es·sar'i·ly

un·nec'es·sar'y

un·need'ed

un·neigh'bor·ly

un·nerve'

un·no'tice·a·ble

un·no'ticed

un·num'bered

un'ob·serv'ant

un'ob·served'

un'ob·tain'a·ble

un·oc'cu·pied

un'of·fi'cial

un·o'pened

un'o·pin'ion·at·ed

un'op·posed'

un·or'ches·trat'ed

un·or'gan·ized
un·or'tho·dox
un'os·ten·ta'tious
un·pac'i·fied
un·pack'
un·paged'
un·paid'
un·paint'ed
un·pal'at·a·ble
un·par'al·leled
un·par'don·a·ble
un·par'doned
un'par·lia·men'ta·ry
un·pas'teur·ized
un·pat'ent·a·ble
un·pat'ent·ed
un'pa·tri·ot'ic
un'pa·tri·ot'i·cal·ly
un'pa·trolled'
un·paved'
un'per·ceived'
un'per'fo·rat·ed
un'per·formed'
un'per·turbed'
un·pit'y·ing
un·pit'y·ing·ly
un·planned'
un·plas'tered
un·play'a·ble
un·pleas'a·ble
un·pleas'ant
un·pleas'ant·ly

un·pleas'ant·ness
un·pleas'ing·ly
un·pledged'
un·plowed'
un·plugged'
un·plumbed'
un'po·et'ic
un'po·liced'
un·pol'ished
un'pol·lut'ed
un'pop'u·lar
un·pop'u·lat'ed
un·pop'u·lous
un·prac'ticed
un'prec'e·dent·ed
un'prec'e·dent·ed·ly
un'pre·dict'a·ble
un·prej'u·diced
un'pre·med'i·tat'ed
un'pre·pared'
un'pre·par'ed·ness
un'pre·pos·sess'ing
un'pre·sent'a·ble
un'pre·tend'ing·ly
un'pre·ten'tious
un'pre·ten'tious·ly
un'pre·ten'tious·ness
un·prin'ci·pled
un·print'a·ble
un·print'ed
un'pro·duced'
un'pro·duc'tive

un'pro·fes'sion·al
un·prof'it·a·ble
un'pro·gres'sive
un·prom'is·ing
un·prompt'ed
un'pro·nounce'a·ble
un'pro·pi'tious
un'pro·tect'ed
un·prov'a·ble
un·proved'
un'pro·vid'ed
un'pro·voked'
un·pub'lished
un·punc'tu·al
un'punc·tu·al'i·ty
un·punc'tu·al·ly
un·pun'ished
un·qual'i·fied
un·quelled'
un·quench'a·bly
un·ques'tion·a·ble
un·ques'tion·a·bly
un·ques'tioned
un·ques'tion·ing·ly
un·ran'somed
un·rav'el
un·rav'eled
un·reach'a·ble
un·read'
un·read'a·ble
un·re'al
un're·al·is'tic

un're·al'i·ty

un're·al·ized

un·rea'son·a·ble

un·rea'son·a·bly

un·rea'soned

un·rea'son·ing·ly

un're·buked'

un're·ceipt'ed

un're·cep'tive

un're·claim'a·ble

un·rec'og·niz'a·ble

un·rec'og·nized

un·rec'og·niz'ing·ly

un·rec'on·cil'a·ble

un're·cord'ed

un're·deem'a·ble

un're·deemed'

un·re·fill'a·ble

un're·fined'

un're·frig'er·at'ed

un're·fut'ed

un·re·gen'er·ate

un·reg'u·lat'ed

un're·hearsed'

un're·lat'ed

un're·lent'ing·ly

un're·li'a·bil'i·ty

un're·li'a·ble

un're·mit'ting

un're·mu'ner·a'tive

un're·mu'ner·a'tive·ly

un·rent'a·ble

un·rent'ed

un're·pent'ed

un're·port'a·ble

un're·port'ed

un'rep·re·sent'a·tive

un're·proach'ing·ly

un're·proved'

un're·quit'ed

un're·served'

un're·serv'ed·ly

un're·sist'ing·ly

un're·solved'

un're·source'ful

un're·spon'sive

un·rest'

un·rest'ed

un're·strained'

un're·strict'ed

un're·veal'ing·ly

un're·ward'ed

un·rhymed'

un·right'eous

un·right'eous·ly

un·right'ful·ly

un·ripe'

un·ri'pened

un·ri'valed

un·roll'

un·rolled'

un·ruf'fle

un·ruf'fled

un·ruled'

un·rul'y

un·sad'dened

un·sad'dle

un·sad'dled

un·safe'

un·said'

un·sal'a·ble

un·sal'a·ried

un·sanc'ti·fied

un·sa'ti·at'ed

un'sat·is·fac'to·ri·ly

un'sat·is·fac'to·ry

un·sat'is·fied

un·sat'is·fy'ing·ly

un·sat'u·rat'ed

un·sa'vor·i·ly

un·sa'vor·y

un·scathed'

un·scent'ed

un·schooled'

un'sci·en·tif'ic

un·scram'ble

un·screw'

un·screwed'

un·scru'pu·lous

un·scru'pu·lous·ly

un·seal'

un·sealed'

un·sea'son·a·ble

un·sea'soned

un·seat'ed

un·sea'wor'thy

un·sec'ond·ed

un'se·cured'

un·see'ing·ly

un·seem'ing·ly

un·seem'ly

un·seen'

un'se·lect'ed

un·self'ish

un·self'ish·ly

un·sen'si·tized

un'sen·ti·men'tal

un·sep'a·rat'ed

un·serv'ice·a·ble

un·set'tle

un·set'tled

un·shack'le

un·shack'led

un·shad'ed

un·shak'a·ble

un·shak'en

un·sharp'ened

un·shav'en

un·sheathe'

un·shed'

un·shel'tered

un·shield'ed

un·ship'

un·shipped'

un·shrink'a·ble

un·shuf'fled

un·sight'ed

un·sight'ly

un·signed'

un·sing'a·ble

un·sink'a·ble

un·sis'ter·ly

un·sized'

un·skilled'

un·skill'ful

un·skimmed'

un·smil'ing·ly

un·smirched'

un·smoked'

un·smudged'

un·snarl'

un·so'cia·ble

un·soft'ened

un·soil'

un·soiled'

un·sold'

un·sol'dier·ly

un'so·lic'it·ed

un'so·phis'ti·cat'ed

un·sought'

un·sound'

un·sound'ly

un·speak'a·ble

un·spe'cial·ized

un·spec'i·fied

un·spoiled'

un·spo'ken

un·sports'man·like'

un·spot'ted

un·sprin'kled

un·sta'ble

un·stained'

un·stamped'

un·stead'i·ly

un·stead'y

un·ster'i·lized

un·stint'ed

un·stint'ing·ly

un·strained'

un·stressed'

un·strung'

un'sub·stan'tial

un'sub·stan'ti·at'ed

un'suc·cess'ful

un·suf'fer·a·ble

un·suit'a·ble

un·sul'lied

un·sum'moned

un·sung'

un'su·per·vised'

un·sure'

un'sur·pass'a·ble

un'sur·passed'

un'sus·pect'ed

un'sus·pect'ing

un'sus·pect'ing·ly

un·swayed'

un·sweet'ened

un·swerv'ing·ly

un·sworn'

un'sym·pa·thet'ic

un·sym'pa·thiz'ing·ly

un'sys·tem·at'ic

un·sys'tem·a·tized

un·taint'ed

un·tal'ent·ed

un·tamed'

un·tan'gle

un·tanned'

un·tast'ed

un·taught'

un·tax'a·ble

un·taxed'

un·teach'a·ble

un·tech'ni·cal

un·tempt'ed

un·ten'ant·a·ble

un·ten'ant·ed

un·tend'ed

un·ter'ri·fied

un·thick'ened

un·think'a·ble

un·think'ing

un·think'ing·ly

un·ti'di·ly

un·ti'dy

un·tie'

un·tied'

un·til'

un·time'ly

un·tint'ed

un·tir'ing·ly

un·ti'tled

un'to

un·told'

un·touch'a·ble

un·touched'

un·to'ward

un·trace'a·ble

un·trad'ed

un·trained'

un·tram'meled

un'trans·lat'a·ble

un·trav'eled

un·tried'

un·trimmed'

un·trod'den

un·trou'bled

un·true'

un·trussed'

un·trust'wor'thy

un·truth'

un·truth'ful

un·tuned'

un·turned'

un·tu'tored

un·twine'

un·twist'

un'un·der·stand'a·ble

un·up·braid'ing·ly

un·us'a·ble

un·used'

un·u'su·al

un·u'su·al·ly

un·ut'ter·a·ble

un·ut'ter·a·bly

un·ut'tered

un·val'i·dat'ed

un·val'ued

un·van'quished

un·var'ied

un·var'nished

un·var'y·ing·ly

un·vaunt'ing·ly

un·veil'

un·veiled'

un·ver'bal·ized

un·ver'i·fied

un·versed'

un·vis'it·ed

un·voiced'

un·walled'

un·war'i·ly

un·warned'

un·war'rant·a·ble

un·war'rant·ed

un·war'y

un·washed'

un·wa'tered

un·wa'ver·ing·ly

un·wea'ried

un·wea'ry·ing·ly

un·wed'

un·wed'ded

un·wel'come

un·well'

un·wept'

un·whole'some

un·whole'some·ly	un·yoked'	up·raised'
un·wield'i·ness	up	up'right'
un·wield'y	u'pas	up'right'ly
un·will'ing	up'beat'	up'right'ness
un·will'ing·ly	up·braid'	up·ris'ings
un·will'ing·ness	up·braid'ed	up'roar'
un·winc'ing·ly	up·braid'ing·ly	up·roar'i·ous
un·wind'	up·bring'ing	up·roar'i·ous·ness
un·wind'ing·ly	up'coun'try	up·root'
un·wink'ing·ly	up'draft'	up·root'ed
un·wise'	up'grade'	up·set'
un·wit'nessed	up'growth'	up·set'ting·ly
un·wit'ting·ly	up·heav'al	up'shot'
un·wom'an·ly	up·held'	up'side'
un·wont'ed	up'hill'	up'stairs'
un·work'a·ble	up·hold'	up'start'
un·work'man·like'	up·hold'er	up'state'
un·world'li·ness	up·hol'ster	up'stream'
un·world'ly	up·hol'stered	up'stroke'
un·worn'	up·hol'ster·er	up'take'
un·wor'ried	up·hol'ster·y	up'-to-date'
un·wor'thi·ly	up'keep'	up'town'
un·wor'thi·ness	up'land'	up·turn'
un·wor'thy	up·lift'	up·turned'
un·wound'	up·lift'ed	up'ward
un·wound'ed	up·lift'ing·ly	up'wind'
un·wrap'	up'most	u·ra'ni·um
un·wrapped'	up·on'	ur'ban
un·wreathe'	up'per	ur·bane'
un·wrin'kled	up'per·most	ur·bane'ly
un·writ'ten	up'pers	ur'ban·ite
un·yield'ing·ly	up·raise'	ur·ban'i·ty

ur'ban·i·za'tion

ur'ban·ize

ur'ban·ized

ur'chin

urge

urged

ur'gen·cy

ur'gent

ur'gent·ly

urg'ings

urn

us

us'a·bil'i·ty

us'a·ble

us'age

use

used

use'ful

use'ful·ly

use'ful·ness

use'less

use'less·ly

use'less·ness

us'er

us'es

ush'er

ush'ered

u'su·al

u'su·al·ly

u'su·fruct

u'su·rer

u·su'ri·ous

u·surp'

u'sur·pa'tion

u·surp'er

u'su·ry

u·ten'sil

u·til'i·tar'i·an

u·til'i·tar'i·an·ism

u·til'i·ties

u·til'i·ty

u'ti·liz'a·ble

u'ti·li·za'tion

u'ti·lize

u'ti·lized

ut'most

u·to'pi·a

u·to'pi·an

u·to'pi·an·ism

ut'ter

ut'ter·ance

ut'tered

ut'ter·ly

ut'ter·most

u'vu·la

u'vu·lar

V

va′can·cy	vag′a·bon′di·a	va·le′ri·an
va′cant	vag′a·bond·ism	val′et
va′cate	vag′a·bond·ize	val′e·tu′di·nar′i·an
va·cat·ed	va·gar′y	Val·hal′la
va·ca′tion	va′gran·cy	val′iant
va·ca′tioned	va′grant	val′id
va·ca′tion·ist	vague	val′i·date
vac′ci·nate	va′guer	val′i·dat′ed
vac′ci·nat′ed	va′guest	val′i·da′tion
vac′ci·na′tion	va′gus	va·lid′i·ty
vac′ci·na′tor	vain	val′id·ly
vac′cine	vain′glo′ri·ous	va·lise′
vac′il·late	vain′glo′ry	val′ley
vac′il·lat′ed	vain′ly	val′or
vac′il·la′tion	vain′ness	val′or·i·za′tion
vac′il·lat′ing·ly	val′ance	val′or·ize
vac′il·la·to′ry	vale	val′or·ous
va·cu′i·ty	val′e·dic′tion	val′u·a·ble
vac′u·ous	val′e·dic·to′ri·an	val′u·a′tion
vac′u·um	val′e·dic′to·ry	val′ue
vag′a·bond	va′lence	val′ued
vag′a·bond′age	val′en·tine	val′ue·less

valve

val'vu·lar

vamp

vam'pire

va·na'di·um

van'dal

van'dal·ism

van'dal·ize

vane

van'guard'

va·nil'la

van'il·lin

van'ish

van'ished

van'ish·ing·ly

van'i·ty

van'quish

van'quished

van'tage

vap'id

vap'id·ly

va'por

va'por·ings

va'por·i·za'tion

va'por·ize

va'por·ized

va'por·iz'er

va'por·ous

var'i·a·bil'i·ty

var'i·a·ble

var'i·ance

var'i·ant

var'i·a'tion

var'i·col'ored

var'i·cose

var'i·cos'i·ty

var'ied

var'i·e·gate

var'i·e·gat'ed

var'i·e·ga'tion

va·ri'e·tal

va·ri'e·ty

va·ri'o·la

var'i·o'rum

var'i·ous

var'i·ous·ly

var'let

var'nish

var'nished

var'nish·ings

var'y

var'y·ing·ly

vas'cu·lar

vase

Vas'e·line

vas'sal

vas'sal·age

vast

vast'er

vast'est

vast'ly

vat

Vat'i·can

vaude'ville

vault

vault'ed

vaunt

vaunt'ed

vaunt'ing·ly

veal

vec'tor

ve·dette'

veer

veered

veg'e·ta·ble

veg'e·tar'i·an

veg'e·tar'i·an·ism

veg'e·tate

veg'e·tat'ed

veg'e·ta'tion

veg'e·ta'tive

ve'he·mence

ve'he·ment

ve'he·ment·ly

ve'hi·cle

ve'hi·cles

ve·hic'u·lar

veil

veiled

vein

veined

vein'ings

vein'let

vel'lum

ve·loc'i·pede

ve·loc'i·ty

ve'lo·drome
ve·lours'
vel'vet
vel'vet·een'
vel'vet·y
ve'nal
ve·nal'i·ty
ve'nal·i·za'tion
ve'nal·ize
ve·na'tion
vend
vend'ed
vend·ee'
ven·det'ta
vend'i·ble
ven'dor
ve·neer'
ve·neered'
ven'er·a·ble
ven'er·ate
ven'er·at'ed
ven'er·a'tion
ven'er·a'tive
Ve·ne'tian
venge'ance
venge'ful
venge'ful·ness
ve'ni·al
ve'ni·al'i·ty
ve'ni·al·ly
ven'i·son
ven'om

ven'om·ous
ven'om·ous·ly
vent
vent'ed
vent'hole'
ven'ti·late
ven'ti·lat'ed
ven'ti·la'tion
ven'ti·la'tor
ven'tral
ven'tri·cle
ven·tric'u·lar
ven·tril'o·quism
ven·tril'o·quist
ven'ture
ven'tured
ven'ture·some
ven'ue
ve·ra'cious
ve·ra'cious·ly
ve·rac'i·ty
ve·ran'da
ver'bal
ver'bal·ism
ver'bal·ist
ver'bal·i·za'tion
ver'bal·ize
ver'bal·ized
ver'bal·ly
ver·ba'tim
ver·be'na
ver'bi·age

ver·bose'
ver·bos'i·ty
ver'dant
ver'dict
ver'di·gris
ver'dure
verge
verged
ver'ger
ver'i·est
ver'i·fi'a·ble
ver'i·fi·ca'tion
ver'i·fied
ver'i·fy
ver'i·ly
ver'i·si·mil'i-
....tude
ver'ism
ver'i·ta·ble
ver'i·ta·bly
ver'i·ties
ver'i·ty
ver'meil
ver'mi·cel'li
ver'mi·cide
ver·mic'u·late
ver·mic'u·la'tion
ver·mic'u·lite
ver'mi·form
ver'mi·fuge
ver·mil'ion
ver'min
ver'min·ous

ver·nac'u·lar
ver'nal
ver'ni·er
ver'sa·tile
ver'sa·til'i·ty
verse
ver'si·cle
ver'si·fi·ca'tion
ver'si·fied
ver'si·fi'er
ver'si·fy
ver'sion
ver'so
ver'sus
ver'te·bra
ver'te·brae
ver'te·brate
ver'tex
ver'ti·cal
ver'ti·cal·ly
ver·tig'i·nous
ver'ti·go
ver'vain
verve
ver'y
ves'i·cle
ves'per
ves'sel
vest
ves'tal
vest'ed
ves·tib'u·lar

ves'ti·bule
ves'tige
ves·tig'i·al
vest'ment
ves'try
ves'ture
vetch
vet'er·an
vet'er·i·nar'i·an
vet'er·i·nar'y
ve'to
ve'toed
vex
vex·a'tion
vex·a'tious
vexed
vi'a
vi·a·bil'i·ty
vi'a·ble
vi'a·duct
vi'al
vi'and
vi·at'i·cum
vi'bran·cy
vi'brant
vi'brate
vi'brat·ed
vi'brat·ing·ly
vi·bra'tion
vi·bra'tion·less
vi·bra'to
vi'bra·tor

vi'bra·to'ry
vic'ar
vic'ar·age
vi·car'i·ate
vi·car'i·ous
vi·car'i·ous·ly
vice
vice'ge'ral
vice'ge'rent
vice'reine
vice'roy
vic'i·nage
vi·cin'i·ties
vi·cin'i·ty
vi'cious
vi'cious·ly
vi'cious·ness
vi·cis'si·tude
vic'tim
vic'tim·ize
vic'tim·ized
vic'tor
Vic·to'ri·an
vic·to'ri·ous
vic·to'ri·ous·ly
vic'to·ry
Vic·tro'la
vict'ual
vi·cu'ña
vid'e·o
vie
vied

view	vin'di·ca'tion	vi·ril'i·ty
viewed	vin·dic'tive	vir'tu·al
vig'il	vine	vir'tu·al·ly
vig'i·lance	vin'e·gar	vir'tue
vig'i·lant	vine'yard	vir'tu·os'i·ty
vig'i·lan'te	vin'i·fi·ca'tion	vir'tu·o'so
vig'i·lant·ly	vi'nous	vir'tu·ous
vi·gnette'	vin'tage	vir'tu·ous·ly
vi·gnett'ed	vint'ner	vir'tu·ous·ness
vig'or	vi'ol	vir'u·lence
vig'or·ous	vi·o'la	vir'u·len·cy
vig'or·ous·ly	vi'o·late	vir'u·lent
vi'kings	vi'o·lat'ed	vi'rus
vile	vi'o·la'tion	vi'sa
vil'er	vi'o·la'tive	vis'age
vil'est	vi'o·la'tor	vis'-à-vis'
vil'i·fi·ca'tion	vi'o·lence	vis'cer·a
vil'i·fi'er	vi'o·lent	vis'cer·al
vil'i·fy	vi'o·lent·ly	vis'cid
vil'la	vi'o·let	vis·cid'i·ty
vil'lage	vi'o·lin'	vis'cid·ly
vil'lag·er	vi'o·lin'ist	vis'cose
vil'lain	vi'o·lon·cel'list	vis·cos'i·ty
vil'lain·ous	vi'o·lon·cel'lo	vis'count'
vil'lain·ous·ly	vi'per	vis'cous
vil'lain·y	vi'per·ous	vise
vil'la·nelle'	vi·ra'go	vis'i·bil'i·ty
vin'ai·grette'	vir'e·o	vis'i·ble
vin'cu·lum	vir'gin	vis'i·bly
vin'di·ca·ble	vir'gin·al	vi'sion
vin'di·cate	vir·gin'i·ty	vi'sion·ar'y
vin'di·cat'ed	vir'ile	vis'it

vis'it·a'tion
vis'it·ed
vis'i·tor
vis'ta
vis'u·al
vis'u·al·i·za'tion
vis'u·al·ize
vis'u·al·ized
vis'u·al·ly
vi'tal
vi·tal'i·ty
vi'tal·ize
vi'tal·ized
vi'tal·ly
vi'ta·min
vi'ti·ate
vi'ti·at'ed
vi'ti·a'tion
vit're·ous
vit'ri·fac'tion
vit'ri·fi·ca'tion
vit'ri·fied
vit'ri·fy
vit'ri·ol
vit'ri·ol'ic
vi·tu'per·ate
vi·tu'per·at'ed
vi·tu'per·a'tion
vi·tu'per·a'tive
vi·tu'per·a'tive·ly
vi·va'cious
vi·va'cious·ly

vi·vac'i·ty
vi·var'i·um
viv'id
viv'id·ly
viv'i·fy
vi·vip'a·rous
viv'i·sect
viv'i·sec'tion
viv'i·sec'tion·ist
vix'en
vix'en·ish
viz'ard
vi·zier'
vo'ca·ble
vo·cab'u·lar'y
vo'cal
vo'cal·ism
vo'cal·ist
vo'cal·i·za'tion
vo'cal·ize
vo'cal·ized
vo'cal·ly
vo·ca'tion
vo·ca'tion·al
vo·ca'tion·al·ly
voc'a·tive
vo·cif'er·ate
vo·cif'er·at'ed
vo·cif'er·a'tion
vo·cif'er·ous
vod'ka
vogue

voice
voiced
voice'less
voice'less·ly
voice'less·ness
void
void'a·ble
void'ed
vol'a·tile
vol'a·til'i·ty
vol'a·til·i·za'tion
vol'a·til·ize
vol'a·til·ized
vol·can'ic
vol·ca'no
vol'can·ol'o·gy
vo·li'tion
vo·li'tion·al
vo·li'tion·al·ly
vol'ley
vol'ley·ball'
vol'leyed
volt
volt'age
vol·ta'ic
volt·am'e·ter
volt'am'me·ter
volt'me'ter
vol'u·bil'i·ty
vol'u·ble
vol'u·bly
vol'ume

vol'u·met'ric	vo·rac'i·ty	voy'aged
vo·lu'mi·nous	vor'tex	voy'ag·er
vo·lu'mi·nous·ly	vor'ti·cal	vul'can·i·za'tion
vo·lu'mi·nous·ness	vor'ti·cal·ly	vul'can·ize
vol'un·tar'i·ly	vo'ta·ry	vul'can·ized
vol'un·tar'y	vote	vul'can·iz'er
vol'un·teer'	vot'ed	vul'gar
vol'un·teered'	vot'er	vul·gar'i·an
vo·lup'tu·ar'y	vo'tive	vul'gar·ism
vo·lup'tu·ous	vouch	vul·gar'i·ty
vo·lup'tu·ous·ly	vouched	vul'gar·i·za'tion
vo·lup'tu·ous·ness	vouch'er	vul'gar·ize
vo·lute'	vouch·safe'	vul'gar·ized
vol'vu·lus	vouch·safed'	vul'gar·iz'er
vom'it	vow	vul'gar·ly
vom'it·ed	vowed	vul'gate
vom'i·to'ry	vow'el	vul'ner·a·bil'i·ty
voo'doo	vow'el·i·za'tion	vul'ner·a·ble
voo'doo·ism	vow'el·ize	vul'ner·a·bly
vo·ra'cious	voy'age	vul'ture

W

wad	wag'gling·ly	wake
wad'ded	Wag·ne'ri·an	waked
wad'dings	wag'on	wake'ful
wad'dle	wag'tail'	wake'ful·ly
wad'dling·ly	waif	wake'ful·ness
wade	wail	wak'en
wad'ed	wailed	wak'ened
wad'er	wail'ing·ly	wak'ing·ly
wa'fer	wail'ings	wale
waf'fle	wain	waled
waft	wain'scot	walk
wag	waist	walked
wage	waist'band'	walk'er
waged	waist'coat'	walk'o'ver
wa'ger	waist'line'	walk'-up'
wa'gered	wait	walk'way'
wa'ger·ings	wait'ed	wall
wag'es	wait'er	wall'board'
wagged	wait'ress	walled
wag'gish	waive	wal'let
wag'gle	waived	wall'eyed'
wag'gled	waiv'er	wall'flow'er

Wal·loon'	ward'ed	war'rant
wal'lop	ward'en	war'rant·a·ble
wal'low	ward'er	war'rant·ed
wal'lowed	ward'robe'	war'ran·tor
wall'pa'per	ward'room'	war'ran·ty
wal'nut	ware'house'	warred
wal'rus	ware'house'man	war'ren
waltz	ware'room'	war'ship'
waltzed	wares	wart
wam'pum	war'fare'	war'time'
wan	war'i·ly	wart'less
wand	war'i·ness	war'y
wan'der	war'like'	was
wan'dered	war'lock	wash
wan'der·er	warm	wash'a·ble
wan'der·ing·ly	warmed	wash'board'
wan'der·ings	warm'er	wash'bowl'
wane	warm'est	wash'cloth'
waned	warm'heart'ed	washed
wan'gle	warm'ly	wash'er
wan'gled	warm'ness	wash'house'
want	war'mon'ger	wash'ings
want'ed	warmth	wash'out'
want'ing·ly	warn	wash'room'
wan'ton	warned	wash'stand'
war	warn'ing·ly	wash'-up'
war'ble	warn'ings	wash'wom'an
war'bled	warp	wasp
war'bler	warp'age	wasp'ish
war'bling·ly	war'path'	was'sail
war'blings	warped	wast'age
ward	war'plane'	waste

waste′bas′ket	wa′ter·log′	wax′i·ness
wast′ed	wa′ter·logged′	wax′ing·ly
waste′ful	Wa′ter·loo′	wax′wing′
waste′ful·ly	wa′ter·man	wax′work′
waste′ful·ness	wa′ter·mark′	wax′y
waste′land′	wa′ter·mel′on	way
waste′pa′per	wa′ter·proof′	way′bill′
wast′er	wa′ter·proofed′	way′far′er
wast′ing·ly	wa′ter·shed′	way′fel′low
wast′rel	wa′ter·side′	way′laid′
watch	wa′ter·spout′	way′lay′
watch′case′	wa′ter·way′	way′side′
watch′dog′	wa′ter·weed′	way′ward
watched	wa′ter·works′	we
watch′er	wa′ter·y	weak
watch′ful	watt	weak′en
watch′ful·ly	watt′age	weak′ened
watch′ful·ness	wat′tle	weak′er
watch′house′	wat′tled	weak′est
watch′keep′er	watt′me′ter	weak′ling
watch′mak′er	wave	weak′ly
watch′man	waved	weak′ness
watch′tow′er	wave′me′ter	weal
watch′word′	wa′ver	wealth
wa′ter	wa′vered	wealth′i·er
wa′tered	wa′ver·ing·ly	wealth′i·est
wa′ter·fall′	wa′ver·ings	wealth′y
wa′ter·find′er	wav′i·ness	wean
wa′ter·fowl′	wav′y	weaned
wa′ter·i·ness	wax	weap′on
wa′ter·ings	waxed	weap′on·less
wa′ter·line′	wax′en	wear

wear'a·bil'i·ty	weed'ed	wel'fare'
wear'a·ble	weed'i·er	wel'kin
wear'er	weed'i·est	well
wea'ried	weed'y	well'born'
wea'ri·er	week	welled
wea'ri·est	week'day'	well'head'
wea'ri·ly	week'end'	well'hole'
wea'ri·ness	week'lies	well'spring'
wear'ings	week'ly	welt
wea'ri·some	weep	welt'ed
wea'ri·some·ness	weep'ing·ly	wel'ter
wea'ry	wee'vil	wel'tered
wea'sel	weft	wen
weath'er	weigh	wench
weath'er·board'	weighed	wend
weath'er·cock'	weigh'ings	wend'ed
weath'ered	weigh'mas'ter	went
weath'er·proof'	weight	wept
weath'er·proofed'	weight'ed	were
weave	weight'i·er	were'wolf'
weav'er	weight'i·est	west
web	weight'ings	west'er·ly
webbed	weight'y	west'ern
web'bings	weir	west'ern·er
wed	weird	west'ward
wed'ded	weird'ly	wet
wed'dings	weird'ness	wet'ness
wedge	wel'come	wet'ta·bil'i·ty
wedged	wel'comed	wet'ta·ble
wed'lock	wel'com·ing·ly	wet'ted
Wednes'day	weld	wet'ter
weed	weld'ed	wet'test

wet'tings	wheez'ing·ly	which
we've	wheez'y	which·ev'er
whack	whelk	which'so·ev'er
whacked	whelp	whiff
whale	whelped	whiffed
whale'back'	when	whif'fle
whale'bone'	whence	whif'fled
whale'man	whence'forth'	Whig
whal'er	when·ev'er	while
wharf	when'so·ev'er	whiled
wharf'age	where	whi'lom
wharf'in·ger	where'a·bouts'	whim
what	where·aft'er	whim'per
what·ev'er	where·as'	whim'pered
what'not'	where·at'	whim'per·ing·ly
what'so·ev'er	where·by'	whim'per·ings
wheat	where'fore	whim'sey
wheat'en	where·from'	whim'si·cal
wheat'worm'	where·in'	whine
whee'dle	where·of'	whined
whee'dled	where·on'	whin'ing·ly
whee'dling·ly	where'so·ev'er	whin'ings
wheel	where'up·on'	whin'nied
wheel'bar'row	wher·ev'er	whin'ny
wheeled	where·with'	whip
wheel'house'	where'with·al'	whip'cord'
wheel'wright'	wher'ry	whipped
wheeze	whet	whip'per·snap'per
wheezed	wheth'er	whip'pet
wheez'i·er	whet'ted	whip'ping·ly
wheez'i·est	whet'stone'	whip'pings
wheez'i·ly	whey	whip'poor·will'

whip'saw'	whit'en	why
whip'stitch'	whit'ened	wick
whip'stock'	white'ness	wick'ed
whip'worm'	white'wash'	wick'ed·ly
whir	white'washed'	wick'ed·ness
whirl	white'wing'	wick'er
whirled	white'wood'	wick'er·work'
whirl'i·gig'	whith'er	wick'et
whirl'ing·ly	whit'ings	wide
whirl'pool'	whit'ish	wide'ly
whirl'wind'	whit'low	wid'en
whirred	whit'tle	wid'ened
whisk	whit'tled	wide'ness
whisked	whit'tlings	wid'er
whisk'er	who	wide'spread'
whisk'ered	who·ev'er	wid'est
whis'ky	whole	wid'ow
whis'per	whole'heart'ed	wid'owed
whis'pered	whole'heart'ed·ly	wid'ow·er
whis'per·er	whole'sale'	wid'ow·hood
whis'per·ing·ly	whole'sal'er	width
whis'per·ings	whole'some	wield
whist	whole'some·ly	wield'ed
whis'tle	whol'ly	wife
whis'tled	whom	wife'hood
whis'tling·ly	whom·ev'er	wife'less
whis'tlings	whom'so·ev'er	wife'ly
whit	whoop	wig
white	whooped	wig'gle
white'cap'	whoop'ing·ly	wig'gled
whit'ed	whose	wig'gler
white'fish'	who'so·ev'er	wig'glings

wight	wind'break'	wing'spread'
wig'mak'er	wind'ed	wink
wig'wag'	wind'er	winked
wig'wam'	wind'fall'	wink'ing·ly
wild	wind'i·ly	win'kle
wild'er	wind'i·ness	win'ner
wil'der·ness	wind'ing·ly	win'ning·ly
wild'est	wind'ings	win'nings
wild'fire'	wind'jam'mer	win'now
wild'ness	wind'lass	win'nowed
wile	wind'mill'	win'some
wil'i·er	win'dow	win'ter
wil'i·est	win'dowed	win'tered
will	win'dow·pane'	win'ter·ize
willed	wind'pipe'	wipe
will'ful	wind'row'	wiped
will'ful·ly	wind'rowed'	wip'er
will'ful·ness	wind'shield'	wire
will'ing·ly	wind'storm'	wired
will'ing·ness	wind'ward	wire'less
wil'low	wind'ward ly	wire'pull'er
wilt	wind'way'	wire'pull'ing
wilt'ed	wind'y	wire'way'
wil'y	wine	wire'work'
win	wine'ber'ry	wire'work'er
wince	wined	wire'worm'
winced	wine'glass'	wir'y
winc'ing·ly	wine'skin'	wis'dom
wind	wing	wise
wind	winged	wise'a'cre
wind'age	wing'fish'	wise'crack'
wind'bag'	wing'less	wise'crack'er

wise'ly	with'ered	woe'be·gone'
wise'ness	with'er·ing·ly	woe'ful
wis'er	with·held'	woe'ful·ly
wis'est	with·hold'	woe'ful·ness
wish	with·hold'ings	wolf
wish'bone'	with·in'	wolfed
wished	with·out'	wolf'hound'
wish'ful	with·stand'	wolf'ish
wish'ful·ly	with·stood'	wol'ver·ine'
wish'ful·ness	wit'less	wolves
wish'ing·ly	wit'less·ly	wom'an
wisp	wit'less·ness	wom'an·hood
wisp'i·er	wit'ness	wom'an·ish
wisp'i·est	wit'nessed	wom'an·kind'
wisp'y	wit'ti·cism	wom'an·like'
wis·te'ri·a	wit'ti·er	wom'an·li·ness
wist'ful	wit'ti·est	wom'an·ly
wist'ful·ly	wit'ting·ly	wom'en
wist'ful·ness	wit'ty	won
wit	wived	won'der
witch	wives	won'dered
witch'craft'	wiz'ard	won'der·ful
witch'er·y	wiz'ard·ly	won'der·ful·ly
witch'ing·ly	wiz'ard·ry	won'der·ing·ly
witch'weed'	wiz'ened	won'der·land'
with	woad	won'der·ment
with·al'	wob'ble	won'der·work'
with·draw'	wob'bled	won'drous
with·draw'al	wob'bli·ness	won'drous·ly
with·drawn'	wob'bling·ly	won't
with·drew'	wob'bly	wont
with'er	woe	woo

wood	word'age	work'peo'ple
wood'bin'	word'build'ing	work'place'
wood'bine'	word'ed	work'room'
wood'chuck'	word'i·er	work'shop'
wood'craft'	word'i·est	work'ta'ble
wood'cut'	word'i·ly	work'wom'an
wood'ed	word'i·ness	work'wom'en
wood'en	word'less	world
wood'en·head'	word'play'	world'li·ness
wood'fish'	word'y	world'ly
wood'land	wore	worm
wood'man	work	wormed
wood'peck'er	work'a·bil'i·ty	worm'hole'
wood'pile'	work'a·ble	worm'i·er
wood'shop'	work'bag'	worm'i·est
woods'man	work'bas'ket	worm'like'
wood'work'	work'bench'	worm'proof'
wood'work'er	work'book'	worm'wood'
wood'worm'	work'box'	worm'y
wooed	work'day'	worn
woo'er	worked	wor'ried
woof	work'er	wor'ried·ly
wool	work'house'	wor'ri·er
wool'en	work'ing·man'	wor'ri·ment
wool'li·er	work'ings	wor'ri·some
wool'li·est	work'less	wor'ri·some·ness
wool'li·ness	work'man	wor'ry
wool'ly	work'man·like'	worse
wool'work'	work'man·ship	wors'en
wool'work'er	work'men	wors'ened
wooz'y	work'out'	wor'ship
word	work'pan'	wor'shiped

wor'ship·er	wrath'ful	wrin'kli·er
wor'ship·ful	wrath'ful·ly	wrin'kli·est
wor'ship·ful·ly	wrath'ful·ness	wrin'kly
worst	wreak	wrist
worst'ed	wreaked	wrist'band'
wor'sted	wreath	wrist'bone'
worth	wreathed	wrist'let
wor'thi·er	wreck	wrist'lock'
wor'thi·est	wreck'age	writ
wor'thi·ly	wrecked	writ'a·ble
wor'thi·ness	wreck'er	write
worth'less	wren	writ'er
wor'thy	wrench	writhe
would	wrenched	writhed
wound	wrest	writh'ing·ly
wound	wrest'ed	writ'ings
wound'ed	wres'tle	writ'ten
wound'ing·ly	wres'tled	wrong
wound'less	wres'tler	wrong'do'er
wove	wretch	wronged
wo'ven	wretch'ed	wrong'ful
wrack	wretch'ed·ly	wrong'ful·ly
wraith	wretch'ed·ness	wrong'head'ed
wraith'like'	wrig'gle	wrong'ly
wran'gle	wrig'gled	wrong'ness
wran'gled	wrig'gling·ly	wrote
wrap	wrig'gly	wroth
wrapped	wring	wrought
wrap'per	wring'er	wrung
wrap'pings	wrin'kle	wry
wrath	wrin'kled	wry'neck'

X Y Z

xe′non	yard′mas′ter	yell
xen′o·phile	yard′stick′	yelled
xen′o·pho′bi·a	yarn	yel′low
xe′ro·der′ma	yar′row	yel′lowed
xe·rog′ra·phy	yat′a·ghan	yel′low·er
xe·ro′sis	yaw	yel′low·est
X ray	yawl	yel′low·ish
xy′lo·phone	yawn	yel′low·ish·ness
xy·loph′o·nist	yawned	yelp
	yawn′ing·ly	yelped
yacht	ye	yeo′man
yachts′man	yea	yeo′man·ry
yak	year	yes
Yale	year′book′	yes′ter·day
yam	year′ling	yet
yam′mer	year′ly	yew
yank	yearn	Yid′dish
Yan′kee	yearned	yield
yard	yearn′ing·ly	yield′ed
yard′age	yearn′ings	yield′ing·ly
yard′arm′	yeast	yield′ing·ness
yard′man	yeast′y	yo′del

yo′deled	youth′ful	ze′ro
yo′del·er	youth′ful·ly	zest
yo′ga	youth′ful·ness	zest′ful
yo′ghurt	youths	zig′zag′
yoke	yt·ter′bi·um	zinc
yoked	yt′tri·um	Zi′on
yoke′fel′low	Yuc′ca	Zi′on·ism
yo′kel	yule	Zi′on·ist
yo′kel·ry	yule′tide′	zip′per
yolk		zir′con
yon	za′ny	zir·co′ni·um
yon′der	zeal	zith′er
yore	zeal′ot	zo′di·ac
you	zeal′ot·ry	zone
young	zeal′ous	zoned
young′er	zeal′ous·ly	zoo
young′est	zeal′ous·ness	zo′o·log′i·cal
young′ish	ze′bra	zo·ol′o·gist
young′ster	ze′broid	zo·ol′o·gy
your	ze′bu	zoom
yours	ze′nith	zoomed
your·self′	ze′o·lite	Zu′lu
your·selves′	zeph′yr	zy′mase
youth	Zep′pe·lin	zy·mol′o·gy

PART TWO

Part Two consists of 1,314 entries of personal and geographical names divided approximately as follows:

835 Geographical Names. The largest group of names consists of the names of American cities and towns that are likely to be encountered in business dictation. The names of the American states are given. A relatively small group of foreign geographical names is given—the foreign countries and cities that are most likely to occur in American business dictation. The lists are not intended to be complete or exhaustive. The attempt has been made, however, to include the geographical names that occur most frequently in ordinary business dictation.

243 Surnames. This small group of names represents the commonest American surnames that are likely to be used in business dictation. There are tens of thousands of surnames in this country, and no attempt can be made to present a complete list.

113 First Names of Women. This list contains the more frequently used feminine first names.

123 First Names of Men. This list contains the more frequently used masculine first names.

The four groups of names listed above are combined in one alphabetical list in Part Two.

With the exception of the states and of a few of the largest cities, the geographical names are written very fully. This is done with the understanding that the writer will use these full outlines for the names that occur only occasionally in the dictation. When some name occurs more frequently in the dictation, an abbreviated form would be used.

The shorthand writer in Oregon would ordinarily have little occasion to use the outline for *Corpus Christi*. The shorthand writer in Texas might use it so frequently that he would abbreviate it to *kk*.

In order to keep the list in Part Two as short and at the same time as useful as possible, the names of many cities and towns are omitted. This is possible because many American city and town names are composed of nouns and adjectives that appear in Part One—for example, such names as *White River Junction* or *Egg Harbor City*.

Many city and town names are formed by adding to the name of another town a word like *Beach, Grove, Hill, City, Park*, or *Spring*. In most cases such names have been omitted, for they would cause no shorthand writing difficulty.

The writing and transcribing of proper names can present many traps for the shorthand writer. When you write in shorthand the name *Pittsburgh,* you will not know whether to transcribe it *Pittsburg* or *Pittsburgh* until you know whether the dictator had in mind *Pittsburg,* Kansas, or *Pittsburgh,* Pennsylvania. You can be tricked similarly by such pairs as *Worcester,* Massachusetts, and *Wooster,* Ohio.

You may confidently write *b-r-ow-n* in your shorthand notes without realizing that the dictator may not be referring to his familiar correspondent, Mr. *Brown,* but to some strange *Browne* or *Braun.*

Martin J. Dupraw, world's champion shorthand writer, tells of an error he made, but caught in time, because of an unusual proper name. He understood the witness to have said: "We gave it the hour test." Mr. Dupraw transcribed it like that, only to find out, just in time, that the witness had really said: "We gave it the Auer test."

Unless the writer is absolutely sure of the identity of the proper names used by the dictator, he should always check them with the greatest possible care. Almost everyone is annoyed when his name or the name of his city or town is spelled incorrectly.

PERSONAL AND GEOGRAPHICAL NAMES

Aaron	Algernon	Anniston
Aberdeen	Allentown	Anthony
Abilene	Allison	Antioch
Abington	Alphonsine	Antoinette
Abraham	Alphonso	Antwerp
Adams	Alton	Appleton
Adelbert	Altoona	Arabia
Adolph	Alvin	Archibald
Agatha	Amanda	Argentina
Aiken	Amarillo	Arizona
Aileen	Amelia	Arkansas
Ainsworth	Amesbury	Arlington
Akron	Amherst	Arnold
Alabama	Amityville	Arthur
Alameda	Amsterdam	Asheboro
Alaska	Anderson	Asheville
Albany	Andover	Ashley
Albert	Angela	Astoria
Albuquerque	Angelica	Atchison
Alexander	Angora	Atkinson
Alfred	Annabel	Atlanta
Algeria	Annapolis	Atlantic

Augusta	Bedford	Blairsville
Augustin	Belfast	Blakely
Aurelia	Belgium	Blanchard
Aurora	Belinda	Bloomington
Austin	Bellefontaine	Bloomsburg
Australia	Belleville	Bluffton
Austria	Bellevue	Bogota
Avery	Bellingham	Boise
Baird	Belmont	Bolivia
Bakersfield	Beloit	Bonham
Baldwin	Belvedere	Boniface
Ballard	Bemidji	Boonville
Baltimore	Benedict	Bordeaux
Bangkok	Benjamin	Boston
Bangor	Bennett	Bosworth
Barberton	Bennington	Boulder
Barcelona	Bentley	Bowen
Barlow	Bergenfield	Bowman
Barnard	Berkeley	Boyd
Barnesville	Bernard	Boyle
Barrington	Bernstein	Braddock
Bartholomew	Bertha	Bradenton
Bartlett	Berwick	Bradford
Bartow	Bethlehem	Bradley
Basil	Beulah	Brattleboro
Batavia	Beverly	Brazil
Batesville	Biloxi	Bremen
Baton Rouge	Binghamton	Bremerton
Bauer	Birmingham	Brenham
Bayonne	Bismarck	Brentwood
Beatrice	Blackstone	Brian
Beckley	Blackwell	Bridgeport

Bridgeton	Camden	Centralia
Brigham	Camilla	Chalmers
Brisbane	Campbell	Chambersburg
Bristow	Canada	Chandler
Brockton	Canfield	Chanute
Bronxville	Cannon	Chapman
Brookfield	Canonsburg	Charleston
Brownsville	Canton	Charlottesville
Brunswick	Caracas	Chattanooga
Bryan	Carbondale	Cheboygan
Bryant	Carlisle	Chelsea
Bucharest	Carlotta	Cherbourg
Budapest	Carlsbad	Cherokee
Buenos Aires	Carlson	Cheyenne
Buffalo	Carlstadt	Chicago
Bulgaria	Carlton	Chicopee
Burbank	Carmel	Childress
Burke	Carnegie	Chillicothe
Burlington	Carol	Chippewa Falls
Burma	Carpenter	Chisholm
Burns	Carrollton	Christabel
Burroughs	Carson	Christchurch
Burton	Carter	Christina
Butte	Cartersville	Christine
Byron	Carthage	Christopher
Cadillac	Casper	Cicely
Caesar	Catharine	Cicero
Calcutta	Catskill	Cincinnati
Calhoun	Cecelia	Claremont
California	Cedarhurst	Clarinda
Callahan	Cedartown	Clarksburg
Calumet City	Celia	Clarksville

Claudia	Connor	Curtis
Clearfield	Conrad	Cuthbert
Clearwater	Constance	Cynthia
Cleburne	Conway	Dagmar
Clement	Cooley	Dalton
Cleveland	Coolidge	Daly
Clifford	Copenhagen	Daniel
Coaldale	Corbin	Danville
Coatesville	Cork	Daphne
Coeur d'Alene	Cornelia	Darby
Coffeyville	Corning	Davenport
Cohen	Corona	Davidson
Coldwater	Corpus Christi	Dawson
Coleman	Cortland	Dearborn
Collier	Corvallis	Deborah
Collingdale	Corwin	Dedham
Collingswood	Costa Rica	Deerfield
Collinsville	Covington	Defiance
Cologne	Crafton	Delaware
Colorado	Crandall	Delhi
Colton	Cranford	Delia
Columbia	Crawford	Denise
Columbus	Creston	Denison
Comstock	Cromwell	Denmark
Concord	Crowley	Denver
Concordia	Cuba	Des Moines
Condon	Cudahy	Detroit
Conklin	Culbertson	Dewey
Conley	Cullman	Dexter
Connecticut	Cumberland	Diana
Connersville	Cummings	Dickinson
Connolly	Cummins	Dillon

District of Columbia	Edwardsville	Enrico
Dolores	Edwin	Enright
Dominic	Effingham	Ernest
Donald	Egan	Ernestine
Donora	Egbert	Erwin
Donovan	Egypt	Esther
Dormont	Eileen	Esthonia
Dorothy	Elbert	Ethel
Dougherty	Eleanor	Ethiopia
Doyle	Electra	Euclid
Dresden	Elgin	Europe
Dublin	Elizabeth	Evangeline
Dubuque	Elizabethton	Evanston
Dudley	Elkhart	Evansville
Duluth	Elkins	Evelina
Dunbar	Ellensburg	Everard
Duncan	Elliott	Everett
Dunkirk	Ellsworth	Exeter
Dunmore	Elmhurst	Fairbanks
Dunn	Elmira	Fairbury
Duquesne	El Paso	Fairfield
Durham	Elvira	Fairmont
Dwight	Elwood	Fargo
Easthampton	Ely	Farrell
Eastman	Elyria	Fayetteville
Easton	Emil	Feldman
Eau Claire	Emily	Ferdinand
Ecuador	Emmanuel	Ferguson
Edgar	Emporia	Ferndale
Edinburgh	Endicott	Findlay
Edmonton	England	Finley
Edward	Englewood	Fisher

Fitchburg	Galion	Greeley
Fitzgerald	Gallagher	Greensboro
Flagstaff	Gallup	Greensburg
Fleming	Galveston	Greenville
Florence	Gardner	Greenwood
Florida	Garfield	Gregory
Floyd	Gasper	Gretchen
Fond du Lac	Gastonia	Griffiths
Ford	Geneva	Grinnell
Fort Atkinson	Genevieve	Guam
Fort Lauderdale	Genoa	Guatemala
Fort Madison	George	Gutenberg
Fort Myers	Georgia	Guthrie
Fort Wayne	Gerald	Hackensack
Fort Worth	Germany	Haggerty
Foster	Gertrude	Halifax
Fostoria	Gettysburg	Hamburg
Framingham	Gibson	Hamilton
Frances	Gifford	Hammond
Francis	Gilbert	Hampton
Frankfort	Girard	Hancock
Franklin	Glasgow	Hanford
Frederic	Gleason	Hannibal
Fredonia	Gloria	Hanover
Freehold	Gloversville	Hanson
Freeport	Goddard	Harding
Fullerton	Godfrey	Harold
Fulton	Goodwin	Harriet
Gabriel	Gordon	Harriman
Gaffney	Gould	Harrington
Gainesville	Grafton	Harrisburg
Galesburg	Great Britain	Harrison

Hartford	Honolulu	Isolde
Hartman	Hopewell	Israel
Hattiesburg	Hopkinsville	Istanbul
Haverford	Horatio	Ithaca
Haverstraw	Hornel	Ivan
Hawaii	Hortense	Jacksonville
Hawthorne	Houston	Jacobs
Hayward	Howard	Jacqueline
Healy	Howell	Jamaica
Hedwig	Hubert	Jamestown
Heloise	Hudson	Janesville
Hempstead	Humboldt	Janet
Henderson	Humphrey	Japan
Henrietta	Hungary	Jason
Herbert	Huntington	Jasper
Herkimer	Huron	Jeannette
Herman	Hutchinson	Jeffersonville
Higgins	Hyattsville	Jeffrey
Hilda	Iceland	Jemima
Hillsboro	Idaho	Jennifer
Hinsdale	Illinois	Jeremiah
Hinton	India	Jersey City
Hobart	Indiana	Jerusalem
Hoboken	Indianapolis	Jessamine
Hoffman	Inglewood	Jessica
Holdenville	Iowa	Jocelin
Hollywood	Ironton	Johnson
Holt	Ironwood	Johnston
Holyoke	Irvington	Johnstown
Homewood	Irwin	Jonathan
Honduras	Isaac	Jonesboro
Hong Kong	Isidore	Joplin

Joseph	La Crosse	Leipsig
Judith	Lafayette	Leningrad
Julian	Lakeland	Lenoir
Juliet	Lakewood	Leominster
Julius	Lambert	Leon
Justin	Lancaster	Leonard
Kalamazoo	Lancelot	Leonia
Kalispell	Lansdale	Leopold
Kankakee	Lansford	Leroy
Kansas	Lansing	Leslie
Kansas City	La Paz	Lettice
Karl	La Porte	Lewiston
Katharine	Larchmont	Lexington
Kathleen	Laredo	Lillian
Kearny	Larksville	Lima
Keith	Larson	Lincoln
Kennedy	La Salle	Lindstrom
Kenneth	Las Vegas	Lionel
Kenosha	Latrobe	Lisbon
Kenton	Laughlin	Litchfield
Kentucky	Laura	Lithuania
Kerrville	Laurel	Liverpool
Keyser	Laurens	Livingston
Kilgore	Lavinia	Llewellyn
Kingsford	Lawrence	Lloyd
Kingston	Lawrenceville	Lockhart
Kirkwood	Lazarus	Lockport
Knoxville	Leah	Lodi
Kokomo	Leavenworth	Logansport
Korea	Lebanon	Lois
Lackawanna	Lehighton	Lombard
Laconia	Lehman	London

Longview	Manila	McCarthy
Lorain	Manistique	McCook
Lorenzo	Manitoba	McCormack
Los Angeles	Mannheim	McDonald
Louis	Manuel	McGregor
Louise	Maplewood	McKenzie
Louisiana	Marblehead	McKinney
Louisville	Marcella	McMillan
Lowell	Marcia	Meadville
Lubbock	Marcus	Medford
Lucretia	Margaret	Melbourne
Ludington	Marian	Melissa
Luella	Marianna	Menasha
Lufkin	Marion	Mercedes
Lumberton	Marlboro	Meriden
Luther	Marquette	Merrill
Luxembourg	Marseilles	Methuen
Lydia	Marshall	Mexico
Lynbrook	Martin	Meyer
Lynchburg	Martinsburg	Miami
Lyndhurst	Martinsville	Michigan
Lynwood	Mason	Middleboro
Lyons	Massachusetts	Midland
Madisonville	Massillon	Mildred
Magdalene	Mathilda	Milford
Maguire	Matthew	Millburn
Mahanoy City	Maxwell	Millbury
Mahoney	Maynard	Milledgeville
Malden	Maysville	Milton
Malvern	Mayville	Milwaukee
Manchester	Maywood	Minersville
Manhattan	McAdoo	Minneapolis

Minnesota	Naomi	New Zealand
Mississippi	Naperville	Niagara Falls
Missouri	Napoleon	Nicaragua
Mitchell	Nashua	Norfolk
Mobile	Nashville	Norma
Monica	Natalie	Norman
Monmouth	Natchez	Northampton
Monroe	Natchitoches	North Carolina
Montana	Nathaniel	North Dakota
Montebello	Natick	Norwalk
Montevideo	Naugatuck	Norway
Montpelier	Nazareth	Norwich
Montreal	Nebraska	Norwood
Mooresville	Needham	Nova Scotia
Moorhead	Nelson	Nyack
Morocco	Neptune	Oakwood
Morris	Netherlands	O'Brien
Morse	Nevada	Ocala
Mortimer	Newark	O'Connor
Moscow	Newberry	Odessa
Moultrie	New Britain	O'Donnell
Moundsville	New Brunswick	Oelwein
Muncie	Newburgh	Ogdensburg
Munhall	New Hampshire	Ohio
Munich	New Haven	Oklahoma
Murdock	New Jersey	Olean
Muriel	New London	Olney
Murray	New Mexico	Olson
Muscatine	New Orleans	Olympia
Muskegon	New Rochelle	Omaha
Myers	Newton	Oneida
Myrtle	New York	O'Neil

Ontario	Pelham	Portsmouth
Ophelia	Pendleton	Portugal
Oregon	Pennsylvania	Potter
Orlando	Pensacola	Pottsville
Oscar	Peoria	Poughkeepsie
Oshkosh	Percival	Powell
Oslo	Perth Amboy	Presque Isle
Ossining	Petaluma	Prichard
Oswald	Petersburg	Princeton
Oswego	Petersen	Priscilla
Ottawa	Peterson	Providence
Owego	Philadelphia	Provo
Owensboro	Philander	Pueblo
Packard	Philippine Islands	Puerto Rico
Paducah	Phillipsburg	Putnam
Painesville	Phoenixville	Quebec
Palestine	Piedmont	Quinn
Pamela	Pittsburgh	Rachel
Panama	Pittsfield	Racine
Paraguay	Pius	Radford
Parkersburg	Plainfield	Rahway
Parsons	Plattsburg	Randall
Pasadena	Pleasantville	Randolph
Passaic	Plymouth	Rankin
Patchogue	Ponca City	Raton
Paterson	Pontiac	Ravenna
Patrick	Portage	Raymond
Pawtucket	Port Arthur	Rebecca
Peabody	Port Chester	Redwood City
Pearson	Porterville	Regina
Peekskill	Port Huron	Reginald
Pekin	Portland	Reinhardt

Rensselaer	Rudolph	Sault Ste. Marie
Reuben	Rupert	Savannah
Revere	Rushville	Sawyer
Reynolds	Russia	Sayreville
Rhea	Rutherford	Schenectady
Rhinelander	Ryan	Schneider
Rhode Island	Ryerson	Schroeder
Richard	Sacramento	Schultz
Richfield	Saginaw	Schuyler
Richmond	St. Albans	Schwartz
Richwood	St. Augustine	Scotland
Ridgeway	St. Joseph	Seattle
Rio de Janeiro	St. Louis	Sedalia
Roanoke	St. Petersburg	Seminole
Robbinsdale	Salisbury	Serena
Robert	Salt Lake City	Seville
Robinson	Sampson	Seward
Rochester	Samuel	Sewickley
Rockford	San Angelo	Sexton
Rockland	San Antonio	Seymour
Rockville	San Diego	Shanghai
Roderick	Sandusky	Sharon
Romania	San Fernando	Sharpsburg
Roosevelt	Sanford	Sheboygan
Rosalind	San Francisco	Sheffield
Rosemary	San Jose	Shelbyville
Roseville	San Luis Obispo	Sheldon
Rossville	San Mateo	Shenandoah
Roswell	San Rafael	Sheridan
Rotterdam	Santa Barbara	Sherman
Rowena	Santiago	Sherwood
Ruby	Sarasota	Shippensburg

Shirley

Shorewood

Shreveport

Siam

Sicily

Silvester

Silvia

Simmons

Simpson

Sinclair

Singapore

Sioux Falls

Solomon

Somerset

Somerville

Sorensen

South America

Southampton

South Carolina

South Dakota

Southington

Sparks

Spartanburg

Spokane

Springfield

Stafford

Stamford

Stanford

Stanley

Statesboro

Staunton

Sterling

Steubenville

Stewart

Stillwater

Stockholm

Stoneham

Stoughton

Stratford

Straus

Stroudsburg

Struthers

Stuart

Sturgis

Stuttgart

Suffolk

Sullivan

Sumner

Sumter

Sunbury

Susan

Sweetwater

Switzerland

Sybil

Sydney

Sylvester

Syracuse

Tacoma

Tallahassee

Tampa

Tampico

Tarrytown

Taunton

Taylorville

Teaneck

Tenafly

Tennessee

Terre Haute

Texas

Thaddeus

The Hague

Theodore

Thomasville

Tifton

Timothy

Tipton

Titusville

Tokyo

Toledo

Topeka

Toronto

Torrington

Trenton

Trinidad

Truman

Tucson

Tulsa

Turkey

Tuscaloosa

Tyrone

Ukraine

Underhill

Union

United Kingdom

United States

Upton

Uruguay	Warsaw	Willmar
Utah	Washington	Wilmette
Utica	Waterbury	Wilmington
Valentine	Waterville	Wilson
Valeria	Watsonville	Winfield
Vanderlip	Waverly	Winifred
Van Horn	Waynesboro	Winnipeg
Venezuela	Weatherford	Winona
Vera Cruz	Webster	Winslow
Vermont	Welch	Winston-Salem
Vernon	Wellesley	Winthrop
Vicksburg	Wellington	Wisconsin
Victoria	Wellsburg	Woburn
Vienna	Westbrook	Woodbury
Vincennes	West Chester	Woodward
Vincent	Westfield	Woonsocket
Viola	Weston	Wooster
Virgil	West Virginia	Worcester
Virginia	Westwood	Worthington
Vivian	Weymouth	Wyoming
Wabash	Wheaton	Xenia
Waddington	Wheeling	Yakima
Wadsworth	Whitman	Yates
Wakefield	Whittier	Yokohama
Walker	Wichita	Yonkers
Wallace	Wilbur	York
Wallington	Wilfred	Youngstown
Walpole	Wilkes-Barre	Ypsilanti
Walsh	Wilkinsburg	Yugoslavia
Walter	Willard	Yuma
Waltham	Williamsport	Zanesville
Warrensburg	Williston	Zion

PART THREE

Part Three consists of a compilation of 1,856 useful business phrases presented in alphabetic order.

These phrases were selected from a study of the phrasing content of 1,500 business letters representing fifty types of businesses. In all, these letters contained 250,143 running words.

Phrases for common expressions are very helpful to the writer seeking to gain shorthand speed. However, they can be a handicap to him if he cannot write them without the slightest hesitation. If the writer must pause for even the smallest fraction of a second in composing or thinking of a phrase, that phrase becomes a speed handicap rather than a help.

If the writer cannot think of the phrase for a combination of words, he will be well advised to write the words separately.

FREQUENTLY USED GREGG
SHORTHAND PHRASES

able to say		after that	
able to see		after that time	
about it		after the	
about its		after these	
about my		after this	
about that		after those	
about that time		along that	
about the		along that line	
about the matter		along the	
about the time		along the line	
about them		along this	
about this		along those	
about this matter		among the	
about this time		among these	
about those		among those	
about which		and are	
about which the		and have	
about your		and his	
above that		and hope	
above the		and hope that	
above you		and I will	
across the		and I will be	

and is		as if the	
and let us		as it has been	
and let us know		as it is	
and my		as it will	
and our		as it will be	
and see		as it will have	
and that		as long	
and that is		as many	
and that the		as much	
and the		as necessary	
and they		as soon as	
and was		as soon as possible	
and will		as soon as the	
and will be		as soon as you can	
and will not		as that	
and write		as that is not	
any of these		as the	
any one		as there has been	
any one of our		as there was	
any one of the		as there will be	
any one of them		as the result	
any one of these		as these	
any one of those		as they	
any other		as they are	
any others		as they can	
any time		as they can be	
any way		as they cannot	
are not		as they come	
are sure		as they did	
are you		as they have	
as a result		as they will	
as if		as this	

as this is		as you may have	
as this may		as you might	
as this may be		as you might be	
as those		as you might have	
as though		as you must	
as time		as you must be	
as to		as you must have	
as to that		as you say	
as to the		as you see	
as to them		as you want	
as to these		as you will	
as to this		as you will be	
as to which		as you will find	
as we		as you will have	
as we are		as you will not	
as we are not		as you will not be	
as we can		as you will see	
as we cannot		as you would	
as well		as you would be	
as yet		as you would be able	
as you		as you would have	
as you are		as you would have been	
as you can		as you would not	
as you cannot		as your	
as you did		ask me	
as you do		ask that	
as you do not		ask the	
as you don't		ask us	
as you have		ask you	
as you know		at a loss	
as you may		at a time	
as you may be		a thousand	

a thousand dollars

a thousand pounds

at last

at least

at length

at such a time

at that

at that time

at the

at the time

at these

at this

at this time

at which time

back and forth

be able

be done

be glad

be glad to know

be glad to see

be sure

been able

before and after

before it is

before me

before many

before many days

before that

before that time

before the

before the time

before these

before they

before they can

before this

before those

before us

before you

before you are

before you can

before your

being able

being done

being sure

between that

between the

between them

between these

between this

between those

between us

bill of sale

business world

by and by

by it

by its

by mail

by me

by means

by Mr.

by myself

by that

by that time

by the

by the time

by the way

by them

by themselves

by these

by this

by this means

by this time

by those

by us

by which

by which it is

by which they are

by which they will

by which time

by which you can

by which you may

by which you will

by you

can be

can be done

can be made

can be sure

can have

can say

can see

can you

can you give

can you give us

cannot be

cannot be done

cannot be made

cannot be sure

cannot have

cannot pay

cannot say

cannot see

can't be

can't be done

can't be sure

centuries ago

Chamber of Commerce

check up

checking up

city of Boston

city of Chicago

city of London

city of New York

city of Pittsburgh

c.o.d.

common stock

Cordially yours

could be

could be done

could be made

could be sure

could have

could have been

could not

could not be

could not say

could not see

could pay

could say

could see

day or two

day or two ago

days ago

Dear Madam

Dear Miss

Dear Mr.

Dear Mrs.

Dear Sir

Dear Sirs

did not

didn't

do it

do not

do not have

do not pay

do not say

do not see

do so

do that

do the

do these

do this

do those

do you

do you know

do you mean

do you think

do you want

don't

does not

does not have

doesn't

doing so

doing that

doing this

due to the

during the last

during the past

during the year

during the years

during which time

each case

each day

each man

each month

each morning

each night

each one

each other

each other's

each time

electric iron

electric motor

electric stove

electric wire

enter into

enter our

enter the

enter your

ever since

ever since the

every day

every minute

every month		for Mrs.	
every one		for most	
every one of the		for my	
every one of them		for myself	
every one of these		for next month	
every one of those		for next year	
every other		for one	
face to face		for one thing	
feel sure		for our	
feeling sure		for so long a time	
few days		for some years	
few days ago		for that	
few minutes		for the	
few minutes ago		for the last	
few moments		for the present	
few moments ago		for the purpose	
few months		for the time	
few months ago		for them	
few times		for there was	
for a few days		for these	
for a few minutes		for this	
for a few months		for this is	
for a long time		for this is not	
for example		for this is the	
for his		for this time	
for it		for those	
for it is		for us	
for it was		for which	
for it will be		for which the	
for its		for whom	
for me		for you	
for Mr.		for your	

for your convenience	
for your information	
for yourself	
from him	
from his	
from it	
from our	
from such	
from that	
from that time	
from the	
from them	
from these	
from this	
from those	
from time	
from us	
from which	
from you	
from your	
gave me	
gave us	
gave you	
give me	
give us	
give you	
giving me	
giving us	
giving you	
glad to have	
glad to hear	
glad to know	

glad to receive	
glad to say	
glad to see	
glad to send	
glad to send you	
good condition	
good deal	
good many	
good many of the	
good many of them	
good many of these	
good many of those	
good morning	
good night	
good time	
good times	
great many	
great many of the	
great many of them	
had been	
had not	
had not been	
half the	
has been	
has been able	
has been done	
has been made	
has come	
has done	
has given	
has gone	
has had	

has made		he can	
has not		he can be	
has not been		he can be sure	
has not been able		he can go	
has not been done		he can have	
has not yet		he can make	
has not yet been		he cannot	
has that		he cannot be	
has the		he cannot have	
has this		he can't	
has to		he could	
has to be		he could not	
has to have		he did	
has tried		he did not	
has written		he did not pay	
have been		he did not say	
have been able		he did not see	
have been done		he didn't	
have done		he does	
have gone		he does not	
have had		he felt	
have made		he finds	
have met		he found	
have not		he gathered	
have not been		he gave	
have not been able		he gives	
have not yet		he goes	
have not yet been		he is	
have you		he is not	
have you made		he knew	
he called		he knows	
he came		he lost	

he made		he will	
he may		he will be	
he may be		he will be able	
he may be able		he will be glad	
he may be sure		he will be sure	
he may have		he will find	
he mentioned		he will have	
he might be		he will not	
he might have		he will not be able	
he might have been		he will pay	
he might not		he will see	
he must		he wished	
he must be		he would	
he must have		he would be	
he needed		he would be able	
he needs		he would be glad	
he said		he would have	
he saw		he would not	
he says		he would not be	
he says that		hear from	
he seemed		hear from him	
he should		hear from you	
he should be		help us	
he should be able		help you	
he should have		here and there	
he should not		here are	
he sold		here is	
he told		here is the	
he took		hope that	
he wanted		hope that the	
he wants		hope you will	
he was		hours ago	

how long		I did	
how long ago		I did not	
how many		I did not say	
how many of the		I did not think	
how many of them		I do	
how many of these		I do not	
how many times		I do not say	
how much		I do not see	
I am		I do not think	
I am glad		I doubt	
I am of the opinion		I enclose	
I am sure		I fear	
I bought		I feel	
I came		I feel sure	
I can		I felt	
I can be		I find	
I can have		I found	
I can say		I gave	
I can see		I get	
I cannot		I give	
I cannot be		I guess	
I cannot be sure		I have	
I cannot have		I have been	
I can't		I have been able	
I come		I have come	
I could		I have done	
I could be		I have given	
I could have		I have had	
I could not		I have made	
I could not be		I have not	
I could see		I have not been able	
I desire		I have not had	

I have not yet		I said	
I have seen		I saw	
I have taken		I say	
I have tried		I see	
I hope		I sent	
I hope it will		I set	
I hope it will be		I shall	
I hope that		I shall be	
I hope to see		I shall be able	
I hope you will		I shall be glad	
I knew		I shall have	
I know		I shall make	
I made		I shall not	
I make		I shall not be	
I may		I shall not be able	
I may be		I should	
I may have		I should be	
I meant		I should have	
I mention		I should say	
I met		I suggest	
I might		I take	
I might be		I talked	
I might have		I thank you	
I must		I thank you for the	
I must be		I think	
I must have		I thought	
I need		I told	
I note		I took	
I notice		I want	
I read		I want to see	
I realize		I wanted	
I regret		I was	

I will		if they can	
I will be		if they cannot	
I will be able		if they may	
I will have		if they would	
I will not		if they would be	
I will not be		if this	
I will not be able		if this is	
I will see		if we	
I wish		if we are	
I would		if we can	
I would be		if we can be	
I would have		if we cannot	
I would not		if we could	
I wrote		if we do	
I wrote you		if we have	
if it		if you	
if it is		if you are	
if it was		if you are not yet	
if it will		if you are sure	
if it will be		if you can	
if my		if you can be	
if not		if you cannot	
if so		if you could	
if that		if you desire	
if that is not		if you did not	
if that will not		if you didn't	
if the		if you do	
if there are		if you do not	
if there is		if you give	
if they		if you have	
if they are		if you haven't	
if they are not		if you know	

if you may		in order to obtain	
if you must		in order to pay	
if you must be		in order to see	
if you need		in our	
if you take		in our opinion	
if you think		in our power	
if you want		in part	
if you will		in particular	
if you will be		in question	
if you will have		in relation	
if you will see		in response	
if you wish		in spite	
if you would		in such	
if you would be		in such a manner	
if you would have		in such a way	
in a few days		in that	
in a few minutes		in the	
in a few months		in the event	
in a position		in the future	
in addition		in the last	
in addition to the		in the past	
in addition to this		in the way	
in behalf		in the world	
in case		in them	
in fact		in these	
in his		in this	
in it		in this case	
in order		in this matter	
in order that		in this way	
in order to be		in time	
in order to be able		in us	
in order to judge		in view	

in which		just a little	
in which case		just as	
in which it is		known as	
in which it was		left hand	
in which the		less and less	
in which you		less than	
in which you are		less than that	
in which you will be		less than the	
into it		let us	
into that		let us have	
into the		let us know	
into this		let us make	
is it		let us say	
is not		let us see	
is not yet		letting us	
is that		letting us know	
is that the		line of business	
is the		line of goods	
is there		long ago	
is this		long time	
is to be		long time ago	
it has been		make the	
it is		make them	
it is the		make this	
it isn't		make up	
it was		make us	
it will		make way	
it will be		making up	
it will have		many of the	
it will not		many of them	
it will not be		many of these	
it will not have		many of those	

many other		next month	
many times		next morning	
may be		next thing	
may be able		next time	
may be done		next year	
may be sure		next year's	
may have		no doubt	
men and women		no less	
might be		no sir	
might be able		no such	
might have		none of the	
might have been		none of them	
might not		not only	
might not be		now and then	
might not be able		of course	
months ago		of course it is	
must be		of course they have	
must be able		of his	
must be done		of its	
must have		of loss	
My dear		of mine	
My dear Madam		of my	
My dear Miss		of our	
My dear Mr.		of ours	
My dear Mrs.		of such	
My dear Sir		of that	
my time		of that time	
need not be		of the	
next day		of their	
next day or two		of them	
next few days		of these	
next meeting		of this	

of this month		one of our	
of those		one of the	
of time		one of the best	
of what		one of the most	
of which		one of them	
of which it is		one of these	
of your time		one or two	
on behalf		one thing	
on his		one time	
on it		one way	
on our		only one	
on our part		only one of these	
on request		other than	
on sale		ought to be	
on such		ought to be able	
on that		ought to be done	
on that day		ought to have	
on the		out of date	
on the part		out of that	
on the question		out of the	
on the subject		out of the question	
on these		out of them	
on this		out of this	
on this case		over it	
on this matter		over our	
on time		over the	
on us		over this	
on which		over to the	
on which the		over which	
on your		over your	
once a month		per gallon	
once or twice		per hundred	

per minute		several months ago	
point of view		several other	
question of time		several times	
quite a few		shall be glad	
quite a little		shall have	
quite right		shall not	
quite sure		shall not be	
reach us		shall not be able	
reach you		shall not have	
real estate		she can	
realize that		she cannot	
realize the		she could	
realizing that the		she could not	
relation to the		she could not be	
Respectfully yours		she is	
safe deposit		she is not	
Saturday morning		she made	
seem to be		she may be	
seems to be		she must	
send him		she must be	
send them		she would	
send this		should be	
send us		should be done	
send you		should be made	
sending the		should have	
sending them		should have been	
sending us		should not	
sending you		should not be	
set forth		should not have been	
several days		should not say	
several days ago		should say	
several months		should see	

shouldn't		take care	
since that time		take the	
since the		taking care	
since this		than the	
Sincerely yours		thank you	
so far		thank you for	
so late		thank you for the	
so little		thank you for your	
so long		thank you for your order	
so long a time		that are	
so long ago		that are not	
so many		that can	
so many of the		that can be	
so many of them		that can be done	
so many times		that do	
so much		that do not	
so that		that does not	
so well		that have	
some of our		that is	
some of that		that is not	
some of the		that is the	
some of them		that is to say	
some of these		that it	
some of this		that it is	
some of those		that its	
some time		that it was	
some time ago		that it will	
some years		that it will be	
some years ago		that may	
such a thing		that may be	
such things		that must	
suggest that		that must be	

that our

that this is

that the

that there are

that there is

that these

that they

that they are

that they have

that they will

that this

that this is

that this is not

that those

that time

that will

that will be

that will not

that would

that would be

that would have

the only thing

the only way

the time

there are

there has been

there have

there is

there may

there may be

there might be

there might have been

there must be

there was

there will

there will be

these are

they are

they are not

they can

they can be

they can have

they cannot

they cannot be

they cannot have

they can't

they come

they could

they could be

they could have

they could not

they did

they did not

they do

they do not

they don't

they have

they have done

they may

they may be

they may be able

they might

they might be

they might be able

they might not		this material	
they must		this matter	
they must be		this may	
they must be able		this may be	
they must have		this may have	
they think		this means	
they want		this month	
they will		this morning	
they will be		this must be done	
they will be able		this one	
they will be glad		this state	
they will have		this thing	
they will not		this time	
they will not be		this was	
they would		this was the	
they would be		this way	
they would be able		this will	
they would be glad		this will be	
they would buy		this would	
they would have		this would be	
this can		through its	
this can be		through that	
this cannot		through the	
this cannot be		through this	
this case		throughout the	
this day		throughout this	
this did not		to balance	
this information		to be	
this is		to be able	
this is not		to be done	
this is the		to be made	
this man		to be sure	

to bear	
to become	
to begin	
to being able	
to believe	
to bind	
to blame	
to borrow	
to bother	
to buy	
to call	
to cancel	
to care	
to carry	
to cash	
to catch	
to cause	
to change	
to charge	
to check	
to choose	
to claim	
to clear	
to close	
to come	
to complete	
to comply	
to continue	
to convince	
to co-operate	
to cover	
to create	

to do	
to do it	
to do so	
to do the	
to do this	
to do your	
to face	
to facilitate	
to fall	
to familiarize	
to favor	
to feature	
to feel	
to figure	
to fill	
to find	
to finish	
to fly	
to follow	
to force	
to forget	
to form	
to forward	
to furnish	
to gain	
to gather	
to get	
to give	
to give me	
to give you	
to give your	
to go	

to grow	to prepare
to have	to present
to have been	to pretend
to have you	to prevent
to his	to print
to increase	to proceed
to it	to produce
to its	to protect
to jar	to prove
to join	to provide
to judge	to publish
to keep	to purchase
to know	to put
to make	to quote
to make the	to sail
to me	to say
to mention	to see
to paint	to see me
to park	to select
to part	to sell
to participate	to separate
to pass	to serve
to pay	to serve you
to perform	to share
to permit	to shift
to persuade	to ship
to place	to show
to plan	to spare
to plant	to speak
to play	to speed
to please	to spend
to point	to spread

to such	
to supply	
to suppose	
to surprise	
to survey	
to take	
to talk	
to tell	
to thank you	
to thank you for	
to thank you for the	
to that	
to the	
to their	
to them	
to these	
to think	
to this	
to those	
to time	
to trade	
to travel	
to try	
to turn	
to us	
to value	
to verify	
to visit	
to which	
to which the	
to which you	
to which you are	

to whom	
to you	
to your	
too much	
Tuesday morning	
twice as much	
two months ago	
two or three	
under a	
under consideration	
under her	
under his	
under my	
under no	
under our	
under question	
under such	
under the	
under their	
under them	
under these	
under this	
under those	
under way	
under which	
under your	
United States	
United States Government	
United States of America	
up to	
up to date	
up to its	

up to the	
up to the minute	
up to this	
up to this time	
upon receipt	
upon request	
upon such	
upon the	
upon the subject	
upon them	
upon this	
upon us	
upon which	
upon you	
Very cordially yours	
very glad	
very glad to hear	
very good	
very important	
very little	
very many	
very much	
Very sincerely	
Very sincerely yours	
very small	
very soon	
Very truly	
Very truly yours	
very well	
want to see	
was done	
was it	

was made	
was that	
was the	
was this	
we are	
we are not	
we are not yet	
we are of the opinion	
we are sending	
we are sure	
we can	
we can be	
we can give	
we can have	
we can make	
we cannot	
we cannot be	
we cannot say	
we cannot see	
we can say	
we can see	
we can't	
we could	
we could be	
we could have	
we could not	
we desire	
we did	
we did not	
we didn't	
we do	
we do not	

we do not say	we feel sure
we do not see	we felt
we do not think	we find
we enclose	we found
we give	we invite
we have	we knew
we have been	we know
we have been able	we made
we have done	we mailed
we have had	we make
we have made	we may
we have not	we may be
we have not been	we may be able
we have not been able	we may have
we have not had	we mean
we have not yet	we mention
we have your order	we might
we hope	we might be
we hope it will	we might be able
we hope it will be	we might have
we hope that	we might have been
we hope that the	we must
we hope the	we must be
we hope these	we must have
we hope they	we need
we hope this	we quoted
we hope this will	we realize that
we hope to have	we shall
we hope you can be	we shall be
we hope you will	we shall be able
we hope you will not	we shall be glad
we feel	we shall have

we shall make		we wish to say	
we shall need		we would	
we shall not		we would be	
we shall not be		we would be glad	
we shall not be able		we would have	
we should		we would not	
we should be		we would not be	
we should be glad		we would not be able	
we should have		we wouldn't	
we should not be able		we wrote	
we should say		weeks ago	
we thank you		week or two	
we thank you for		week or two ago	
we thank you for the		well known	
we thank you for your		well written	
we think		were not	
we think that		were sure	
we tried		what are	
we try		what has been	
we want		what is	
we wanted		what our	
we will		what was	
we will be		what will	
we will be able		what will be	
we will have		when that	
we will not		when the	
we will not be		when these	
we will not be able		when they	
we will see		when this	
we will send		when those	
we will send you		when you	
we wish		when you are	

which does		who have done	
which has		who have had	
which has not		who have made	
which have		who have not	
which have not		who is	
which is		who is not	
which is the		who knew	
which may		who know	
which may be		who knows	
which means		who made	
which must		who make	
which they have		who may	
which was		who may be	
which way		who might	
which we		who might be	
which we are		who might have	
which would not		who might have been	
which you can		who must	
which you cannot		who need	
which you may		who needs	
who are		who should	
who are not		who should be	
who can		who should have	
who can be		who should not	
who cannot		who takes	
who could		who taught	
who could be		who think	
who could not		who want	
who desire		who wanted	
who didn't		who will	
who do not		who will be	
who have		who will be able	

who will have

who will not

who will not be

who will not have

who would

who would be

who would have

who would have been

who would not

why not

will be

will be able

will be done

will be glad

will find

will have

will not be

will not be able

will not have

will see

will you

will you please

wish to say

with him

with his

with our

with such

with that

with the

with them

with these

with this

with those

with us

with which

with which it is

with which the

with whom

with you

within our

within the

within this

would be

would be able

would be done

would be glad

would be made

would have

would have been

would not

would not be

would not have been

would not say

written us

written you

years ago

years of age

you are

you are not

you are not yet

you are sure

you aren't

you can

you can be

you can be sure

you can get

you can give

you can have

you can make

you cannot

you cannot have

you cannot pay

you cannot see

you come

you could

you could be

you could be sure

you could have

you could have been

you could see

you could not

you could not have

you couldn't

you desire

you did

you did not

you did not say

you did not see

you do

you do not

you don't

you gave

you have

you have been

you have done

you have had

you have made

you have not

you have not been

you have not been able

you have seen

you knew

you know

you made

you make

you may

you may be

you may be able

you may be sure

you may have

you mention

you might

you might be

you might not

you must

you must be

you must be able

you must be sure

you must have

you must see

you need

you order

you say

you see

you shall have

you should

you should be

you should be able

you should be sure		you would	
you should have		you would be	
you should have been		you would be able	
you should not		you would be glad	
you take		you would be sure	
you think		you would have	
you want		you would have been	
you wanted		you would not	
you will		you would not be able	
you will be		you would not have	
you will be able		your inquiry	
you will be glad		your name	
you will be sure		your order	
you will find		your orders	
you will have		Yours cordially	
you will not		Yours respectfully	
you will not be		Yours sincerely	
you will not be able		Yours truly	
you will not have		Yours very sincerely	
you will see		Yours very truly